# Lecture Notes of the Institute for Computer Sciences, Social Informatics and Telecommunications Engineering    471

The LNICST series publishes ICST's conferences, symposia and workshops.

LNICST reports state-of-the-art results in areas related to the scope of the Institute. The type of material published includes

- Proceedings (published in time for the respective event)
- Other edited monographs (such as project reports or invited volumes)

LNICST topics span the following areas:

- General Computer Science
- E-Economy
- E-Medicine
- Knowledge Management
- Multimedia
- Operations, Management and Policy
- Social Informatics
- Systems

Sachi Nandan Mohanty · Vicente Garcia Diaz ·
G. A. E. Satish Kumar

Editors

# Intelligent Systems and Machine Learning

First EAI International Conference, ICISML 2022
Hyderabad, India, December 16–17, 2022
Proceedings, Part II

 Springer

*Editors*
Sachi Nandan Mohanty ⓘ
VIT-AP University
Amrāvati, Andhra Pradesh, India

Vicente Garcia Diaz ⓘ
University of Oviedo
Oviedo, Spain

G. A. E. Satish Kumar ⓘ
Vardhaman College of Engineering
Hyderabad, India

ISSN 1867-8211 ISSN 1867-822X (electronic)
Lecture Notes of the Institute for Computer Sciences, Social Informatics
and Telecommunications Engineering
ISBN 978-3-031-35080-1 ISBN 978-3-031-35081-8 (eBook)
https://doi.org/10.1007/978-3-031-35081-8

This Springer imprint is published by the registered company Springer Nature Switzerland AG
The registered company address is: Gewerbestrasse 11, 6330 Cham, Switzerland

# Preface

We are delighted to introduce the proceedings of the first edition of the 2022 European Alliance for Innovation (EAI) International Conference on Intelligent Systems and Machine Learning (ICISML 2022). ICISML 2022 is the premier conference in the field of emerging technologies. In today's world, intelligent systems are a new and rapidly growing technology. A large volume of data can be generated and made available for analysis. Humans lack the cognitive ability to comprehend such massive volumes of data. Humans can use machine learning (ML) to process enormous volumes of data and get insights into how the data behaves. These machines can learn from their mistakes and do human-like tasks.

The 75 papers presented were selected from 209 submissions. The conference has four different technical tracks: Track 1: Image Recognition, Track 2: Machine Learning, Track 3: Intelligent Systems and Machine Learning Applications, and Track 4: Intelligent Communications Networks. The technical programme also featured four keynote talks and one technical workshop. The title of the technical workshops organised in collaboration with the software industry, "CORTEVA Agriscience," has the theme "Sequences to Satellites: Applications of Artificial Intelligence and Machine Learning in the Agriculture Domain." The average number of papers per reviewer was three. Around 192 technical experts participated in the review process from across the globe. Three experts in various fields reviewed each paper. A technical programme committee member finally took the decision and communicated it to the authors as per reviewer reports.

Coordination with the general chair, Vicente Garcia Diaz, University of Oviedo, Spain, was essential for the success of the conference. We sincerely appreciate their constant support and guidance. It was also a great pleasure to work with such an excellent organising committee team and we appreciate their hard work in organising and supporting the conference.

We strongly believe that the ICISML 2022 conference provided a good forum for all researchers, developers, and practitioners to discuss all application aspects of science and technology that are relevant to smart grids. We also expect that future ICISML conferences will be as successful and stimulating as indicated by the contributions presented in this volume.

July 2023

Sachi Nandan Mohanty
Vicente Garcia Diaz
G. A. E. Satish Kumar

# Conference Organization

## Steering Committee

| | |
|---|---|
| Imrich Chlamtac | Bruno Kessler Professor, University of Trento, Italy |
| T. Vijender Reddy (Chairman) | Vardhaman College of Engineering, Hyderabad, India |
| M. Rajasekhar Reddy (Vice Chairman) | Vardhaman College of Engineering, Hyderabad, India |
| T. Upender Reddy | Vardhaman College of Engineering, Hyderabad, India |
| E. Prabhakar Reddy | Vardhaman College of Engineering, Hyderabad, India |
| J. V. R. Ravindra | Vardhaman College of Engineering, Hyderabad, India |

## Organizing Committee

### General Chair

| | |
|---|---|
| Vicente Garcia Diaz | University of Oviedo, Spain |

### General Co-chairs

| | |
|---|---|
| G. A. E. Satish Kumar | Vardhaman College of Engineering, Hyderabad, India |
| Milos Stojmenovic | Singidunum University, Serbia |
| George Tsaramirsis | Higher College of Technology, Abu Dhabi, UAE |
| Sachi Nandan Mohanty | Singidunum University, Serbia |

### Technical Program Chairs

| | |
|---|---|
| G. A. E. Satish Kumar | Vardhaman College of Engineering, Hyderabad, India |
| Tanupriya Choudhury | University of Petroleum & Energy Studies, Dehradun, India |

| | |
|---|---|
| Sachi Nandan Mohanty | Singidunum University, Serbia |
| Sven Groppe | University of Lübeck, Germany |

## Technical Program Co-chairs

| | |
|---|---|
| Mohammed Altaf Ahmed | Prince Sattam Bin Abdulaziz University, Saudi Arabia |
| Adil O. Khadidos | King Abdulaziz University, Jeddah, Saudi Arabia |
| Sanjay Misra | Covenant University, Nigeria |
| Maria Spichkova | RMIT University, Australia |

## Web Chair

| | |
|---|---|
| A. Pramod Kumar | Vardhaman College of Engineering, India |

## Publicity and Social Media Chairs

| | |
|---|---|
| Sarika Jain | NIT Kurukshetra, India |
| Nonita Sharma | Indira Gandhi Delhi Technical University for Women, New Delhi, India |
| Monika Mangala | Dwarkadas J. Sanghvi College of Engineering Mumbai, India |
| Suvendu Kumar Pani | Krupajala Engineering College, Bhubaneswar, India |

## Organizing Chair

| | |
|---|---|
| A. Pramod Kumar | Vardhaman College of Engineering, Hyderabad, India |

## Convenors

| | |
|---|---|
| M. Naresh Kumar | Vardhaman College of Engineering, Hyderabad, India |
| D. Krishna | Vardhaman College of Engineering, Hyderabad, India |

## Special Session Chairs

| | |
|---|---|
| Sarita Mohanty | CPGS, Odisha University Agriculture University, Bhubaneswar, India |
| Tejaswini Kar | KIIT, Bhubaneswar, India |

**Website Chair**

D. Praveen Kumar        Vardhaman College of Engineering, Hyderabad, India

**Registration Chairs**

Ch. Sulakshana        Vardhaman College of Engineering, Hyderabad, India

Sangeeta Singh        Vardhaman College of Engineering, Hyderabad, India

**Finance Chairs**

J. Krishna Chaithanya        Vardhaman College of Engineering, Hyderabad, India

B. Srikanth        Vardhaman College of Engineering, Hyderabad, India

**Workshops Chair**

Nonita Sharma        NIT Jalandhar, India

**Sponsorship and Exhibits Chairs**

Jatin Kumar Das        SRM-AP University, Andhra Pradesh, India

I. Babu        Vardhaman College of Engineering, Hyderabad, India

M. Nagarjuna        Vardhaman College of Engineering, Hyderabad, India

**Publication Chair**

Suneeta Satpathy        Sri Sri University Odisha, India

Priya Gupta        JNU New Delhi, India

**Panel Chair**

Mohammed Altaf Ahmed        Prince Sattam Bin Abdulaziz University, Saudi Arabia

**Local Chair**

J. Krishna Chaitanya          Vardhaman College of Engineering, Hyderabad,
                              India

## Technical Program Committee

| | |
|---|---|
| Sanjay Misra | Covenant University, Nigeria |
| Milos Stojmenovi | Singidunum University, Serbia |
| Georgios Tsaramirsis | Higher Colleges of Technology Women's Campus, Abu Dhabi, UAE |
| Sven Groppe | University of Lübeck, Germany |
| Mohammad Yamin | King Abdulaziz University, Saudi Arabia |
| Mukesh Misra | Massey University, New Zealand |
| Neha Mohanty | New Jersey Institute of Technology, USA |
| Aleksandar Jevremovic | University of Lübeck, Germany |
| Jinghua Groppe | University of Lübeck, Germany |
| Abdulrhman M. Alshareef | King Abdulaziz University, Saudi Arabia |
| Gourav Sen Gupta | Massey University, New Zealand |
| S. K. Ramesh | California State University, USA |
| María José Navarro Avilés | Gijon Hospital, Spain |
| Ishani PriyaDarshini | UC Berkeley, USA |
| Laxmidhar Behera (Director) | Indian Institute of Technology Mandi, India |
| Santunu Choudhury | IIT Jodhpur, India |
| Durga Prasad Mohapatro | NIT Rourkela, India |
| Debasis Samanta | IIT Kharagpur, India |
| E. Laxmi Lydia | Vignan's Institute of Information Technology, Visakhapatnam, India |
| Mukta Jagdish | Vardhaman College of Engineering, Hyderabad, India |
| Mahendran Arumugam | IIT Saveetha, India |
| Mrutyunjaya Panda | Utkal University, India |
| Abdulsattar Abdullah Hamad | Hamad Imam University College, Iraq |
| Bhagirathi Nayak | Sri Sri University, India |
| Bunil Kumar Balabantaray | National Institute of Technology, Meghalaya, India |
| Priya Gupta | Jawaharlal Nehru University, India |
| Martine Gadille | AMU, France |
| Deepak Gupta | National Institute of Technology, Arunachal Pradesh, India |

| Gouse Baig | Vardhaman College of Engineering, Hyderabad, India |
| Sanjay Kuamr Panda | NIT Warangal, India |
| Deepak Gupta | Maharaja Agrasen Institute of Technology, India |

# Contents – Part II

# Contents – Part I

## Digital Forensic and Network Security

## Intelligent Communication Wireless Networks

# Emerging Applications

# A Model for Engineering, Procurement, and Construction (EPC) Organizations Using Vendor Performance Rating System

Sujit Kumar Panda[1], Sukanta Kumar Baral[2], Richa Goel[3,4], and Tilottama Singh[5]([⊠])

[1] Department of Computer Science and Engineering, GIFT Autonomous College,
Bhubaneswar, Odisha, India
sujit.panda@gift.edu.in
[2] Department of Commerce, Faculty of Commerce and Management, Indira Gandhi National
Tribal University (A Central University), Aamarkantak, Madhya Pradesh, India
sukanta.baral@igntu.ac.in
[3] SCMS, Noida, Noida, India
richasgoel@gmail.com
[4] Symbiosis International University Pune, Pune, India
[5] Department of Management, Uttaranchal University, Dehradun, Uttarakhand, India
tilottamasingh2101@gmail.com

**Abstract.** Assurance in Quality deals beardly with multi sourcing as well as vendor expansion undertakings. The vendors present in the system are reviewed for extension of their agreement. There are fairly a big number of suppliers available for various items distributed as per directorates, by means of limited number of resources; it turns into hard to prepare review report in time. For requirement of transparent structure, different cases need to deal or handle equivalently as well as visits are being systematized. The dealer assessment device may offer with a transparent device by using that; selection can be done to allocate with ground visits for re-evaluation. The preferred additionally specify that require for improvement of supplier assessment system need to be categorical with retaining cost of vendor rating gadget against expected returns as well as other aspects in assessment. Consequently, the rating gadget primarily centered on four vital elements viz. Quality, Service, Delivery in addition to Machine might be well enough to achieve the necessity. The rating device can be employed in different decision-making equipment additionally.

**Keywords:** Vendor · Performance Rating · Engineering · Procurement and Construction

## 1 Introduction

The term vendor rating (or rating of vendor) as it from time to time mentioned in a EPC business used to define the procedure of measuring a firm's vendor abilities as well as performance (Asadabadi et al., 2020). Rating of vendor formulates a portion of a firm's

S. Nandan Mohanty et al. (Eds.): ICISML 2022, LNICST 471, pp. 3–12, 2023.
https://doi.org/10.1007/978-3-031-35081-8_1

vendor relationship management program. Such schemes use to vary in the standards that are to be measured; this generally comes under quantitative as well as qualitative categories which may use as when conducting vendor rating. The procedure differs from one firm to another firm. The method of rating i.e. alternative common standards often include: Quality (for example number of right time deliveries and good raw materials), Service, Delivery (schedule adherence), Cost/Price and Capability.

Outcomes of respective variables are then weighted into a concluding score generally in a percentage form, permitting vendors to rank. Vendor rating is a continuing action; vendors are time and again evaluated constantly or occasionally (i.e. evaluating the last year's trading). Numerous measures can examine within vendor rating systems as a common method that is to be used Cost Quality as well as delivery procedures in addition to apply weighting against standards in agreement with company necessities. Firms then frequently group providers rendering to effects which can obviously use to highlight poor performing providers in sequence that they can remove from use (Tsaramirsis, 2010). Vendor score consequences may generate development programs on providers that score low. Trend analysis is frequently applied to vendor score which permits agencies to observer adjustments in provider complete performance during the time horizon. Both vendors as well as buyers have to follow vendor ratings device to force performance as well as develop the business relationship.

Actual vendor rating calls for a constant as well as goal method wherein rating standards are open to interpretation inaccuracy can be added. This is especially wherein particular complaint from shoppers is added into the score procedure. History isn't constantly a manual to future performance in addition to vendors ought to be referred as a part of the evaluation.

## 2   Literature Review

Operating in surroundings of risky, uncertain, complex and ambiguous conditions, EPC corporations are going through unsustainable degrees of stress.

From onerous contracting models that discourage collaboration, to unpredictable commodity fees that undermine the splendor of the world as an organization, the motives are many and complex. Combined, those stressors are the forces to be able to reshape the enterprise over the next decade (Chavan et al., 2020).

This situation leaves a lot of thought for innovators—the subsequent era of ambitious engineers and managers who need to work on alternate methods and enhance overall performance within their companies and throughout the industry? Studies have identified five characteristics to be able to define the successful EPC companies of the future. These key developments will assist agencies effectively manual investment and spur innovation all through the virtual transformation journey (Ara et al., 2021). Striving to embody these characteristics will pressure nice adjustments in careers, groups and the industry, making the EPC phase of 2030 stronger, extra innovative and increasingly more worthwhile (Niayeshnia et al., 2020).

Viable gain of critical firm is based deeply upon the routine of the providers. Efficacy of choosing, and gauging movements of providers is a considerable aspect in reaching corporations' desires ((Kabirifar and Mojtahedi, 2019)). In commonplace, supply recital, which relies upon on deliver behavior, has the possessions of multi size in addition to multi-scales, regarding to numerous dimensions. So, the performance evaluation of a seller is not handiest inclusive, however is also problematic beneath a steady scale (Wang et al., 2009). Evaluation strategies provide an output essential to the carriers' recital, but a number of the providers' behaviors can degree explicitly rendering to its description (consisting of unit rate as well as defect). Some cannot represent with an in-depth numeric fee (which include functionality on R & D in addition to quality), conversely, tons of the information related to vendor performance evaluation is not quantifiable further to detailed with crunchy limitations. Somewhat, this evidence is offered in expressions or words in normal language then without precision (Asher et al., 2021). The winds of alternate had been blowing inside the EPC enterprise since 2014. If there may be one component of which we may be positive, it's far that the pace of trade will handily accelerate over the next decade (Tsaramirsis, et al., 2016).

Much of discussion about the future is focused on new technologies and digitalization (Wagner et al., 2020). Certainly, using technology to higher manage methods and records is a prerequisite for advancement. However, even as the beyond decade has been more centered on records acquisition and optimization inside silos, the following may be focused on connecting statistics threads across events, databases and challenge levels— and leveraging that statistics to optimize average outcomes for a mission (Kantaros et al., 2022).

Untapped price will pressure a exchange in the nature of the connection between proprietors and EPC firms toward one that is extra collaborative. The end result can be higher designs and facilities, and a extra comprehensive expertise of project economics across the lifecycle, with fewer surprises for all parties.

Customers and contractors provide various weights to different success criteria, with contractors giving more emphasis to cost and duration minimization than their clients, and clients giving more weight to stakeholder satisfaction than contractors (Bryde & Robinson, 2005).

Finally, via 2030, younger, pragmatic engineers will see the potential to help acquire significant and vital change in an industry that embraces era, innovation and collaboration to help society meet its strength and cloth needs in a manner that is more sustainable for future generations (Eke et al., 2020).

## 3  Objectives of the Study

The study envisaged on the following objectives-

1. The dealer assessment device may offer with a transparent device by using that; selection can be done to distribute with field visits for re-evaluation,
2. The rating device can be employed in different decision-making equipment additionally

## 4  Research Methodology

Execution assessments of provider are difficult; numerous standards and norms that are included ought to be measured. In actuality, provider choice is the quintessences' of inventory network the executives; meanwhile, appraisal of supply execution turns into the fundamental action of provider choice (Lau et al, 2002). Choi and Hartley assessed "providers dependent on consistency, unwavering quality, relationship, adaptability, value, administration, innovative capacity and funds and furthermore tended to 26 provider determination criteria" (Choi, Hartley, 1996). Verma and Pullman positioned the significance of the provider characteristics of value, on time conveyance, cost, lead-time as well as adaptability (Verma, Pullman, 1998). Vonderembse and Tracey portrayed that provider in addition to assembling execution were controlled through provider choice standards in addition to provider association (Vonderembse, Tracey, 1999). It was presumed that the provider choice standards can be assessed by quality, accessibility, dependability and execution. Provider contribution could assess by item R&D and development, in addition to provider execution can assess by stoppage, conveyance, harm as well as quality. Moreover, fabricating execution can assess by cost, quality, stock in addition to conveyance. Tracey and Tan created provider determination criteria, including quality, conveyance, dependability, execution and value (Tracey, Tan, 2001).

The criteria are likewise used to survey consumer loyalty dependent on value, quality, assortment and conveyance. Besides, Kannan and Tan decided provider choice dependent on responsibility, needs, ability, fit and trustworthiness, and built up a framework for provider assessment dependent on conveyance, quality, responsiveness and data sharing (Kannan, Tan, 2002). Kannan and Tan additionally assessed provider determination and execution dependent on the loads of assessment qualities or criteria with fresh qualities that rely upon emotional individual decisions. Muralidharan et al analyzed the points of interest and confinements of nine recently created strategies for provider rating, and joined various criteria dynamic and applied investigative progressive system procedures to build multi-criteria cooperative choice making model for provider rating (Muralidharan et al, 2002) The traits of value, conveyance, value, strategy capacity, funds, mentality, office, adaptability and administration were utilized for provider assessment, and the characteristics of information, aptitude, demeanor and experience were utilized for singular appraisals. Anyway, numerous variables have been considered in provider choice and assessment, including operational, culture, innovation, relationship, cost, quality, time and adaptability. Right now, criteria are grouped in six classes as appeared in Table 1 and are utilized in the introduced model. It is the way toward estimating, breaking down and dealing with the provider execution to exceed expectations on the serious parameters of the business (Tables 2, 3 and 4).

**Table 1.** Importance of Criteria

|   | Criteria | Relative | Importance |
|---|---|---|---|
| 1 | Quality | C1 | 1 |
| 2 | On time delivery | C2 | 0.6 |
| 3 | Technological ability | C3 | 0.4 |
| 4 | Competitive cost & Financial situation | C4 | 0.8 |
| 5 | Product design Ability | C5 | 0.9 |
| 6 | After sale services | C6 | 0.7 |

# 5 Importance of Vender Management

- Forthcoming competitiveness can n determine by firm's capability to create policies to optimally line up as well as manage a large network of vender relationships.
- Firm's performance will be progressively determined through (as well as reliant upon) the performance of external supply partners.
- The real management of these large supply network requires firms to apply approaches for gauging well as refining the performance of network.

In this study, a model has developed by taking vender performance rating system into consideration with differ criteria. The different criteria are explained as follows: Vendor Performance Rating System-Model.

A supplier can be rated based on the below four Parame through a Point Rating Model.

- Adherence to Delivery
- Adherence to Technical Specifications
- Landed Price
- Responsiveness & Customer Satisfaction

The Vendor Rating is proposed to be done Based on the criteria:

1. Quality performance of vendor: Based on Quality Products produced during period under consideration
2. Delivery Performance of Vendor: Based on sup performance of vendor against orders within delivery Perio
3. Service & System performance of vendor: Based General Performance Such as reassessment, Upda infrastructure etc. and maintenance of Quality control system
Point rating system – an illustration
4. Adherence to Delivery                       35 points
5. Adherence to Technical Specifications    30 points
6. Landed Price                                    15 points
7. Responsiveness & Customer Satisfaction 20 points

Total 100 points

Vendor rating is the sum total of the points scored out of 100.

Adherence to Delivery

- Maximum Points - 35
- Compare Actual Delivery vs. Contractual for each item in the PO.
- If the delivery is within contractual period and within grace period, supplier to get 35 points.
- For every day delay beyond grace period, supplier lose 1 point
- (Max. 30)
- For everyday early before grace period, supplier lose 0.5 point
- (Max. 15) - Optional

Adherence to Technical Specifications & Quality

- Maximum Points - 30
- Outright Rejection - 0 points
- Complete Acceptance - 20 points
- Acceptance with deviation – 0 - 15
- Rejection points for rework is 0 - 15.
- Calibrated Equipment with calibration history – 5 points (max)
- Trained employee with training hour history – 5 points (max)

**Table 2.** Acceptance with Deviation

| Rejection Code | Description | Rejection Points |
|---|---|---|
| C - 01 | Machining: Undersize | 8 |
| C - 02 | Machining: Oversize | 4 |
| F - 01 | Fabrication: Welding defects | 10 |
| F -02 | Fabrication: Not meeting requirements | 15 |
| M- 01 | Material: Lamination observed | 10 |
| M - 02 | Material: Excessive Pitting | 10 |
| M- 03 | Material: Not meeting specification | 12 |
| M - 04 | Material: Received in damage condition | 5 |
| M- 05 | Material: Dimension deviation | 5 |
| M - 06 | Material: Poor Workmanship | 8 |
| M- 07 | Material: Improper Packing | 2 |
| M - 08 | Material: Damage Packing | 5 |
| M - 09 | Material: Physical Test Failed | 15 |
| M - 10 | Material: Chemical Analysis Failed | 10 |
| M - 11 | Material: HT not done as required | 10 |
| M - 12 | Material: Stamping not matching | 3 |
| M - 13 | Material: Original stamping not available | 6 |
| M - 14 | Material: 3rd party stamping not available | 2 |
| PRV | Provisionally cleared | 5 |

**Rework**

- **For every 20 shop/field man-hour spent on rework - 1 point to be deducted**

Landed Price
**Maximum Points - 15**

- Lowest quoted landed price - 15 points
- Higher than the lowest bid up to 5% - 12 points
- Higher than the lowest bid up to 10% - 9 points
- Higher than the lowest bid up to 15% - 6 points
- Higher than the lowest bid > 15% - 3 points

**Table 3.** Landed Price Categorization

| Code | Description | Points |
|------|-------------|--------|
| Type-1 | Rate Contract & L1 | 15 |
| Type-2 | Rate Con-tract & L2 | 12 |
| Type-3 | Rate Contract & L3 & Onwards | 9 |
| Type-4 | L1 on quotations received | 13 |
| Type-5 | L2 on quotations received | 10 |
| Type-6 | L3 on quotations received & Onwards | 7 |
| Type-7 | Repeat Order & L1 | 15 |
| Type-8 | Repeat Order other than L1 | 12 |
| Type-9 | Initiator / Customer Recommendation | 10 |
| Type-10 | OE Item | 12 |
| Type-11 | Monopoly Supplier/Controlled price | 10 |
| Type-12 | Emergency buying on single offer | 5 |

## Customer Satisfaction

- Maximum Points – 20
- ISO certification / Registered Exporter - 5 points
- Customer satisfaction (Buyer) - 5 points
- (Vendor responsiveness)
- Local Supplier/Vendor from SC/ST/Backward classes/Physically challenged - 5 points
- Customer satisfaction (Accounts) – 5 points
- Customer satisfaction (Inspection) – 5 points
- Customer satisfaction (Stores) – 5 points
- Adherence to Delivery 35points (20)
- Adherence to Technical Specifications 30 points (25)
- Landed Price15 points (12)
- Responsiveness & Customer Satisfaction 20 points (15)

## Vendor inclusion criteria

- Minimum order value or Minimum orders is the criteria for a supplier to be included in VPRS

- Applicable for all the suppliers of Service as well as non-service items
- Categorization of vendors

**Table 4.** Categorization of Vendors

| Supplier Category | Description | Supplier Category | Description |
|---|---|---|---|
| CAT - 1 | Raw Material | CAT - 16 | Gearboxes |
| CAT - 2 | Forging | CAT – 17 | Drive components |
| CAT - 3 | Pipe - Manufacturers | CAT – 18 | Pulleys & Idlers |
| CAT - 4 | Pipe - Stockiest | CAT – 19 | Conveyor & Components |
| CAT - 5 | Pipe - Fittings | CAT – 20 | Sub- Contracting |
| CAT - 6 | Fasteners | CAT – 21 | Piling |
| CAT - 7 | Electrodes | CAT – 22 | Pile - Capping & Concreting |
| CAT - 8 | Paints | CAT – 23 | Civil- Foundation |
| CAT - 9 | Gases | CAT – 24 | Heavy Fabrication |
| CAT - 10 | Cement | CAT – 25 | Medium & Light Fabrication |
| CAT - 11 | Rebar | CAT – 26 | Shot Blasting & Painting |
| CAT - 12 | Structural | CAT – 27 | Electrical Services |
| CAT - 13 | Refractory | CAT – 28 | Erection |
| CAT - 14 | Instruments & Values | CAT – 29 | Commissioning |
| CAT - 15 | Motor | CAT - 30 | Misc Services |

**Benefits**

- Provided valuable inputs for Internal Analysis
- Individual Supplier rating
- Average Rating for all Suppliers
- Reinforcement

## 6  Conclusion

This research creates an assessment strategy to assess vendor performance in vendor rating form. Various factors used in the vendor assessment procedure are as well as problematic to quantify. There are great advantages in the usage of the model provided by the paper which is contemporary. It is also relatively flexible, permitting the decision maker to apply a comprehensive range of linguistic factors further to modifiers for better judgment or to make versions to membership standards and vendor overall performance categories. Lastly, it's far an ideal device while the decision maker is tackled with a chain of sub-decisions anywhere where obtainable data is based on ambiguity, uncertainty, as well as opinion. These sub-decisions are then mixed into an average device for provider performance assessment. The flexibility of the model permits the decision maker to introduce vagueness, uncertainty, and subjectivity into the provider overall performance evaluation system. This examination points out an elective strategy for the provider execution assessment framework.

## 7 Future Implications

Future implications of this research study is expected to build up a technique for relating provider execution esteems to etymological factors in provider execution assessment, just as testing the affectability of provider execution esteems and their effect on the result and helps industry professionals become more aware of the important aspects that affect a project's effectiveness and suggests practical methods for preserving optimal alignment between project and product objectives as well as encouraging end-user involvement including vendors.

## References

Asadabadi, M.R., et al.: Hidden fuzzy information: Requirement specification and measurement of project provider performance using the best worst method. Fuzzy Sets Syst. **383**, 127–145 (2020)

Ara, R.A., Paardenkooper, K., van Duin, R.: A new blockchain system design to improve the supply chain of engineering, procurement and construction (EPC) companies–a case study in the oil and gas sector. J. Eng., Design Technol. (2021)

Asher, S.W., Jan, S., Tsaramirsis, G., Khan, F.Q., Khalil, A., Obaidullah, M.: Reverse engineering of mobile banking applications. Comput. Syst. Sci. Eng. **38**(3), 265–278 (2021)

Baldwin, J. F., "Fuzzy Logic", John Wiley & Sons, New York, (1996), N.Y

Bryde, D.J., Robinson, L.: Client versus contractor perspectives on project success criteria. Int. J. Project Manage. **23**(8), 622–629 (2005)

Choi, T.Y., Hartley, J.L.: An exploration of supplier selection practices across the supply chain. Journal of Operation Management **14**(4), 333–343 (1996)

Chavan, G., Chaudhuri, R., Johnston, W.J., Garner, B.: Purchasing performance of engineering procurement and construction companies using a fuzzy quality function deployment approach. J. Bus. Indust. Market. **36**(5), 849–66 (2020)

Eke, J., et al.: The global status of desalination: An assessment of current desalination technologies, plants and capacity. Desalination **495**, 114633 (2020)

Kannan, V.R., Tan, K.C.: Supplier selection and assessment: their impact on business performance. J. Supply Chain Manag. **38**(4), 11–21 (2002)

Klir, G.J., Yuan, B.: Fuzzy Sets and Fuzzy Logic. Prentice-Hall, Upper Saddle River, NJ (1995)

Muralidharan, C., Anantharaman, N., Deshmukh, S.G.: A multicriteria group decision making model for supplier rating. J. Supply Chain Manag. **38**(1), 22–33 (2002)

Niayeshnia, P., Damavand, M.R., Gholampour, S.: Classification, prioritization, efficiency, and change management of EPC projects in Energy and Petroleum industry field using the TOPSIS method as a multi-criteria group decision-making method. AIMS Energy **8**(5), 918–934 (2020)

Tracey, M., Tan, C.L.: Empirical analysis of supplier selection and involvement, customer satisfaction, and firm performance. Supply Chain Manag. **6**(3–4), 174–188 (2001)

Verma, R., Pullman, M.E.: An analysis of the supplier selection process. Omega **26**(6), 739–750 (1998)

Vonderembse, M.A., Tracey, M.: The impact of supplier selection criteria and supplier involvement on manufacturing performance. J. Supply Chain Manag. **35**(3), 33–39 (1999)

Wang, S.Y., Chang, S.L., Wang, R.C.: Assessment of supplier performance based on product-development strategy by applying multi-granularity linguistic term sets. Int. J. Manage. Sci. **37**(1), 215–226 (2009)

Wagner, R.F.: EPC 4.0: The quest for reducing CAPEX in EPC projects. Org., Technol. Manage. Construct.: an Int. J **12**(1), 2245–2255 (2020)

Yao, F., et al.: Evaluation of informatization performance of construction industrialization EPC enterprises in China. Advances in Civil Engineering (2020)

Tsaramirsis, G., Karamitsos, I., Apostolopoulos, C.: Smart parking: An IoT application for smart city. In: 2016 3rd International Conference on Computing for Sustainable Global Development (INDIACom), pp. 1412–1416. IEEE (2016, March)

Tsaramirsis, G.: Bridging the Divide: Transforming Business Requirements into Component-based Architectures (Doctoral dissertation, University of London), (2010)

Kantaros, A., et al.: 3D printing: Making an innovative technology widely accessible through makerspaces and outsourced services. Mater. Today: Proc. **49**, 2712–2723 (2022)

# F2PMSMD: Design of a Fusion Model to Identify Fake Profiles from Multimodal Social Media Datasets

Bhrugumalla L. V. S. Aditya[1]([✉]), Gnanajeyaraman Rajaram[2],
Shreyas Rajendra Hole[3], and Sachi Nandan Mohanty[1]

[1] School of Computer Science and Engineering (SCOPE), VIT-AP University, Amaravati,
Andhra Pradesh, India
aditya.22phd7023@vitap.ac.in
[2] Department of AI & ML, Saveetha School of Engineering, SIMATS, Chennai, India
[3] School of Electronics Engineering (SENSE), VIT-AP University, Amaravati, Andhra Pradesh,
India
rajendra.20phd7078@vitap.ac.in

**Abstract.** Modern-day social media is one of the most used platforms by millennials for sharing personal, and professional events, thoughts & other entities. These entities include photos, texts, videos, locations, meta data about other users, etc. Thus, securing this content from fake-users is of utmost importance, due to which a wide variety of techniques are proposed by researchers that includes but is not limited to, deep learning models, high density feature processing models, bioinspired models, etc. But these models are either highly complex, or require large user-specific datasets in order to improve their detection capabilities. Moreover, most of these models are inflexible, and cannot be scaled for large social networks with multiple parameter sets. To overcome these issues, this text proposes the design of a novel fusion model to identify fake profiles from multimodal social media datasets. The proposed model initially collects multimodal information about users that includes the presence of profile pic, username length ratios, number of words in the full name, length of their personal description, use of external URLs, account type, number of posts, number of followers & following users, etc. These information sets are pre-processed via a Genetic Algorithm (GA) based feature selection model, which assists in the identification of highly variant feature sets. The selected feature sets are classified via a fusion of Naïve Bayes (NB) Multilayer Perceptron (MLP), Logistic Regression (LR), Support Vector Machine (SVM), and Deep Forest (DF) classifiers. Due to a combination of these classifiers, the proposed model is capable of showcasing an accuracy of 98.5%, precision of 94.3%, recall of 94.9%, and F-measure score of 94.7% across multiple datasets. Due to such a high performance, the proposed model is capable of deployment for a wide variety of social media platforms to detect fake profiles.

**Keywords:** Social · Media · Fake · Profile · Genetic · Algorithm · NB · MLP · LR · SVM · DF · Precision · Recall · Accuracy · F-measure · Fusion · Features

© ICST Institute for Computer Sciences, Social Informatics and Telecommunications Engineering 2023
Published by Springer Nature Switzerland AG 2023. All Rights Reserved
S. Nandan Mohanty et al. (Eds.): ICISML 2022, LNICST 471, pp. 13–23, 2023.
https://doi.org/10.1007/978-3-031-35081-8_2

# 1   Introduction

Identification of fake profiles in social media is a multidomain task that involves user tracing, context analysis, analysis of user posts, their login patterns, personal profile update patterns, image metadata patterns, etc. A typical social network analysis model (Krishnan et al. 2020) that uses network activity logs, profile attributes, graph analysis, ranking models, network information sets, etc. is depicted in Fig. 1, wherein a threshold-based ranking of profiles is done for identification of normal profiles from fakes. In this model, researchers were able to combine multiple data sources, and extract their nodes, edges, weights, and other parameters for improving classification performance under different scenarios. But these models showcase moderate accuracy, and cannot be scaled for larger network deployments. To overcome these issues, researchers have proposed multiple deep learning and machine learning based classification models, that aim at dynamically modifying their performance based on contextual requirements. A survey of such models (Latha et al. 2022), (Harris et al. 2021), (Patel et al. 2020) in terms of their functional nuances, contextual advantages, application-specific drawbacks, and deployment-specific future scopes is discussed in the next section of this text.

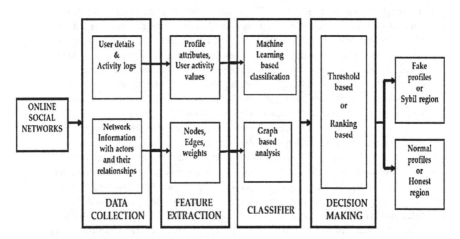

**Fig. 1.** Design of a threshold-based model for identification of fake profiles

Based on this discussion, it was observed that these models are either highly complex, or require large user-specific datasets in order to improve their detection capabilities. Moreover, most of these models are inflexible, and cannot be scaled for large social networks with multiple parameter sets. To overcome these issues, Sect. 3 of this text proposes design of a novel fusion model to identify fake profiles from multimodal social media datasets. The proposed model was validated in Sect. 4, wherein its performance was compared with other models in terms of accuracy, recall, F-measure, and precision metrics. Finally, this text is concluded with some contextual observations about the proposed model, and also recommends methods to further improve its performance under different network types.

## 2  Related Work

A wide variety of models are proposed for analysis of social media profiles, and each of them varies in terms of their internal performance characteristics. For instance, work in (Siva Rama Krishna et al. 2022), (Parihar et al. 2021) proposes use of C4.5 Decision Tree (CDT), and Collaborative Filtering that assists in identification of fake profiles for Twitter, but cannot be extended to other networks. To overcome this limitation, work in (Kulkarni et al. 2022) proposes use of Artificial Neural Networks (ANNs) that can be extended to multiple network types. Similar models are discussed in (Bhattacharya et al. 2021), (Ajesh et al. 2021), (Antonio Theophilo, Rafael Padilha, Fernanda A. Andal, 2022) which propose use of Deep Learning, ensemble of Deep Forest, Support Vector Machine (SVM) with Optimized Naïve Bayes (ESDN), and Authorship Attribution sets, which aim at incorporating multiple parameters for improved social media analysis. Extensions to these models are discussed in (Rathod, 2022), (Ekosputra et al. 2021), (Hosseini Moghaddam & Abbaspour, 2022) which propose use of Author Profiling, ANN, and botnet-based detection, which assists in automating the detection process under different network types. Similar methods that use Random Walk (Le et al. 2020), Adversarial Model of Network Disruption (AMND) (Chen and Racz, 2022), and Particle Swarm Optimization with Deep Reinforcement Learning (PSO DRL) (Lingam et al. 2021) that aims at incorporating multiple deep learning models with extended feature processing techniques for identification of fake profiles are also discussed and applied for different use cases. Based on this discussion, it can be observed that these models are either highly complex, or require large user-specific datasets in order to improve their detection capabilities. Moreover, most of these models are inflexible, and cannot be scaled for large social networks with multiple parameter sets. To overcome these issues, next section proposes design of a novel fusion model to identify fake profiles from multimodal social media datasets. The proposed model was also validated on multiple datasets, and compared with various state-of-the-art methods under different scenarios.

## 3  Data Set Description

The proposed model uses a combination of multimodal information sets along with Genetic Algorithm for feature selection, and ensemble classifier for identification of fake profiles. To validate its performance, the model was tested on the following datasets,

- Social Network Fake Account Dataset, which is available at https://www.kaggle.com/datasets/bitandatom/social-network-fake-account-dataset
- Instagram fake spammer genuine accounts Dataset, which is available at https://www.kaggle.com/datasets/free4ever1/instagram-fake-spammer-genuine-accounts

## 4  Design of the Proposed Fusion Model to Identify Fake Profiles from Multimodal Social Media Datasets

Following a review of the existing models, it can be observed that these models are either very complex or call for sizable user-specific datasets to enhance their detection capabilities. In addition, the majority of these models lack flexibility and are incapable of scaling to large social networks with multiple parameter sets. The design of a novel fusion model to identify fake profiles from multimodal social media datasets is suggested in this section as a solution to these problems. The proposed model's process is shown in Fig. 2, where it can be seen that it begins by gathering multimodal data about users, such as whether they have profile pictures, how long their usernames are on average, how many words are in their full names, how long their personal descriptions are, whether they use external URLs, what kind of accounts they have, how many posts they have made, how many followers and users they follow, etc. These data sets are pre-processed using a feature selection model based on a Genetic Algorithm (GA), which helps identify feature sets with a high degree of variation. A combination of Naive Bayes (NB), Multilayer Perceptron (MLP), Logistic Regression (LR), Support Vector Machine (SVM), and Deep Forest (DF) classifiers is used to categorize the chosen feature sets.

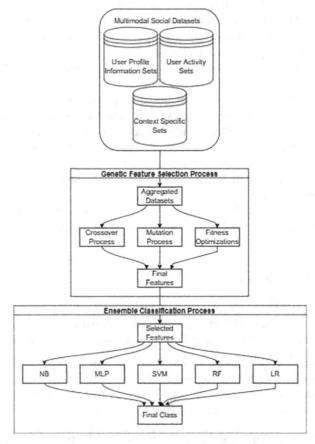

**Fig. 2.** Overall flow of the proposed fake-profile identification process

The process initially collects multimodal information sets from different sources, and applies a Genetic Algorithm (GA) for the identification of other f optimal feature sets. These feature sets are obtained via the following process,

4.1 Initially, setup the following optimization parameters,
    4.1.1 Iterations needed for GA optimization ($Ni$)
    4.1.2 Solutions to be generated for optimization ($Ns$)
    4.1.3 Rate at which the model will learn ($Lr$)
    4.1.4 Number of features extracted from the multimodal datasets ($Nf$)
4.2 To start the process, generate $Ns$ solutions as follows,
    4.2.1 Stochastically select $N$ features from the dataset via Eq. 1,

$$N = STOCH(Lr * Nf, Nf) \tag{1}$$

where, *STOCH* is a stochastic Markovian process, that generates value sets between given ranges.

4.3 Based on the selected features, identify class-level variance (or fitness of solution) via Eq. 2,

$$f = \sqrt{\frac{\sum_{a=1}^{m} (fa - \frac{\sum_{i=1}^{m} \sqrt{\frac{\sum_{j=1}^{n} (f_j - \frac{\sum_{a=1}^{n} fa}{n})^2}{n-1}}}{m})^2}{m-1}} \tag{2}$$

where, $m, n$ represents feature values in current class and other classes respectively such that $N = m + n$, while $fa$ represents selected features.

4.4 Once all solutions are generated, then identify optimization fitness threshold via Eq. 3,

$$f_{th} = \sum_{i=1}^{N_s} f_i * \frac{L_r}{N_s} \tag{3}$$

4.5 Check fitness of all solutions, and mark solutions with $f > f_{th}$ as 'Crossover', while mark others as 'Mutate'
4.6 Once the distinction is done, then scan all solutions for $Ni$ iterations, and regenerate 'Mutate' solutions via Eq. 1 and 2
4.7 Repeat this process for $Ni$ iterations

At the end of final iteration, select solution with maximum fitness, and use its features for classification process. This classification process is performed via a combination of Naive Bayes (NB), Multilayer Perceptron (MLP), Logistic Regression (LR), Support Vector Machine (SVM), and Deep Forest (DF) classifiers. The parameters used for these classifiers are indicated in Table 1 as follows,

**Table 1.** Parameters used for different classifiers

| Classifier | Parameters |
|---|---|
| NB | Priors = Interclass Fitness Levels<br>Smoothing = 1e-9 |
| LR | Normalization = True |
| MLP | Hidden Layers = Number of classes<br>Solver = Stochastic Gradient Descent Learning Rate = $Lr$ |
| SVM | Regularization parameter = 0.5<br>Kernel = Sigmoid Class Weights = Balanced |
| DF | Number of trees = 100*Number of classes<br>Maximum Forest Depth = 10 |

These parameters were selected via 'hit & try' method, which assisted in identification of classification parameters for optimal accuracy levels. Classification results of these classifiers are combined via Eq. 4,

$$C_{out} = C(NB) * A(NB) + C(LR) * A(LR) + C(MLP) * A(MLP) + C(SVM) * A(SVM) + C(DF) * A(DF) \quad (4)$$

where, $C$ & $A$ represents output class, and testing accuracy for given classifiers. Based on this process, classification is performed on different social media sets. Results of this classification, can be observed from the next section of this text.

## 5   Results and Discussion

The sets were combined to form a total of 2000 entries, out of which 1500 were used for training, while 250 for testing and 250 for validation purposes. The model's performance was compared with CDT (Siva Rama Krishna et al., 2022), ESDN, and PSO DRL (Lingam et al. 2021)in order to identify its efficiency over standard implementations. Based on this strategy, accuracy (A) of fake profile detection w.r.t. Number of Test entries (NT) can be observed from Table 2,

**Table 2.** Accuracy evaluation for different fake profile detection models

| NT | 100 | 200 | 300 | 400 | 500 | 600 | 750 | 900 | 1000 | 1200 | 1500 | 2000 |
|---|---|---|---|---|---|---|---|---|---|---|---|---|
| CDT | 87.7 | 88.31 | 88.84 | 89.22 | 89.45 | 89.57 | 89.61 | 89.65 | 89.69 | 89.78 | 89.95 | 90.15 |
| ESDN | 86.87 | 87.76 | 88.32 | 88.73 | 88.96 | 89.2 | 89.49 | 89.8 | 90.23 | 90.6 | 90.93 | 91.25 |
| PSO DRL | 86.09 | 86.83 | 87.36 | 87.76 | 87.99 | 88.17 | 88.32 | 88.5 | 88.73 | 88.95 | 89.18 | 89.44 |
| F2PM SMD | 95.58 | 96.4 | 96.99 | 97.43 | 97.68 | 97.89 | 98.05 | 98.25 | 98.52 | 98.76 | 99.02 | 99.31 |

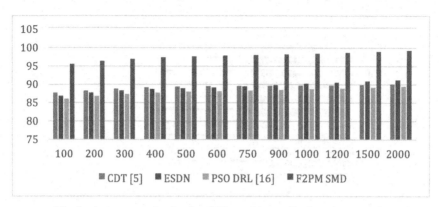

**Fig. 3.** Accuracy evaluation for different fake profile detection models

Based on this evaluation and Fig. 3, it can be observed that the proposed model showcases 9.2% better accuracy than CDT (Siva Rama Krishna et al. 2022), 8.3% better accuracy than ESDN and 9.5% better accuracy than PSO DRL (Lingam et al. 2021), which makes it highly useful for a wide variety of fake profile detection use cases. This is due to selection of optimal feature sets, that aim at improving classification performance for different scenarios. Similarly, precision (P) of evaluation can be observed from Table 3 as follows,

**Table 3.** Precision evaluation for different fake profile detection model

| NT | 100 | 200 | 300 | 400 | 500 | 600 | 750 | 900 | 1000 | 1200 | 1500 | 2000 |
|---|---|---|---|---|---|---|---|---|---|---|---|---|
| **CDT**(Siva Rama Krishna et al., 2022) | 87.7 | 88.31 | 88.84 | 89.22 | 89.5 | 89.57 | 89.61 | 89.7 | 89.7 | 89.78 | 89.95 | 90.2 |
| **ESDN** | 86.87 | 87.76 | 88.32 | 88.73 | 89 | 89.2 | 89.49 | 89.8 | 90.2 | 90.6 | 90.93 | 91.3 |
| **PSO DRL**(Lingam et al., 2021) | 86.09 | 86.83 | 87.36 | 87.76 | 88 | 88.17 | 88.32 | 88.5 | 88.7 | 88.95 | 89.18 | 89.4 |
| **F2PM SMD** | 95.58 | 96.4 | 96.99 | 97.43 | 97.7 | 97.89 | 98.05 | 98.3 | 98.5 | 98.76 | 99.02 | 99.3 |

Based on this evaluation and Fig. 4, it can be observed that the proposed model showcases 8.5% better precision than CDT (Siva Rama Krishna et al. 2022), 8.3% better precision than ESDN and 9.4% better precision than PSO DRL (Lingam et al. 2021), which makes it highly useful for a wide variety of fake profile detection use cases. This is due to selection of optimal feature sets and use of ensemble learning, that aim at improving classification performance for different scenarios. Similarly, recall (R) of evaluation can be observed from Table 4 as follows,

Based on this evaluation and Fig. 5, it can be observed that the a) of evaluation can be observed from Table 5 as follows,

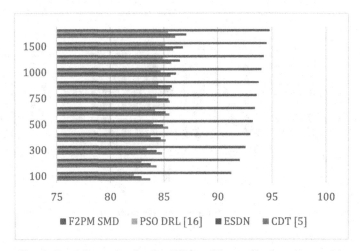

**Fig. 4.** Precision evaluation for different fake profile detection models

**Table 4.** Recall evaluation for different fake profile detection models

| NT% | | 100 | 200 | 300 | 400 | 500 | 600 | 750 | 900 | 1000 | 1200 | 1500 | 2000 |
|---|---|---|---|---|---|---|---|---|---|---|---|---|---|
| R | CDT (Siva Rama Krishna et al., 2022) | 85.14 | 85.72 | 86.24 | 86.61 | 86.83 | 86.95 | 86.98 | 87.03 | 87.07 | 87.15 | 87.31 | 87.51 |
| R | ESDN | 84.32 | 85.19 | 85.73 | 86.13 | 86.35 | 86.59 | 86.87 | 87.17 | 87.59 | 87.94 | 88.26 | 88.57 |
| R | PSO DRL (Lingam et al., 2021) | 83.57 | 84.29 | 84.8 | 85.19 | 85.41 | 85.58 | 85.73 | 85.9 | 86.13 | 86.34 | 86.57 | 86.82 |
| R | F2PM SMD | 92.78 | 93.58 | 94.15 | 94.57 | 94.82 | 95.02 | 95.18 | 95.38 | 95.63 | 95.87 | 96.12 | 96.4 |

**Table 5.** F-measure evaluation for different fake profile detection models

| NT(%) | | 100 | 200 | 300 | 400 | 500 | 600 | 750 | 900 | 1000 | 1200 | 1500 | 2000 |
|---|---|---|---|---|---|---|---|---|---|---|---|---|---|
| F | CDT (Siva Rama Krishna et al., 2022) | 84.42 | 85 | 85.51 | 85.88 | 86.1 | 86.22 | 86.25 | 86.3 | 86.34 | 86.4 | 86.6 | 86.77 |
| F | ESDN | 83.62 | 84.47 | 85.01 | 85.4 | 85.63 | 85.86 | 86.14 | 86.4 | 86.86 | 87.2 | 87.5 | 87.83 |
| F | PSO DRL (Linga m et al., 2021) | 82.86 | 83.58 | 84.09 | 84.47 | 84.7 | 84.86 | 85.01 | 85.2 | 85.4 | 85.6 | 85.8 | 86.09 |
| F | F2PM SMD | 92.15 | 92.8 | 93.36 | 93.78 | 94.02 | 94.22 | 94.38 | 94.6 | 94.83 | 95.1 | 95.3 | 95.59 |

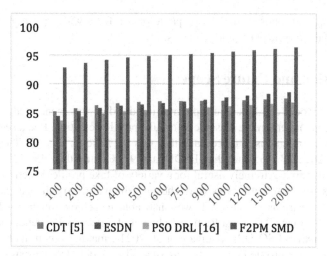

**Fig. 5.** Recall evaluation for different fake profile detection models

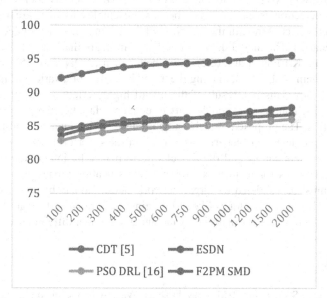

**Fig. 6.** F-measure evaluation for different fake profile detection models

Based on this evaluation and Fig. 6, it can be observed that the proposed model showcases 9.8% better F-measure than CDT (Siva Rama Krishna et al. 2022), 8.5% better F-measure than ESDN and 9.5% better F-measure than PSO DRL (Lingam et al. 2021), which makes it highly useful for a wide variety of fake profile detection use cases. This is due to use of high efficiency classifiers & selection of optimal feature sets, that aim at improving classification performance for different scenarios. Due to this performance enhancements, the proposed model is capable of use for a wide variety of real- time social media fake profile detection scenarios.

## 6  Conclusion and Future Scope

The suggested model combines multiple multimodal data sets, genetic algorithms for feature selection and ensemble classifiers for fake profile detection. Because of this, the model was able to demonstrate accuracy that was 9.2% better than CDT (Siva Rama Krishna et al. 2022), 8.3% better than ESDN, and 9.5% better than PSO DRL (Lingam et al. 2021), making it extremely useful for a variety of fake profile detection use cases. This is because the best feature sets were chosen, which aims to enhance classification performance for various scenarios. It was also able to achieve precision levels that were 8.5% better than CDT (Siva Rama Krishna et al. 2022), 8.3% better than ESDN, and 9.4% better than PSO DRL (Lingam et al. 2021), making it extremely beneficial for a variety of fake profile detection use cases. The model also demonstrated recall improvements of 8.3% over CDT (Siva Rama Krishna et al. 2022), 7.5% over ESDN, and 9.5% over PSO DRL (Lingam et al. 2021), making it extremely useful for a variety of fake profile detection use cases. This is because ensemble classifiers are used and the best feature sets are chosen with the intention of enhancing classification performance in various scenarios. The model demonstrated an F-measure that was 9.8% better than CDT (Siva Rama Krishna et al. 2022), 8.5% better than ESDN, and 9.5% better than PSO DRL (Lingam et al. 2021), making it extremely useful for a variety of fake profile detection use cases. This is a result of the use of highly effective classifiers and the choice of the best feature sets, which aims to enhance classification performance for various scenarios. The proposed model can be used for a wide range of real-time social media fake profile detection scenarios as a result of these performance improvements. In future, researchers can extend the model's performance by integration of multiple bioinspired techniques for feature extraction & classification processes. The model's performance must be validated on larger network sizes, and can be enhanced via use of hybrid deep learning techniques like Q-Learning, Generative Adversarial Networks (GANs), etc. which will assist in accuracy enhancement under different use cases.

## References

Ajesh, F., Aswathy, S.U., Philip, F.M., Jeyakrishnan, V.:  A hybrid method for fake profile detection in social networkusing artificial intelligence. Security Issues and Privacy Concerns in Industry 4.0 Applications, 89–112 (2021). https://doi.org/10.1002/9781119776529.ch5

Theophilo, A., Padilha, R., Fernanda, A.A., Rocha, R.: Explainable Artificial Intelligence For Authorship Attribution On Social Media  Artificial Intelligence Lab . ( Recod . ai ) Institute of Computing , University of Campinas , Br. ICASSP 2022 - 2022 IEEE International Conference on Acoustics, Speech and Signal Processing (ICASSP), pp. 2909–2913 (2022)

Bhattacharya, A., Bathla, R., Rana, A., Arora, G.: Application of machine learning techniques in detecting fake profiles on social media. In: 2021 9th International Conference on Reliability, Infocom Technologies and Optimization (Trends and Future Directions), ICRITO 2021, pp. 1–8 (2021). https://doi.org/10.1109/ICRITO51393.2021.9596373

Chen, M.F., Racz, M.Z.: An adversarial model of network disruption: maximizing disagreement and polarization in social networks. IEEE Trans. Netw. Sci. Eng. **9**(2), 728–739 (2022). https://doi.org/10.1109/TNSE.2021.3131416

Ekosputra, M.J., Susanto, A., Haryanto, F., Suhartono, D.: Supervised machine learning algorithms to detect instagram fake accounts. In: 2021 4th International Seminar on Research of Information Technology and Intelligent Systems. ISRITI 2021, pp. 396–400 (2021). https://doi.org/10.1109/ISRITI54043.2021.9702833

Harris, P., Gojal, J., Chitra, R., Anithra, S.: Fake instagram profile identification and classification using machine learning. In: 2021 2nd Global Conference for Advancement in Technology, GCAT 2021, pp. 1–5 (2021). https://doi.org/10.1109/GCAT52182.2021.9587858

Hosseini Moghaddam, S., Abbaspour, M.: Friendship preference: scalable and robust category of features for social bot detection. IEEE Trans. Depend. Sec. Comput. **5971**(c), 1–14 (2022). https://doi.org/10.1109/TDSC.2022.3159007

Krishnan, P., John Aravindhar, D., Reddy, P.B.P.: Finite automata for fake profile identification in online social networks. In: Proceedings of the International Conference on Intelligent Computing and Control Systems (2020)

ICICCS 2020, Iciccs, 1301–1305. https://doi.org/10.1109/ICICCS48265.2020.9121086

Kulkarni, V., Aashritha Reddy, D., Sreevani, P., Teja, R.N.: Fake profile identification using ANN, pp. 375–380 (2022). https://doi.org/10.1049/icp.2022.0372

Latha, P., Sumitra, V., Sasikala, V., Arunarasi, J., Rajini, A. R., Nithiya, N. Fake profile identification in social network using machine learning and NLP. In: 2022 International Conference on Communication, Computing and Internet of Things, IC3IoT 2022 - Proceedings, pp. 20–23 (2022). https://doi.org/10.1109/IC3IOT53935.2022.9767958

Le, N.C., Dao, M.T., Nguyen, H.L., Nguyen, T.N., Vu, H.: An application of random walk on fake account detection problem: a hybrid approach. Proceedings - 2020 RIVF International Conference on Computing and Communication Technologies, RIVF 2020 (2020). https://doi.org/10.1109/RIVF48685.2020.9140749

Lingam, G., Rout, R.R., Somayajulu, D.V.L.N., Ghosh, S.K.: Particle swarm optimization on deep reinforcement learning for detecting social spam bots and spam-influential users in twitter network. IEEE Syst. J. **15**(2), 2281–2292 (2021). https://doi.org/10.1109/JSYST.2020.3034416

Parihar, P., Devanand, Kumar, N.: Fake profile detection from the social dataset for movie promotion. In: Proceedings of the IEEE International Conference Image Information Processing, 2021-Novem, 495–498 (2021). https://doi.org/10.1109/ICIIP53038.2021.9702684

Patel, K., Agrahari, S., Srivastava, S. Survey on fake profile detection on social sites by using machine learning algorithm. In: ICRITO 2020 - IEEE 8th International Conference on Reliability, Infocom Technologies and Optimization (Trends and Future Directions), 1236–1240(2020). https://doi.org/10.1109/ICRITO48877.2020.9197935

Rathod, S.: Exploring Author Profiling for Fake News Detection, pp. 1614–1619 (2022). https://doi.org/10.1109/compsac54236.2022.00256

Siva Rama Krishna, S., Umakanth, K., Anji Reddy, T., Saiteja, A., Sumanjali, R.: Detection of fake and clone accounts in twitter using classification and distance measure algorithms. In: Reddy, A.N.R., Marla, D., Favorskaya, M.N., Satapathy, S.C. (eds.) Intelligent Manufacturing and Energy Sustainability. SIST, vol. 265, pp. 391–399. Springer, Singapore (2022). https://doi.org/10.1007/978-981-16-6482-3_39

# A Novel Model to Predict the Whack of Pandemics on the International Rankings of Academia

Nidhi Agarwal[1,2] and Devendra K. Tayal[1(✉)]

[1] Indira Gandhi Delhi Technical University for Women, Delhi, India
devendrakumartayal@gmail.com
[2] Delhi Technical Campus, Greater Noida, India
http://www.delhitechnicalcampus.ac.in

**Abstract.** Pandemics bring physical life to a complete standstill; people are bound to remain confined to their homes. Students suffer a lot academically due to closure of educational institutes worldwide due to pandemic fear. In such a scenario, imparting adequate education to them so that their academics is not affected, is a big challenge. During the COVID-19 pandemic time, educational institutions have really played a good role in imparting online education to students. Their career and academic tenure were not affected. It is contrary to the past pandemics throughout the world history where students' academic years were lost. All this has been possible because of advancement in technologies related to Human Computer Interaction. The educational institutions tried to cope up a lot with the current educational mode but lacked in some or the other international ranking parameters. This brought sudden dips in their international ranks which can be regained only in long periods of time with major extra efforts. This research work provides an insight on the slipped off international ranks of higher educational institutions during global disruptive conditions like pandemics (COVID-19 and combatting with future pandemics). The novel model proposed in this work helps academicians in predicting the impact of pandemics on their overall international rankings so that recovery decisions and plans can be taken timely by academicians to combat with the situation. The work involves developing a model based on Machine Learning advanced algorithms with the inclusion of a humongous ranking dataset. Strong empirical results support the high efficiency as sensitivity = 97.98, Accuracy = 97.54, F1 value = 97.82, Kappa-score = 0.95. Using the proposed model. To the best of our knowledge, till now none of the researchers have proposed any such pioneering tool for academicians using advanced Machine Learning algorithms.

**Keywords:** University rankings · COVID-19 · Pandemics · Machine Learning Models · Higher Educational Institutions

S. Nandan Mohanty et al. (Eds.): ICISML 2022, LNICST 471, pp. 24–38, 2023.
https://doi.org/10.1007/978-3-031-35081-8_3

# 1  Introduction

Past pandemics in the world history brought academia to a complete standstill. There were huge academic losses to students in the form of year loss, zero-education, delayed admissions and even no admissions. But the academia industry played completely different role during the current pandemics "COVID-19". The sole credit goes to advancement in technologies related to Human Computer Interaction. Students were connected virtually to their schools, classrooms, teachers and most importantly with their peers [1–4]. The technological advancements even provided them ways to attempt quizzes, assignments, tutorials etc. both graphically and textually. Even the video-call based applications provide students with the facility to keep their classroom-customised background where they can have a complete classroom feel [5–8]. All this lead "COVID-19" not hamper the students' higher level academia. All this could help educational institutions to continue their aacademia uninterruptedly but there were various factors at the international level which were neglected during the pandemics. These are those factors which actually contribute for the international ranking of the various higher educational institutions (HEIs). A large chunk of students which comes from various other countries known as "international students" was unable to be catered by all the academia.

There are various Australian and European countries whose major chunk of student contribution is from the international market. The universities of these countries were affected badly by the closure of borders. They were unable to cater the international students which remarkably reduced their international ranking scores. In this way, a major ranking parameter which is dependent on "international students" was undoubtedly reduced. The various other factors related to publications, citations, visits as resource persons in various other academia which have a great contribution in the international ranking parameters were also hampered. The various educational institutions dealing with traditional modes of education were completely neglected by the admission aspirant student community. The new entrants were totally unwilling to take admission in traditional educational institutions. Various HEIs demanding higher fees were also neglected by the new student community. As we all know that the privately owned educational institutions are dependent mainly on the fee which they get from students, so their growth and their stay in international market were also hampered. Finance also plays a major role in the advancement of any educational institution because it has a major contribution for procuring new tools, technologies, softwares and infrastructure. All this lead to significant reduction in the ranks of various educational institutions especially if we talk about the privately owned ones. This work would provide an insight to combat with current and future pandemics regarding Higher Educational Institutions students. The study involves only those working professionals who are pursuing higher studies also.

# 2  Overview of the Related Work

At the very onset of year 2020 the various HEIs were forced to go for online mode of education with a sudden shift from the offline one. This forced the educational institutions to put their major emphasis and energy on how to accelerate the new mode of education.

All the resources, energy, time, resources were consumed in implementing this mode of education in a proper and best possible manner. Due to this, the various parameters on which the institutions and academicians used to focus during pre-pandemic times to gain higher rankings was neglected. Also, the number of students being catered as "international students" was reduced significantly due to the physical closure of the universities. As during the pandemic time people suffered from a lot many financial losses so continuing or opting for high fee based educational institutions for their wards proved to be quite difficult for majority of the parents. In such a scenario even in developed countries like United States, according to the study [9], the parents preferred not to opt for very high fee demanding higher educational institutions. In most of the high fee demanding higher educational institutions the enrolment ratio even dropped to half during the 2 years of pandemics. These universities which were affected majorly by the COVID-19 pandemic. In the absence of adequate finances, the universities were unable to maintain many parameters for sustainability in the international ranking fight. Even if we look at the various highly reputed Australian, American, or European universities, many of them had to face these challenges [10, 11].

The Australian and the European universities were majorly affected by this pandemic scenario and faced a significant dip in the international rankings [12, 13]. Lack of adequate finances which comes majorly from the "international student" cult stopped them from taking various progressive steps which can compete them in the international market [14, 15]. The Australian universities have highest number of international students in their campus. According to a report for these universities the international students contribute to even 1/4 of the total number of enrolments in Australia in the years prior to COVID-19. But this percentage dipped significantly during the post COVID time and reduced to even 2% to 3% for the years 2020 and 2021 enrolments 9 [16, 17]. As these are the major countries which faced pandemic to a greater extent and lockdown continued in these countries for a longer duration and so the quarantine period. So, the campuses were almost deserted with minimal enrolments as discussed above. If we see the pre-pandemic scenario for these countries, then the enrolments for the masters and the doctorate degree programmes were even higher as compared to that for graduate degree programs [18, 19]. It summarises that during the pre -pandemic times, the enrolments were fairly good for the graduate programs (around 25%) but they were excellent for the postgraduate and doctorate programs (reaching even up to 50% of the total enrolments) [12].

If we talk about the Indian students who used to take admission in China based HEIs by the year 2019, then it was around 60% but during the tenure of pandemics, this value reduced even to 10% to 15% [18]. According to an Australian universities survey, around 6500 academicians lost their jobs during the pandemics because of lesser turn ups of students in higher educational institutions, this data even involves some of the best Australian universities [30]. In this context, China also faced significant financial losses because of the early outbreak covid in China as well as due to long duration of covid restrictions due to closure of international borders [20].Their academic business process model has been shattered because of the pandemics. The money from international students, which was used to raise the rankings of the universities, could not be generated [19]. Many senior academicians anticipate that if the same condition prolongs for one or two more years, then major Australian universities will have to lower their academic standards in various parameters which would substantially impact the international ranking scores [23]. This is a very alarming situation which needs to be addressed especially for Australian based universities.

The research fundings have also been reduced which has led to the reduction in thousands of research-oriented jobs for the Australian universities, which has again significantly reduced their international rankings. To combat with this situation many of the Australian best universities have started switching to the short-term courses (with the help of some local educators) and online lectures in partnership with the local people. But this has no not been able to solve the problem entirely. All this has no doubtedly impacted educational standards and thus also impacted the overall international ranking of these institutions. This will take a long time to help these universities regain their international stay in the academia market. Academicians also fear that the top universities may permanently lose their international rankings as would not be able to recover themselves at all with these alarming situations. If we talk about UK based higher education institutions, then they have comparatively low ratio of "international students" as compared to Australia based universities. But they have a good contribution of "international students" as compared to various other countries of the world. The major turn-ups for these UK based universities are for bachelor's and master's degree programs [24]. Europe has always offered very high scholarships which has attracted good percentage of international students[25]. This has been the prime attraction among the international students to opt for these universities. But during the pandemic, even after offering scholarships the students had not turned up to the mark. The major reason behind this goes to the closing of international borders[24]. Various parameters on which these universities work come from the student contribution in which the mixed knowledge sharing and working on interdisciplinary projects by the mixture of international and national students matters a lot. But this collaboration reduced significantly because of the above stated reasons[27].

Most of the UK based HEIs depend majorly on the funds given by the government [27, 28] but during the pandemics, these funds have been reduced which led to a great dip in the international ranking scores for these universities. The recruitments were also affected a lot because of the pandemics. This restricted students to not opt for the satisfactory jobs as they were deserving. The layouts of the staff and the faculty members has also taken place to a great extent during these times due to which academic retention ratio has been reduced which is a major contributor in the international rankings of most of the ranking bodies. All these reasons discussed about various universities in the world, be it public sector or private sector based, higher ranking based, or lower ranking based, their rankings dipped significantly during the pandemics. The fear is that many of these universities will take years to combat with the situation and few of them might not even be able to recover themselves for longer duration. This is a bitter fact which most of the academia has faced during the pandemics.

# 3   Proposed Methodology and Design

The dataset used in the research work is taken from the Kaggle repository and contains a vast collection of international ranking parameters data of various academia of 5 years viz for years 2017–2022. This includes the data of all reputed HEIs which have been able to place themselves in the international ranking fight for last 5 years including the current year 2022.The data comprises of total 6482 universities for 5 years out of which 1368 are distinct universities at international ranking level. The dataset contains 6482 rows and 15 columns. The various parameters on which these universities are categorized are the research output from faculty, students and staff faculty student ratio, number of international students, size of the university, the count of the faculty members. As is indicative from these parameters that research plays a very important role in the international ranking of various educational institutions. The number of faculty members per specified number of students also contributes a lot to the same. No doubt the number of "international students" taking admission in any higher educational institution in a particular year also contributes a lot for international rankings. As is indicative from the data through the data set that the number of international students has dipped considerably during the pandemic years. All this will be discussed in detail in Sect. 4 in the results part.

The universities are categorised as public sector based at private sector based. The research output is taken in 3 categories as high, low, and very high. The university size is taken as small, large, extra-large. Faculty count is also of great importance in contributing to the international ranking parameters of the university. The proposed methodology is shown in Fig. 1, as we can see that the first step is to load our database which is in the form of a CSV file to the pandas data frame. Then we divide the data set into the training and test datasets to make the predictions. Usually, the preferred values to divide the training and the test dataset is 70% and 30%. As the data is quite humongous which is running in thousands of number of rows and tens of columns, so it may be possible that some of the data values are missing. Thus, an important part is to check for the missing data which is done as the next step. Then we go for the data pre-processing where we first normalise the data to bring it to a uniform scale and then deal with the imbalanced data problem. Imbalanced data refers to the presence of outliers in the dataset for a particular attribute. The presence of outliers makes the predictions biased, so we need to handle and remove it properly so that our predictions are not affected. Then, finally we deploy the model based on the proposed approach.

Here the approach which we are using to deploy the model is a computationally strong, effective, and efficient supervised machine learning supervised model called XGBoost model. This model has a very high predictive power and thus has been adopted as our proposed methodology. The various other models were also tried but the results generated by them were not so satisfactory. So, we have adopted this XGBoost model-based approach in our proposed methodology. It is a computationally strong model and is capable of dealing with humongous amount of data. Then after the model deployment the predictions are made to check the efficacy of the proposed model. Then a comparative analysis is made to depict the comparison of the proposed model with the various other approaches. Then finally the model is evaluated on the basis of various important parameters to ascertain the enhanced predictive power generated using our proposed approach. The various steps followed by the proposed methodology are summarised below.

## 3.1  Loading the Dataset

The data is present in various formats in the dataset. It may be a text file format, excel file or a comma separated file. The data is loaded in csv format using Python pandas and the required function readcsv will be used to load and retrieve data from the pandas dataframe. The data is loaded in the form of a 2D matrix.

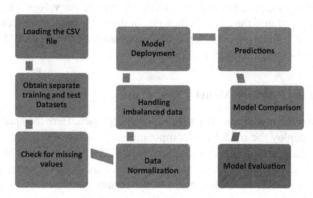

**Fig. 1.**  Proposed Methodology

## 3.2  Splitting the Dataset

After loading the dataset, one needs to break it down to corresponding training and testing components. The training component gives inputs to out prediction model while the testing component checks for the efficacy of the proposed model. The aim of machine learners is to produce higher efficacy models on the basis of various important parametric attributes.

## 3.3  Data Pre-processing: Checking for Missing Data

Since we are dealing with a humongous dataset which comprises of total 6482 universities for 5 years out of which 1368 are distinct universities at international ranking level. The dataset contains 6482 rows and 15 columns. The various parameters on which these universities are categorized are the research output from faculty, students and staff faculty student ratio, number of international students, size of the university, the count of the faculty members. There are possibilities of missing data values in various blocks. To deal with this situation, one needs to devise methodologies so that the meaning of data is not affected.

### 3.4 Data Pre-processing: Data Normalization

The data many a times needs to be normalized to bring it to a uniform scale. This helps in making the predictions more easily and efficiently without even changing the meaning of data.

### 3.5 Data Pre-processing: Handling Imbalanced Data

Sometimes the data is quite imbalanced, some major values belong to one class and minor to another class. Data imbalance may also be observed with multiclass where some classes contain many output categories and others contain lesser values. This makes the predictions biased and thus the overall efficiency of the model may be reduced. We have many ways to deal with it, out of which the solution adopted by us is SMOTE analysis (Synthetic Minority Oversampling Technique).

### 3.6 Deploying the Proposed Model

Finally, we deploy the model based on the proposed approach. Here the approach which we are using to deploy the model is a computationally strong, effective, and efficient supervised machine learning supervised model called XGBoost model. This model has a very high predictive power and thus has been adopted as our proposed methodology. The various other models were also tried but the results generated by them were not so satisfactory. So, we have adopted this XGBoost model-based approach in our proposed methodology. It is a computationally strong model and is capable of dealing with humongous amount of data.

### 3.7 Make Predictions

The proposed model is used to make predictions whether during the pandemic time, the international rankings of various HEIs all over the world dipped or not. All major international ranking parameters are considered and 1368 universities at international level are considered for a span of 5 years. So, in total 6482 values for universities are used for 5 years data from year 2017–2022. The fit () function from XGBoost Classifier-model fits model by taking 2 input values as set of input variables which are used to make predictions and the end-target variable. Here the input variables comprise of those attributes which depict the underlying features of that attribute. In this work, the following attributes in the dataset describing the various ranking parameters for past 15 years act as input values.

**Type of University**
**Research Output**
**Student-Faculty Ratio**
**International Students**
**Size of University**
**Faculty Count**
**Total Score**

Here the "**Total score**" describes the sum total of the quantitative measure based on above metrices. All the above metrices are either categorized as numeric or non-numeric. The numeric metrics are added directly by multiplying them with their corresponding weights. Corresponding weights are obtained based on a particular international ranking criteria. The non-numeric attributes are first converted to some pre-specified numeric values, and then added to the total score by multiplying with the corresponding weights. The conversion factor and corresponding weights are also obtained based on a particular international ranking criteria.

## 3.8   Model Comparison with Other Models

Then a comparative analysis is made to depict the comparison of the proposed model with the various other approaches. As we can see in Sect. 4 that the various other models are not generating satisfactory results in terms of various parameters as compared to the proposed model.

## 3.9   Evaluate the Model

The proposed model is evaluated on the basis of various parameters like accuracy, sensitivity, specificity, f1-value, kappa-statistics etc. The empirical results for all the important parameters will be discussed in Sect. 4. These results ascertain the enhanced predictive power generated using the proposed model as compared to the other models.

The various attributes on the basis on which the model is evaluated are depicted in Table 1. A (2*2) matrix called the confusion matrix is depicted in Table 1 which shows the binary classification in the form of values 0 and 1, where 0 represents those universities, whose ranks didn't dip during the two academic years effected by pandemics viz 2021 and 2022. The value 1 represents those universities which did not account for dipped ranks during two pandemic effected academic years. The various parameters deciding the predictive power of the proposed model are discussed in detail in Table 1.

**Table 1.** Evaluative Parameters

| | | Actual output values | |
|---|---|---|---|
| | Total values | Positive Condition | Negative Condition |
| | Predicted values match | TP *(Correctly identified universities whose ranks dipped)* | FP *(Incorrectly identified universities whose ranks dip)* |
| | Predicted values don't match | FN *(Incorrectly identified universities whose ranks didn't dip)* | TN *(Correctly identified universities whose ranks didn't dip)* |
| | $Precision = \dfrac{TP}{TP+FP}$ | $Recall\ or\ Sensitivity \dfrac{TP}{TP+FN}$ | $f1-score = 2 * \dfrac{Precision * Recall}{Precision + Recall}$ |

Predicted output values

Here output values are those which decide whether the ranks dipped or not during 2 pandemic years of academia. The various other attributes like accuracy, precision, recall, True_positives, False_positives etc. are calculated according to the formulae shown in Table 1. The Table 1 also contains the elaboration of these attributes. The TP (True_Positives) define the number of those HEIs which are rightly identified by the proposed model that their ranks have dipped during the pandemic academic years. The FP (False_Positives) define the number of those HEIs which are wrongly identified by the proposed model that their ranks have dipped during the pandemic academic years. The FN (False_Negatives) define the number of those HEIs which are wrongly identified by the proposed model that their ranks haven't dipped during the pandemic academic years. Similarly, the TN (True_Negatives) define the number of those HEIs which are rightly identified by the proposed model that their ranks haven't dipped during the pandemic academic years. The various other measures are calculated on the basis of these 4 measures only according to.

## 4    Empirical Setup with Implementation Details

The proposed model is used to make predictions whether during the pandemic time, the international rankings of various HEIs all over the world dipped or not. All major international ranking parameters are considered and 1368 universities at international level are considered for a span of 5 years. So, in total 6482 values for universities are used for 5 years data from year 2017–2022. The fit () function from XGBoost Classifier-model fits model by taking 2 input values as set of input variables which are used to make predictions and the end-target variable [29–31]. Here the input variables comprise of those attributes which depict the underlying features of that attribute. In this work, the various attributes in the dataset describing the various ranking parameters for past 15 years act as input values are Type of University, Research output, Student-faculty ratio, Number of International students, Size of University, Faculty count and the total score.

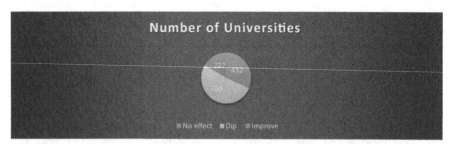

**Fig. 2.**  Number of universities whose ranks Dipped, Improved, remained same during COVID

As is evident from Fig. 2 that the total number of universities is 1368 out of which 227 improved their rankings during the pandemic academic years, 432 maintained their rankings consistently before and after pandemic and there was many 709 which is approximately 50% of universities whose ranks dipped considerably during pandemic academic years. This is a big number which majorly forced us to provide a solution to such HEIs through this research work. All the HEIs are categorized as private and public universities. As is evident from Fig. 2 that out of total, 13% are privately owned and 87% are publicly owned and the dip is not related to this category. One can easily deduct from Fig. 4 that the universities in our dataset, which fight for international ranks, have been consistently able to maintain highly satisfactory faculty student ratio. The majority of universities i.e. more than 50% are able to maintain the ration in the range 1–10. Around 35% maintain the ratio from 11–20 (Fig. 3).

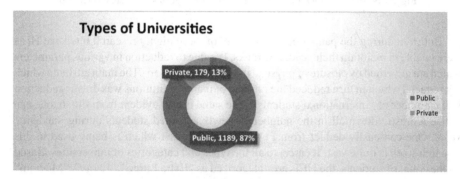

**Fig. 3.** Types of universities

And the remaining 15% contribute to ratio higher than 20. This value is quite satisfactory from the university and more importantly from student point of view as they get more individual attention from their teachers.

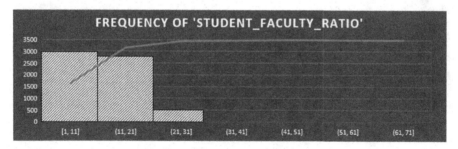

**Fig. 4.** Student-faculty ratio frequency

Another major attribute is the "research output" which is categorized into 4 attributes viz "Very High", "High", "Medium" and "Low". As is quite clear that the research has a strong contribution in the total score of all the national and international rankings bodies. The higher the research contribution, the greater would be the "total_score" leading to higher rankings. As is very clear from Fig. 5 that 4586 out of 6482 values in the dataset account for "Very High" research output. It implies that all these are research intensive universities.

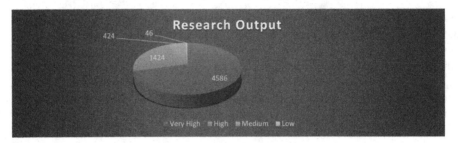

**Fig. 5.** Number of universities having various categories of Research Output

But even during the pandemic years, many of these highly research intensive HEIs were unable to maintain their academic ranks. It is due to reduction in various parameters which are governed by closure of physical international borders. The main attribute which got reduced which in turn reduced the ranking of many institutions was drastic reduction in the number of "international students". The same is also evident from Fig. 6, one can notice a drastic downfall in the number of newly admitted students during pandemic years. One can easily deduct from Fig. 7 that the dataset which is being used in this research work is quite vast. It caters to all the types and categories of universities. Based on the count of students, the HEIs are categorized as "Extra Large", "Large", "Medium" and "Small". The maximum percentage is for "Large" category of universities. Then is the percentage of universities with "Extra Large" size.

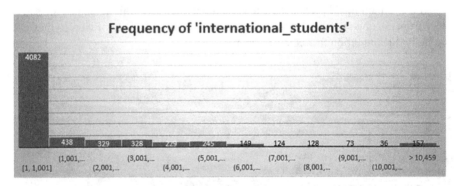

**Fig. 6.** Frequency of international students

The Table 2 shows the predictive values obtained using the proposed model by adopting XGBoost model for making the predictions. The various values are as *Specificity = 98.56, Sensitivity = 97.98, Accuracy = 97.54, F1 value = 97.82, Kappa-score = 0.95.* The values of various parameters are quite satisfactory. We have been able to achieve higher values for accuracy which is 97.54%. This value is achievable using the proposed model only. As will be discussed in next section, these high predictive values are obtained using the proposed model only. For other machine learning models, the obtained values are comparatively lower. A comparative analysis for the same is also available in next section in tabular and bar graph form.

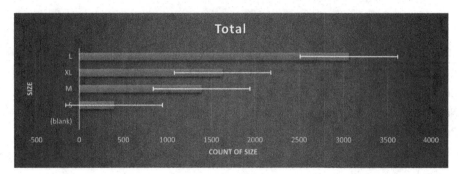

**Fig. 7.** Size of universities

**Table 2.** Statistical Parameters Obtained Using Proposed Model

| Model Adopted | Specificity | Sensitivity | Accuracy | F1-value | Kappa-score |
|---|---|---|---|---|---|
| **Proposed Model** | **98.56** | **97.98** | **97.54** | **97.82** | **0.95** |

## 5 Collating with State-of-Art

If the proposed model undergoes prediction using Random Forest Classifier method, Logistic Regression and Naïve Bayes then the values of various statistical parameters are depicted in Table 3 and Fig. 8.

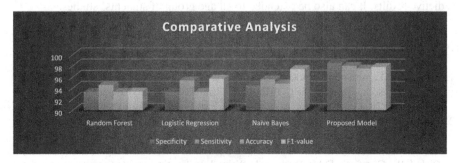

**Fig. 8.** Comparison of Proposed Model with other algorithms.

As is clearly indicative that using the proposed model, we can obtain the highest values for all statistical measures like *f1-score, sensitivity, specificity, accuracy and kappa score.* The bar graph showing a comparative analysis of all three models with our proposed model is shown in Fig. 8.

**Table 3.** Statistical Parameters' Comparative Analysis

| Model Adopted | Specificity | Sensitivity | Accuracy | F1-value | Kappa-score |
| --- | --- | --- | --- | --- | --- |
| **Random Forest** | 93.3 | 94.53 | 93.3 | 93.37 | 0.78 |
| **Logistic Regression** | *93.3* | 95.4 | 93.3 | 95.7 | 0.87 |
| **Naïve Bayes** | 94.43 | 95.55 | 94.8 | 97.43 | 0.93 |
| **Proposed Model** | 98.56 | 97.98 | 97.54 | 97.82 | 0.95 |

## 6 Deductions and Subsequent Work

In this paper, a novel model is proposed to help academicians in predicting the impact of pandemics on the overall international rankings as it is observed that due to physical closure of HEIs, their rankings dipped considerably. Through this research work, the recovery decisions and plans can be taken timely by academicians to combat with the situation. The work involves developing a model based on XGBoost Machine Learning model on the basis of a humongous international ranking dataset. Strong empirical results showed the high efficiency and accuracy of the proposed model. Till now none of the researchers have proposed any such pioneering tool for academicians using advanced Machine Learning algorithms. Though we have been able to obtain higher accuracy value of 97.54% using the proposed model, we can work in future to obtain even higher values for it. To achieve this, an ensembled model can be explored for implementation which involves more than one machine learning and deep learning models working together. The work cab be enhanced further in future by using deep learning models also for better predictive results. It can also be extended to all age group of students' studies.

## References

1. Alhadreti, O.: Assessing academics' perceptions of blackboard usability using SUS and CSUQ: A case study during the COVID-19 pandemic. Int. J. Hum.-Comput. Interact. **37**(11), 1003–1015 (2021)
2. Callaghan, F.V.O'., Neumann, D.L., Jones, L., Creed, P.A.: The use of lecture recordings in higher education: A review of institutional, student, and lecturer issues. Educ. Inf. Technol. **22**(1), 399–415 (2017)
3. Park, S.W., Cornforth, D.M., Dushoff, J., Weitz, J.S.: The time scale of asymptomatic transmission affects estimates of epidemic potential in the COVID-19 outbreak. Epidemics **31**, 100392 (2020)
4. Scagnoli, N.I., Choo, J., Tian, J.: Students' insights on the use of video lectures in online classes. Br. J. Edu. Technol. **50**(1), 399–414 (2019)
5. Lwoga, ET., Komba, M.: Antecedents of continued usage intentions of web-based learning management system in Tanzania. Education+ training (2015)
6. Agarwal, N., Tayal, D.K.: FFT based ensembled model to predict ranks of higher educational institutions. Multimedia Tools Appli. **81**, 34129–34162 (2022)
7. Nguyen, N.T., Chinn, J., Nahmias, J., Yuen, S., Kirby, K.A., Hohmann, S., Amin, A.: Outcomes and mortality among adults hospitalized with COVID-19 at US medical centers. JAMA Netw. Open. **4**(3), e210417- e210417-e210417 (2021)

8. Marín, D.V., Cabero, A.J.: Las redes sociales en educación: desde la innovación a la inves-
tigación educativa. RIED. Revista Iboeroamericana de Educación a Distancia. **22** (2), 25–33
(2019)
9. Belkin, D.: Is This the End of College as We Know It?, in The Wall Street Journal (2020)
10. Duffy C.: Humanities degrees to double in cost as government funnels students into "job-
relevant" uni courses. ABC News (2020)
11. Ratten, V.: Coronavirus (Covid-19) and the entrepreneurship education community. J.
Enterprising Commun. People Places Global Econ. (2020)
12. Feuerlicht, G., Beránek, M., Kovář, V.: Impact of COVID-19 pandemic on Higher Education.
In: 2021 International Conference on Computational Science and Computational Intelligence
(CSCI), pp. 1095–1098. IEEE (2021)
13. Jackson, C.: DATA SNAPSHOT: 2019, Universities Australia (2021)
14. De, W.H., Adams, T.: Global competition in higher education: A comparative study of
policies, rationales, and practices in Australia and Europe, in Higher education, policy, and
the global competition phenomenon, pp. 219–233. Springer (2010)
15. De, W.H.: Trends, issues and challenges in internationalisation of higher education. Centre
for Applied Research on Economics and Management, School of Economics (2011)
16. Update C. 11,965,661 Cases and 546,988 Deaths from COVID-19 Virus Pandemic-
Worldometer. Доступно на (2020). https://www.worldometers.info/coronavirus/#countries.
17. AEN. Student Numbers at Australian Universities Australian Universities.com.au.
(.2020) https://www.australianuniversities.com.au/directory/studentnumbers/
18. OECD. International Student in Australia Statistics - Study Abroad in Australia. (2019) 2019–
12–13 https://www.studying-inaustralia.org/international-student-in-australia-statistics/
19. Ross, J.: Economic ramifications of the COVID-19 pandemic for higher education: a circuit
breaker in Australian universities' business model? Higher Educ. Res. Developm., 1–6 (2020)
20. Ferguson, H., Love, S.: Universities and COVID – Parliament of Australia. (2020).
(12 Oct 2020]. https://www.aph.gov.au/About_Parliament/Parliamentary_Departments/Par
liamentary_Library/FlagPost/2020/August/Universities_and_COVID
21. Ferguson, R.: Group of Eight warns of 'brain drain' with 7000 jobs set to go, in The Australian.
2020, News Corp Australia: Australia (2020)
22. Tertiary Education Quality and Standard Agency (TESQA). Key financial metrics on
Australia's higher education sector (2018)
23. Ferguson, R.: Crisis leaves unis facing global crash: Craven, in The Australian (2021),
@australian
24. Study Portal. Tuition Fees at Universities in Europe in 2020 - Overview and Comparison -
MastersPortal.com. (2020). https://www.mastersportal.com/articles/405/tuition-fees-atuniv
ersities-in-europe-in-2020-overview-and-comparison.html
25. Eurostat. Learning mobility statistics - Statistics Explained. (2020). https://ec.europa.eu/eur
ostat/statistics%20explained/index.php/Learning_mobility_statistics
26. Brendan, O.M.: Education exports worth almost £20 billion to the UK, in University World
News (2020)
27. Estermann, T., Pruvot, E.B., Kupriyanova, V., Stoyanova, H.: The Impact of the Covid-19
Crisis on University Funding in Europe: Lessons Learnt from the 2008 Global Financial
Crisis. European University Association, Briefing (2020)
28. Lederman, D.: Will shift to remote teaching be boon or bane for online learning. Inside Higher
Ed. 18 (2020)
29. Agarwal, N., Srivastava, R., Srivastava, P., Sandhu, J., Singh, P.P.: Multiclass classification
of different glass types using random forest classifier. In: 6th International Conference on
Intelligent Computing and Control Systems (ICICCS) 2022, pp. 1682–1689. IEEE (2022)

30. Agarwal, N., Singh, V., Singh P.: Semi-supervised learning with GANs for melanoma detection. In: 6th International Conference on Intelligent Computing and Control Systems, ICICCS 2022, pp. 141–147. IEEE (2022)
31. Agarwal, N., Jain, A., Gupta, A., Tayal, DK.: Applying xgboost machine learning model to succor astronomers detect exoplanets in distant galaxies. In: International Conference on Artificial Intelligence and Speech Technology 2021, pp. 385–404. Springer, Cham (2021). https://doi.org/10.1007/978-3-030-95711-7_33

# Credit Risk Assessment - A Machine Learning Approach

Thumpala Archana Acharya[1]([✉]) [ID] and Pedagadi Veda Upasan[2] [ID]

[1] Vignan's Institute of Information Technology (A), Duvvada, Visakhapatnam,
Andhra Pradesh 530046, India
taamphil@gmail.com
[2] Wipro Infotech ltd., Gachibowli, Hyderabad, Telangana 500032, India

**Abstract.** Banks are foregoing their present reserves for future sources of Revenue. This source is associated with a risk called credit default risk which increases defaulting conditions called the Non-performing assets(loans) thus leading to the financial crisis. Machine Learning, a branch of Artificial Intelligence, is the upcoming technology with promising solutions to present limitations of the systems eliminating the human errors or emotions with precision by way of training and testing. The present study is focused on predicting defaulting loans using algorithms of Machine learning. The dataset is preprocessed for dropping the missing values. Further three models - Logistic Regression, KNN and XGBoost are applied for predicting defaulters based on precision, recall and F1-score. The findings of the research concluded that the XGBoost model performed best among the three models for assessment of credit risk which will waive off the crisis situation.

**Keywords:** Artificial Intelligence · Machine Learning · Credit Risk · KNN · Logistic Regression · XGBoost · Default Risk

## 1 Introduction

Credit risk is the root cause for financial crisis. Credit risk arises due to disbursement of loans by banks. For banks, loans are the primary source operating revenue in form of interest and processing fee paid by the borrower. On the basis of collateral banks provide loans to the borrowers. The repayment depends on the borrower's income generation. The crisis situation comes into picture due to uncertainty of repayments which is called credit risk or default risk [1] where the banks not only lose their revenue (interest amount) but also their principal also [2].

Credit risk or default risk can be waived off if properly predicted. Machine Learning Algorithms which is part of Artificial Intelligence, the future ruler of the technology, gives a means for assessment of credit risk. Training the system with existing cases eliminates many limitations of disbursement and recovery of loan process such as personal biases. In the present paper a prediction model is developed using Machine Learning Algorithms for credit risk assessment.

© ICST Institute for Computer Sciences, Social Informatics and Telecommunications Engineering 2023
Published by Springer Nature Switzerland AG 2023. All Rights Reserved
S. Nandan Mohanty et al. (Eds.): ICISML 2022, LNICST 471, pp. 39–54, 2023.
https://doi.org/10.1007/978-3-031-35081-8_4

## 2 Understanding the Concept of Credit Risk and Machine Learning Algorithms

### 2.1 What is Credit Risk?

The probable loss for lending institutions emerging due to failure of repayment of the loan by the borrower. In simple terms, a failure of contractual commitment of the borrower due to inability of repayment.[19] The following table shows the list of factors contributing to credit risk (Table 1)

**Table 1.** Factors contributing to Credit risk [20]

| Internal | External |
| --- | --- |
| Inappropriate lending practices | Government interference |
| Limited Institutional capacity | Volatile interest rates |
| Credit policies | Inappropriate laws |
| Poor management | Massive licensing of banks |
| Low capital and liquidity levels | Inadequate supervision by the central bank |
| Direct lending | |
| Poor loan underwriting | |
| Laxity in credit assessment | |

The different types of credit risk include.

1. Credit default risk - non-repayment by individual and exceeding 90 days from due date
2. Concentration risk - non-repayment by companies due to large losses of industry
3. Country risk or sovereign risk - non-repayment by sovereign states due to foreign currency commitments

Credit default risk is primarily influenced by microeconomic factors listed above; Concentration risk is influenced both by micro and macro economic factors and the Country risk or Sovereign risk is influenced primarily by macroeconomic factors.

The primary cause is inappropriate risk assessment and followed by disbursement to specific borrowers - single specific individuals, groups of individuals, companies, industries, sectors etc. leading credit concentration. Lenders can waive off credit risk through mitigation such as Risk-based Pricing, agreements called as covenants which specify - periodic report of borrower's financial status, making prepayment in case of unfavorable changes, availability of funding pool to diversify the risk, Insuring the credit and arranging for alternative credit. All the mitigation is an attempt to address the credit risk but at the primary level a prediction required to do mitigation. Credit risk analysis helps to forecast the ability of borrower's repayment which helps for further mitigation through covenants and minimizes the loss quantifiably. As part of Basel III execution these techniques help in increasing the proficiency in measuring, identifying and regulating credit risk [19].

## 2.2 What is Machine Learning?

Machine learning is the process of learning by machine how humans respond to the specific condition. This process basically helps in training the machine to imitate humans. This technology helps in highly vulnerable areas where human intervention is highly risky for the life of humans or creates large losses to the economy in terms of financial crisis.

Machine learning is a branch of Artificial intelligence [6] which applies algorithms to represent humans. The more the training the more is the accuracy.

In general, large volumes of flooding data (Big data) is increasing the scope of applications of machine learning algorithms due to the limited approach of humans and in particular to the Banking Industry [7] (Fig. 1 and 2).

### 2.2.1 Classifiers of Machine Learning

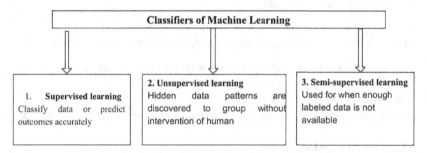

**Fig. 1.** Classifiers of Machine Learning [21]

### 2.2.2 Working of Machine Learning Algorithm

There are three main parts in the algorithm [6].

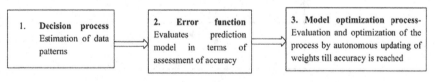

**Fig. 2.** Working of Machine Learning Algorithm [21]

### 2.2.3 KNN Model

K Nearest Neighbour algorithm is a supervised classification algorithm also a lazy algorithm no learning or decision but only similarity based classification using euclidean distance which is a proximity measure [8] (Fig. 3 and 4).

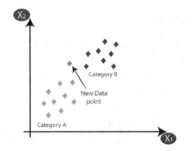

**Fig. 3.** Working of KNN Algorithm [24]

*Algorithm of KNN.*

1. Load Data - xls, csv
2. Initialise K value
3. Every sample in the training lab.

   Distance between query point & the current point is calculated.
   Distance & the index of the example are added to the ordered collection.

4. Distances& Indexes of Ordered collection are sorted in ascending order.
   1. First K entries from sorted collection are picked
   2. Labelling Of selected K entries
   3. Returns K Labels Mean in case of regression and Mode in case of classification.

### 2.2.4 Logistic Regression Model

It is a regression model under supervised classification algorithm criteria decision based on threshold value using sigmoid function [10].

1. High Recall or Low Precision where the number of false negatives are reduced.
2. Low Recall or High Precision where the number of false positives are reduced.

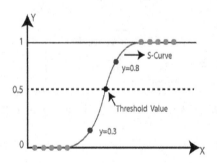

**Fig. 4.** Working of Logistic Regression Algorithm [26]

### 2.2.5 XGBoost Model

It is a powerful model under supervised learning model. The statement is validated based on.

1. Objective function
2. Base Learners

The objective function which contains a loss function and a regularization term. Further the difference between the actual and predicted values is calculated to obtain the results which gives accuracy level of the model. The loss functions include:

1. Regression problems
2. Binary classification

The base learners also called as Ensemble - a single prediction is obtained based on training and combining individuals. In the process predictions are combined so that bad predictions are eliminated and finally good predictions is formed. The key members of metrics include:

1. Root-mean-squared error (RMSE)
2. Mean-squared-error (MAE) [13]

## 3  Literature Review

**Table 2.** Literature review [3–17]

| Year | Authors | Title | Methodology | Result |
|---|---|---|---|---|
| 2022 | Pontus Lindqvist Dariush Khailtash [32] | The Impact AI on Bank's Risk Management Approach | Dynamic Risk Management Framework & Multi-Level Perspective | New risks-organisational and regulatory identified with AI implementation |
| 2021 | Iryna Yanenkova Yuliia Nehoda Svetlana Drobyazko Andrii Zavhorodnii Lyudmyla Berezovska [3] | Modeling of Bank Credit Risk Management Using the Cost Risk Model [3] | fuzzy programming and symbiotic methodical support | At a very early point Predicting defaulting loans while monitoring using change of indicators |
| 2020 | Chun and Lejeune [4] | Risk-Based Loan Pricing: Portfolio Optimization Approach with Marginal Risk Contribution [4] | Statistical method | Analyzing factors help banks to minimize lending risk |

(*continued*)

**Table 2.** (*continued*)

| Year | Authors | Title | Methodology | Result |
|------|---------|-------|-------------|--------|
| 2020 | Drobyazko et al.; Nosratabadi et al.[5] | Risk Management in the System of Financial Stability of the Service Enterprise. Journal of Risk and Financial Management [5] | Statistical method | No appropriate monitoring and forecasting system with respect to operating risk |
| 2019 | Kaya, Or,cun et al. [31] | Artificial intelligence in banking | Review | Key process automation - Detecting fraud pattern, personal banking, anti-money laundering (AML) |
| 2019 | Zinisha, OS, Ivanenko, IN, and Avdeeva, RA [30] | Artificial Intelligence As A Factor To Improve Bank Eciency | Robots | Saving cost upto 87% by investing in robos than hiring employees fultime and increasing efficiency of work |
| 2019 | Sarfo-Manu, Philip & Siaw, Gifty & Appiahene, Peter. [29] | Intelligent System for Credit Risk Management in Financial Institutions | Data Mining Algorithm, Decision Tree, Domain Expert, Expert System | Rate of Accuracy 70% for predicting Client eligibility for loans |
| 2019 | Allen and Luciano [6] | Risk Analysis and Portfolio Modelling [6] | Qualitative Analysis | Financial indicators help banks to obtain information about credit risk and defaulting borrowers based on previous default history |
| 2018 | Naoyuki Yoshino and Farhad Taghizadeh-Hesary [7] | A Comprehensive method for the credit risk assessment of small and Medium-sized enterprises based on Asisn Data [7] | Cluster analysis Principal component analysis | Taking Finanical health as basis the customers of SME are grouped. Each group is unique with interest rates and ceilings of lending |

(*continued*)

**Table 2.** (*continued*)

| Year | Authors | Title | Methodology | Result |
|------|---------|-------|-------------|--------|
| 2018 | Wilhelmsson and Zhao [8] | Risk Assessment of Housing Market Segments: The Lender's Perspective [8] | Statistical method | Overstating the interest rate and levy surcharges of different types helps in minimizing the risk and transferring it on to responsible borrowers |
| 2017 | Giordana and Schumacher [9] | An Empirical Study on the Impact of Basel III Standards on Banks' Default Risk: The Case of Luxembourg. [9] | Statistical method | Accuracy of the borrower assessment is important for granting a loan with grant amount |
| 2016 | Natalija Konovalovalneta Ineta Kristovska Marina Kudinska [10] | Credit risk management in commercial banks [10] | Factor analysis | In commercial banks based on internal credit ratings there was improvement in management of credit risk |
| 2016 | Sirus Sharifi. Arunima Haldar S.V.D. Nageswara Rao [11] | The relationship between credit risk management and non-performing assets of commercial banks in India [11] | Multiple linear regression | Negative relation between growth of NPAs or loans and identification of credit risk |
| 2015 | Yoshino, Taghizadeh-Hesary, and Nili [12] | Estimating Dual Deposit Insurance Premium Rates and Forecasting Non-Performing Loans: Two New Models. ADBI [12] | PCA - Principal component analysis and Cluster analysis | Predicting Non-Performing Loans |

(*continued*)

**Table 2.** (*continued*)

| Year | Authors | Title | Methodology | Result |
|---|---|---|---|---|
| 2014 | Addo Boye Michael Kwabena [13] | Credit Risk Management in Financial Institutions: A Case Study of Ghana Commercial Bank Limited [13] | Regression model | Positive relationship between ROE and NPAs and negative relationship between lower loan losses and higher interest |
| 2013 | Orsenigo and Vercellis [14] | Linear versus Nonlinear Dimensionality Reduction for Banks' Credit Rating Prediction. Knowledge-Based Systems [14] | Quantitative methods | Identification of determinants of Banks' rating which help for assessing the creditworthiness |
| 2007 | Ravi Kumar and Ravi [15] | A comprehensive survey of the application of statistical and intelligent techniques to predicting the likelihood of default among banks and firms [15] | Statistical techniques | Prediction of credit ratings |
| 2007 | Maechler et al. [16] | Decomposing Financial Risks and Vulnerabilities in Eastern Europe [16] | Statistical method | High credit risk calls for approaches and systematic methods for forecasting and identification of risk |
| 1999 | Poon, Firth, and Fung [17] | A Multivariate Analysis of the Determinants of Moody's Bank Financial Strength Ratings [17] | Logistic regression models | Moody's ratings help in predicting value based on profitability indicators, risk and Loan provision information |

From the literature review it can be summarized that all most the previous studies highlighted on prediction models of identifying credit risk based on different statistical methods, regression models, clustering analysis etc. In most of the studies indicators such as profitability ratios, Non performing assets (NPAs), ROE, Credit rating etc. are taken for study purpose. No study gave a prediction of credit risk. The present suggested model is based on machine learning algorithms for training the system with dataset and providing prediction based on Precision, Recall and F1 score (Table 2).

## 4   Research Problem or Gap

Default risk or credit risk is reaching its heights due to many limitations in the process of disbursement. There is no proper mechanism to forecast the risk. As the process is executed with human interventions which is having the threat of emotions, biasing etc. which is the root cause for the interrupted revenue generation and increases the collection cost. To address this machine learning models are used to predict the default probability.[18].

## 5   Objectives of Study

1. To understand the concept of credit risk and Machine learning algorithms
2. To analyse credit risk using machine learning algorithms

## 6   Research Methodology

**Dataset**
For the study purpose credit_risk_dataset.csv (1) Dataset is taken from Kaggle. The following table shows the description of variables (Table 3).

**Table 3.** Type of variables used

| S. No | Variable | Variable type | Units |
| --- | --- | --- | --- |
| 1 | Age | numerical | Years |
| 2 | Income | numerical | INR |
| 3 | status of Home | categorical | "rent", "mortgage" or "own" |
| 4 | Experience | numerical | Years |
| 4 | Intent of Loan | categorical | "education", "medical", "venture", "home improvement", "personal" or "debt"consolidation" |

(continued)

**Table 3.** (*continued*)

| S. No | Variable | Variable type | Units |
|---|---|---|---|
| 5 | Amount of Loan | numerical | INR |
| 6 | Grade of Loan | categorical | "A", "B", "C", "D", "E", "F" or "G" |
| 7 | Rate of Interest | numerical | Percentage |
| 8 | Loan to income ratio | numerical | 0 and 1 |
| 9 | Default credit history | binary categorical | "Y" or "N" |
| 10 | Status of Loan (target variable) | binary, numerical | 0 - no default<br>1- default |

The data exploration and preprocessing is done in order to drop the missing values from the data. The study is based on descriptive statistics using function describe(). For visualization of the relationships, a scatterplot matrix is used. Further to find out the relation between the variables and the loan status Blox plot is used. For testing and training three algorithms - logistic regression, K-Nearest Neighbourhood and XGBoost are used (Fig. 5 and 6).

The following is the model developed:

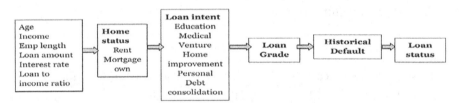

**Fig. 5.** Research model Source: author's proposal

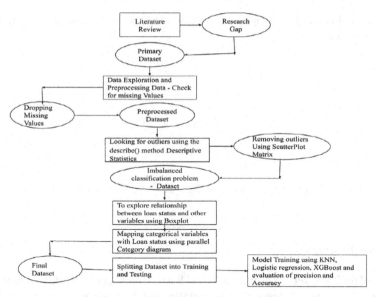

**Fig. 6.** Research Design Source: The author's proposal

# 7 Experimental results

## • Data Analysis

Step 1: Data Exploration & Preprocessing: In this step Missing values are identified in two variables - employment length and interest rates which are considered.

**St**ep 2: Identifying Outliers: Using describe() and scatter plot matrix 3 outliers identified - Age, Employment length and income which are eliminated. The following descriptive statistics is calculated.

|  | Age | Income | Employment_Length | Loan_Amount | Interest_Rate | Loan_Status | loan_percent_income |
|---|---|---|---|---|---|---|---|
| count | 28638.000000 | 2.863800e+04 | 28638.000000 | 28638.000000 | 28638.000000 | 28638.000000 | 28638.000000 |
| mean | 27.727216 | 6.664937e+04 | 4.784482 | 9656.493121 | 11.039867 | 0.216600 | 0.169488 |
| std | 6.310441 | 6.235845e+04 | 4.095491 | 6329.683361 | 3.229372 | 0.411935 | 0.106393 |
| min | 20.000000 | 4.000000e+03 | 0.000000 | 500.000000 | 5.420000 | 0.000000 | 0.000000 |
| 25% | 23.000000 | 3.948000e+04 | 2.000000 | 5000.000000 | 7.900000 | 0.000000 | 0.090000 |
| 50% | 26.000000 | 5.595600e+04 | 4.000000 | 8000.000000 | 10.990000 | 0.000000 | 0.150000 |
| 75% | 30.000000 | 8.000000e+04 | 7.000000 | 12500.000000 | 13.480000 | 0.000000 | 0.230000 |
| max | 144.000000 | 6.000000e+06 | 123.000000 | 35000.000000 | 23.220000 | 1.000000 | 0.830000 |

Source: Research work

Step 3: Step 3: Generating target variable:In the dataset 78.4% are non-default cases when compared default cases meaning imbalanced classification. To handle this imbalance classification firstly, Status of Loan - Loan to income ratio is the indicator variable to identify default borrowers. Boxplot is used to draw the relationship between the loan status and other variables. From the following Boxplot figure it can be drawn that borrowers (Grade G) with low loan to income ratio didn't default and repaid their loans.

Secondly, Parallel category diagram is used to identify the relation of the categorical variables with loan status.

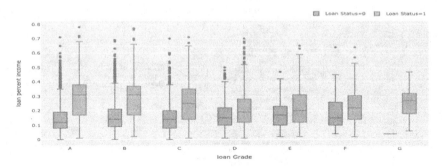

Source: Research work

Most of the borrowers have attained A and B as common grades while very borrowers were graded as F and G. From the home status of rent, mortgage and owners, firstly highest defaulters were rented borrowers, Secondly it is followed by the mortgage and finally by the owners with least number of defaulters. Coming to the loan intent of the borrowers majority of them took loan for the purpose of Educational loans where as for home improvement was the least. Defaulting conditions were more in case of borrowers with loan intent of consoliation of debt and expenses incurred for medical purposes. Further three models KNN, Logistic regression and XGBoost were applied to attain precision and Accuracy.

## 8   Result Analysis

KNN, Logistic regression and XGBoost models are used for training and testing of imbalanced dataset. The main focus is to have a common metric that is accuracy. The metrics of evaluation is based firstly on precision( ratio of true positives to total positives) where the positive symbolizes default cases, second on Recall (true positive rate - true positives to total number of elements) which give false positives predicting default or not, third F1 score gives combined score of both Precision and Recall (Table 4).

**Table 4.** Precision, Recall, F1 - score values based on models

| KNN Model | | Precision | Recall | F1- Score | Support |
|---|---|---|---|---|---|
| | 0 | 84.0% | 96.0% | 90.0% | 4448 |
| | 1 | 74.0% | 38.0% | 50.0% | 1260 |
| | Accuracy | | | 83.0% | 5708 |
| | Macro Average | 79.0% | 60.0% | 7.0% | 5708 |
| | Weighted Average | 82.0% | 83.0% | 81.0% | 5708 |
| Logistic Regression Model | 0 | 81.0% | 99.0% | 89.0% | 4448 |
| | 1 | 79.0% | 17.0% | 29.0% | 1260 |
| | Accuracy | | | 81.0% | 5708 |
| | Macro Average | 80.0% | 58.0% | 59.0% | 5708 |
| | Weighted Average | 80.0% | 81.0% | 76.0% | 5708 |
| XGBoost Model | 0 | 92.0% | 99.0% | 96.0% | 4448 |
| | 1 | 94.0% | 72.0% | 81.0% | 1260 |
| | Accuracy | | | 93.0% | 5708 |
| | Macro Average | 93.0% | 85.0% | 88.0% | 5708 |
| | Weighted Average | 93.0% | 93.0% | 92.0% | 5708 |

Source: Research work

**Table 5.** Summary of Precision, Recall, F–score

| | Precision | Recall | F1-Score | Accuracy |
|---|---|---|---|---|
| **KNN Model** | 74.0% | 38.0% | 50.0% | 83.0% |
| **Logistic Regression Model** | 79.0% | 17.0% | 29.0% | 81.0% |
| **XGBoost Model** | 94.0% | 72.0% | 81.0% | 93.0% |

Source: Research work

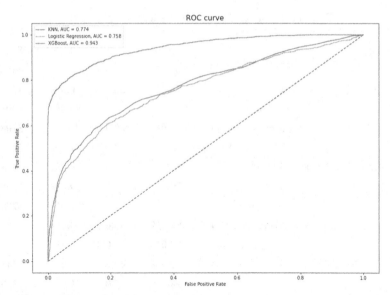

Source: Research work

From the above table the result of training and testing the dataset using KNN model resulted with prediction of 74%, Recall with 38% and F1-Score with 50%. The accuracy is about 83 percent. Using Logistic Regression model resulted with prediction of 79 percent, Recall with 17 percent and F1-Score with 29%. The accuracy is about 81%. Using XGBoost model resulted with prediction of 94 percent, Recall with 72 percent and F1-Score with 81%. The accuracy is about 93% (Table 5).

From the above table and chart out of the metrics of 3 models XGBoost gave the best result of precision 94 percent, Recall with 72 percent, F1 score with 81 percent and the Accuracy of 93 percent.

## 9   Conclusion

Among the three prediction models - Logistic Regression, K Nearest Neighbour and XGBoost - XGBoost model gave highest accuracy - precision in assessment of credit risk. Thus it can be concluded that assessment of credit risk helps in waiving off the financial crisis. So, in real-time with 93% of accuracy the proposed prediction model can be implemented for assessment of credit risk by banks.

## References

1. https://www.investopedia.com/terms/c/creditrisk.asp
2. https://www.investopedia.com/terms/d/defaultrisk.asp#:~:text=Default%20risk%20is%20the%20risk,all%20forms%20of%20credit%20extensions
3. Yanenkova, I., Nehoda, Y., Drobyazko, S., Zavhorodnii, A., Berezovska, L.: Modeling of bank credit risk management using the cost risk model. J. Risk Finan. Managem. **14**(5), 211 (2021). https://doi.org/10.3390/jrfm14050211"

4. Chun, S.Y., Lejeune, M.A.: Risk-based loan pricing: portfolio optimization approach with marginal risk contribution. Manage. Sci. **66**, 3735–3753 (2020)
5. Drobyazko, S., Barwinska-Malajowicz, A., Slusarczyk, B., Chubukova, O., Bielialov, T.: Risk management in the system of financial stability of the service enterprise. Journal of Risk and Financial Management **13**, 300 (2020)
6. Allen, D.E., Luciano, E.: Risk analysis and portfolio modelling. Journal of Risk Financial Management **12**, 154 (2019)
7. https://www.adb.org/sites/default/files/publication/473006/adbi-wp907.pdf
8. Wilhelmsson, M., Zhao, J.: Risk assessment of housing market segments: the lender's perspective. Journal of Risk and Financial Management **11**, 69 (2018)
9. Giordana, G.A., Schumacher, I.: An empirical study on the impact of basel iii standards on banks' default risk: the case of luxembourg. Journal of Risk Financial Management **10**, 8 (2017)
10. https://www.researchgate.net/publication/304669880_Credit_risk_management_in_commercial_banks
11. https://www.researchgate.net/publication/308610434_Credit_risk_management_practices_in_Indian_Banks. (Accessed 09 May 2022)
12. Yoshino, N., Taghizadeh-Hesary, F., Nili, F.: Estimating Dual Deposit Insurance Premium Rates and Forecasting Non-Performing Loans: Two New Models. ADBI Working Paper. No. 510. ADBI: Tokyo (2015)
13. Kwabena, A.B.M.: Credit risk management in financial institutions: a case study of Ghana commercial bank limited. Res. J. Fina. Account 5(23) (2014). www.iiste.org, ISSN 2222–1697 (Paper) ISSN 2222–2847 (Online)
14. Orsenigo, C., Vercellis, C.:. Linear versus nonlinear dimensionality reduction for banks' credit rating prediction. Knowl. Based Syst. **47**, 14–22 (2013)
15. Ravi Kumar, P., Ravi, V.: Bankruptcy prediction in banks and firms via statistical and intelligent techniques–a review. Eur. J. Oper. Res. **180**(1), 1–28 (2007)
16. Maechler, A.M., Srobona, M., Delisle, W.: Decomposing Financial Risks and Vulnerabilities in Eastern Europe. IMF Working Paper. Washington, DC, USA: International Monetary Fund, WP/07/248, pp. 1–33 (2007)
17. Poon, W.P.H., Firth, M., Fung, H.G.: A multivariate analysis of the determinants of moody's bank financial strength ratings. J. Int. Finan. Markets. Inst. Money **9**, 267–283 (1999)
18. https://towardsdatascience.com/a-machine-learning-approach-to-credit-risk-assessment-ba8eda1cd11f
19. https://www.educba.com/credit-risk/
20. https://journals.univ-danubius.ro/index.php/oeconomica/article/view/3027/3209#:~:text=The%20main%20source%20of%20micro,loan%20underwriting%2C%20laxity%20in%20credit
21. https://www.ibm.com/in-en/cloud/learn/machine-learning
22. https://www.springerprofessional.de/en/a-stitch-in-time-saves-nine-a-big-data-analytics-perspective/17846200
23. https://www.geeksforgeeks.org/k-nearest-neighbours/
24. https://www.google.com/search?q=KNN+Algorithm&tbm=isch&ved=2ahUKEwi3gOzVmdD3AhWZKbcAHbibCa8Q2-cCegQIABAA&oq=KNN+Algorithm&gs_lcp=CgNpbWcQAzIECAAQQzIECAAQQzIFCAAQgAQyBQgAEIAEMgUIABCABDIFCAAQgAQyBQgAEIAEMgUIABCABDIFCAAQgAQyBQgAEIAEOgcIIxDvAxAnULUKWLUKYMYaaABwAHgAgAGnAYgBlQKSAQMwLjKYAQCgAQGqAQtnd3Mtd2l6LWltZZ8ABAQ&sclient=img&ei=R993YvfAJ5nT3LUPuLem-Ao&bih=880&biw=1920&rlz=1C1CHBF_enIN983IN985#imgrc=_wWUhdyKGVGvWM
25. https://www.geeksforgeeks.org/understanding-logistic-regression/

26. .https://www.google.com/search?q=logistic+regression+algorithm+in+machine+learning+
pdf&rlz=1C1CHBF_enIN983IN985&sxsrf=ALiCzsbsf4mPxIBZZ8X2SkTdLl3jPkhsqQ:
1652023058259&source=lnms&tbm=isch&sa=X&ved=2ahUKEwiQgLG8mdD3AhVL
R2wGHR4rDBoQ_AUoAnoECAEQBA&biw=1920&bih=880&dpr=1#imgrc=LuaHnfur7
6i8eM
27. https://www.geeksforgeeks.org/xgboost-for-regression/?ref=gcse
28. https://www.google.com/search?q=xgboost+algorithm+in+machine+learning&tbm=isch&
ved=2ahUKEwjHurjYm9D3AhWH8DgGHYOHB8sQ2-cCegQIABAA&oq=xgboost+
algorithm&gs_lcp=CgNpbWcQARgBMgcIIxDvAxAnMgUIABCABDIFCAAQgAQyB
QgAEIAEMgUIABCABDIFCAAQgAQyBggAEAcQHjIGCAAQCBAeMgQIABAYMg
QIABAYUABYAGDPC2gAcAB4AIABcIgBcJIBAzAuMZgBAKoBC2d3cy13aXotaW1n
1nwAEB&sclient=img&ei=ZeF3Yof0Oofh4-EPg4-e2Aw&bih=880&biw=1920&rlz=1C1
CHBF_enIN983IN985#imgrc=QZ9NELxuymJ7gM
29. Sarfo-Manu, P., Siaw, G., Appiahene, P.: Intelligent system for credit risk management in
financial institutions. Int. J. Artifi. Intell. Mach Learn. **9**, 57–67 (2019). https://doi.org/10.
4018/IJAIML.2019070104
30. Zinisha, O.S., Ivanenko, I.N., Avdeeva, R.A.: Artificial Intelligence As A Factor To ˙ Improve
Bank Eciency. Indo Am. J. Pharm. Sci. **6**(3), 6917–6919 (2019)
31. Kaya, O., et al.: Artificial intelligence in banking. Artifi. intell. (2019)
32. Khailtash, P.L.D.: The Impact AI on Bank's Risk Management Approach. In thesis report
submitted to KTH Industrial Engineering and Management (2022)

# Development of Analytical DataMart and Data Pipeline for Recruitment Analytics

Ashish Chandra Jha[✉], Sanjeev Kumar Jha, and J. B. Simha

REVA Academy for Corporate Excellence, Bengaluru, India
{ashish.ba05,sanjeev.ba05,jb.simha}@reva.edu.in

**Abstract.** The HR department handles all the data regarding the recruitment process while also analyzing them to select suitable candidates for the organization. The HR department interacts with the data regarding the recruitment using many tools for data analysis and interpretation. Such data should be organized properly to ensure the screening of candidates. Each system gives their own report in their own format. Data is not integrated and aggregated at proper granularity suitable for analysis. This can be mitigated by the use of Dimensional and Analytical DataMarts. The dimensional DataMarts will contain transitional data modified for analysis with dimensions and facts. These DataMarts can be used for any adhoc analysis like drill down/roll up, slice and dice, drill through, comparative analysis etc. The analytical DataMart will contain the aggregated data in one row per employee format. This will be task specific like Quality of Hire modeling, Cost of Hire, Time to Hire, demand prediction etc.

This paper has focused on creating a recruitment DataMart for Human Resource Department with the assistance of the data modeling technique. This Paper has also discussed the exploratory data analysis and model building in relation to the DataMarts for the recruitment.

**Keywords:** HR Analytics · Recruitment · DataMart · Analytical DataMart · Dimensional DataMart

## 1 Introduction

The success and growth of any organization primarily depend on its employees. Without employees, no organization can run as they are the workforce for the organization. Various employees take up different roles in the organization and perform the duties assigned to their positions. The employees of an organization are crucial for the organization and therefore the department that majorly deals with them becomes crucial as well. This department is the Human Resource Department of an organization. The HR department is responsible for almost all aspects concerning the workforce of an organization. The importance of employees for an organization makes the HR department very important. The Human Resource Department is responsible for the effective administration of the employees of an organization to help in its overall growth. Moreover, an organization can only succeed if competent people are recruited in it. This department needs to carefully examine and select suitable persons for the various roles in the organization.

© ICST Institute for Computer Sciences, Social Informatics and Telecommunications Engineering 2023
Published by Springer Nature Switzerland AG 2023. All Rights Reserved
S. Nandan Mohanty et al. (Eds.): ICISML 2022, LNICST 471, pp. 55–65, 2023.
https://doi.org/10.1007/978-3-031-35081-8_5

## 1.1 Recruitment Process

Recruitment can be defined as the overall process of choosing the right candidates for job positions at an organization based on several criteria. The recruitment process is usually handled primarily by the Human Resource department of an organization. This process might differ for every organization but there are certain general steps involved in it that most organizations seem to follow. These are Job Description Preparation, Sourcing, Screening, Selecting, Hiring, and Onboarding.

### 1.1.1 JD Preparation

Job description refers to the details of the job position for which the recruitment is taking place. It contains all the necessary information regarding the job such as-

- Qualifications required for the job
- Skills required to perform the necessary functions of the job
- Different responsibilities that the selected candidate has to take care of
- Suitable characteristics for the candidates for the job such as age, experience, etc.
- Salary expectations concerning the job
- Working hours

The job description is an important aspect of the recruitment process as it notifies the interested candidates with all the necessary information about the job. It is the primary source of attracting candidates for the job position.

### 1.1.2 Sourcing

Sourcing is the process of collection of data relevant to the position for which recruitment is being done. In other words, this process involves the collection of resumes or data of various candidates who are suitable for the concerned position. The HR department scrambles through multiple portals for data collection such as Naukri.com, LinkedIn, monsterindia.com, etc. This process does not involve the selection of the candidates, it only involves the collection of the information of the relevant candidates for further screening and selection.

### 1.1.3 Screening

Screening is the first assessment of the candidates with the necessary qualifications for the job position. All the resumes and data that are collected in the sourcing process are reviewed and screened by the HR department. This stage finds out those candidates who will be advancing to the next level of selection. Screening the resumes of candidates and selecting the top ones from the whole lot is the usual activity in this process.

### 1.1.4 Selecting

Selecting is the main stage of choosing the most suitable candidate for the job for which the recruitment is being done. Those candidates who passed the screening stage have to go through this phase of selection which might involve multiple tests. Personal tests, group discussions, aptitude tests are some of the most common tests that are used to select the most suitable candidate for the job post. The candidate who is selected also gets to negotiate his/her salary with the HR department in this phase itself. The best candidate is selected for the job and no more candidates are assessed after this selection stage.

### 1.1.5 Hiring

The candidate who is finally selected in the selecting stage is hired by the company. This occurs in this phase called hiring. The concerned candidate is presented with the offer letter from the organization's HR department. All the terms and conditions of the job along with other necessary information regarding the job are presented to the chosen candidate at this stage. If the organization and the chosen candidate agree on all the terms and conditions set forward, the candidate is hired into the organization.

### 1.1.6 Onboarding

Onboarding is the last phase in the recruitment process and by this stage, a suitable candidate is already selected and hired for the concerned job position. In this phase, the new employee is welcomed into the organization by the HR department. Onboarding is the process of introducing the new employee to the organization, its cultures, rules & regulations, his/her role, other employees, and the way of working. It is a way of familiarizing the new employee about the various aspects of the organization and the job role.

HR Analytics is defined as a HR process which uses the HR data (e.g. recruitment data) and domain knowledge to do start predicting the performance and cost involved of the people on the basis of their work (Kailash).

## 2   Literate Review

According to the Gartner, human resource leader has begun analyzing the HR data at each level to improve the HR efficiency, recruitment efficiency and enhance employee experience (George 2012). In the fast-growing world with their emerging new challenges, it is very difficult to hire skilled people which will be in the organization for a decent span of time. To create such system, we need good quality of data backed by domain knowledge to provide analytical suggestion to hire a candidate. To create such analytical system, the business data should be extensively available to the hiring manager to work align to find the suitable candidate (Kimball 2016).

For a smooth functioning of an organization, their strategic decision should be backed by data. Data helps us to find the insights or patterns among the people or work. This data should be properly created and organized in such a way that it can be further used to perform any analytical tasks. The success of human resource department with the help of analytics can be measured as the success of the organization. HR department tries to understand the business requirement and ensure the finding of right candidate according to their skills and qualifications. To hire such a niche level people we need to create a precise DataMart and use its data for analytical view. Human resource (HR) DataMart is the base stone for building an enterprise data warehouse. The paper presents the implementation process of HR DataMart starting from implementing DataMart schema to online analytical processing (OLAP) reports (Kimball 2016).

There are quite a few DataMarts available in the market these days. Among them, quite popular are the Kim Kimball HR DataMart which is the base for many available DataMarts, Oracle HR DataMart, SAP HR DataMart.

## 2.1 HR DataMart by Ralph Kimball

The Kimball HR DataMart is based on the ideology of Ralph Kimball according to whom the data warehouses should be model using dimensional models such as the star schema or snowflake schema. Kimball's approach was the bottom-up approach that involved creating DataMarts first to allow quick analysis and interpretation of the data in them. These small DataMarts can later be combined to form a normal data warehouse. Kimball focused on the use of dimensional models to improve the performance of the users of the data warehouse (Oracle, Recruiting Data Mart Dimension Tables, n.d.).

In order to understand Kimball's HR DataMart, we have to look at the star schema dimension model. A star schema is a tool for dimensional modeling of data by organizing it to allow analytical operations to run on it. The star schema presents the data in the form of fact tables and dimension tables. The fact tables contain the primary data regarding the business process, in our case, the recruitment data, which are termed as 'facts'. The other tables or dimension tables contain the data associated with the primary fact tables. The dimension table contains 'dimensions' which sort of describe the data in the facts table.

The dimensional tables surround the fact table depicting the descriptive nature of the facts. The multiple dimension tables around the fact table make this model look something like a star due to which it is known as the star schema.

Kimball's HR DataMart focused on doing the harder things in the beginning while keeping the easy things for the end. Below is the Employees tracking DataMart from Kimball. I could not find anything specific to only recruitment in Kimball DataMart, which we will be disusing inferring Kimball DataMart concept (Kimball 2016). Kimball HR DataMart is shown in Fig. 1.

## 2.2 HR DataMart by Oracle

Then we have Oracle DataMart. Oracle Recruitment DataMart is a data storehouse of enlistment also, staffing drives, status, costs, and results. This information store contains more outlined data and all current and memorable well-known enrolment drives including open positions, orders, candidates, applications, results, and enrolment cost. Recruitment measurements can be reported and investigated by a wide assortment of credits, including specialty unit, division, work code, area, status, status reason, reference class, and subcategory, etc. The Recruiting information store furnishes staff and the board with data expected to settle on informed choices with respect to current and future recruitment drives (Oracle, Recruiting Data Mart Dimension Tables, n.d.).

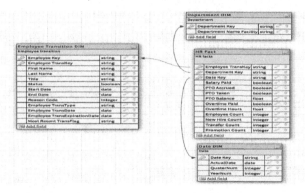

**Fig. 1.** Kimball HR DataMart (Kimball 2016)

Oracle gives a total and self-administration arrangement that permits business groups to get the profound, reliable, information-driven experiences they need to settle on speedy choices. Business groups can rapidly join all vital information across various sources and organizations, including spatial and diagram, in a combined data set to drive secure cooperation around a solitary wellspring of truth given by information stores. Analysts can without much of a stretch influence self-administration information devices and implanted AI—with zero coding needed—to speed up information stacking, change, and readiness, consequently find examples and patterns, make expectations, and gain experiences dependent on information with straightforward ancestry (Prado 2010) (Hamoud 2020). Oracle DataMart has been shown in Fig. 2.

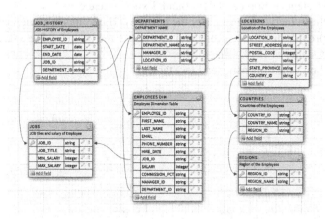

**Fig. 2.** Oracle HR DataMart (Oracle, Recruiting Data Mart Dimension Tables n.d.)

## 3  Methodology

The following point consists of the proposed methodology (Fig. 3):-

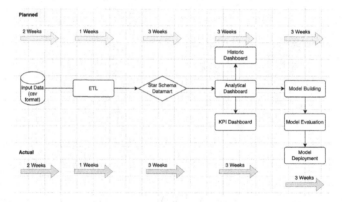

**Fig. 3.** Pipeline

## 3.1  Load the Data

At this stage, the data will be load to the system. Here we are accepting only csv file as input data for now.

## 3.2  ETL and Finding Fact and Dimension Tables

Data exploration and further cleaning as per the requirement. Ingest the clean data into system. Dimension table the tables of a star schema which store the attributes that describes the object. Here dimension tables are Candidate Reference Id, Manager Id, Job Role, Job Category, Source, Salary Band, Experience etc.

Facts are the numeric dimensions of the business. They support numerical computations used to provide details regarding and investigate the business. Here fact tables are Cost of Hire, Quality of Hire, Time to Hire.

Figure 4 shows the dimension and fact tables.

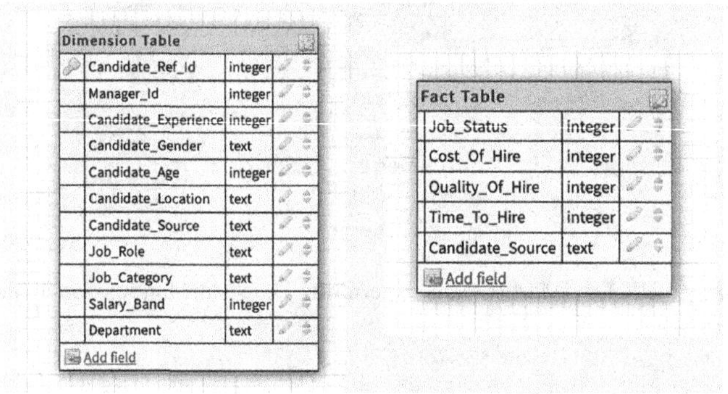

**Fig. 4.** Dimension & Fact Tables

### 3.3  Star Schema DataMart

The clean data will be used to find the dimension and fact tables. Further star schema DataMart will be created.

Figure 5 shows the star schema for recruitment process. Star schema has been taken under consideration for this paper. Snowflake schema is just to understanding in detail purpose. Figure 6 shows Snowflake schema.

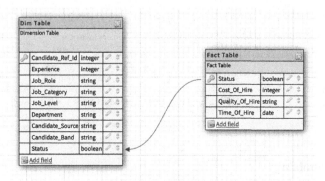

**Fig. 5.**  Star Schema

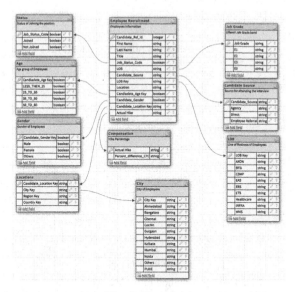

**Fig. 6.**  Snowflake

### 3.4  Creating Analytical Dashboards

Analytical dashboard, historic dashboard and KPI dashboard will be created. Analytical DataMart helps us to create decision management platforms where data scientists can use the analytical DataMart for their analysis. Analytical DataMart Example has been shown in Fig. 7.

- Application Tracking
  - Number of Candidate seen the application
  - Number of candidate filled up the application

- Interview Tracking
  - Number of interview schedule
  - Number of interview rescheduled
  - Number of interview taken
  - Number of interviews completed
  - Number of selections

- Recruitment Source Analytics
  - Application Sourced Directly
  - Application Sourced by Employee Referral
  - Application Sourced by Agency

- Notice Period Tracking
  - Notice period
  - Joined

**Fig. 7.** Analytical DataMart

### 3.5 Model Building

After data modelling by building DataMart, segmentation has been done using K-Mean Algorithm. To check the number of clusters, elbow method has been used which is shown in Fig. 8.

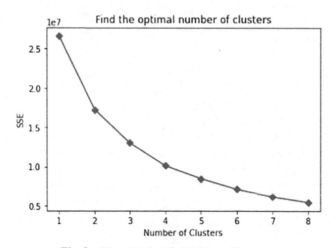

**Fig. 8.** Elbow Method for K-Mean Clustering

Once the data is segmented in clusters, historic dashboard has been built on data studio tool. The Historic Dashboard has been shown below in below figure. Historic Dashboard shows the historic trend of the recruitment referring to other features like cost of hire, hiring cost and hiring time. Historic Dashboard has been shown in Fig. 9.

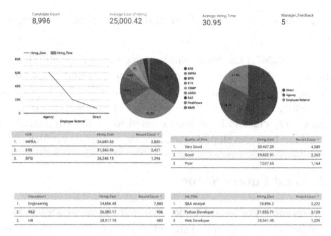

**Fig. 9.** Historic Dashboard

## 3.6 Deployment

The DataMart has been designed on dbdesigner which generates the SQL code which can be further developed in any database tool like Microsoft SQL server management studio or oracle database or can be built on any cloud like Amazon Web Services, Google Cloud Platform, Microsoft Azure. Various dashboards like historic and predictive dashboards have been made on Datastudio which is a free tool from Google. Alternately one can use Power BI or Tableau as a substitute of Datastudio. For segmentation (modeling), K-Means algorithm has been used to build the model. The model has not been deployed as of now.

## 4   Results and Discussion

After A DataMart is the access layer of a data warehouse used to offer data to users in business intelligence. Small chunks of the data warehouse are often referred to as Data-Mart. Data warehouses typically hold enterprise-wide data, whereas DataMart typically store data unique to a department or team. The primary goal of DataMart is to offer the most relevant data for BI to the business user in the shortest time feasible. Millions of records can be stored in a DataMart, which necessitates terabytes of storage. The following are some of the benefits of employing a DataMart:

- Allows users to have access to the precise type of data they require, which improves end-user response time.
- A data warehouse that has been compacted and narrowed in scope.
- Each one is devoted to a single item or function.
- Implementing a full data warehouse is more expensive.
- Contains a lot of information.
- It is less crowded and simply contains necessary company information and data.
- Assists in the integration of all data sources

- The building and use of a DataMart result in a significant amount of data summarization.

In this paper, a DataMart has been built up referring to Kimball HR DataMart and Oracle recruitment DataMart. A star schema with facts and dimension tables has been built up to develop KPI DataMart and analytical DataMart. Further, segmentation model has been created using K-Mean algorithm to cluster the similar kind of candidates. As per elbow method, five clusters have been created to segment the candidates. Later, historic dashboard has been developed to analyze the candidate profiles in details.

## 5  Conclusion and Future Scope

Different human resource Datamart like Kimball HR Datamart, Oracle HR Datamart, SAP- HANA Datamart has been studied and inferred. Based on inferences from popular Datamart, industry expert experience and through research done, a new Datamart for recruitment has been created. This Datamart will be a good option to start building the recruitment Datamart. The K-Mean algorithm has been used to build a model on recruitment data. Candidates are segmented under 5 classes with different features. Historic and predictive analytical dashboard has been created on recruitment dataset.

Future work will be extending recruitment process to other human resource process like Employee Lifecycle, Employee Exit (Retention) etc. Will be creating Datamart, create dashboards and build model for the same process.

## References

Kailash, M.P.: HR Analytics methodical measurement of HR processes. Int. J. Innov. Sci. Res. Technol. (2020)

George, S.: Inmon or Kimball: which approach is suitable for your data warehouse, 14 April 2012. https://www.computerweekly.com/tip/Inmon-or-Kimball-Which-approach-is-suitable-for-your-data-warehouse

Kimball, M.R.: Data warehousing, business intelligence, and dimensional modeling primer. In: Kimball, M.R. (ed.) The Data Warehouse Toolkit, 3rd edn., pp. 7–16. Wiley (2016)

Kimball, M.R.: Employees tracking for profile. In: The Data Warehouse Toolkit: The Definitive Guide to Dimensional Modeling, 3rd edn., pp. 263–265. Wiley (2016)

Oracle. Recruiting Data Mart Dimension Tables (n.d.). https://docs.oracle.com/cd/E41507_01/epm91pbr3/eng/epm/phcw/concept_HCMWarehouseStructure-399b81.html

Kimball, M.R.: Data warehousing. In: Business Intelligence, and Dimensional Modeling Primer, in Kimball The Data Warehouse Toolkit, 3rd edn., pp. 7–16. Wiley (2016)

Kimball, R., Ross, M.: Employees tracking for profile. In: The Data Warehouse Toolkit: The Definitive Guide to Dimensional Modeling, 3rd edn., pp. 263–265. Wiley (2016)

Prado, A., Freitas, C., Sbrici, T.R.: Using OLAP tools for e-HRM: a case study. Int. J. Technol. Human Interact. (2010)

Hamoud, A.K., Ulkareem, M.A., Hussain, H.N., Mohammed, Z.A., Salih, G.M.: Improve HR decision-making based on data mart and OLAP. J. Phys. Conf. Ser. (2020)

Udhay Kailash, M.P.: HR analytics methodical measurement of HR processes. Int. J. Innov. Sci. Res. Technol. (2020)

Alexandra: 25 Practical Tips for Building and Managing a Solid Recruitment Funnel, 27 August 2019. https://harver.com/blog/recruitment-funnel/

Kimball, R., Ross, M.: Data warehousing, business intelligence, and dimensional modeling primer. In: Kimball The Data Warehouse Toolkit, 3rd edn., pp. 7–16. Wiley (2016)

SAP: SAP HANA as Data Mart, 24 January 2018. https://help.sap.com/doc/e95f6750b0fd10148e a5c6be75016694/1.0.12/en-US/SAP_HANA_Master_Guide_en.pdf

Gartner: Gartner Identifies Three Most Common AI Use Cases in HR and Recruiting, June 2019. https://www.gartner.com/en/newsroom/press-releases/2019-06-19-gartner-identi fies-three-most-common-ai-use-cases-in-

ttttt (n.d.). Retrieved from Gartner Identifies Three Most Common AI Use Cases in HR and Recruiting

Google (n.d.). www.google.com

Inuwa, I.: Design of a data warehouse model for a university decision support system. J. Inf. Knowl. Manage. **5** (2015)

Gabcanova, I.: Human resources key performance indicators. J. Competitiveness (2012)

Oracle: Installing Human Resources Schema on Autonomous Database (2020). https://docs. oracle.com/en/cloud/paas/autonomous-data-warehouse-cloud/dw_hr_analytics/run-analytics/ run-analytics.html#setting-up-the-human-resource-analytics-paper-in-oac

Vulpen, E.V.: Human Resources KPIs: An In-depth Explanation with Metrics & Examples (n.d.). https://www.aihr.com/blog/human-resources-key-performance-indicators-hr-kpis/

Datapine: 19 KPIS That Every HE Manager Should Use (n.d.). https://www.datapine.com/kpi-examples-and-templates/human-resources

# Data Homogeneity Dependent Topic Modeling for Information Retrieval

Keerthana Sureshbabu Kashi[✉], Abigail A. Antenor,
Gabriel Isaac L. Ramolete, and Adrienne Heinrich

Aboitiz Data Innovation, Goldbell Towers, 47 Scotts Road, Singapore, Singapore
{keerthana.sureshbabu,abigail.antenor,gabriel.ramolete,
adrienne.heinrich}@aboitiz.com

**Abstract.** Different topic modeling techniques have been applied over the years to categorize and make sense of large volumes of unstructured textual data. Our observation shows that there is not one single technique that works well for all domains or for a general use case. We hypothesize that the performance of these algorithms depends on the variation and heterogeneity of topics mentioned in free text and aim to investigate this effect in our study. Our proposed methodology comprises of i) the calculation of a homogeneity score to measure the variation in the data, ii) selection of the algorithm with the best performance for the calculated homogeneity score. For each homogeneity score, the performances of popular topic modeling algorithms, namely NMF, LDA, LSA, and BERTopic, were compared using an accuracy and Cohen's kappa score. Our results indicate that for highly homogeneous data, BERTopic outperformed the other algorithms (Cohen's kappa of 0.42 vs. 0.06 for LSA). For medium and low homogeneous data, NMF was superior to the other algorithms (medium homogeneity returns a Cohen's kappa of 0.3 for NMF vs. 0.15 for LDA, 0.1 for BERTopic, 0.04 for LSA).

**Keywords:** Topic modeling · Topic Discovery · Technique selection · Information retrieval · NMF · LDA · LSA · BERTopic · Homogeneity · Heterogeneity

## 1 Introduction

Topic modeling methods are a set of text-mining and information retrieval approaches that have been vastly utilized in natural language processing (NLP) for segmented text analysis. It serves best for several use cases: organizing vast volumes of text, the retrieval of information from unstructured or semi-structured documents, feature extraction through creating representations of latent classes, and clustering of documents. Topic model algorithms scan a set of documents called a corpus, examine how words and phrases co-occur, and group the words that best describe the document. These words often represent a coherent theme, categorized in a topic. A variety of topic models, from Bayesian

© ICST Institute for Computer Sciences, Social Informatics and Telecommunications Engineering 2023
Published by Springer Nature Switzerland AG 2023. All Rights Reserved
S. Nandan Mohanty et al. (Eds.): ICISML 2022, LNICST 471, pp. 66–84, 2023.
https://doi.org/10.1007/978-3-031-35081-8_6

probabilistic topic models (BPTMs) such as Latent Dirichlet Allocation (LDA) [1] to neural topic models (NTMs) such as variational autoencoders [2,3] and generative adversarial nets (GANs) [4–6], have been utilized in language models, text summarization, and text generation, identifying concealed semantics in heaps of semantic data [7,8].

Numerous researchers leverage on topic modeling techniques to easily derive topics from corpora. Often, the corpora used for topic modeling contain enormous amounts of text data resulting from open-ended survey questions and manual logging of complaints. For instance, Nguyen and Ho aim to evaluate how Latent Dirichlet Allocation (LDA) analyzes experience in customer service [9]. Various algorithms have attempted to demystify social media posts on Facebook and Twitter according to human interpretation [10–12].

While topic modeling can help automate the conception of ideas and abstractions, it is inevitable for these algorithms to pick up on noise or linguistically meaningless correlations of words found in documents. Recent papers which review topic modeling methods on different text lengths and domains suggest that not all topic modeling algorithms perform consistently. Vayansky and Kumar suggest that LDA, while versatile and often gravitated upon, does not befit complex data relationships [13]. Sbalchiero and Eder experiment the capability of different algorithms on different text lengths [14]. Hu et al. even propose an interactive topic modeling framework which inputs user feedback on initial model outputs to further optimize the topic modeling solutions [15]. Validation metrics such as accuracy, Cohen's kappa coefficient, and coherence scores can be used to optimize these models and may return numerically sufficient performance, but vague semantic outputs may hinder or misguide human interpretation.

To illustrate this further, consider the topic keywords generated with Non-negative Matrix Factorization (NMF) [10], a commonly known topic model, and its subjective observation as shown in Table 1. This is applied to a set of complaints sourced from a dataset further discussed in Sect. 3.1. It can be observed that when data consisting of only two complaint categories is considered ('Late payment' and 'Fraud'), a user can easily assign a description and action point to the topic inferred from the topic key words.

**Table 1.** Keywords generated by NMF for two complaint categories

| Topic ID | Topic Key words | Topic Description | Impact |
|---|---|---|---|
| 0 | payment, interest, fee, late | Late payment | Complaints are sent to late payments dept. |
| 1 | report, theft, identity theft | Fraud | Complaints are sent to fraud dept. |
| 2 | card, charge, credit, fraudulent | Fraud | Complaints are sent to fraud dept |

However, in Table 2, using the same NMF topic modeling technique now on three complaint categories ('Late payment', 'Fraud' and 'Closing account'), some topic keyword groups can result in mixed context words; in Topic ID 0, the mixed content seems to address both 'fraud' and 'late payment'. It may be seen that as the variation in the data increases, the value of the interpretations arising from the topic keywords can alter.

**Table 2.** Keywords generated by NMF for three complaint categories

| Topic ID | Topic Key words | Topic Description | Impact |
|---|---|---|---|
| 0 | charge, late, payment, merchant, card, fraud | Mixed context words | Some of the complaints in this cluster are sent to late payments instead of fraud dept. |
| 1 | statement, payment, past due, found late | Late payment | Complaints are sent to late payments dept. |
| 2 | account, credit, close, credit card, close account | Closing account | Complaints are sent to closing accounts dept. |
| 3 | account, information, card, contact, fraudulent | Fraud | Complaints are sent to fraud dept. |
| 4 | payment, fee, late, late fee, pay, paid, interest, due | Late payment | Complaints are sent to fraud dept |

Similar examples of the issue illustrated above could be seen in the contrasting best performance models for large text [16], sentence classification [17], and short text topic modeling [18]. Although previous papers can suggest that techniques such as LDA, NMF, and even Latent Semantic Analysis (LSA) perform best for certain scenarios [17,18], no technique appears to have the best average performance on a variety of data assortments and purposes.

The goal of this paper is to investigate and propose a topic modeling selection method that is dependent on the data homogeneity. With this in place, the best topic modeling techniques can be identified for particular scenarios given a broad set of data variations in topic-laden corpora. The text content variety is measured based on a homogeneity score. Suggesting the best performing algorithm for certain scenarios will help researchers and organizations mitigate the risk of misidentifying topics on various corpora, which consequently lessens wasted resources and time.

In this paper, Sect. 2 describes the state-of-the-art approaches regarding preprocessing steps, the intuition behind different topic modeling algorithms, and the formulation of a homogeneity score used in the experimentation. Section 3 details the experimental setup while Sect. 4 discusses the results of the experiment. Section 5 concludes on the observed performance of the algorithms and how our proposed method can help users in selecting an appropriate algorithm based on data homogeneity.

## 2   Review of Related Literature

### 2.1   Prevalence of Topic Modeling in Scientific and Corporate Settings

Topic modeling has applications in many fields, such as literature review, software engineering, and linguistic science. For example, organizing qualitative works, including opinion and sentiment analysis for marketing, discourse analysis in media studies, and blog usage for sociological studies, have shown to improve through the usage of an Interval Semi-supervised Latent Dirichlet Allocation (ISLDA) approach, with the help of defining a term frequency-inverse document frequency (TF-IDF) coherence score [19]. A variety of authors, such as DiMaggio et al. [20], Grimmer [21], Quinn et al. [22], Jockers and Mimno [23], Baum [24], Elgesem et al. [25], have shown the usage of topic modeling approaches for identifying concepts, subjects of discussion, or sentiments through data such as newspapers, press releases, speeches, books, blogs, and tweets. Other researchers have also shown topic modeling expertise with respect to software traceability [26], coupling of classes in object-oriented software systems [27], and mining source code histories [28,29].

Outside of natural and social sciences, topic modeling use cases are also prevalent in corporate settings. Voice-of-customer processing with topic modeling for extracting actual customer needs has been remarked by Özdağoğlu et al. [30]. Barravecchia et al. [31]. At the same time, topic modeling has also been observed to define service quality attributes, content marketing topics, sentiment analysis towards products, and issues in customer reviews [32–35]. Other applications of topic modeling were studied by Asmussen & Møller, focusing on the Latent Dirichlet allocation model in particular. A bibliometric analysis performed over topic modeling-focused researched papers in 2000–2017 observed that while computer science and engineering comprised of the majority of publications, topic modeling has emerged in other subjects such as medical informatics, telecommunications, business economics, operations research, biochemistry and molecular biology, remote sensing, and photographic technology [36].

## 2.2 Homogeneity and Heterogeneity

The heterogeneity of texts in a corpus can be perceived using the concept of entropy, a measure of the level of complexity and randomness of any system with various interdependent components [37]. The formula for Shannon's Entropy is shown in Eq. (1).

$$S = -\sum_{i=1}^{T} p_i ln(p_i), \tag{1}$$

where $S$ indicates entropy, $p$ denotes the probabilities of occurrence, $T$ corresponds to types of different components, and $i$ conform to the number of tokens of a text [37,38].

In this system, the texts are observed as communicative functions that drive the evolution of the corpus' entropic process. The complex nature of the corpus is shown in various aspects such as semantic, syntactic, discourse, chaotic interactions, and possible self-organizational mechanisms. In essence, homogeneity produces criteria for classifying texts with common linguistic characteristics. They may share the same features, such as lexical distance, word choice, or genre [39].

Using Shannon's Entropy, a homogeneity score denoted as $H$ is calculated. A lower homogeneity score is computed when the topic variation increases with the number of categories. The formula is shown in Eq. (2).

$$H(X) = \sum_{i=1}^{N} P(x_i) \cdot \log \frac{1}{P(x_i)} \tag{2}$$

Considering a dataset $X$ with elements $x_i$, fitting the formula to this use case, let $N_C$ be the number of categories (labels) and $C_i$ be a set of data points in a category (label). Defining probability for each element $P(x_i) = \frac{|C_i|}{N}$, the entropy equation can be transformed to Eq. (3).

$$H(X) = \sum_{i=1}^{N_C} \frac{|C_i|}{N} \cdot \log \frac{N}{|C_i|} \tag{3}$$

With this, the homogeneity score of the data set could be derived as the inverse of its Shannon's entropy shown in Eq. (4).

$$h(x) = \begin{cases} \infty & \text{if } H(X) = 0 \\ \frac{1}{H(X)} & \text{otherwise} \end{cases} \tag{4}$$

If $h(X) = \infty$, then $X$ is fully homogeneous. So, the higher the value of $h(X)$, the data set $X$ is said to be more homogenous. A lower homogeneity score is computed when the topic variation increases with the number of categories.

## 2.3   Preprocessing Techniques

Before modeling, preprocessing techniques are used to transform text inputs into machine-readable elements. Such steps are described below:

**Tokenization.** Tokenization is a preprocessing technique that cuts text into sentences and breaks them down into words. Uppercase letters are converted to lowercase letters, then punctuation marks are removed [40].

**Part-of-Speech (POS) Tagging.** This preprocessing technique tags words by their context in a sentence, whether they are nouns, verbs, adjectives, or other forms [41]. In this paper, POS taggers are used to study large tagged text corpora and make an abstract level of analysis from reliable low-level information.

**Word Lemmatization.** Lemmatization is a linguistic term defined as grouping words with the same root or lemma. While there are concerns that the real meaning of words in the sentence could be out of context, lemmatization preempts this complication. Therefore, it is a preferred option for topic modeling compared to stemming. Stemming only cuts off the derived affixes of the word, thus losing the true intention of the word in the sentence [40].

**Term Frequency-Inverse Document Frequency (TF-IDF).** Words with a high relative term frequency value have high importance in documents. TF-IDF illustrates the correlation and relationship of words on the corpus by calculating similar degrees among documents and deciding on search rank. With this, getting the inverse of document frequency means we are identifying the terms with high importance [42].

## 2.4 Modeling Techniques

With the advent of data-driven approaches toward understanding customer feedback efficiently, various topic modeling techniques have been developed to optimize the topic identification problem in information retrieval. State-of-the-art and commonly used topic algorithms include Non-negative Matrix Factorization, Latent Dirichlet Allocation, Latent Semantic Analysis, and BERTopic [10].

**NMF.** Non-negative Matrix Factorization (NMF) is a linear algebraic method on decompositional non-probabilistic algorithms [10]. The goal of NMF is to decrease the data dimension and to identify its principal components to represent the chaotic and complex data as an interpretable information cluster [43].

NMF breaks down the input term-document matrix $V$ to term-topics matrix $W$ and topics-document matrix $M$. This factorization was initiated by Paatero and Tapper from 1994 to 1997 [44], commenced with Lee and Seung in 1999 to 2001 [45]. It incorporates non-negative constraints that enhance semantic explainability with the parts-based representation [43]. See Eq. (5).

$$V_{i\mu} \approx (WM)_{i\mu} = \sum_{a=1}^{r} W_{ia}M_{a\mu} \qquad (5)$$

Compared to LDA, this method utilizes Term Frequency-Inverse Document Frequency (TF-IDF) to represent the importance of each word in a corpus and not just solely rely on the raw word frequency. According to Egger and Yu, NMF outperforms LDA by producing clearly defined topics but is relatively standard compared to algorithms working on word embeddings [10].

**LDA.** Latent Dirichlet Allocation (LDA) is an unsupervised generative probabilistic model of a corpus, representing topics by word probabilities [1]. LDA assumes that each document is a probabilistic distribution over latent subjects and that topic distribution in all documents share a common Dirichlet prior. Each latent topic in the LDA model is also a probabilistic distribution over words. Thus, the word distributions of issues share a common Dirichlet prior.

**LSA.** Latent Semantic Analysis (LSA) is another older method for extracting the contextual meaning of words and phrases in sizeable text compilations. Known for reducing the dimensionalities of matrices during information retrieval procedures [46], LSA aims to take advantage of an implicit latent semantic form found in sentences and documents, estimated through singular-value decomposition to remove random "noise". When larger portions of data are in play, terms that may not appear in an individual document may still be linked to the document semantically [47].

**BERT and BERTopic.** The Bidirectional Encoder Representations from Transformers (BERT), classified as a transformer-based NLP technique, aims to improve on other fine-tuning approaches in applying pre-trained language representation [48]. Variations of BERT went with both clustering procedures and a class-based variation of the TF-IDF algorithm to create logical topic representations, coined BERTopic by Grootendorst in 2022 [49]. BERTopic utilizes pre-training or creating general-purpose language representation models fine-tuned on smaller-data NLP activities. These activities include next sentence prediction, sentiment analysis, question-answer responses, and other tasks found in the General Language Understanding Evaluation (GLUE) benchmark [50].

The architecture of BERT follows a self-attention mechanism [51] and is pre-trained using a Masked Language Model (MLM) and Next Sentence Prediction (NSP), two unsupervised tasks. Each document is converted to its embedding representation by clustering a version of the embeddings with reduced dimensionality and extracting the topics with a class-based TF-IDF iteration. This accounts for the clusters of documents as shown in Eq. (6).

$$W_{t,c} = tf_{t,c} \cdot log(1 + \frac{A}{tf_t}), \tag{6}$$

wherein the frequency of a term $t$ inside a class $c$, or a collection of documents transformed into a single document cluster, is modeled. The logarithm of the mean words of each class $A$ divided by $t$ across all classes made, adding one to positive output values, is used to measure the amount of information the term $t$ provides to the class $c$ [49].

## 2.5    Evaluation Metrics

To determine the most suitable topic modeling algorithm for various levels of topic variation, accuracy and Cohen's kappa coefficient were used as evaluation metrics and to find the optimal number of topics for various variations in the data set coherence score was applied.

**Coherence Score.** A coherence score is applied to find the degree of semantic similarity between high-scoring words in the topic. To calculate, the formula used is shown in Eq. (7).

$$C(t : V^{(t)}) = \sum_{m=2}^{M} \sum_{l=1}^{m-1} \log \frac{D(v_m^{(t)}, v_l^{(t)}) + 1}{D(v_l^{(t)})} \tag{7}$$

where $D(v)$ denotes the document frequency of word type $v$, and $D(v, v')$ corresponds to the co-document frequency of the word types $v'$, and $v$, and $V^{(t)}$ depicts the list of M most probable words in topic $t$. When the most significant and comprehensive words found for a certain topic have a high rate of co-occurrence, this results in high coherence score [52].

**Accuracy.** A common evaluation metric for text classification is accuracy. It measures the correct classifications over the total number of classifications. The formula for accuracy is shown in Eq. (8).

$$accuracy = \frac{TP + TN}{TP + TN + FP + FN} \tag{8}$$

where TP stands for True Positive, TN for True Negative, FP for False Positive, and FN for False Negative [53].

**Cohen's Kappa Coefficient.** This formula calculates the kappa coefficient, denoted by $\kappa$ shown in Eq. (9).

$$\kappa = \frac{Pr(a) - Pr(e)}{1 - Pr(e)} \tag{9}$$

where Pr(a) is the proportion of units in which the raters agreed, and Pr(e) is the proportion for which the agreement is expected by likelihood, as found in Eq. (9). For topic modeling purposes, the agreements could be interpreted as how close the predicted value and the true value concur with one another. As $\kappa$ positively increases, there is a larger chance of the predicted value and the ground truth agreeing. If there is no agreement, then $\kappa$ is negative [54]. Along with accuracy, Kappa's coefficient is an additional evaluation metric for classifiers as it considers the presence of imbalanced data [55]. Therefore in this experiment, the better-performing classifiers should have higher values of $\kappa$ [56].

## 3  Experimental Setup

### 3.1  Data Source

The consumer complaint data used in the experiments was sourced from the Consumer Financial Protection Bureau of 2012–2017, particularly the "Credit Card complaints.csv" dataset [57]. It contains thirty (30) unique categories such as Billing disputes, Balance transfer, Delinquent accounts, Identity theft/Fraud/Embezzlement, and Late fee in the 'Issue' column. These were considered annotated compliant categories, while the topic modeling algorithms used the'Consumer complaint narrative' column to generate topic keywords.

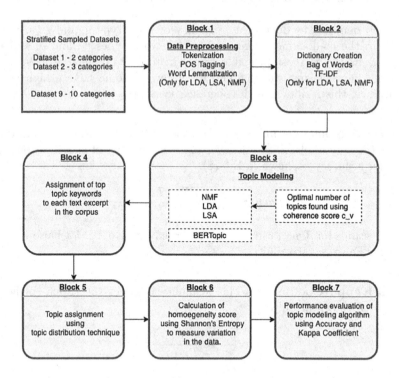

**Fig. 1.** Experimental Setup

## 3.2 Methodology

Figure 1 explains the setup used in this experiment. Nine (9) stratified sampled data sets, containing complaint categories between two and ten, are obtained from the complaints dataset discussed in Sect. 3.1. After the dataset is created, a set of preprocessing steps, shown in Block 1, is applied to each stratified dataset sample. These include Tokenization, Parts-of-Speech Tagging, and Word Lemmatization. The preprocessing steps mentioned are only required for NMF, LDA, and LSA, not for BERTopic, as the latter uses pre-trained language and representation models.

After data is preprocessed, a dictionary and Bag of Words (BOW) are created, containing all words in the corpus represented as keys and the frequency of the occurrence of the words identified as values. Following the BOW is the TF-IDF identification, which carries information on which words are more critical. After documents are vectorized, the topic modeling method is implemented. In our case, the topic modeling techniques NMF, LDA and LSA utilize the coherence score calculation to find the optimal number of topics, while BERTopic internally calculates the optimal number of topics to be used.

The topic keywords, generated by executing the topic modeling algorithms, are then mapped against the annotated categories as shown in Blocks 4 and 5. As an example from our dataset, topics such as Advertising and marketing, Closing/Cancelling Accounts, Identity Theft, Rewards/Memberships, will be assigned based on the maximum value of the distribution among all annotated topics within each cluster formed by the topic modeling algorithms.

An example of keywords generated by NMF is shown in Table 3. The first four columns show the distribution of existing annotated categories with each cluster of documents. The cluster of documents formed by the generated Topic ID 0 has 10% of total Reward/Memberships complaints/inquiries, 8% of inquiries on closing accounts, 7% on Advertising and marketing, and 3% of Identity theft/Fraud complaints. Since the majority of complaints within this cluster of Topic ID 0 are inclined towards inquiries on Reward/Memberships, the generated topic is assigned to Rewards/Memberships.

**Table 3.** Sample distribution of annotated categories for each generated topic by algorithm NMF. The first four columns denote the text excerpt frequency.

| Advertising and Marketing | Closing /Cancelling account | Identity theft / Fraud | Rewards /Memberships | Categories with highest frequency of text excerpts | Topic ID |
|---|---|---|---|---|---|
| 7% | 8% | 3% | **10%** | Rewards /Memberships | 0 |
| 2% | 8% | **11%** | 0% | Identity theft /Fraud | 1 |
| 0% | **36%** | 3% | 2% | Closing /Cancelling account | 2 |

**Table 4.** Top keywords generated by NMF for each topic

| Topic ID | Topic Keywords | Subjective Observation |
|---|---|---|
| 0 | express, american express, american, point, membership reward, spend, card, offer, express credit, receive | Talks about Rewards and membership |
| 1 | capital, fraud, report, charge, bureau, line | Talks about Fraudulent activities |
| 2 | account, close, balance, account, open, without, credit, citibank | Talks about account closure |

To verify the topic assigned to each topic ID, the model-generated top topic keywords, as shown in Table 4, are also manually interpreted using eyeballing techniques. Table 3 shows that the manual inference is matched with the aforementioned topic allocation using the distribution method.

Steps from Block 1 to Block 6 were ran nine (9) times for all homogeneity scores, generated by the equations in Sect. 2.2. This set of iterations was performed for each topic modeling algorithm for further comparisons. Accuracy and Cohen's kappa coefficient, found in Eq. (8) and (9), were used to evaluate the performance of each topic modeling algorithm, as shown in Block 7.

# 4   Results and Discussion

## 4.1   Outcome of Experiments

**Table 5.** Homogeneity and accuracy values for NMF, LDA, LSA and BertTopic

| Normalized Homogeneity Score | Kappa Coefficient | | | | Normalized Accuracy | | | |
|---|---|---|---|---|---|---|---|---|
| | LSA | BERTopic | LDA | NMF | LSA | BERTopic | LDA | NMF |
| 1.00 | 0.06 | 0.42 | 0.25 | 0.35 | 0.77 | 1.00 | 0.82 | 0.91 |
| 0.47 | 0.14 | 0.24 | 0.04 | 0.35 | 0.63 | 0.70 | 0.27 | 0.74 |
| 0.32 | 0.06 | 0.24 | 0.07 | 0.35 | 0.35 | 0.45 | 0.23 | 0.68 |
| 0.15 | 0.03 | 0.16 | 0.07 | 0.39 | 0.16 | 0.35 | 0.26 | 0.65 |
| 0.11 | 0.04 | 0.10 | 0.15 | 0.30 | 0.12 | 0.26 | 0.32 | 0.50 |
| 0.09 | 0.09 | 0.12 | 0.13 | 0.35 | 0.20 | 0.11 | 0.15 | 0.55 |
| 0.05 | 0.03 | 0.15 | 0.16 | 0.28 | 0.11 | 0.19 | 0.26 | 0.41 |
| 0.02 | 0.02 | 0.13 | 0.07 | 0.26 | 0.00 | 0.19 | 0.04 | 0.37 |
| 0.00 | 0.04 | 0.13 | 0.05 | 0.23 | 0.03 | 0.13 | 0.01 | 0.33 |
| **Average Score** | **0.06** | **0.19** | **0.11** | **0.32** | **0.26** | **0.38** | **0.26** | **0.57** |

Table 5 shows how the performance of NMF, LDA, LSA, and BERTopic vary depending on heterogeneity of the data. Classification accuracy and Kappa's coefficient as calculate. Equation (8) and (9) are used as the metrics to evaluate the performance of these algorithms. The accuracy and homogeneity scores are normalized to set a common scale for a new diversified set of corpora. It can be seen that, when the homogeneity score changed from 1 to 0.47, the accuracy for LDA dropped by 55%, BERTopic by 30%, LSA by 14%, and NMF by 17%. Even though LSA has the most negligible change, it is relatively less performing than NMF, to begin with. Furthermore, as the homogeneity scores changed from 0.47 to 0.32, the normalized accuracy for LSA and BERTopic continued to plummet. For LSA, it dropped by 28%. For BERTopic it decreased by 25%. These drops in normalized accuracy are highlighted in red text in Table 5.

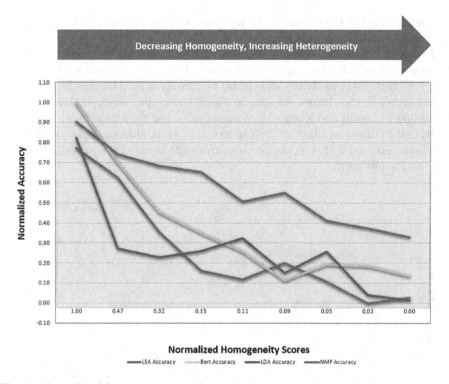

**Fig. 2.** Normalized homogeneity vs Normalized accuracy for the investigated topic modeling algorithms. BERTopic outperforms other algorithms for highly homogeneous data and NMF is superior to other algorithms for low-medium homogeneity scores

The results shown in Fig. 2 and Fig. 3 add to this claim, illustrating that as the homogeneity score decreases, the normalized accuracy and Kappa's coefficient also decrease. However, there are exceptions. For instance, when the homogeneity scores range between 0.15 and 0.05, the normalized accuracy bounces back in Fig. 2 for some algorithms.

As seen in Fig. 2, NMF seems to be the most accurate and suitable algorithm as topic variation increases. While its normalized accuracy decreases, it stays above the other algorithms tested somewhere after the 0.47 mark of the normalized homogeneity. Moreover, the gap for the normalized accuracy between NMF and the others after this point ranges from 15% to 47%. This significant difference further solidifies the claim that NMF is better in increasingly varying topics. However, when the homogeneity score is at its highest value, or when the variability in the topic is least, BERTopic outperforms NMF by 9%. Thus for topics with more similarities, it can be claimed that BERTopic is the best algorithm to use, followed by NMF, LDA, then LSA.

The performance of the algorithms between homogeneity scores of 0.05 and 0.15 shows some insight. While NMF still surpasses the others, LDA appears to be the second best option, beating BERTopic and LSA. It can therefore be concluded that for the corpus with moderate topic variations, NMF and LDA are the desirable algorithms to use.

In addition to accuracy, the Kappa coefficient is an added evaluation metric. As seen in Sect. 2.5, the Kappa coefficient $\kappa$ helps users evaluate the performance of each topic modeling algorithm, becoming more reliable when there is an imbalance in the classes. As seen in Fig. 3, the graph conveyed three ranges. According to Landis and Koch, [58], a kappa value less than 0 indicates no agreement, 0–0.20 draws as slight, 0.21–0.40 as fair, 0.41–0.60 as moderate, 0.61–0.80 as substantial, and 0.81–1 as the perfect agreement between the predicted values and the ground truth.

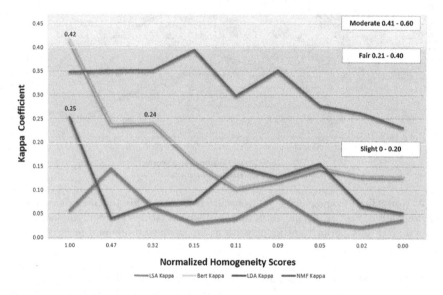

**Fig. 3.** Normalized homogeneity vs Kappa coefficient for investigated topic Modeling algorithms.

For datasets similar to the one at hand, NMF still is the desirable algorithm to use after the 0.47 mark in the homogeneity score. It consistently exhibits fair agreement, meaning that the predicted and actual values are concurring equitably. For the highest homogeneity score tested, BERTopic seems to provide a good Kappa score slightly above the fair range and over the minimum point in the moderate range, thus it can be used more than the NMF at this stage. BERTopic could be used until the 0.32 homogeneity score but not beyond. It already went under the slight range with LSA and LDA. LSA is almost always in the slight range, therefore this could be the last option to take across the whole range.

In summary, the accuracy of topic modeling algorithms must be viewed as dependent on the present homogeneity in the data. For this dataset, NMF is the best algorithm for low and medium homogeneity. But alternatively, LDA could be used for medium homogeneity and BERTopic for high homogeneity. BERTopic performs best for the most homogeneous data, but the performance deteriorates as the homogeneity in data decreases.

**Table 6.** Topic Keywords for Identity theft/Fraud/Embezzlement with Homogeneity Score of 1.00

| Topic | Topic Keywords | Subjective Observation | Remarks |
|---|---|---|---|
| Homogeneity Score: 1.00 | | | |
| NMF | | | |
| Identity theft / Fraud /Embezzlement | account, report, credit, identity, debt, credit report, reporting, open, theft, identity theft | Correct Interpretation | |
| Identity theft / Fraud / Embezzlement | card, charge, credit, credit card, company, call, fraudulent, receive, fraud, card company | Correct Interpretation | |
| Identity theft / Fraud / Embezzlement | capital one, capital, one, one credit, theft, reporting, merchandise, resolve, secure | Correct Interpretation | 100 % topics gives correct interpretation |
| LDA | | | |
| Identity theft / Fraud / Embezzlement | credit, account, card, charge, bank, call, get, information, would, number | Cannot Interpret | |
| Identity theft / Fraud / Embezzlement | card, credit, one, payment, account, make, capital, month, sent, state | Cannot Interpret | |
| Identity theft / Fraud / Embezzlement | payment, balance, would, tv, delivery, purchase, make, best, pay, check | Cannot Interpret | |
| Identity theft / Fraud / Embezzlement | card, credit, account, charge, call, would, receive, time, fraud, told | Correct Interpretation | Only 25% of topics give correct interpretation |
| LSA | | | |
| Identity theft / Fraud / Embezzlement | credit, card, account, charge, call, payment, would | Cannot Interpret | Zero topic with correct interpretation |
| BerTopic | | | |
| Identity theft / Fraud / Embezzlement | credit, card, account, not, fraud, charges, bank | Correct Interpretation | 100% of topics give correct interpretation and clusters all the fraud into one definite cluster, instead of creating many clusters like NMF |

Alongside the comparison of evaluation metrics, a sample set of tables of an "Identity Theft/Fraud/Embezzlement" topic with its generated topic keywords are shown for a homogeneity score of 1.00 and a homogeneity score of 0.32. Aside from the accuracy and Kappa coefficient, a subjective observation will aid in validating the effectiveness of using the recommended algorithms. The subjective validation will also support the use of suitable performance measures for this study.

In Table 6, BERTopic and NMF are able to give 100% correct interpretation for the topic 'Identity theft/Fraud/Embezzlement.' under a homogeneity score of 1.00. However, BERTopic performs best as it could give precisely one definite cluster with correct interpretation from the keywords generated, while NMF gave three clusters with proper interpretation. On the other end, LDA showed 25% correct interpretations and LSA produced keywords that are not as interpretable. In Table 7, which showcases topic keywords for the same topic for the homogeneity score of 0.32, it is apparent that NMF performs the best among LDA, LSA, and BERTopic. NMF gave two-thirds topics worth of correct interpretations, while the three others had either mixed words or uninterpretable keywords.

**Table 7.** Topic Keywords for Identity theft/Fraud/Embezzlement with Homogeneity Score of 0.32

| | Homogeneity Score: 0.32 | | |
|---|---|---|---|
| Topic | Topic Keywords | Subjective Observation | Remarks |
| NMF | | | |
| Identity theft / Fraud / Embezzlement | call, say, would, time, bill, money, get, phone, pay | Contains Mixed Words | |
| Identity theft / Fraud / Embezzlement | capital, capital one, one, one bank, fraud, information, judgment, someone, wallet, charge back | Correct Interpretation | |
| Identity theft / Fraud / Embezzlement | identity, theft, identity theft, report, debt, victim, open, account, victim identity, information | Correct Interpretation | 66% topics give correct interpretation |
| LDA | | | |
| Identity theft / Fraud / Embezzlement | credit, account, card, report, charge, bank, call, close, fraudulent, receive | Contains Mixed Words | Zero topics with correct interpretation |
| LSA | | | |
| Identity theft / Fraud / Embezzlement | card, credit, bank, account, charge, call, one, capital, amex | Cannot Interpret | |
| Identity theft / Fraud / Embezzlement | one, charge, american, express, bank, call, paypal, time, make, capital | Cannot Interpret | Zero topics with correct interpretation |
| BERTopic | | | |
| Identity theft / Fraud / Embezzlement | credit, card, account, had, would, payment | Cannot Interpret | Zero topics with correct interpretation |

The boundaries and algorithm rankings may vary for other data sets unrelated to bank customer complaints or inquiries. A similar experiment should be conducted to understand the generalizability of this study's findings.

## 4.2   Recommended Data Homogeneity Dependent Topic Modeling Process

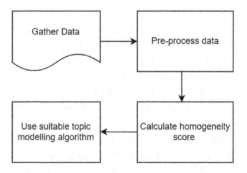

**Fig. 4.** Proposed methodology to select a topic modeling algorithm for a new data

Figure 4 shows the recommended steps a user new to a dataset can apply to determine how homogeneous the data at hand is and which topic modeling algorithm should be considered depending on the homogeneity score. If the user's data is more homogeneous with a normalized homogeneity score greater than 0.5, BERTopic is recommended for similar datasets to the one discussed in this work. If the data moves to a homogeneity score of less than 0.5, NMF can be applied, followed by LDA. LSA is the last choice to take.

# 5  Conclusion

Despite many years of advancements in topic modeling algorithms, there are still apparent drawbacks dealing with conceptually spurious or multi-context words generated by the topic modeling algorithms. These constraints escalate with increasing topic variation in given text corpora, which hinder coherence and usability especially in organizations with large free-text such as in banking and customer feedback. To address this limitation, a homogeneity score based on Shannon's entropy was formulated to capture the topic variation in a data set for each set of annotated categories. The performances of four commonly used state-of-the-art topic modeling algorithms, namely Non-negative Matrix Factorization (NMF), Latent Dirichlet Allocation (LDA), Latent Semantic Analysis (LSA), and Bidirectional Encoder Representation from Transformers for Topic modeling (BERTopic), were evaluated using Accuracy and Cohen's kappa coefficient scores on different levels of data variation explained by the calculated homogeneity scores.

From the results above, it can be concluded that there is no single topic modeling algorithm among the four that perfectly works for increasing topic variation/heterogeneity. Comparatively, BERTopic outperforms other algorithms (Cohen's kappa of 0.42 vs. 0.06 for LSA) for high data homogeneity. For medium and low homogeneous data, NMF is superior to the other algorithms (medium homogeneity returns a Cohen's kappa of 0.3 for NMF vs. 0.15 for LDA, 0.1 for BERTopic, 0.04 for LSA). The methodology described in this paper aims to help users calculate the topic variation in their dataset which is derived from the proposed homogeneity score. The user can choose among most widely used algorithms, not limited to the four topic modeling techniques aforementioned, to get the best coherent interpretation from the topic keywords generated.

# References

1. Jelodar, H., et al.: Latent Dirichlet Allocation (LDA) and topic modeling: models, applications, a survey. Multimedia Tools Appl. **78**(11), 15169–15211 (2019)
2. Srivastava, A., Sutton, C.: Autoencoding variational inference for topic models, arXiv preprint arXiv:1703.01488 (2017)
3. Joo, W., Lee, W., Park, S., Moon, I.-C.: Dirichlet variational autoencoder. Pattern Recogn. **107**, 107514 (2020)
4. Jabbar, A., Li, X., Omar, B.: A survey on generative adversarial networks: variants, applications, and training. ACM Comput. Surv. (CSUR) **54**(8), 1–49 (2021)
5. Glover, J.: Modeling documents with generative adversarial networks, arXiv preprint arXiv:1612.09122 (2016)
6. Wang, R., Zhou, D., He, Y.: ATM: adversarial-neural topic model. Inf. Process. Manag. **56**(6), 102098 (2019)
7. Zhao, H., Phung, D., Huynh, V., Jin, Y., Du, L., Buntine, W.: Topic modelling meets deep neural networks: a survey. arXiv preprint arXiv:2103.00498 (2021)
8. Doan, T.-N., Hoang, T.-A.: Benchmarking neural topic models: an empirical study. In: Findings of the Association for Computational Linguistics: ACL-IJCNLP 2021, pp. 4363–4368 (2021)

9. Nguyen, H.-H., Thanh, H.: Analyzing customer experience in hotel services using topic modeling. J. Inf. Process. Syst. **17**, 586–598 (2021)

10. Egger, R., Yu, J.: A topic modeling comparison between LDA, NMF, Top2Vec, and BERTopic to demystify Twitter posts. Frontiers Sociol. **7** (2022)

11. Tan, S., et al.: Interpreting the public sentiment variations on Twitter. IEEE Trans. Knowl. Data Eng. **26**(5), 1158–1170 (2013)

12. Xu, Z., Liu, Y., Xuan, J., Chen, H., Mei, L.: Crowdsourcing based social media data analysis of urban emergency events. Multimedia Tools Appl. **76**(9), 11567–11584 (2017)

13. Vayansky, I., Kumar, S.A.: A review of topic modeling methods. Inf. Syst. **94**, 101582 (2020)

14. Sbalchiero, S., Eder, M.: Topic modeling, long texts and the best number of topics. Some problems and solutions. Qual. Quant. **54**(4), 1095–1108 (2020)

15. Hu, Y., Boyd-Graber, J., Satinoff, B., Smith, A.: Interactive topic modeling. Mach. Learn. **95**(3), 423–469 (2014)

16. Suri, P., Roy, N.R.: Comparison between LDA & NMF for event-detection from large text stream data. In: 2017 3rd International Conference on Computational Intelligence & Communication Technology (CICT), pp. 1–5 (2017)

17. Anantharaman, A., Jadiya, A., Siri, C.T.S., Adikar, B.N., Mohan, B.: Performance evaluation of topic modeling algorithms for text classification. In: 2019 3rd International Conference on Trends in Electronics and Informatics (ICOEI), pp. 704–708 (2019)

18. Qiang, J., Qian, Z., Li, Y., Yuan, Y., Wu, X.: Short text topic modeling techniques, applications, and performance: a survey. IEEE Trans. Knowl. Data Eng. **34**(3), 1427–1445 (2022)

19. Nikolenko, S.I., Koltcov, S., Koltsova, O.: Topic modelling for qualitative studies. J. Inf. Sci. **43**(1), 88–102 (2017)

20. DiMaggio, P., Nag, M., Blei, D.: Exploiting affinities between topic modeling and the sociological perspective on culture: application to newspaper coverage of us government arts funding. Poetics **41**(6), 570–606 (2013)

21. Grimmer, J.: A Bayesian hierarchical topic model for political texts: measuring expressed agendas in senate press releases. Polit. Anal. **18**(1), 1–35 (2010)

22. Quinn, K.M., Monroe, B.L., Colaresi, M., Crespin, M.H., Radev, D.R.: How to analyze political attention with minimal assumptions and costs. Am. J. Polit. Sci. **54**(1), 209–228 (2010)

23. Jockers, M.L., Mimno, D.: Significant themes in 19th-century literature. Poetics **41**(6), 750–769 (2013)

24. Baum, D.: Recognising speakers from the topics they talk about. Speech Commun. **54**(10), 1132–1142 (2012)

25. Elgesem, D., Feinerer, I., Steskal, L.: Bloggers' responses to the Snowden affair: combining automated and manual methods in the analysis of news blogging. Comput. Support. Coop. Work (CSCW) **25**(2), 167–191 (2016)

26. Asuncion, H.U., Asuncion, A.U., Taylor, R.N.: Software traceability with topic modeling. In: 2010 ACM/IEEE 32nd International Conference on Software Engineering, vol. 1, pp. 95–104. IEEE (2010)

27. Gethers, M., Poshyvanyk, D.: Using relational topic models to capture coupling among classes in object-oriented software systems. In: 2010 IEEE International Conference on Software Maintenance, pp. 1–10. IEEE (2010)

28. Thomas, S.W.: Mining software repositories using topic models. In: Proceedings of the 33rd International Conference on Software Engineering, pp. 1138–1139 (2011)

29. Tian, K., Revelle, M., Poshyvanyk, D.: Using latent Dirichlet allocation for automatic categorization of software. In: 2009 6th IEEE International Working Conference on Mining Software Repositories, pp. 163–166. IEEE (2009)
30. Özdağoğlu, G., Kapucugil-Ikiz, A., Celik, A.F.: Topic modelling-based decision framework for analysing digital voice of the customer. Total Qual. Manag. Bus. Excellence **29**(13–14), 1545–1562 (2018)
31. Barravecchia, F., Mastrogiacomo, L., Franceschini, F.: Digital voice-of-customer processing by topic modelling algorithms: insights to validate empirical results. Int. J. Qual. Reliab. Manag. (2021)
32. Ding, K., Choo, W.C., Ng, K.Y., Ng, S.I.: Employing structural topic modelling to explore perceived service quality attributes in Airbnb accommodation. Int. J. Hosp. Manag. **91**, 102676 (2020)
33. Putranto, Y., Sartono, B., Djuraidah, A.: Topic modelling and hotel rating prediction based on customer review in Indonesia. Int. J. Manag. Decis. Mak. **20**(3), 282–307 (2021)
34. Gregoriades, A., Pampaka, M., Herodotou, H., Christodoulou, E.: Supporting digital content marketing and messaging through topic modelling and decision trees. Expert Syst. Appl. **184**, 115546 (2021)
35. Sánchez-Franco, M.J., Arenas-Márquez, F.J., Alonso-Dos-Santos, M.: Using structural topic modelling to predict users' sentiment towards intelligent personal agents. An application for Amazon's echo and Google home. J. Retail. Consum. Serv. **63**, 102658 (2021)
36. Li, X., Lei, L.: A bibliometric analysis of topic modelling studies (2000–2017). J. Inf. Sci. **47**(2), 161–175 (2021)
37. Angel, M.M., Rey, J.-M.: On the role of Shannon's entropy as a measure of heterogeneity. Geoderma **98**(1–2), 1–3 (2000)
38. Torres-García, A.A., Mendoza-Montoya, O., Molinas, M., Antelis, J.M., Moctezuma, L.A., Hernández-Del-Toro, T.: Pre-processing and feature extraction. In: Torres-García, A.A., Reyes-García, C.A., Villaseñor-Pineda, L., Mendoza-Montoya, O. (eds.) BioSignal Processing and Classification Using Computational Learning and Intelligence, pp. 59–91. Academic Press (2022)
39. Zhang, Y.: Modelling the lexical complexity of homogenous texts: a time series approach. Qual. Quant. (2022)
40. Manning, C.D., Raghavan, P., Schütze, H.: Introduction to Information Retrieval. Cambridge University Press (2019)
41. Mitkov, R.: The Oxford Handbook of Computational Linguistics. Oxford University Press (2021)
42. Kim, S.-W., Gil, J.-M.: Research paper classification systems based on TF-IDF and LDA schemes. Hum. Centric Comput. Inf. Sci. **9**(1) (2019)
43. Wang, Y.-X., Zhang, Y.-J.: Nonnegative matrix factorization: a comprehensive review. IEEE Trans. Knowl. Data Eng. **25**(6), 1336–1353 (2013)
44. Paatero, P., Tapper, U.: Positive matrix factorization: a non-negative factor model with optimal utilization of error estimates of data values. Environmetrics **5**(2), 111–126 (1994)
45. Lee, D.D., Seung, H.S.: Learning the parts of objects by non-negative matrix factorization. Nature **401**(6755), 788–791 (1999)
46. Dumais, S.T., et al.: Latent semantic analysis. Annu. Rev. Inf. Sci. Technol. **38**(1), 188–230 (2004)
47. Deerwester, S., Dumais, S.T., Furnas, G.W., Landauer, T.K., Harshman, R.: Indexing by latent semantic analysis. J. Am. Soc. Inf. Sci. **41**(6), 391–407 (1990)

48. Devlin, J., Chang, M.-W., Lee, K., Toutanova, K.: BERT: pre-training of deep bidirectional transformers for language understanding, arXiv preprint arXiv:1810.04805 (2018)
49. Grootendorst, M.: BERTopic: neural topic modeling with a class-based TF-IDF procedure. arXiv preprint arXiv:2203.05794 (2022)
50. Wang, A., Singh, A., Michael, J., Hill, F., Levy, O., Bowman, S.R.: GLUE: a multi-task benchmark and analysis platform for natural language understanding. arXiv preprint arXiv:1804.07461 (2018)
51. Vaswani, A.: Attention is all you need. In: Advances in Neural Information Processing Systems, vol. 30 (2017)
52. Mimno, D., Wallach, H., Talley, E., Leenders, M., McCallum, A.: Optimizing semantic coherence in topic models. In: Proceedings of the 2011 Conference on Empirical Methods in Natural Language Processing, pp. 262–272 (2011)
53. Ge, J., Lin, S., Fang, Y.: A text classification algorithm based on topic model and convolutional neural network. J. Phys: Conf. Ser. **1748**(3), 032036 (2021)
54. Cohen, J.: A coefficient of agreement for nominal scales. Educ. Psychol. Measur. **20**(1), 37–46 (1960)
55. Adhitama, R., Kusumaningrum, R., Gernowo, R.: Topic labeling towards news document collection based on latent Dirichlet allocation and ontology. In: 2017 1st International Conference on Informatics and Computational Sciences (ICICoS), pp. 247–252 (2017)
56. Vieira, S.M., Kaymak, U., Sousa, J.M.: Cohen's kappa coefficient as a performance measure for feature selection. In: International Conference on Fuzzy Systems (2010)
57. Consumer Financial Protection Bureau: Credit card complaints. https://data.world/dataquest/bank-and-credit-card-complaints (2018)
58. McHugh, M.L.: Interrater reliability: the Kappa statistic. Biochemia Medica, pp. 276–282 (2012)

# Pattern Discovery and Forecasting of Attrition Using Time Series Analysis

Saumyadip Sarkar[(⊠)] and Rashmi Agarwal[iD]

REVA Academy of Corporate Excellence, REVA University, Bangalore, India
{saumyadip.ba05,rashmi.agarwal}@reva.edu.in

**Abstract.** Attrition is a burning problem for any industry and if the rate of attrition is very high, it creates enormous pressure on the process to function effectively. This is precisely what a leading organization's transportation Line of Business (LOB) is going through where attrition is averaging around 34% for the last three years. Time and again, it has struggled with managing a healthy attrition rate. As a result, there has been a constant occurrence of missed Service Level Agreements (SLAs) resulting in huge penalties. For managers, managing workload has become extremely tedious in the current context.

To tackle this problem, this study aims to forecast attrition using time series analysis at various levels based on only the attrition data available for the last fourteen months. The hypothesis here is, if probable attrition is forecasted well in advance, a plan can be put in place to hire employees and make them available whenever there is demand from contract managers. This in turn can help individual contract managers manage their workload efficiently, and reduce their missed SLAs, thereby reducing penalties.

The proposed solution is to compare various Time Series Forecasting techniques like Auto-Regressive Integrated Moving Average (ARIMA), Seasonal Auto-Regressive Integrated Moving Average (SARIMA), Exponential Smoothing (ES), Holt-Winters (HW), Moving Average, Ratio to Moving Average, based on attrition data and compared to arrive at the best possible solution.

The novelty of this study is the use of time series forecasting techniques to forecast future attrition trends specifically based on attrition data, which has not been explored much. This forecasted data can be used to better workload management which in turn is expected to reduce missed SLAs and penalties.

**Keywords:** Forecasting · Time series · ARIMA · Seasonal ARIMA · Exponential Smoothing · Holt-Winters · Data Discovery · Pareto · Trend Analysis · Regression · Moving Average · LSTM

## 1 Introduction

For any organization, finding the right candidate is of paramount importance. However, this is just the first step. Then there starts a long journey of fitting the candidate into the right job. This is not only time intensive, but also involves a huge cost of orientation and

© ICST Institute for Computer Sciences, Social Informatics and Telecommunications Engineering 2023
Published by Springer Nature Switzerland AG 2023. All Rights Reserved
S. Nandan Mohanty et al. (Eds.): ICISML 2022, LNICST 471, pp. 85–98, 2023.
https://doi.org/10.1007/978-3-031-35081-8_7

training [1]. However, when the same candidate decides to leave the organization within a year, it creates a huge void jeopardizing the entire setup with a cascading effect going down till contract termination.

That is the condition the transportation LOB is going through. With attrition going up the roof, the transportation LOB is struggling to meet its SLAs resulting in a huge outflow of money in form of penalties.

The hypothesis here is that if probable attrition is forecasted well in advance at various levels, a plan can be put in place to hire employees and make them available whenever there is demand from contract managers.

In recent times, human resource departments of various organizations have been trying to map the employee life cycle which involves a lot of phases [2]. Using machine learning algorithms, predictions are being made about employee tenure within organizations [3]. However, when there is a lack of good Human Resource (HR) data, the scope becomes limited.

The study aims to find an easy-to-use attrition forecast solution which in turn could help individual contract managers manage their workload efficiently, and reduce their missed SLAs, thereby reducing penalties.

To have a better understanding of the attrition problem and various time series techniques, a detailed literature review has been conducted as discussed in the next section.

## 2 Literature Review

Employee attrition is a very costly affair for any industry. The direct costs of workforce turnover include the cost of hiring new employees, the cost of training new employees, the time it takes to transition, the cost of temporary employees, the cost of lost expertise, and the cost of the job itself [4].

Several studies have been conducted on employee attritions. However, most of the employee attrition studies have concentrated on using various Machine Learning Algorithms using several factors. In the study [5], several machine learning algorithms like Decision Tree, Support Vector Machine (SVM), Random Forests have been used to estimate if an employee will leave or not.

In another study [6], Gaussian Naïve Bayes classifier has been used to classify if an employee will attrit or not. XGBoost classifier has also been used to classify employee attrition [7].

As seen in most of the studies related to attrition predictions, classification is the most used approach. However, using time series techniques to forecast future attrition has not been explored enough based on the observations during the literature review. This establishes a unique opportunity for this study.

Generating scientific projections based on data with historical time stamps is known as time series forecasting. It entails creating models through historical study, using them to draw conclusions and guide strategic decision-making in the future [8].

Timeseries analysis and forecasting are important for a variety of applications, including business, the stock market and exchange, the weather, electricity demand, cost, and usages of goods like fuels and electricity, etc., and in any setting where there are periodic, seasonal variations [9].

There are several time series techniques available, notably Moving Average, Exponential Smoothing, Holt-Winters Smoothing method, ARIMA, Seasonal ARIMA, LSTM, etc.

One well-known technical indicator, the moving average, is employed in time series analysis to forecast future data. Researchers have produced numerous variations and implementations of it during its evolution [10]. Another variation of the moving average is the Ratio to Moving Average, which is superior to the simple average method and is predicated on the idea that seasonal variance for any given month is a continuous component of the trend. Moving average methods reduce periodic movements if any [11].

Another immensely popular time series technique is Exponential Smoothing. Its popularity is based on the fact that surprisingly accurate forecasts can be obtained with minimal effort. This has been proved in this study as well where time series forecasting methods are used via an Excel (FORECAST.ETS) function. The superior efficacy of this model has been nicely illustrated in the paper by Dewi Rahardja. With this Excel function, forecasting is simple and quick while considering the model's level (intercept), trend (slope), and seasonality [12].

Another variation of the Exponential Smoothing technique popularly known as Holt-Winters after the name of the inventors is very effective when there is both trend and seasonality in the data. The two primary HW models are multiplicative for time series exhibiting multiplicative seasonality and additive for time series exhibiting additive seasonality [13].

However, there are times when, for the same number of data, a Long Short-Term Memory (LSTM) multivariate machine learning model outperforms a Holt-Winters univariate statistical model [14]. By utilizing the nonlinearities of a particular dataset, LSTM networks can overcome the constraints of conventional time series forecasting methods and produce state-of-the-art outcomes on temporal data [15].

From a statistical modeling perspective, another time series technique that produces a robust result in short-term prediction is ARIMA, first introduced by Box and Jenkins in 1970. It consists of a series of steps for locating, calculating, and diagnosing ARIMA models using time series data. A very well-researched paper available in this context is [16], which shows ARIMA's strength in predicting future stock prices. The limitation of ARIMA model is however the number of periods. It is recommended to employ at least 50 and ideally 100 observations [17].

While ARIMA has its own strength, when it comes to seasonal data, there is a variation of ARIMA available commonly known as SARIMA or seasonal ARIMA. For climate-related data, SARIMA has been a valuable tool [18].

With a lot of statistical techniques already being widely used in forecasting techniques, recent studies have now been conducted using Deep Learning (DL) models showing outstanding results when compared to traditional forecasting techniques. A comparative study [19] has shown that the DL method significantly improves upon Machine Learning (ML) models.

# 3   Problem Statement

It has been observed that, in the last 14 months, close to $2,082k has been paid in terms of penalties in transportation LOB. Penalties are incurred when SLAs are not being met.

One of the main reasons identified is "attrition" which presently stands at 34%. This has almost remained constant for the last three years.

With constant churn at top management and lack of HR support, there seems almost no headway in managing attritions. Ironically, the lack of HR support is due to the fact that HR department has failed to manage its own attrition rate.

The problem is further exacerbated due to the lack of proper data collection at the HR end. With the limited data and considering the present problem area, this study aims to do the following:

1. Identify the required attrition dataset. In this case, only the attrition data for the last 14 months are available.
2. Study data at various levels and categories to identify trends, patterns, and top contributors which then will be used to create subsets of the main dataset for modeling.
3. Explore various time series techniques to identify the best time series forecasting model which can be used to forecast future attrition.

# 4   Methodology

This study uses Cross-Industry Standard Process for Data Mining (CRSIP-DM) framework which is discussed below.

The first phase is to understand the business in context. For this study, the transportation LOB is considered which is reeling under huge attrition for the last 3 years.

The next phase in CRISP-DM process is data understanding. Here, the data is the employee attrition record captured for the last 14 months. The other data points are missed SLA numbers at contract levels and penalties paid at contract levels for the last 14 months.

The third phase involves data preparation. The goal here is to identify if the data is fit for time series analysis. This involves looking at trends to see if there are any strong upward or downward trends. Along with this, the data is further analyzed for any seasonal trends. Based on the findings, data transformation can be done to make the data stationary.

The main approach in the modeling phase is to select the best time series forecasting technique like Moving Average, ARIMA, SARIMA, Exponential Smoothing, and Holt Winters.

Post modeling technique, the evaluation phase starts. In this phase, the efficacy of the various time series forecasting techniques is assessed. The one which most accurately mimics the test data would be finalized.

In the deployment phase, the forecasted numbers can be used to hire a pool of employees. These employees will then be suitably placed in various contracts based on the current need.

## 4.1 Business Understanding

The transportation LOB is one of the most profitable units in this organization. It provides the following solutions as depicted in Table 1 to its client.

**Table 1.** Transportation Solutions

| Solutions | Description |
|---|---|
| Automated Tolling | Captures vehicle details when a tolling both is crossed and bills customer accordingly. A team also works on dispute resolutions pertaining to technical failure, failed auto-debit attempts, customer complaints, etc. |
| Automated Parking | It provided intelligent parking solutions mainly for governments. The solution involves fee collections, dynamic pricing, enforcement solutions, etc. |
| Public Safety | It provides automated photo enforcement, traffic violation solutions, etc. |

However, the biggest challenge is the abnormal attrition rate for the last 3 years which on average is around 34%. Managers are finding it difficult to manage their workload efficiently.

Apart from providing technological solutions, there are dedicated teams working on resolving disputes pertaining to technological failures, missed billing, payment disputes, failed payments, etc. There are agreed Turnaround Time (TAT) for resolving disputes which are part of SLAs with individual contracts.

There are also several SLAs linked to penalties. A missed SLA incurs penalties to be paid to the client. It has been observed that almost $ 2,082k penalties is paid in the last 14 months by the accounts reeling under huge attritions.

Since dispute resolution is manually intensive work, more employees are needed during peak times. But with a lack of available manpower due to high attrition, dispute resolutions often lead to missed TAT, and missed TAT leads to penalties being levied at contract levels.

This study aims to forecast probable attrition, which can help plan workload management efficiently thereby can help control missed SLAs and bring down penalties to an acceptable level.

## 4.2 Data Understanding

The attrition data collected for this study contains some important parameters as described below.

- Employee details – ID, Employee Name, Salary, Last Performance Rating
- Employment Details – Employee Type (Regular or Contract), Joining Date, Termination Date, Employee Level, Type of Termination, Termination Code, Cost Centre, Job Name

- Contract Details – Contract Name, Sector, Business Category, Location City, Country

For this analysis, the focus is on the contract level. The following plot as appears in Fig. 1 shows a Pareto Chart of Attrition vs Contracts. It clearly shows top 6 which represents 15% of overall contracts are contributing to more than 80% of attrition.

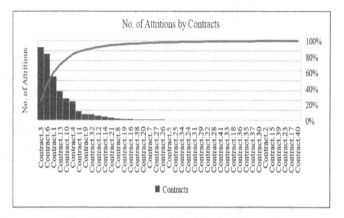

**Fig. 1.** Pareto – No. of Attrition by Contracts

It is also observed that the penalties paid by the top 6 contracts which total to $1,051k representing ~50% of overall penalties.

There is also a strong correlation of 0.93 exists between contract level attrition numbers and missed SLAs. Figure 2 shows a scatter plot relation between attrition numbers and missed SLAs at contract levels.

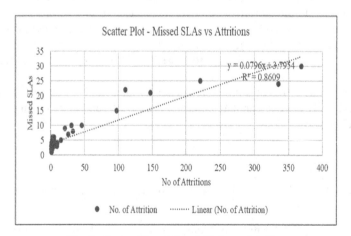

**Fig. 2.** Scatter Plot - Missed SLAs vs Attrition

An almost similar strong correlation is detected between missed SLAs and penalties paid at contract levels as shown in Fig. 3.

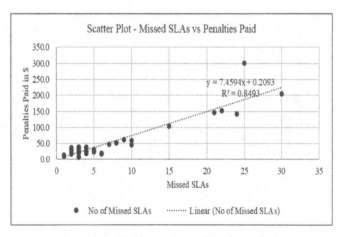

**Fig. 3.** Scatter Plot - Missed SLAs vs Penalties

Another key point that came out prominently is that close to 90% of attrition is at the junior most level (C01). Figure 4 highlights this fact.

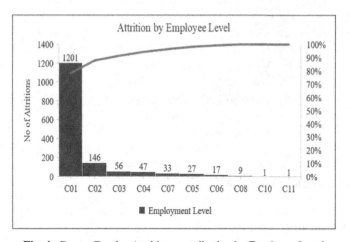

**Fig. 4.** Pareto Graph - Attrition contribution by Employee Level

This finding remains consistent with the overall contract level attrition trend.

A few other levels that are considered for this study are location-wise attrition and salary range. At various locations, Fig. 5 shows that the top 11 cities contributed to 80% of attritions in the last 14 months.

Attrition at the pay level is the last set of data that is examined. The salary bucket is created to identify a certain range causing attrition. The salary range of $20k to $40k is the one that causes the most attrition as shown in Fig. 6.

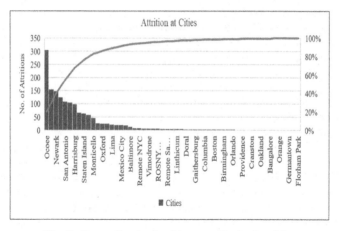

**Fig. 5.** Pareto Graph - Attrition contribution by cities

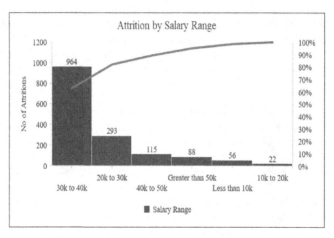

**Fig. 6.** Pareto Graph - Attrition contribution by salary bucket

### 4.3   Data Preparation

Based on termination date, the attrition data is divided into five quarters with each quarter consist of three months of data. The first 12 months of data have been used for modeling and the last 2 months of data have been used for testing forecast accuracy.

Again, based on the termination date, the month with "MMM-YY" format is created. The quarter and the month form the basis of forecasting data.

The salary bucket is created to understand if there is any particular salary range that is contributing to high attrition. The buckets created here are "Less than 10k", "10k to 20k","20k to 30k", "30k to 40k", "40k to 50k" and "Greater than 50k".

To summarize, the data is divided into the following six categories for forecasting purpose. This was done in order to account for every level that could significantly affect the forecasting outcomes.

1. Overall attrition by quarter and month-wise.
2. Attrition by top contracts, quarter and month-wise.
3. Attrition by top employment levels, quarter and month-wise.
4. Attrition by top contracts and top employment level, quarter and month-wise.
5. Attrition by top cities, quarter and month-wise.
6. Attrition by top salary ranges, quarter, and month-wise.

The above categorizations form the basis of the forecast modeling.

## 4.4  Modeling

Considering the limitation of the available information in the dataset, various time series forecasting techniques are considered on each of the categorized levels of data and compared. The top technique is chosen to predict future attrition. The forecasted attrition result is further used as the input of regression to predict missed SLAs numbers and the predicted missed SLAs to predict probable penalties. These approaches are discussed in detail in the following sections.

The modeling approach starts by taking the overall data and by checking for stationarity of the data using Dickey-Fuller (DF) test. The low p-value of 0.0395 observed during DF test which is less than 0.05 indicates that the data has no unit root and is stationary. This result remains consistent for all other 5 datasets.

Then a quick check on the trend graph shows an overall upward trend as appears in the Fig. 7. This is a bit contradictory to the findings in Dickey-Fuller test. However, this trend is observed for the other 5 subsets of the data.

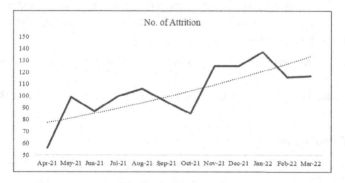

**Fig. 7.**  Attrition trend

The first technique used is Moving Average (MA), which is followed by ratio-to-moving-average and Exponential Triple Smoothing (ETS) using Microsoft Excel's FORECAST.ETS formula.

In the MA, the moving average of three months is considered. This is done since the months are divided into quarters with each quarter consisting of three months.

Building on MA, the next technique that is used in ratio-to-moving-average. This contains some additional steps like deseasonalizing the data and building a regression model on the deseasonalized data to forecast. This method is frequently used to show the data's overall movement without taking seasonal effects into account.

The next forecasting technique considered is Microsoft Excel's in-built forecast algorithm. It uses FORECAST.ETS function and allows for auto-detection of seasonality. The other in-built function FORECAST.ETS. STAT is used to show some important stats related to FORECAST.ETS predictions.

The ARIMA, Holt-Winters (Smoothing 1, Smoothing 2 Additive & Multiplicative, Smoothing 3 Additive and Multiplicative), and LSTM techniques are also explored using python. For ARIMA, the auto ARIMA is used to find the best combination of the order (p,d,q). The best order found is (1,0,0) using AIC as order selection criteria. This order is used in ARIMA Model to forecast attrition.

Since ARIMA could not perform as expected, it led to another technique called LSTM. It is a kind of recurrent neural network that can pick up order dependence in situations involving sequence prediction. The data is divided into train and test data. After selecting test and train data, "MinMax" preprocessing technique is used on both datasets. The LSTM technique has not performed as expected on the given dataset and hence the technique is dropped for consideration on other datasets.

Finally, Holt-Winters smoothing technique is used to see if the forecast can be improved. It uses a modified version of exponential smoothing to account for a linear trend. Simple smoothing is used where the result observed is poor.

The Holt-Winter Exponential Double Smoothing is then tried to see if the forecast can be improved further. Though, the results improved but not as expected.

The last Holt-Winter Exponential Smoothing technique used is Triple Smoothing to see if the forecast can be further improved upon Excel's FORECAST.ETS function.

Finally, the forecasted attrition data is used to create a regression model to predict the missed SLAs as shown in Eq. (1). The predicted missed SLAs then become the input to Eq. (2) to predict penalties.

$$\text{Predicted Missed SLAs} = (0.07958 * \text{Forecasted Attrition}) + 3.7954 \quad (1)$$

$$\text{Predicted Penalties} = (7.45942 * \text{Predicted Missed SLAs}) + 0.20933 \quad (2)$$

## 4.5  Model Evaluation

Once all the forecast techniques are used, a summary showing the model performance is presented in Table 2.

When overall attrition data is considered, the best forecast technique is the Moving Average for which the MAPE is 9%.

The graph in Fig. 8 shows how well the forecasted values perform against the original values.

The same approach is used for the other datasets to check if there is any significant difference between the various time series technique used.

**Table 2.** Model Performance on overall attrition data

| TS Models | MAD | RMSE | MAPE |
|---|---|---|---|
| Moving Average (3) | 9.6 | 10.9 | 9% |
| Ratio-to-Moving-Average | 11.0 | 12.9 | 12% |
| ETS | 13.2 | 14.0 | 10% |
| ARIMA | 15.8 | 18.7 | 14% |
| Holt Winters ES1 | 27.5 | 30.5 | 25% |
| Holt Winters ES2_ADD | 12.1 | 13.5 | 13% |
| Holt Winters ES2_MUL | 18.9 | 25.0 | 18% |
| Holt Winters ES3_ADD | 16.9 | 19.1 | 16% |
| Holt Winters ES3_MUL | 21.3 | 24.3 | 20% |

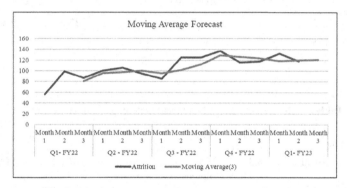

**Fig. 8.** Moving Average performance on overall attrition

## 5   Analysis and Results

The forecasting techniques are tested on the actual attrition data of the following two months (Month 1 and Month 2). When the overall data is used, the Moving Average model is giving MAPE as 17% shown in Table 3 compared with the result received at the time of modeling which is 9%.

Since there is a difference of 8% between the actual versus the model prediction, the ETS is used to compare the results with the Moving Average. The ETS shows better performance on the actual numbers as shown in Table 4.

For top contracts, both Moving Average and ETS can be used as their results are almost similar with MAPE for ETS is 6% whereas for Moving Average it is 5%. The results are shown in Table 5 and Table 6 respectively.

For the rest of the datasets, the ETS model result is considered since it gives the best and most consistent results across all datasets.

**Table 3.** Moving Average Model Outcome for Overall dataset

| Overall Data | | | | | |
|---|---|---|---|---|---|
| Month | Attrition - Actual | MA (Forecast) | MAD | RMSE | MAPE |
| Month 1 | 132 | 118.8 | **25.8** | **28.6** | 17% |
| Month 2 | 158 | 119.7 | | | |
| Month 3 | | 120.6 | | | |

**Table 4.** ETS Model Outcome for Overall dataset

| Overall Data | | | | | |
|---|---|---|---|---|---|
| Month | Attrition - Actual | ETS (Forecast) | MAD | RMSE | MAPE |
| Month 1 | 132 | 128.7 | **14.0** | **17.5** | 9% |
| Month 2 | 158 | 133.4 | | | |
| Month 3 | | 138.2 | | | |

**Table 5.** Moving Average (MA) Model Outcome for Top 6 Contracts

| Top 6 Contracts | | | | | |
|---|---|---|---|---|---|
| Month | Attrition - Actual | MA (Forecast) | MAD | RMSE | MAPE |
| Month 1 | 116 | 103.8 | **6.3** | **8.6** | 5% |
| Month 2 | 126 | 125.6 | | | |
| Month 3 | | 111.4 | | | |

**Table 6.** ETS Model Outcome for Top 6 Contracts

| Top 6 Contracts | | | | | |
|---|---|---|---|---|---|
| Month | Attrition - Actual | ETS (Forecast) | MAD | RMSE | MAPE |
| Month 1 | 116 | 111.9 | **7.1** | **7.6** | 6% |
| Month 2 | 126 | 116.0 | | | |
| Month 3 | | 120.2 | | | |

Finally, using the regression Eq. (1) and Eq. (2), predicted missed SLAs and penalties on overall attrition data are calculated respectively as shown in Table 7. The same concept can be used for all other 5 datasets.

**Table 7.** Predicted Missed SLAs and Penalties

Overall Data

| Month | ETS (Forecast) | Predicted Missed SLAs | Predicted Penalties in ($ k) |
|---|---|---|---|
| Month 1 | 128.7 | 14 | 104.9 |
| Month 2 | 133.4 | 14 | 107.7 |
| Month 3 | 138.2 | 15 | 110.6 |
| **Total** | | **43** | **323.2** |

# 6  Conclusions and Recommendations for Future Work

Attrition remains a burning problem in any sector, and it can have profound consequences when it is way above a tolerable limit.

Numerous research has been done to address this issue, however, when there is little information available, a simple solution can sometimes work wonders.

As seen here, the time series forecasting technique is used to predict future attritions across several datasets. Since this is a novel method for predicting attrition, multiple forecasting approaches are applied to a variety of datasets to determine the effectiveness of this method.

This study has shown that future attrition can be forecasted accurately even when only attrition statistics are available. The main forecasting method for all datasets has been FORECAST.ETS, a built-in Excel function.

To conclude, sometimes a seemingly tough problem can be tackled through simple approaches, in this case, attrition forecasting using time series techniques. This will help plan future workload effectively and reduce missed SLAs and penalties.

However, this approach is suitable only when the data dimension is less. In an ideal scenario, there can be several factors that may affect a company's attrition, but with limited data, this approach is a way out as it uses monthly attrition data to forecast probable attritions for the next 3 months.

Just like with any other data modelling technique, this work has to be replicated on new datasets to determine its validity. More the data, the better the result expected as it may throw up additional trends which are probably missing in the current context.

Due to the novelty of this strategy in the current AI/ML era, the approach used in this study would open the door for similar studies in attrition predictions.

# References

1. Ner, W.: The Official Publication of Training Magazine Network Training Temperature Check (2020). www.trainingmag.com
2. Smither, L.: Managing Employee Life Cycles To Improve Labor Retention (2003). www.tho mas-staffing.com/survey99/retention_TABLE2.htm
3. Singh Sisodia, D., Vishwakarma, S., Pujahari, A.: Evaluation of machine learning models for employee Churn prediction (2017)
4. Chakraborty, R., Mridha, K., Nath Shaw, R., Ghosh, A.: Study and prediction analysis of the employee turnover using machine learning approaches; study and prediction analysis of the employee turnover using machine learning approaches. In: 2021 IEEE 4th International Conference on Computing, Power and Communication Technologies (GUCON), 2021, doi: https://doi.org/10.1109/GUCON50781.2021.9573759
5. Jain, P.K., Jain, M., Pamula, R.: Explaining and predicting employees' attrition: a machine learning approach. SN Appl. Sci. **2**(4), 1–11 (2020). https://doi.org/10.1007/s42452-020-2519-4
6. Fallucchi, F., Coladangelo, M., Giuliano, R., de Luca, E.W.: Predicting employee attrition using machine learning techniques (2020). https://doi.org/10.3390/computers9040086
7. Jain, R., Nayyar, A.: Predicting employee attrition using XGBoost machine learning approach; predicting employee attrition using XGBoost machine learning approach (2018)
8. Time Series Forecasting: Definition & Examples|tableau (2020). https://www.tableau.com/learn/articles/time-series-forecasting. Accessed 7 Aug 2022
9. Mahalakshmi, G., Sridevi, S., Rajaram, S.: A survey on forecasting of time series data; a survey on forecasting of time series data (2016). https://doi.org/10.1109/ICCTIDE.2016.772 5358
10. Hansun, S.: A New Approach of Moving Average Method in Time Series Analysis (2013). https://doi.org/10.1109/CoNMedia.2013.6708545
11. Sailaja, M., Prasad, A.R.: Identification of seasonal effects through ratio to moving average method for the number of train passengers and income of South Central Railway Zone. Int. J. Math. Trends Technol. **65**, 11 (2019). http://www.ijmttjournal.org
12. Rahardja, D.: Statistical Time-Series Forecast via Microsoft Excel (FORECAST.ETS) Built-In Function (2021). www.questjournals.org
13. Kalekar, P.S.: Time series Forecasting using Holt-Winters Exponential Smoothing (2004)
14. Ueno, R., Calitoiu, D., Calitoiu@forces, D.: Forecasting Attrition from the Canadian Armed Forces using Multivariate LSTM; Forecasting Attrition from the Canadian Armed Forces using Multivariate LSTM (2020). https://doi.org/10.1109/ICMLA51294.2020.00123
15. Chimmula, V.K.R., Zhang, L.: Time series forecasting of COVID-19 transmission in Canada using LSTM networks. Chaos Solitons Fractals **135** (2020). https://doi.org/10.1016/j.chaos.2020.109864
16. Adebiyi, A.A., Adewumi, A.O., Ayo, C.K.: Stock price prediction using the ARIMA model. In: 2014 UKSim-AMSS 16th International Conference on Computer Modelling and Simulation (2014). https://doi.org/10.1109/UKSim.2014.67
17. Box, G.E.P., Jenkins, G.M., Reinsel, G.C.: Time Series Analysis Forecasting and Control, 4th edn. (1976)
18. Dimri, T., Ahmad, S., Sharif, M.: Time series analysis of climate variables using seasonal ARIMA approach. J. Earth Syst. Sci. **129**(1), 1–16 (2020). https://doi.org/10.1007/s12040-020-01408-x
19. Sezer, O.B., Gudelek, M.U., Ozbayoglu, A.M.: Financial time series forecasting with deep learning: a systematic literature review: 2005–2019. Appl. Soft Comput. **90**, 106181 (2019). http://arxiv.org/abs/1911.13288

# Resume Shortlisting and Ranking
# with Transformers

Vinaya James[(✉)] [iD], Akshay Kulkarni[iD], and Rashmi Agarwal[iD]

REVA Academy for Corporate Excellence (RACE), REVA University, Bangalore, India
{vinayajames.AI01,akshaykulkarni}@race.reva.edu.in,
rashmi.agarwal@reva.edu.in

**Abstract.** The study shown in this paper helps the human resource domain eliminate the time-consuming recruitment process task. Screening resume is the most critical and challenging task for human resource personnel. Natural Language Processing (NLP) techniques are the computer's ability to understand spoken/written language. Now a day's, online recruitment platform is more vigorous along with consultancies. A single job opening will get hundreds of applications. To discover the finest candidate for the position, Human Resource (HR) employees devote extra time to the candidate selection process. Most of the time, shortlisting the best fit for the job is time-consuming and finding an apt person is hectic. The proposed study helps to shortlist the candidates with a better match for the job based on the skills provided in the resume. As it is an automated process, the candidate's personalized favor and soft skills are not affected by the hiring process. The Sentence-BERT (SBERT) network is a Siamese and triplet network-based variant of the Bidirectional Encoder Representations from Transformers (BERT) architecture, which may generate semantically significant sentence embeddings. An end-to-end tool for the HR domain, which takes hundreds of resumes along with required skills for the job as input and provides the better-ranked candidate fit for the job as output. The SBERT is compared with BERT and proved that it is superior to BERT.

**Keywords:** Natural Language Processing · Sentence-BERT · Automatic Recruitment Process · Sentence Embedding

## 1 Introduction

In a business or organization, it is indeed critical to make the proper hiring decisions for particular positions for Human Resources Manager or Head-hunter [1]. Recruitment tools like "LinkedIn" and "Monster" search for skills and identify candidates who are qualified for open positions. The list of resume search results may be lengthy. All resumes should be manually reviewed to identify possible applicants. Especially, large companies like "Google" frequently receive hundreds of thousands of resumes each year for job applications. As a result, automation is introduced to make the work easy with time-saving.

© ICST Institute for Computer Sciences, Social Informatics and Telecommunications Engineering 2023
Published by Springer Nature Switzerland AG 2023. All Rights Reserved
S. Nandan Mohanty et al. (Eds.): ICISML 2022, LNICST 471, pp. 99–108, 2023.
https://doi.org/10.1007/978-3-031-35081-8_8

The introduction of NLP simplifies the process of automatic sentence or test recognition from papers or resumes [2]. In general vector, representations have become an ever-existing entity in the NLP context. Word embedding properties have seen major developments in the recent past, such as the superposition of word contexts [3], pointwise linkages to shared data values between related words, and linear substructures [4]. However, locating sentences that are comparable based on context, meaning, subject, etc. is a problem in naturally occurring language processing, which leads to the issue of statement integration. The text can be organized, produced, processed, etc., and based on this, it converts the vectors of the words into a vector representation of the sentence. In contrast, an embedding definition is a numerical representation of a word, phrase, sentence, or longer natural language utterance in a particular space. Additionally, word embeddings distributed semantic vector representations of words have drawn a lot of interest in recent years and have undergone a lot of changes [5]. The word embeddings were developed by analyzing the word distribution among arbitrary text data, and because they are familiar with word semantics, they are a crucial part of many semantic similarity algorithms.

Compared to word embeddings, sentences encompass a higher level of information: the complete semantics and syntactic declarations of the sentence. The word2vec model, which is one of the most popular models, employs neural networks to create word embeddings [6]. Recent transformer-based models' pre-trained word embeddings provided cutting-edge outcomes in a variety of NLP tasks, including semantic similarity. Based on this, modern language models like RoBERTa, BERT [7, 8], and ALBERT use transformers to traverse the underlying corpus in both directions and create vector representations of text data. In 2009, the BERT transformer model outperformed the best results available for different NLP tasks, including semantic similarity. The BERT model is typically tuned to serve a specific NLP task using labeled training data. Multilingual BERT is enhanced by the alignment method suggested by Cao et al. [9]. Thus, the BERT models produce bilingual illustrations of words that consider the word's context in both directions.

Performing sentence pair regression, like clustering and semantic search [10], can be time-consuming with BERT due to the large corpus size. Converting a sentence into a vector that encodes the semantic meaning of the sentence is one efficient technique to address this issue. Transformers are the guide to a state-of-art model, and the next section discusses more works accomplished on the NLP concept.

## 2 State of Art

As sentence embeddings are more realistic representations of text, recent papers on sentence embedding transformers have focused on the mechanics of recognition. Fast Text is a model that incorporates a character-based n-gram model in addition to the established word embedding techniques Word2Vec and GloVe [11]. This makes it possible to calculate word embeddings from the vocabulary.

Vaswani et al. [12] suggested the Transformer, a self-attention network, as a remedy for the neural sequence-to-sequence issue. When a self-attention network is used to visualize a phrase, each word is represented by a scaled sum of all the other words in the phrase. Liu et al. [13] used a sentence's inner attention to show that self-attention pooling existed before self-attention networks. By generalizing scalar attention to vectors, Cho et al. [14] devised a fine-grained attention approach for neural machine translation. Natural Language Inference (NLI) and other supervised transfer tasks can help complex phrase encoders that are often pre-trained like language models. The Universal Sentence Encoder improves unsupervised learning by training a transformer network on the Stanford NLI (SNLI) dataset. According to Giorgiet al. [15], the task that sentence embeddings are trained on greatly influences their quality. The SNLI datasets, according to Conneau et al. [16], are appropriate for training sentence embeddings.

Therefore, to successfully develop the Chinese Depth Approximation Networking (DAN) and transformers, Parameswa et al. [17] offer an approach that uses Internet responses. Naseem et al. [18] fed the static word embeddings GloVe through the deep neural networks and carried out a controlled neural interpretation operation to obtain the perspective encoding. The Remiers et al. [19] ELMo model is a method for a deeper summarized description. The internal states of words are used to teach a deep bidirectional Language Model (biLM) that has already been trained on a large text corpus. Pre-trained language models of the fine-tuning variety have unfrozen pretrained parameters that can be changed for a new assignment. The text presentation is no longer extracted using this approach. Two significant tasks were introduced by Devlin et al. [20] in their autoencoding pre-trained language model BERT, a deep bidirectional Transformers model: Mask Language Model (MLM) and Next Sentence Prediction (NSP). During the tuning stage, the only activities that deviate from one another are those at the input and output layers. Dai, Zihang, et al. [21] proposed the Transformer-XL generalized autoregressive pretrained language model, which can learn bidirectional contexts by maximizing expected likelihood across all possible factorization order permutations. Additionally, two groups of the pre-trained language model can be identified based on the pre-training procedure: Auto Encoding (AE) and Auto-Regressive (AR). AR language models like ELMo and XLNet aim to estimate the probability distribution of a text corpus by employing an autoregressive model. However, AE language models like BERT and its variations like RoBERTa by Liu, Yinhan, et al. [22] seek to recreate the original data from corrupted input without resorting to explicit density estimates.

One major problem with BERT-type models is the introduction of fictitious symbols like MASK during pretraining, despite their complete absence from the final output text. The pre-trained model effectively illustrates how words or phrases link to one another and access various data. Thus, embedding-based key phrase extraction has recently demonstrated strong performance. Lee et al. [23] suggested a Deep Belief Network (DBN) to model the hierarchical relationship between key phrase embeddings. It is simple to distinguish the target document from others using this strategy. Reference Vector Algorithm (RVA) by Papagiannopoulou et al. [24] is a key phrase extraction technique that uses local word vectors as a guiding principle, employing an average of the embeddings trained on distinct files using GloVe as the reference vector for all candidate phrases. The score used to rank the candidate key phrases is then determined by calculating how closely the embeddings of each candidate key phrase match those of the reference vector.

Bennani-Somerset et al. proposed EmbedRank [25] based on the cosine similarity between the candidate key phrase's embeddings and the document's sentence embeddings. EmbedRank creates a document representation using the phrase embedding models Doc2Vec and Sent2Vec. They employ Maximal Marginal Relevance (MMR) to further broaden the keyword's applicability. Pre-trained language models, in particular, BERT, have recently gained popularity and significantly enhanced performance for several NLP applications. Pre-trained BERT and its variations have mostly proved successful in the English language. A language-specific model might be retrained using the BERT architecture for other languages, or one could employ pre-trained multilingual BERT-based models.

## 3  Problem Definition

Identifying a qualified candidate for the job is a complex undertaking. Typically, manual processes are used in the traditional hiring process. The HR department's qualified recruiters and other significant resources are needed for the manual recruitment process. Businesses sometimes receive a substantial volume of resumes for each job opening, some of which may not even be suitable for the position. Additionally, these hiring procedures take a lot of time and effort to discover qualified applicants for open positions.

Therefore, manually selecting the most pertinent applicants from a lengthy list of potential candidates is difficult. Numerous recent research has focused on the drawbacks of the manual hiring process. Dealing with resumes in the advertising of job specifications and hiring procedures. Selecting people who fit a given job profile is a vital task for most firms. As online hiring becomes more common, traditional hiring methods become less successful.

Recruiting the most pertinent multilingual candidates through the manual hiring process is one of the most critical issues in multilingual job offers and resumes.

The proposed model investigates developing a resume shortlisting and ranking with Transformers to address the difficulty of selecting the right candidate out of two hundred resumes. An automated recruiting system is essential to make it easier for job seekers to access recruitment opportunities and to minimize the amount of human effort involved in the hiring process.

The main goal is to improve the current resume ranking scheme and make it more adaptable for both parties.

1. *Those who were hired as candidates:* Candidates who have recently graduated and are looking for a job. A significant portion of those applicants is so desperate that they are willing to work in any position unrelated to their skill set and abilities.
2. *The client organization that recruits the applicants:* A job recruiter's objective is to select the top candidate from all qualified applicants based on the Job Description (JD). The process takes time for both the individual and the business. With an automatic resume sorting system, the business may produce the finest candidate list possible based on the limits and requirements they gave for that particular role. Since the appropriate person will be hired for the position, this hiring method will benefit both

the candidate and the organization. Therefore, neither the client firm nor the hired candidate would have any regrets.

The three objectives of this study are:

1. *Collect the resumes as per the defined JD:* The resumes are collected by HR from online job platforms, referrals from existing employees, and third-party consultancies. But getting the exact JD-related resumes are challenging. For this model two hundred resumes have been collected.
2. *Build a custom algorithm to shortlist the resume as per the JD given:* The skills are extracted to a *pandas* data frame with the help of *ResumeParser*. The resume matches will be shortlisted and added to a list based on the JD that HR has provided.
3. Create a ranking *algorithm to get the best out of shortlisted resumes:* JDs and candidates' skill sets are compared, and the most suitable individual with the necessary skills is shortlisted. The model is trained using SBERT and BERT model encodings, and the top N resumes are sorted according to their cosine similarity to sentences and words, respectively.

## 4  Proposed Method

Finding the "right" applicant for a position has never been simple. In addition to having the required training and work experience, a prospective employee typically needs to fit in with the current team and support the company's vision. A new dilemma has emerged with the rise of internet job boards and globalization. Today's recruiting professionals frequently need to analyze hundreds of online profiles and resumes only to pick whom to approach due to how simple it has become to build an online profile and apply to a position with a few clicks.

It is not surprising that various technology solutions have been offered to aid recruiters in addressing the problem of candidate screening because automating the shortlisting of candidates can lead to lower costs and higher recruiter productivity. To rank the resume successfully, an efficient context test-based embedding is needed. To achieve textual similarity, transfer-based models like BERT and XLNet are used. In addition, an efficient pre-trained model is required due to its poor accuracy. SBERT, a version of the BERT network that can produce semantically significant sentence embeddings by combining Siamese and triplet networks, is employed in this way [26]. The suggested architecture is depicted in Fig. 1.

The number of resumes is the input used in this proposed model methodology to shortlist the most suitable individuals. *ResumeParser* is used to extract the required details of jobseekers, like Name, Mobile Number, Email Address, and Skills. Exploratory Data Analysis (EDA) is used to remove duplicates, locate databases, and predict and remove missing or null values from text or sentences in resumes. The next step is data pre-processing. At this step, improper words are eliminated, the text is normalized, and the words are prepared for further processing with stop words, Stemming, Lemmatization, and Latent Dirichlet Allocation (LDA). Making vector representations of all words and documents and collectively embedding them in a common vector space is the first step in the extraction of relevant skills and expertise. Then SBERT and BERT are used to create a model.

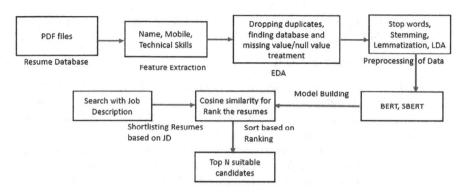

**Fig. 1.** Proposed Model

The produced embedding vectors can be subjected to the Semantic Textual Similarity (STS) task employing metrics such as the Manhattan distance, Cosine similarity, and Euclidean distance. BERT, Siamese networks, and Pooling layer are the three key principles that the SBERT architecture employs. Using a pre-training method called MLM, which typically masks a portion of the tokens in a sentence and predicts them based on their context. BERT is a deep bidirectional transformer because MLM predicts that tokens will approach it from both directions. This is different from traditional left-to-right models, which only work one way. The JD is then matched with terms described in skills to get a cosine similarity score that may be used to rank and shortlist candidates appropriately in the HR field.

## 5  Modeling

The term "dictionary" refers to a list of distinct words for each category of documents after the stop words have been eliminated and the words have been stemmed. These stemmed nonstop words can easily address several fields in a database by adding field names to them. Both words with several grammatical forms and words with similar meanings derived from them are handled by an algorithm. Taking all these stages into account, the techniques employed in the example are:

*Step 1:* Divide the text into words.

*Step 2:* Eliminate all punctuation and symbols and, if desired, lowercase all words.

*Step 3:* Eliminate the stop words.

*Step 4:* Use the Snowball Stemming Algorithm to stem the words.

*Step 5:* Add parenthesis to each word before adding the field names (if appropriate).

Two hundred resumes are gathered from various sources as part of the data collection process. All the necessary features, including Name, Email address, Mobile Number, and abilities, are retrieved with the aid of *ResumeParser.* A model for BERT and SBERT is constructed based on the JD following EDA and data preprocessing. The *N* number of resumes with the highest ranking is listed using the cosine similarity between the skill set and required JD. The proposed software design is described in Fig. 2.

SBERT for the STS task permits two steps in the prediction of similarity:

*Step 1:* First, using a sentence encoder, obtain sentence embeddings for each sentence.

*Step 2:* Next, as the model-predicted similarity SBERT and BERT, compute the cosine similarity between the two embeddings of the input sentence. SBERT used *the bert-base-nli-mean-tokens* model and is compared to the BERT *bert-base-uncased* model.

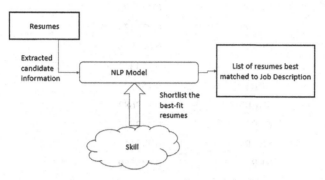

**Fig. 2.** Software Design

## 6 Analysis and Results

Sentence embedding that outperforms the Classical Least Squares (CLS) vector is obtained by the average of the SBERT context embedding's one or two layers. The average of the last two layers of SBERT, denoted by *last2avg*, consistently yields better results than the average of the last layer of BERT. Since unsupervised learning methods like topic modeling do not guarantee that their results can be understood, correlation metrics have gained popularity among text-mining experts.

The degree of semantic similarity among top-ranking terms in each topic is measured by correlativity. It determines the co-occurrence scores of words in the modeled documents. As coherence also works with syntactic information with the aid of a sliding window that traverses across the corpus and checks occurrences. The notion behind coherence calculation is strongly related to embedding representations of text. Different methods can be used to calculate the correlation. SBERT gives a better solution than BERT when a comparison of top ten ranked resumes based on JD.

Table 1 shows the consistency and alignment of different sentence embedding models (BERT and SBERT) and their averaged STS results. Among BERT and SBERT, models with superior alignment and homogeneity outperform in comparison with the models which do not have alignment and homogeneity. Scores for each pair of sentences are calculated by applying the cosine similarity scoring function to the sentence vectors. The SBERT method is used to arrange the sentences to maximize the sum of their similarities. The findings of this method show that the SBERT method always performs better than the BERT method.

**Table 1.** Coherence value comparison for BERT and SBERT

| Data Set | Model | Correlation value for Similarity |
|----------|-------|----------------------------------|
| STS1 | SBERT | 0.42649 |
|      | BERT  | 0.194206 |
| STS2 | SBERT | 0.378602 |
|      | BERT  | 0.119996 |
| STS3 | SBERT | 0.377433 |
|      | BERT  | 0.047986 |
| STS4 | SBERT | 0.374302 |
|      | BERT  | 0.156387 |
| STS5 | SBERT | 0.373682 |
|      | BERT  | 0.182748 |
| STS6 | SBERT | 0.373111 |
|      | BERT  | 0.048559 |

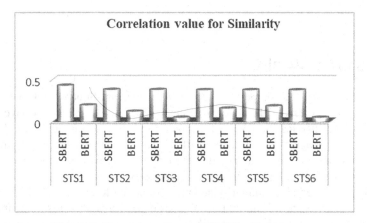

**Fig. 3.** Performance analysis of SBERT with Coherence

Based on Table 1, the graphical representation is provided in Fig. 3.

Table 1 analysis reveals that the SBERT performs better than the BERT in terms of correlation. Compared to SBERT, the similarity variation is lower, as depicted in Fig. 3. Resumes in the STS3 dataset exhibit a relatively low similarity variance. As a result, the SBERT executes the ideal sentence embedding to rank the candidate's information with the JD of the job provider in the minimum similarity variance.

## 7 Conclusion and Future Works

The proposed SBERT transformer helps recruiters screen resumes more quickly and effectively, cutting the cost of hiring. Thus, the company will then have access to a potential applicant who will be successfully placed in a business that appreciates the candidate's skills and competencies. These days, many applicants submit applications for interviews. Every interview should include a review of resumes. Going through each resume one by one is not a good idea. It becomes quite difficult for the HR team to narrow down candidates for the following stage of the hiring process. The SBERT streamlines the process by summarizing resumes and classifying them by how closely they match the organization's necessary skills and requirements.

The proposed method evaluates candidates' skills and ranks them by the JD and skill requirements of the employing organization. A summary of their resume is supplied to provide a fast overview of each candidate's qualifications. One of the main issues is when a candidate lists skills for which they have no experience because the model focuses on the skill set listed on the resume submitted by the candidate. Artificial Intelligence techniques or any other effective sentence embedding transformers can be used for further improvement.

## References

1. Siddique, C.M.: Job analysis: a strategic human resource management practice. Int. J. Human Resour. Manage. **15**(1), 219–244 (2004)
2. Sanabria, R., et al.: How2: a large-scale dataset for multimodal language understanding. arXiv preprint arXiv:1811.00347 (2018)
3. Arora, S., Li, Y., Liang, Y., Ma, T., Risteski, A.: A latent variable model approach to PMIbased word embeddings. Trans. Assoc. Comput. Linguist. **4**, 385–399 (2016)
4. Rieck, B., Leitte, H.: Persistent homology for the evaluation of dimensionality reduction schemes. Comput. Graph. Forum **34**(3) (2015)
5. Stein, R.A., Jaques, P.A., Valiati, J.F.: An analysis of hierarchical text classification using word embeddings. Inf. Sci. **471**, 216–232 (2019)
6. Mishra, M.K., Viradiya, J.: Survey of sentence embedding methods. Int. J. Appl. Sci. Comput. **6**(3), 592 (2019)
7. Chernyavskiy, A., Ilvovsky, D., Nakov, P.: Transformers: "The End of History" for natural language processing? In: Oliver, N., Pérez-Cruz, F., Kramer, S., Read, J., Lozano, J.A. (eds.) ECML PKDD 2021. LNCS (LNAI), vol. 12977, pp. 677–693. Springer, Cham (2021). https://doi.org/10.1007/978-3-030-86523-8_41
8. Suryadjaja, P.S., Mandala, R.: Improving the performance of the extractive text summarization by a novel topic modeling and sentence embedding technique using SBERT. In: 2021 8th International Conference on Advanced Informatics: Concepts, Theory and Applications (ICAICTA), pp. 1–6 (2021). https://doi.org/10.1109/ICAICTA53211.2021.9640295
9. Cao, S., Kitaev, N., Klein, D.: Multilingual alignment of contextual word representations. arXiv preprint arXiv:2002.03518 (2020)
10. Choi, H., Kim, J., Joe, S., Gwon, Y.: Evaluation of BERT and ALBERT sentence embedding performance on downstream NLP tasks. In: 2020 25th International Conference on Pattern Recognition (ICPR), pp. 5482–5487 (2021). https://doi.org/10.1109/ICPR48806.2021.9412102

11. Dharma, E.M., et al.: The accuracy comparison among word2vec, glove, and fasttext towards convolution neural network (CNN) text classification. J. Theor. Appl. Inf. Technol. **100**(2), 31 (2022)
12. Vaswani, A., et al.: Attention is all you need. In: Advances in Neural Information Processing Systems, vol. 30 (2017)
13. Liu, Y., Sun, C., Lin, L., Wang, X.: Learning natural language inference using bidirectional LSTM model and inner-attention. arXiv preprint arXiv:1605.09090 (2016)
14. Choi, H., Cho, K., Bengio, Y.: Fine-grained attention mechanism for neural machine translation. Neurocomputing **284**, 171–176 (2018). ISSN 0925-2312
15. Giorgi, J., et al.: DeCLUTR: deep contrastive learning for unsupervised textual representations. arXiv preprint arXiv:2006.03659 (2020)
16. Conneau, A., et al.: Supervised learning of universal sentence representations from natural language inference data. arXiv preprint arXiv:1705.02364 (2017)
17. Parameswaran, P., Trotman, A., Liesaputra, V., Eyers, D.: Detecting the target of sarcasm is hard: really?? Inf. Process. Manage. **58**(4), 102599 (2021)
18. Naseem, U., Musial, K.: DICE: deep intelligent contextual embedding for Twitter sentiment analysis. In: 2019 International Conference on Document Analysis and Recognition (ICDAR), pp. 953–958 (2019). https://doi.org/10.1109/ICDAR.2019.00157
19. Reimers, N., Gurevych, I.: Alternative weighting schemes for elmoembeddings. arXiv preprint arXiv:1904.02954 (2019)
20. Devlin, J., Chang, M.-W., Lee, K., Toutanova, K.: BERT: pre-training of deep bidirectional transformers for language understanding. In: Proceedings of the 2019 Conference of the North American Chapter of the Association for Computational Linguistics: Human Language Technologies, vol. 1 (Long and Short Papers), Minneapolis, Minnesota, pp. 4171–4186. Association for Computational Linguistics (2019)
21. Dai, Z., Yang, Z., Yang, Y., Carbonell, J., Le, Q.V., Salakhutdinov, R.: Transformer-Xl: attentive language models beyond a fixed-length context. arXiv preprint arXiv:1901.02860 (2019)
22. Liu, Y., et al.: Roberta: a robustly optimized BERT pretraining approach. arXiv preprint arXiv:1907.11692 (2019)
23. Jo, T., Lee, J.H.: Latent keyphrase extraction using deep belief networks. Int. J. Fuzzy Logic Intell. Syst. **15**(3), 153–158 (2015)
24. Papagiannopoulou, E., Tsoumakas, G.: Local word vectors guiding keyphrase extraction. Inf. Process. Manage. **54**(6), 888–902 (2018)
25. Bennani-Smires, K., Musat, C., Hossmann, A., Baeriswyl, M., Jaggi, M.: Simple unsupervised keyphrase extraction using sentence embeddings. In: Proceedings of the 22nd Conference on Computational Natural Language Learning, Brussels, Belgium, pp. 221–229. Association for Computational Linguistics (2018)
26. Reimers, N., Gurevych, I.: Sentence-BERT: sentence embeddings using Siamese BERT-networks. arXiv preprint arXiv:1908.10084 (2019)

# Hybrid Deep Learning Based Model on Sentiment Analysis of Peer Reviews on Scientific Papers

Ritika Sarkar[1], Prakriti Singh[1], Mustafa Musa Jaber[2], Shreya Nandan[1],
Shruti Mishra[1]([✉]), Sandeep Kumar Satapathy[1], and Chinmaya Ranjan Pattnaik[3]

[1] School of Computer Science and Engineering, Vellore Institute of Technology, Chennai,
Vandalur-Kelambakkam Road, Chennai, Tamil Nadu, India
{ritika.sarkar2019,prakriti.singh2019,
shreya.nandan2019}@vitstudent.ac.in, shrutim2129@gmail.com
[2] Department of Medical Instruments Engineering Techniques, Al-Farahidi University,
Baghdad 10021, Iraq
mustafa.musa@alfarahidiuc.edu.iq
[3] Department of Computer Science and Engineering, Ajay Binay Institute of Technology
(ABIT), Cuttack, Odisha, India

**Abstract.** The peer review process involved in evaluating academic papers submitted to journals and conferences is very perplexing as at times the scores given by the reviewer may be poor in contrast with the textual comments which are in a positive light. In such a case, it becomes difficult for the judging chair to come to a concrete decision regarding the accept or reject decision of the papers. In our paper, we aim to extract the sentiment from the reviewers' opinions and use it along with the numerical scores to correlate that in order to predict the orientation of the review, i.e., the degree of acceptance. Our proposed methods include Machine learning models like Naive Bayes, Deep learning models involving LSTM and a Hybrid model with BiLSTM, LSTM, CNN, and finally Graph based model GCN. The dataset is taken from the UCI repository consisting of peer reviews in Spanish along with other parameters used for judging a paper. Bernoulli's Naive Bayes was the model that fared the highest amongst all the approaches, with an accuracy of 75.61% after varying the parameters to enhance the accuracy.

**Keywords:** Peer reviews · Sentiment analysis · Natural Language Processing · AI algorithms

## 1 Introduction

Sentiment analysis is the way in which we detect whether a statement indicates a positive, negative or neutral emotion. It is the method of imparting some emotional intelligence to the machines with the help of Artificial Intelligence algorithms and Natural Language Processing. A positive emotion indicates that the person who spoke or wrote the text can

S. Nandan Mohanty et al. (Eds.): ICISML 2022, LNICST 471, pp. 109–116, 2023.
https://doi.org/10.1007/978-3-031-35081-8_9

be happy, a negative emotion shows he/she may be angry or sarcastic, and a neutral one indicates that he/she is indifferent. The application of sentiment analysis in businesses and industries is done as an indicator of how well the products and commodities are received in the market by using customer feedback. Sometimes, the number of criteria for judging the sentiment of the text is increased and mapped to a scale of five in order to gain more insights. The knowledge of emotions from written text is especially helpful while drafting notices or emails in the corporate and academic world.

Over the years, sentiment analysis has been applied to use cases like social media monitoring like Twitter sentiment analysis, obtaining the voice of the customer in major customer-centric businesses, monitoring brands, and market research. In this paper, we are going to deviate from these market and customer-centric analyses and move towards the analysis of paper reviews. Sentiment analysis of paper reviews is a complex and important domain which has not been explored greatly. The comments given by peer reviews are seldom considered in the final decision for publishing the article or paper in a journal or conference. Hence, we attempt to derive the sentiment from these reviews in order for them to be considered as well as the final accept or reject decision of a paper.

We aim to employ machine learning methods like the different types of Naive Bayes, namely Gaussian [11], Multinomial [12], Bernoulli's [13] and Complement [14], deep learning algorithm LSTM [15], Graph-based algorithm GCN [16] and draw comparisons between them, finally identifying the most suited algorithm for the paper reviews domain in sentiment analysis.

## 2 Literature Review

Chakraborty et al. [1] provide a comprehensive evaluation of implicit aspect sentiments in the peer-reviewed content of works submitted to/published at one of the leading machine learning conferences – ICLR. The paper holds the upper hand over other publications in the same category by creating a non-pre-existing database through the annotation of around 25000 reviews of data. The downside of the generated model was that it could only attain a maximum accuracy of 65%. The accuracy only suffered more as a result of removing the features. In Keith et al. [2] the classification of 382 reviews of research articles presented at an international conference was accomplished utilizing supervised and unsupervised methodologies along with a hybrid technique. The hybrid approach, the HS-SVM, is more robust than most, relative to the number of classes, which is among the paper's merits. The paper's shortcoming is that the dataset examined was quite limited, rendering the approach's viability uncertain. Furthermore, when additional classes were introduced, the performance began to deteriorate. Kang et al. [3] outline the data gathering strategy and reflect on observed occurrences in peer reviews, as well as NLP tasks centered around the dataset. The paper's key benefit is that its most optimum classifier consistently beats the majority model, exhibiting up to a 22% reduction in error. Their models are inadequately nuanced to judge the quality of the work reported in a given publication; this could imply that some of the features they specify are associated with favorable papers, or that reviewers' opinions are persuaded by them. Anta et al. [4] utilizes a corpus of Spanish tweets and presents a near examination of various methodologies and grouping procedures for these problems. The information is preprocessed utilizing strategies and apparatuses proposed in the literature, together with others explicitly proposed here that consider the qualities of Twitter. Then, popular classifiers have been used. (In particular, all classifiers of WEKA have been assessed. Aue et al. [5] surveys four different approaches to customizing a sentiment analysis system to a new target domain in the absence of large amounts of labeled data. The paper bases the experiments on data from four different domains. After establishing that Naive Bayes classification results in poor classification accuracy, they compare results obtained by using each of the four approaches and discussing their advantages, disadvantages, and performance. Baccianella et al. [6] present SENTIWORDNET 3.0 which is a lexical resource used in sentiment classification and opinion mining applications. It is a result of when wordnet synsets are automatically annotated to positive, negative, or neutral sentiments. The sentiwordnet 3.0 gives 20% more accuracy than the 1.0 version. Through comparative analysis of the above literature, the proposed work introduces exhaustive implementations using three learning paradigms of AI, which is the first of its kind in the analysis of paper reviews. The method achieves good accuracy despite the small dataset, in contrast to the above works [1–3, 5].

## 3  Proposed Method

The implementation of the proposed method is outlined in Fig. 1 on a dataset of paper reviews, taken from the UCI repository which consists of anonymous reviews on papers submitted to an international conference on computer science. The dataset contains most of the reviews in Spanish and a few in English in a JavaScript Object Notation format. The reviews are then translated from Spanish to English using Microsoft Azure's Translator Text API by creating a resource in Cognitive Services. The translated JSON dataset is converted into CSV and the non-null textual values of the reviews are utilized for the sentiment analysis task. After pre-processing the reviews, they are fed to the four Naive Bayes algorithms and the LSTM models. For the graph model, first a graph is created out of the cleaned corpus which is then fed to the Graph Convolution network. The accuracies on the test set are compared for this task.

## 4  Methodology

### 4.1  Dataset Description

The original dataset from UCI has fields like timespan, paper id, preliminary decision, and the following fields for each review for a paper: review id, text and remarks in Spanish or English, language, orientation, evaluation, confidence in JSON format. Out of these fields, we use the text as our feature input to the classifier, and the preliminary decision as our class label.

### 4.2  Pre-processing

Data preprocessing is the procedure for prepping raw data to be used in a machine learning model. In this paper, all basics of data preprocessing [21] have been covered in order to make the data suitable for all the proposed models. Exploratory Data Analysis is done

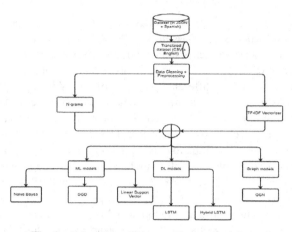

**Fig. 1.** A flowchart of the working methodology.

for visualization in order to get a better understanding of data such as removing null and duplicate values if any and performing feature reduction. Papers having review 0 are only permitted to be fed into the model so that data is more balanced. After noticing the drastic class imbalance in our dataset (173 total samples), we came to a consensus to provide sentiment value '0' to all those papers having the preliminary decision as "accept", 115 in count, and '1' to those having the preliminary decision "reject", "probably reject" and "no decision", 56 in total, which balanced it a little. Furthermore, we perform data cleaning [21] like stopwords removal, tokenization, lemmatization, etc., in order to increase the model's accuracy. Consequently, we reach at 109 for positive sentiment '0' and 55 for the negative sentiment '1'.

### 4.3 Implementation

**Implementation of Machine Learning Models.** Sentiment analysis is a machine learning technology [18, 19] that looks for polarities in texts, ranging from positive to negative. For sentiment analysis categorization, Naive Bayes is a relatively simple collection of probabilistic techniques that assigns a probability that a specific word or phrase should be regarded as positive or negative [11]. In mathematical terms, in order to find the probability of y given input features X we use Eq. 1.

$$p(y/X) = [p(X/y) * p(y)]/p(X) \tag{1}$$

In this paper, we have tried to implement various variations of the Naive Bayes algorithm, namely Multinomial, Gaussian, Bernoulli, and Complement, in order to check which one gives us the highest accuracy. Multinomial Naive Bayes [12], after plane counter vectorization, only gives us 56.10% accuracy which is not desirable by far. Hence, we further try to improve the accuracy by tweaking the n-grams range but the maximum we achieve is 73.17%. On implementation of the other variations, Bernoulli Naive Bayes [13] technique gave us the highest accuracy of 75.61%. Even alternative approaches like TF-IDF vectorization and other algorithms like SGD and Linear SVM

[17] (on both TF-IDF and CV fitted data) weren't able to reach an accuracy higher than 75%. Also, in addition to the accuracy scores, precision, recall and f1 scores were also calculate to see whether the two kinds of vectorizations would provide any difference in these parameters but they turned up to be the exact same.

**Implementation of Deep Learning Model.** Deep learning models are used in extracting abstract features, increasing performance measures and performing analytical tasks with the help of neural networks. We have used the LSTM (Long Short-Term Memory), which is a special kind of RNN (recurrent neural network) capable of perceiving long-term dependencies, for sentiment analysis consisting of 3 layers: Embeddings, LSTM and Dense with Softmax. After training the model on the dataset for a total of 15 epochs, the model is used to predict on the test set to measure the accuracy scores. The results show that the f1-score for the negative sentiments is 0.85 whereas, for the positive ones, it is 0. We perform re-sampling with substitution next to make a layer without any weights; it duplicates the data so that it may be utilized in the generation of the model followed by the convolutional layer. Test-set needs to be separated before up-sampling as it creates multiple copies of the same data. Up-sampling reduces the class imbalance and improves the f1-score i.e., 0.07 for negative sentiments and 0.49 for positive sentiments. On running a few more epochs, the f1-score improves greatly, as shown in Table 1.

**Implementation of Graph-Based Model.** Text_gcn [10], where a large heterogeneous text graph is constructed considering the number of nodes as the corpus size in addition to the number of unique words in the corpus, is used on our dataset. The words are one hot encoded and are inputted to the GCN. An edge connects two nodes based on the occurrence of the word in the whole corpus, and it is added between two nodes if their pointwise mutual information (PMI) is positive, as that indicates a high correlation between the words. The weight of the edges is taken as TF-IDF and PMI of the words. For a graph $G = (V, E)$, where $V$ is the set of nodes and $E$ is the set of edges, let $A$ be an adjacency matrix, with the degree matrix $D = \sum_j (A_{ij})$. The feature matrix $H$ for the $(l + 1)$th GCN layer is given by Eq. 2.

$$H^{(l+1)} = \sigma(D^{-1/2}AD^{-1/2}H^{(l)}W^{(l)}) \tag{2}$$

where $W$ is the weight matrix and $\sigma$ is the ReLu activation function. The GCN model consists of two GCN layers [16] and a final Dense layer with softmax activation. The model allows the passage of messages to a maximum of two nodes away and helps in capturing the semantic relationships between the words in the reviews.

**Implementation of Hybrid Model.** The proposed ensemble model is a hybrid of bidirectional LSTM and CNN for generating the final feature representation. CNN, for its ability to extract features from the text and LSTM/BiLSTM, for maintaining the sequential control between words and having the ability to overlook unnecessary words utilizing the forget gate, are combined as it uses the strengths of the two to give the accuracy. The CNN extracted features are then fed to the LSTM as input. The model consists of the Embedding layer, Spatial Dropout, a BiLSTM, a LSTM, 2 blocks of 1D CNN and Average Pooling, Dropout, Flatten and Dense layers. In the convolution layer, filters act as n-gram finders; each filter looks for a particular class of n-grams and appoints them high scores. The identified grams with most elevated score pass the max pooling function. The convolution layer applies the Rectified Linear Unit to replace the negative output with a 0 in order to remove the non-linearity of the model. Optimization is used to change the attributes such as weights, and learning rate in order to reduce the losses. The model uses Adaptive Moment Estimation optimizer that uses learning rate to optimize the network that converges quickly. The BiLSTM layer maintains the sequential order between the information. It permits connecting the links between the past inputs and outputs. The input of this layer is the connection of the max pooling outputs.

## 5  Results Analysis

The Machine Learning [18] models gave us various accuracies through the implementation of several Naive Bayes variants, the highest being 75.61% achieved by Bernoulli Naive Bayes approach. The LSTM model, after up-sampling the class imbalance gave an F1 score of 0.69 for negative sentiments and 0.37 for positive sentiments. The GCN model trained for 200 epochs gives an accuracy of 73.171% on the test set which consisted of 25% of the dataset considered for the study. Figure 2 visualizes the training accuracy and loss for the Hybrid model. After training for 100 epochs, it is seen that the training accuracy oscillates between 0.97 and 1.0 and gives a f1-score of 0.73 for negative sentiments and 0.44 for positive sentiments.

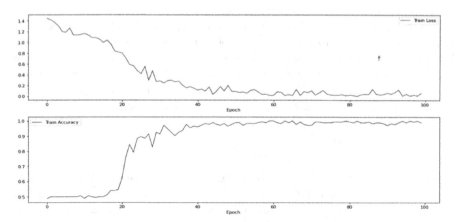

**Fig. 2.** Plot of the training of the Hybrid model

Table 1 summarizes the accuracy scores of the respective models created using the mentioned algorithms. It is observed that Bernoulli's Naive Bayes gives the highest accuracy out of all the models. Since the dataset is small with only 163 non-null observations, the ML models are observed to perform better. The Hybrid model is proposed to give better results for a larger test set, as it is observed that on increasing the size of the test set the accuracy increases. The GCN model is also very promising on this kind of problem. Hence, we put forward the Bernoulli's Naive Bayes as the best model in our study on this peer reviews dataset.

**Table 1.** Result comparison of all the Models.

| Sl. No. | Model name | Accuracy (in %) |
|---------|------------|-----------------|
| 1a | Multinomial NB | 73.17 |
| 1b | Bernoulli's NB | 75.61 |
| 1c | Complement NB | 73.17 |
| 1d | Linear Support Vector CV | 73.17 |
| 1e | Stochastic Gradient Descent CV | 73.17 |
| 2 | Hybrid Model | 63.00 |
| 3 | GCN | 73.17 |

## 6    Conclusion and Future Work

Sentiment analysis of peer reviews on conference papers is very useful for automating the task of the judging chair in considering both the numerical scores and the textual comments given by the reviewers and capturing any conflicts between the scores and comments. To make a competent system, we performed graded multilingual sentiment analysis, which is a complex task. Hence Microsoft's Translator Text which has free academic access has been used for the translation of the reviews. A number of pre-processing techniques have been experimented and the one giving the best accuracy in the classifiers has been recorded. It is observed that the Machine learning Bernoulli's Naive Bayes classifier using N-grams vectorizer has given the best accuracy. In a future study, we aim to compare the predicted sentiments with the numerical scores given by the reviewers and correlate them to the final decision taken by the judging chair.

## References

1. Chakraborty, S., Goyal, P., Mukherjee, A.: Aspect-based sentiment analysis of scientific reviews. In: Proceedings of the ACM/IEEE Joint Conference on Digital Libraries in 2020, pp. 207–216. Association for Computing Machinery, New York, NY, USA (2020)
2. Keith, B., Meneses, C.: A hybrid approach for sentiment analysis applied to paper reviews (2017)
3. Kang, D., et al.: A dataset of peer reviews (PeerRead): collection, insights and NLP applications. In: NAACL 2018 (2018)
4. Fernández Anta, A., Morere, P., Chiroque, L.F., Santos, A.: Techniques for sentiment analysis and topic detection of Spanish tweets: preliminary report. In: Spanish Society for Natural Language Processing Conference (SEPLN 2012), September 2012
5. Aue, A., Gamon, M.: Customizing sentiment classifiers to new domains: a case study. In: Proceedings of Recent Advances in Natural Language Processing (RANLP), vol. 1, no. 3.1, p. 2-1, September 2005
6. Baccianella, S., Esuli, A., Sebastiani, F.: SentiWordNet 3.0: an enhanced lexical resource for sentiment analysis and opinion mining. In: Proceedings of the Seventh International Conference on Language Resources and Evaluation (LREC 2010) (2010)

7. Shi, H., Zhan, W., Li, X.: A supervised fine-grained sentiment analysis system for online reviews. Intell. Autom. Soft Comput. **21**(4), 589–605 (2015)

8. Tang, D., Qin, B., Liu, T.: Document modeling with gated recurrent neural network for sentiment classification. In: Proceedings of the 2015 Conference on Empirical Methods in Natural Language Processing, pp. 1422–1432, September 2015

9. Zhang, L., Ghosh, R., Dekhil, M., Hsu, M., Liu, B.: Combining lexicon-based and learning-based methods for Twitter sentiment analysis. HP Laboratories, Technical report HPL-2011 89, pp. 1–8 (2011)

10. Yao, L., Mao, C., Luo, Y.: Graph convolutional networks for text classification. In: Proceedings of the AAAI Conference on Artificial Intelligence, vol. 33, no. 01, pp. 7370–7377, July 2019

11. Kök, H., İzgi, M.S., Acılar, A.M.: Evaluation of the artificial neural network and Naive Bayes Models trained with vertebra ratios for growth and development determination. Turk. J. Orthod. **34**(1), 2 (2021)

12. Kibriya, A.M., Frank, E., Pfahringer, B., Holmes, G.: Multinomial Naive Bayes for text categorization revisited. In: Webb, G.I., Yu, X. (eds.) AI 2004. LNCS (LNAI), vol. 3339, pp. 488–499. Springer, Heidelberg (2004). https://doi.org/10.1007/978-3-540-30549-1_43

13. Singh, M., Bhatt, M.W., Bedi, H.S., Mishra, U.: Performance of Bernoulli's Naive bayes classifier in the detection of fake news. Mater. Today Proc. (2020)

14. Seref, B., Bostanci, E.: Sentiment analysis using Naive Bayes and complement Naive Bayes classifier algorithms on Hadoop framework. In: 2018 2nd International Symposium on Multidisciplinary Studies and Innovative Technologies (ISMSIT), pp. 1–7. IEEE, October 2018

15. Zhou, C., Sun, C., Liu, Z., Lau, F.: A C-LSTM neural network for text classification. arXiv preprint arXiv:1511.08630 (2015)

16. Zhang, S., Yin, H., Chen, T., Hung, Q.V.N., Huang, Z., Cui, L.: GCN-based user representation learning for unifying robust recommendation and fraudster detection. In: Proceedings of the 43rd International ACM SIGIR Conference on Research and Development in Information Retrieval, pp. 689–698, July 2020

17. Satapathy, S.K., Jagadev, A.K., Dehuri, S.: An empirical analysis of training algorithms of neural networks: a case study of EEG signal classification using Java framework. In: Jain, L.C., Patnaik, S., Ichalkaranje, N. (eds.) Intelligent Computing, Communication and Devices. AISC, vol. 309, pp. 151–160. Springer, New Delhi (2015). https://doi.org/10.1007/978-81-322-2009-1_18

18. Mishra, S., Mishra, D., Satapathy, S.K.: Fuzzy frequent pattern mining from gene expression data using dynamic multi-swarm particle swarm optimization. In: 2nd International Conference on Computer, Communication, Control and Information Technology (C3IT 2012), Published in Journal Procedia Technology, vol. 4, pp. 797–801, February 2012

19. Chandra, S., Gourisaria, M.K., Harshvardhan, G.M., Rautaray, S.S., Pandey, M., Mohanty, S.N.: Semantic analysis of sentiments through web-mined Twitter corpus. In: Proceedings of the International Semantic Intelligence Conference 2021 (ISIC 2021), New Delhi, India, 25–27 February 2021. CEUR Workshop Proceedings, vol. 2786, pp. 202, 122–135 (2021). CEUR-WS.org

# Artificial Intelligence Based Soilless Agriculture System Using Automatic Hydroponics Architecture

Aveen Uthman Hassan[1], Mu'azu Jibrin Musa[2](✉), Yahaya Otuoze Salihu[3], Abubakar Abisetu Oremeyi[4], and Fatima Ashafa[5]

[1] Department of Communication, Sulaimani Polytechnic University, Sulaymaniyah, Iraq
[2] Department of Electronics and Telecommunication, Engineering, Ahmadu Bello University, Zaria, Nigeria
mjmusa@abu.edu.ng
[3] Department of Computer Engineering, Kaduna Polytechnic, Kaduna, Nigeria
[4] Department of Computer Engineering, School of Engineering, Kogi State Polytechnic Lokoja, Itakpe Campus, Lokoja, Nigeria
[5] Department of Electrical and Electronics Engineering, Federal Polytechnic, Nasarawa, Nigeria

**Abstract.** The conventional practices of farming vegetables are inherently associated with the shortage of vegetables due to its seasonal nature, limited farming land and continuous demand. The introduction of artificial means of vegetable production is labor-intensive because of the processes involved in this paper an Artificial Intelligence (AI) based Nutrient Film Technique (NFT) hydroponics system will be designed to mitigate the shortage of vegetable production and minimizes labor. AI will be coded into the ATMEGA328P microcontroller using C++ to provide the required automatic control necessary for the NFT pumps and valves, while Attention Commands (AT) will be used for the interfaced Sim900 Global System for Mobile Communication (GSM) modem for sending Short Message Service (SMS) to the farm operator in case of any malfunction. The improved NFT is found to maximize farmland sine layers of plants can be arranged on one another at a given distance apart, which varies from plant to plant. The AI minimizes human intervention and provides exact mixing and supply of balanced nutrients to plants for fast growth and healthy plants. Continuous production throughout the year using precise AI techniques was designed. Therefore, an improved user-friendly NFT was achieved by utilizing AI embedded in a microcontroller.

**Keywords:** Artificial intelligence · Microcontroller · Hydroponics · NFT · Soilless agriculture

## 1 Introduction

With the advancement of technology in various aspects of our daily lives which aims to improve our standard of living, the need to find a suitable technological solution to the endearing increase in dwindling supply of agricultural products became imminent. With

S. Nandan Mohanty et al. (Eds.): ICISML 2022, LNICST 471, pp. 117–130, 2023.
https://doi.org/10.1007/978-3-031-35081-8_10

the plant rapid increase in industrialization, which in turn results in the reduction of fertile farmlands and urbanization resulted in the overtake of most of the nearby farmlands. Therefore, a solution was developed termed as hydroponics which allows for vegetables and other farm produce to be grown anywhere even in cities as an alternative to conventional agriculture. This is so to meet the daily food requirements in the community [1]. Conventional farming practice is faced with several problems that need to be improving to mitigate with the shortage of seasonal food, fix size of farmland and lack of balanced nutrients for plant growth [2].

This paper aims at providing the solution to continuous production throughout the year, providing the plants with an automatic mixing of the required nutrients elements in the desire proportions and deliver the exact requirements to the plant roots. The stated factures will be addressed using artificial intelligence (AI) embedded in ATMEGA328P. The automation will be carried out using an embedded system, which will be preprogrammed with a suitable mixing formula for the plant to be served. Some degree of freedom will be given which will enable a preset through the graphical user interface (GUI). The GUI will provide flexibility in adjusting the mixture proportions of the nutrients for various stages of plant growth.

The rest of this paper is structured as follows. Section 2 covers the background of the hydroponics; Sect. 3 discusses the design overview and the process flow of the proposed NFT system was explained in Sect. 4. Section 5 provides the conclusion.

## 2   Background of Hydroponics

The background of the hydroponics is provided in the subheadings to enable a clearer understanding of the proposed design.

### 2.1   Introduction to Hydroponics

Hydroponics is a type of agricultural system under the subset of hydro-culture. It is known as a method whereby plants are grown in the absence of soil, by using mineral nutrient solutions in a water solvent. The roots of the plant can either be directly exposed to the nutrient solution or can be supported by inert materials [3]. As a result of the nature of hydroponics, plants can be grown all through the year. Figure 1 shows the Sample of the proposed hydroponics system, whereby variety of vegetables are planted in layers. This configuration leads to space maximizing to about three times the size of the land. The plant grown through hydroponics are healthy and free from pests.

### 2.2   Advantages of Hydroponics to Conventional Soil Agriculture

With the increasing indulgence of researchers in hydroponics agriculture, results have been obtained which shows that hydroponics is very advantageous in various respects, in terms of crop output, expenses, use of resources, etc. Besides the fact that it makes plant cultivation possible in any environment, research has also shown that plants grown with hydroponics are bigger, stronger, healthier, more nutritious, and increased yield of plant produce. Hydroponics also reduces the use of resources, about 70% less water

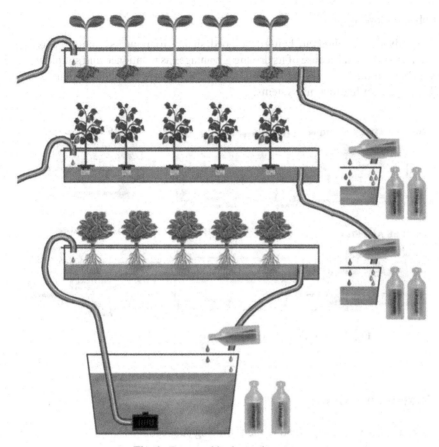

**Fig. 1.** Proposed hydroponics system.

is needed in hydroponics than in conventional farming [4]. Moreover, there is a high reduction in the use of fertilizers (minimal amounts are needed), the use of pesticides is highly reduced [1, 4]. Other advantages of the system include faster growth rate which results in higher rate of production and complete knowledge of the system in case of any infection in the plant since it is a controlled system [5], the problem can easily be detected. Also, in automated hydroponics, the amount of supervision by the farmer is brought to a minimum and birds cannot get direct access to the plants.

## 2.3 Types of Hydroponic Systems

There are six (6) basic types of hydroponics systems [6], which include.

- Wick System
- Drip System
- Water Culture System
- Aeroponics System
- Nutrient Film Technique (NFT)

• Ebb and Flow System

New advanced methods are being developed, such as fogponics systems. In this paper, the NFT was adopted because of its driving advantages as mentioned and simplicity. The AI was built in the NFT via the ATMEGA328P to increase efficiency. Figure 2 shows the basic types of hydroponic systems.

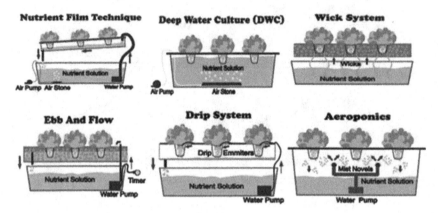

**Fig. 2.** Conventional setups of basic hydroponic systems [7].

## 3 Design Overview

The design overview is explained in the following subheadings.

### 3.1 Nutrient Film Technique

In this paper, the Nutrient Film Technique (NFT) was used in combination with AI. It was chosen because it is simple to implement, and its design arrangement allows for easy automation and maximizing land usage as well as AI is incorporated as the highest and full automation approach [8]. The NFT is also called the continuous-flow solution culture because nutrient solution constantly flows passes the roots and is drained back to the reservoir from where it is pumped again. Figure 3 shows the features of the adopted NFT [9].

The NFT system is simple, and it eliminates some of the challenges of other setups [11]. Because of its continuous flow, no timer is required for the submersible pumps. It also does not require any growing medium i.e., inert materials used in other setups. The NFT makes used of only plastic baskets to support the plant and the roots are immersed directly in the nutrient solution passing through the channel. Despite its advantages, the NFT system has shortcomings such as susceptibility to power outages and pump failures. Once any of the two happens, then the roots become dry shortly. Due to the critical of the said shortcomings, the AI was deployed to address the problems by triggering alarm of unpleasant frequencies to alert the operator and an immediate Short Message Service

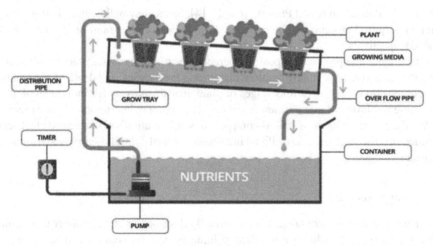

**Fig. 3.** The basic setup of the NFT system [10].

(SMS) will also be sent for urgent response. Figure 4 shows the NFT plant grow trays using PVC materials and film channels for the planting. The PVC was selected because they are lighter than other hydroponic system materials like steel, and moreover they are not toxic and soluble.

**Fig. 4.** PVC pipes for NFT plant grow tray and film channel [12].

## 3.2 Nutrient Solution Mixture

The basis of hydroponics is the replacement of the natural soil with a suitable nutrient solution that contains all the plant needs. Research has shown that the plant needs about 16 elements for growth [13]. These include carbon, hydrogen, oxygen, phosphorus, potassium, nitrogen, sulfur, calcium, iron, magnesium, boron, manganese, copper, zinc, molybdenum, and chlorine. These nutrients can be gotten from water, air, and fertilizers or by getting liquid solutions of the individual elements. The major elements however are

Nitrogen N, Potassium K and Phosphorous P [14], hence they will be used in this paper and their required mixture will be done via AI in the percentage ratio of 7%-9%-5% of N-P-K respectively.

The correct and precise composition percentages of these elements are required for the nutrient mixture else it may result in distortion, deficiencies, and death of the plants. The compositions vary at various stages of plant growth and vary for individual plants. The nutrient solution mixture is therefore a very key aspect of hydroponics hence precise is placed in maintaining the nutrients compositions, the solution's pH value and electrical conductivity always. Hence an artificial intelligence-based control is employed to enable the exact process.

### 3.3  Plant Reservoir

The plant reservoir is a container that is specially designed or any container that could serve the purpose of holding a required volume of nutrient solutions. It also houses the air pump, air stone, EC sensor, pH sensor, submersible nutrient pumps and other components. Figure 5 shows the plant reservoir.

**Fig. 5.**  Plant reservoir [15].

### 3.4  Submersible Pumps

These are pumps that can be powered electrically and can be controlled by the control unit equipped with AI. The pumps are driven by a direct current (DC) motor, which is controlled by the AI. They are used to deliver the nutrient solution by pumping the required solution as instructed by the AI from the reservoir to the plant tray (Fig. 4) and pump nutrient element solutions from their various tanks into the reservoir. Figure 6 shows a submersible DC pump.

**Fig. 6.** Submersible Electric Pump [16].

### 3.5 EC Sensor

The EC meter known as the electrical conductivity meter is a meter used to measure the electrical conductivity of solutions. The EC meter is especially useful in hydroponics to determine the number of nutrients, salt, or other impurities present in the nutrient solution [17]. The standard unit for measuring electrical conductivity is milli-Siemens per centimeter (mS/cm). For a typical hydroponic nutrient solution, the value of electrical conductivity is around 2.0 mS/cm.

The EC meter returns the value of its readings of the electrical conductivity of the nutrient solution to the control unit where the AI will decide considering the value of the readings whether the nutrient solution in the reservoir needs to be changed. Though the EC meter can measure the strength of the nutrient solution, but it cannot give the nutrient balance of the solution and cannot also read the strength of non-ionic compounds such as carbon compounds [17], hence the introduction of the AI as an improvement measure ahead of research of its kind.

### 3.6 pH Sensor

The pH meter is also important for this research work. It is used to measure the hydrogen-ion activity in water-based solutions, indicating its acidity or alkalinity expressed as pH, which is useful in hydroponics agriculture [17]. Its readings are necessary because the pH value in the reservoir must be maintained at a balance in growing plants [18]. Hence, the control unit of an automatic hydroponics system takes the inputs of the pH meter and applies measures where necessary to balance the pH value. This is mostly done by adding a chemical pH balancing solution. In most hydroponics systems the optimum pH range is within 5.8–6.2 [19].

### 3.7 Oxygenation of the Nutrient Solution

After the proper composition of the nutrient mixture in the reservoir, another important task to be done is the oxygenation of the nutrient solution. This is necessary because the plant needs a proper amount of oxygen to breathe otherwise it dies out. There are a couple of methods used to oxygenate the nutrient solution. Some hydroponic users adopt the use of hydrogen peroxide, which is not amazingly effective. It creates dissolved oxygen which has a short life and is not well circulated. Also, O2- is created which can damage healthy plant cells [20].

A better oxygenation approach is to introduce natural air to the reservoir, which reacts with the solution to form enough dissolved oxygen (DO) molecules needed by the plant. This is done by using air pumps and air stones to aid in better circulation of the dissolved oxygen molecules. Supplementary, stirring pumps can be added for better circulation.

### 3.8  Air Pumps and Air Stones

As discussed in the section above, one other important aspect of implementing a successful hydroponics system is the oxygenation of the nutrient solution. This is done using air pumps and air stones. What the air pump does is pump air into the nutrient reservoir, when the air meets the water; it diffuses into the water which supplies it with oxygen to undergo oxygenation. The air pump pumps air through a plastic tube or pipe to the bottom of the reservoir where its end is attached to an air stone as shown in Fig. 7 and Fig. 8. The purpose of the air stone is to catalyze the oxygenation reaction by passing out the pumped air in the shape of small size bubbles for the effective circulation of air into the nutrient solution to form dissolved oxygen, which is needed by the plant roots.

**Fig. 7.** Air pumps pumping air through air stones [21].

**Fig. 8.** Air Stones [22].

## 4   Process Flow of the NFT System

Pump P3, P4 and P5 are controlled via the AI, which is embedded in the ATMEGA328P to supply nutrients (Nitrogen, Phosphorous, and Potassium) in the required proportions to the reservoir. Water and are pumped via P6. From the reservoir, a nutrient pump (P7) is used to pump the nutrients to the nutrient film channel which is maintained at a fixed slope to achieve a constant and desired flow rate. After the nutrient solutions have passed through the roots of the plants it is then returned to the reservoir where it will be pumped up again. 'AT' commands are used for the Global System for Mobile Communication (GSM) modem Sim900, which is cooperated to establish communication via SMS to the operator when malfunction occurs. This describes the unique character of the proposed improved NFT system, whereby nutrients solutions are reused, and wastage is eliminated, and the roots are constantly supplied with adequate amounts of water, oxygen, and nutrients. It can also be seen from the schematic diagram shown in Fig. 9 that two sensors (meters) are used, the EC meter and pH meter. These two (M1 and M2) meters determine the pH level of the nutrient solution and the electrical conductivity, respectively. If the values fall below a certain threshold at which the solution does not deliver proper nutritious content to the plants, the current solution will be drained to the waste reservoir through valve S2, and new nutrients will be pumped and mixed in the reservoir [20]. The repetition of the entire process is done via AI. Proposed NFT system was explained in Sect. 4. Section 5 provides the conclusion.

### 4.1   Control Unit

The ATMEGA328P was used due to its inherent advantages in addition to being easy to program using Arduino development boards [23]. It is also the main component of the control unit where the intelligence was coded in it using the C++ and AT commands. The DC motor switches use to control the water, nutrient and air pumps are controlled by the ATMEGA328P. The DC motors are interfaced with the I/O ports through a switching circuit. The ATMEGA328P controls the switching circuit following the intelligence

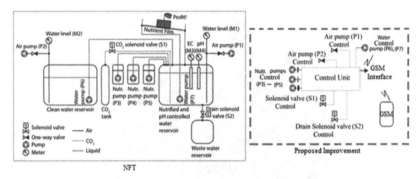

**Fig. 9.** Artificial intelligence process flow schematic for an NFT hydroponic system

embedded in the coding. Figure 10 shows the pins configurations and ports for the ATMEGA328P.

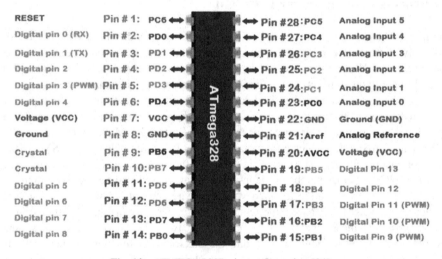

**Fig. 10.** ATMEGA328P pin configuration [24].

## 4.2 Display Unit (16 × 2 LCD)

The 16 × 2 liquid crystal display (LCD) was used to provide visualization of the percentage of the composition mixture of the nutrient solution. The quality of the current nutrient solution in the reservoir as measured by the EC and pH sensors and which mixture type is currently in use are displayed for easy monitoring.

## 4.3 Mixture Types

The diverse types of composition mixtures of the nutrients to form solution are referred to as the states. There are three States A, B and C. These states are included in other to improve the versatility of the system by giving the user the freedom to choose from diverse types of mixtures. These states A, B and C denote different composition mixtures of nutrients required for various stages of plant growth from germination to full growth. The states are selected by pushing dedicated button switches which inform the controller that a state has been selected and that the nutrient mixture should be done accordingly. Figure 11 shows the Proteus schematic circuit diagram for the control.

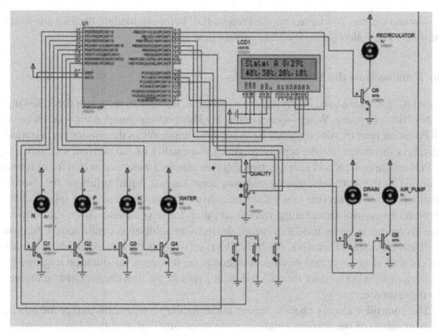

**Fig. 11.** The schematic diagram for the control circuit of the plan

## 4.4   Developed Software

Two applications software were used to implement the software aspect of this paper. First, the Arduino Compiler was used to write the program code. Secondly, the Proteus 8 Professional was used to simulate the hardware circuit of the work.

## 4.5   Arduino Compiler

Arduino compiler is that which uses the C++ programming language. It is commonly used to write program codes for Arduino-based controllers. The Arduino compiler interface is simple and hex files are easily generated and uploaded on the controller in the Proteus environment.

### 4.6 Proteus 8 Professional

Proteus 8 Professional is an interactive development environment (IDE) developed by Labcenter Electronics. It is used for the development and simulation of electronic circuits. It has the advantages of pre-implementation in loop tests and corrections.

### 4.7 Simulation

The simulation was conducted on the Proteus IDE before uploading the Hex file to the controller. The following subsystems explain how it is done.

### 4.8 Brief on How the Simulation Works

Seven DC motors are used in this paper's simulation, the motors represent the following: N – Nitrogen pump, Water – Water pump, P – Phosphorous pump, drain – Drain valve, K – Potassium pump, Air pump and Recirculation pump. When the simulation is started, it displays the state (i.e., the type of mixture), the quality of the nutrient solution, and the Percentage of N, K and P, respectively. It then pumped water and mixes the nutrients according to the state selected, by pumping their various liquid solutions for specific durations into the reservoir using flow rate. After the nutrient has been mixed in the reservoir, the control circuit triggered the air pump for oxygenation. Since the Nutrient Film Technique is being used that means the nutrient solution is continuously pumped into the film channel. Therefore, the controller is set to pump the nutrient solution into the film channel after every one minute. Assuming one minute is the duration required for the nutrient solution to slide through the plant's root in the film channel and be drained into the reservoir.

The controller always checks, before initiating the recirculation pump, the quality (nutrient value) of the nutrient solution in the reservoir. This quality value is measured by the EC and pH sensors and feedback to the controller, which are represented by a variable resistor in this simulation. If the quality is below 30% the control circuit, then initiates the drain pump to drain this low-value solution and then mix a new nutrient solution into the reservoir then initiates the recirculation pump. This process is repeated continuously.

## 5 Conclusion

It can be concluded that a soilless agriculture system using the proposed AI enhanced NFT hydroponics system can provide an improvement over the conventional NFT. The improved NFT maximizes farmland, minimizes human intervention, provides fast growth of plants due to balance nutrients at all the time, resulting in healthy plants free from pests, and birds and permits continuous production throughout the year using the precise AI techniques.

## 6 Limitation and Recommendation

Every good engineering design has some number of limitations, which give room for future improvement to increase its reliability and effectiveness. Some of the future work may include:

i. Physical implementation of the prototype.
ii. Frequent updating the IoT related to this research finding is necessary as technology rapidly changes with time.

## References

1. Rajeev, L.M., Preet, J.: Design and implementation of automatic hydroponics system using ARM Processor. Int. J. Adv. Res. Electr. Electron. Instrum. Eng. 4(8), 6035–6940 (2015). https://www.ijareeie.com/upload/2015/august/16_Design.pdf
2. Al-Darraji, I., et al.: Adaptive robust controller design-based RBF neural network for aerial robot arm model. Electronics 10(7), 831 (2021). https://www.mdpi.com/2079-9292/10/7/831
3. Santos, J.D., et al.: Development of a vinasse nutritive solutions for hydroponics. J. Environ. Manage. 114(15), 8–12 (2013). https://www.sciencedirect.com/science/article/pii/S03 01479712005506
4. Vijendra, S., Preet, J.: Automated hydroponic system using psoc4 prototyping kit to deliver nutrients solution directly to roots of plants on time basis. Int. J. Adv. Res. Electr. Electron. Instrum. Eng. 4(11), 8765–8770 (2015). https://www.ijareeie.com/upload/2015/november/32_Automated.pdf
5. Al-Darraji, I., Ali K., Sadettin, K.: Optimal control of compliant planar robot for safe impact using steepest descent technique. In: Proceedings of the International Conference on Information and Communication Technology, pp. 233–238 (2019). https://dl.acm.org/doi/10.1145/3321289.3321313
6. Mohammed, B.S., Sookoo, R.: Nutrient film technique for commercial production. Agric. Sci. Res. J. 6(11), 269–274 (2016). http://resjournals.com/journals/agricultural-science-res earch-journal.html
7. Nosoilsolutions: Hydroponic systems 7 Different types of hydroponic systems. https://www.nosoilsolutions.com/6-different-types-hydroponic-systems/. Retrieved 8 Nov 2022
8. Al-Darraji, I., et al.: A technical framework for selection of autonomous UAV navigation technologies and sensors. CMC-Comput. Mater. Continua 68(2), 2771–2790 (2016). https://www.techscience.com/cmc/v68n2/42212
9. Michael, G.W., Tay, F.S., Then, Y.L.: Development of automated monitoring system for hydroponics vertical farming. J. Phys. Conf. Ser. 1–8 (2021). https://iopscience.iop.org/art icle/10.1088/1742-6596/1844/1/013024
10. Altine: Top 20 Nutrient Film Technique Advantages and Disadvantages-You need to be aware of. https://plantsheaven.com/nutrient-film-technique-advantages-and-disadvantages/. Retrieved 8 Nov 2022
11. Atmel-42735-8-bit-AVR-Microcontroller-ATmega328-328P_Datasheet, pp. 1–10. https://www.alldatasheet.com/view.jsp?Searchword=ATMEGA328P&sField=4. Retrieved 8 Nov 2022
12. Alibaba.com. PVC pipes for NFT plant grow tray and film channel. https://www.alibaba.com/product-detail/Customized-sizes-hydroponic-tube-square-PVC_60646336032.html. Retrieved 8 Nov 2022

13. Beckman C.: Beckman Coulter Product Milestones, 13 May 2009. https://www.biospace.com/article/releases/beckman-coulter-inc-pending-acquisition-of-b-olympus-diagnostics-systems-b-passes-milestone-with-u-s-regulatory-approval-/. Retrieved Aug 2021
14. James, L., Matthew, D., Khalid, A., Justin, W.: Leaf alone hydroponics system. Department of Electrical Engineering and Computer Science, University of Central Florida, Orlando, Florida 32816-2450, pp. 1–8 (2014). https://www.ece.ucf.edu/seniordesign/sp2014su2014/g09/documents/Group%209%20Conference%20Paper.pdf
15. Supercloset Super Ponics 16 Hydroponic System. https://supercloset.com/product/hydroponics-systems/superponic-system/superponics-16-hydroponic-grow-system/?doing_wp_cron=1667940478.9332089424133300781250. Retrieved 8 Nov 2022
16. IndiaMART. Electric Submersible Pump. https://dir.indiamart.com/impcat/electric-submersible-pump.html. Retrieved 8 Nov 2022
17. George, J.H., Robert, C.H.: Nutrient solution formulation for hydroponic (perlite, rockwool, NFT) tomatoes in Florida. Horticultural Sciences Department, University of Florida, Institute of Food and Agricultural Sciences, Gainesville, HS796, pp. 1–10. https://edis.ifas.ufl.edu/pdf/CV/CV21600.pdf. Reviewed Aug 2021
18. Hardeep, S., Bruce, D., Mark, P.: Hydroponic pH modifiers affect plant growth and nutrient content in leafy greens. J. Hortic. Res. **27**(1), 31–36 (2019). https://sciendo.com/pdf/10.2478/johr-2019-0004
19. Rodolfo, D.R., et al.: Water and fertilizers use efficiency in two hydroponic systems for tomato production. Horticultura Brasileira. **38**(1), 47–52 (2020). https://www.scielo.br/j/hb/a/KxB8v57FNgjvDdZP3P9tL4f/?lang=en&format=pdf
20. Edi, S.P., Jamaludin, J., Djalu, M.D.: Comparison of hydroponic system design for rural communities in Indonesia. J. Arts Humanit. **7**(9), 14–21 (2018). https://www.theartsjournal.org/index.php/site/article/view/1490/681
21. Petzlife: World Air pumps pumping air through air stones. https://www.indiamart.com/petzlifeworld/oxygen-plate.html
22. Daraz.: Air stones. https://www.daraz.com.bd/products/4-50mm-50mm-i180151177-s1121334292.html?spm=a2a0e.searchlistcategory.list.47.548a28b6BxUtev&search=1. Retrieved 8 Nov 2022
23. Wenke, L., Lingyan, Z., Yubin, Z.: Growth and nutrient element content of hydroponic lettuce are modified by LED continuous lighting of different intensities and spectral qualities. MDPI Agronomy **10**(11), 1–11 (2020). https://www.mdpi.com/2073-4395/10/11/1678
24. David, W.: Introduction to ATmega328. https://www.theengineeringprojects.com/2017/08/introduction-to-atmega328.html. Retrieved 8 Nov 2022

# Mining Ancient Medicine Texts Towards an Ontology of Remedies – A Semi-automatic Approach

João Nunes[1] ⓘ, Orlando Belo[1]([⊠]) ⓘ, and Anabela Barros[2] ⓘ

[1] ALGORITMI Research Centre/LASI, University of Minho, Campus of Gualtar,
4710-057 Braga, Portugal
a82300@alunos.uminho.pt, obelo@di.uminho.pt
[2] Centre for Humanistic Studies, CEHUM, University of Minho, Campus of Gualtar,
4710-057 Braga, Portugal
aldb@elash.uminho.pt

**Abstract.** Over the last years, ontology learning processes have gained a vast space for discussion and work, providing essential tools for discovering knowledge, especially from textual information sources. One of the most currently used techniques for extracting ontological elements from textual data is through the application of lexical-syntactic patterns, which aim to explore formalities of the language in which texts are written, for removing hyperonym/hyponym pairs that can be used to identify and characterize ontology concepts and create valuable semantic networks of terms. We applied a lexical-syntactic patterns approach in a set of medicine texts, written in classical Portuguese, during the 16th and 17th centuries, with the goal of extracting hyperonym/hyponym pairs to establish a medicine ontology of the time. In this paper, we discuss the most relevant aspects of an ontology learning system we implemented for extracting the referred ontology, which has the ability for characterizing the knowledge expressed in ancient medicament texts.

**Keywords:** Ontology Learning · Linguistic Ontologies · Extracting Knowledge from Textual Data · Natural Language Processing · Linguistic Patterns · Graph Databases

## 1 Introduction

In computer science, ontologies are data structures having a concise and explicit semantics in a given knowledge domain, which integrate different categories of data and metadata elements, such as classes, concepts, and relationships, among others. Ontologies [1, 2] are very useful instruments for supporting assumption or inference processes about their application domain, which greatly facilitates the understanding of its elements and the domain they represent and sustain. Additionally, allow for creating simple visualization methods on the data represented in an ontology's structure, providing a clear representation of all ontological elements and relationships. Inserting, updating or removing

© ICST Institute for Computer Sciences, Social Informatics and Telecommunications Engineering 2023
Published by Springer Nature Switzerland AG 2023. All Rights Reserved
S. Nandan Mohanty et al. (Eds.): ICISML 2022, LNICST 471, pp. 131–146, 2023.
https://doi.org/10.1007/978-3-031-35081-8_11

ontological elements are easy tasks to do, due to the flexibility of the structure of an ontology, being very scalable in this type of operations [3]. Furthermore, an ontology can easily receive and represent a model of a given domain of knowledge, easily to be share with other systems [4].

Nowadays, the popularity of ontologies, as well as the recognition of their utility, is due to the successful application of ontological systems in knowledge-based systems that provide information retrieval, natural language processing or machine learning services [5]. Thus, over the last years, ontology learning processes have gained a vast space for discussion and work, being essential tools for discovering knowledge, especially from textual information sources. Ontology learning [6, 7] can be defined as the set of methods or techniques used for constructing, maintaining or extending ontologies in an automatic way. To do this, a very diversified set of machine learning techniques is used on ontology learning processes, especially natural language processing, to identify, for example, terms, concepts, properties, and relationships that are present in data [8, 9]. Afterwards, all these elements can be used to compose an ontology, housing a given knowledge domain. However, the process of extracting an ontology can be very complex and demanding, both in terms of human and computational resources. Today, carrying out a process like this in a fully automatic way is already possible, but stills is very difficult to design and implement, requiring in most cases the attention of one or more specialists to validate, evaluate or adjust, in particular, the tasks of identification and extraction of the various elements of the knowledge involved. The difficulty of these processes is considered as complicated as the final knowledge granularity that we pretend include in the ontology structure and semantics. As referred, ontology learning processes are commonly used on unstructured texts. These texts are difficult to deal with, because most of the knowledge they contain can rise very different interpretations, from person to person, even when same words are used [10].

One of the techniques we can use for extracting ontological elements from textual data is through the application of lexical-syntactic patterns [11], which aim to explore formalities of the language in which texts are written, for removing hyperonym/hyponym pairs that can be used to identify and characterize ontology concepts and create valuable semantic networks of terms. We applied a lexical-syntactic patterns approach over a set of remedy texts [12, 13], written in classical Portuguese, during the 16th and 17th centuries, with the goal of extracting hyperonym-hyponym pairs to establish a remedy ontology of the time. After an exhaustive analysis of the remedy texts, edited in semidiplomatic version (respecting the classical language and orthography, with all its normal variation), and using ontological tools, it was possible to identify a significant set of linguistic patterns. These patterns allowed, with a very high degree of confidence, the automatic extraction of a large diversity of ingredients of the remedies and other relate data from those texts. All of this sustained the generation of a specialised ontology about remedies, prepared and used at the time the codex was written.

In this paper, we discuss the most relevant aspects of an ontology learning system we implemented for extracting a remedy ontology, characterizing the knowledge expressed in the remedy texts referred above. The ontology we got incorporates a large diversity of medicine elements that allow for knowing botanical specimens, animals and minerals, in addition to the medicinal, daily, agricultural and veterinary practices of the referred period. It offers a very rich field of research for students, professors, researchers and individual users, offering a very interesting view of the remedy knowledge of 16th and 17th centuries to pharmacological and medicinal research in the 21st century [14]. The remaining part of this paper is organized as follows. Section 2 exposes the domain of ontologies, their methodologies and applications, Sect. 3 discusses ontology learning processes, approaching task models organization and functioning, Sect. 4 documents our application case and reveals how we extract the ontology of remedies on ancient remedy texts, and, finally, Sect. 5, presents conclusions and points out some research lines for future work.

## 2  Ontologies, Methodologies and Applications

Technological advances taken place over the last few years have given rise to a large number of applications, somewhat dispersed across a large variety of knowledge fields, which raised an impressive volume of data, especially in the global network, the Internet. Almost proportionally to this volume of information, the types and models of data (and metadata) soared extraordinary, emerging large information sources of a very diverse nature. The vastness of this information, structured, semi-structured or unstructured, aroused the curiosity of many researchers and companies that saw that this information would bring them value for their innovation, development and business activities.

Currently, much of this information is available for exploration. However, given the large volume, diversity and variation over time, this information cannot be explored in a conventional way. It needs sophisticated and expeditious mechanisms of extraction, preparation, storage, and analysis, being capable of dealing with the nature of this data. This raised numerous questions and challenges. The representation of the knowledge contained in these data is just one of those problems, one of those challenges. Although not easy, it is a very important issue. The knowledge that data can provide, in order to be identified, needs special mechanisms capable of working with different types of data, recognizing concepts, properties and relationships, among other things, and then storing them in adequate structures that allow for a useful and expeditious exploration. The lack of an adequate storage structure usually makes impossible to explore the knowledge we acquired.

Nowadays, one of the most sophisticated structures we have access to accommodate this knowledge are ontologies [1, 2]. These can be seen as representative elements of a given knowledge domain [15]. When well defined, an ontology is a primordial structure in any knowledge-based system, allowing for exploring various strands of knowledge, sustained by the concepts and relationships acquired, taking into account the characteristics and semantics of knowledge elements. Through an ontology, we can share or reuse an explicit representation of knowledge for other purposes, partially or fully.

There are many other perspectives for defining ontologies, addressing many different aspects, but always having the same common denominator, the representation of knowledge. Uschold and Gruninger [16] defined an ontology for sharing knowledge about a given domain of interest, allowing for the encapsulation of a global perspective on that domain, involving the conceptualization of a set of concepts, in the form of entities, attributes and relationships. In turn, Borst [17] defined an ontology as a formal specification of a shared conceptualization, emphasizing the fact that there has to be an agreement regarding the conceptualization of the ontology. Finally, the definition given by Gruber [18], in general terms, is the most consensual definition in the field of Computer Science.

Ontologies prove to be advantageous in terms of knowledge structures for making assumptions and inferencing methods over data, which may allow the creation of simple visualization methods for the data represented in the ontology's structure. Regarding the insertion of new elements in an ontology, due to the flexibility of its structure, an ontology can be easily extended, being scalable for any conventional data manipulation operations [3]. Additionally, different users or systems can easily share its structure [4].

Ontologies can be very useful tools for solving problems in the most diverse areas. The use of applications supported by ontologies can be divided into several categories, taking into account a very diverse range of aspects, such as, for example, the creation of data structures and associated semantics or the exchange and sharing of knowledge contained in an ontology. Today, we can easily found worldwide applications of ontologies, ranging from Music to Medicine and Biology. However, the process of developing an ontology [19] is not an easy process to execute. It requires the use of concrete strategies and methods that should be applied from its idealization, to its implementation and subsequent exploitation stages. Over the years, researchers in the field have been proposing and developing different types of approaches, not only for conceptualization but also for the implementation of ontologies. There are some ideas and aspects shared by the different ontology learning approaches, concerning the creation and development of ontologies. Considering alternatives in the idealization of the knowledge domain, knowing that the development of an ontology is an iterative process, or knowing that classes and relationships expressed in an ontology must always belong to a domain of knowledge, are only two examples of such ideas. In the next section, we will look at the ontology learning process in more detail.

## 3   Ontology Learning Processes

The design and implementation of an ontology learning process should not carried out in an *ad hoc* manner. By nature, they are quite complicated processes using different types of strategies and methods from different domains of working, for extracting knowledge from textual data, which often require natural language processing techniques [20], text mining [21], and machine learning mechanisms [22]. Due to their nature, all these domains are quite complicated and require a high level of knowledge for using and applying their tools and working methods. For overcoming ontology learning process implementation difficulties, we may use different types of approaches and methodologies. Despite their differences, they all share a set of common tasks, which regulates how an ontology learning process is built [4]. Basically, we need to take into account one must consider several alternatives in the idealization of the domain of knowledge, since there are also several possibilities, more or less complex, of conceptualizing an ontology. Furthermore, we must remember that an ontology development process is iterative, which according to the implementation requirements will allow to increase or decrease the structure of the ontology, influencing its final complexity. The ontology's classes and relationships must always belong to the domain of knowledge we are dealing with, otherwise the ontology will not be useful since it did not respect the knowledge domain. Some common ontology development methodologies are Tove [23, 24], Uschold [25] and Methontology [4].

However, the ontology learning process is not limited to the choice of a methodology and its consequent application. In turn, the ontology has to be evaluated based on an established framework, knowledge representation, data types and extraction requirements. Reyes-Peña and Tovar-Vidal [25] argued that a methodology must be verified and evaluated in terms of the model it incorporates. For carrying on this verification, it is necessary to analyze, for example, all the lexical aspects related to the dictionaries of terms created and used, the semantic aspects referring to the consistency of the terms, and the structural aspects related to the ontology structure itself, to verify, for example, if there are loops in the ontology structure. Data driven and application driven [27] are two of the techniques that can be used to validate an ontology. In the first technique, we use textual data from the same domain of knowledge of the ontology for comparing the data with the elements defined and integrated in the ontology. In the second technique, we combine the ontology created with a given application for evaluating the performance of the ontological application, measuring the quality of the responses given by the application.

Ontologies can be extracted from texts manually or automatically. The manual construction of an ontology has costs of different nature, caused by the modeling and capture of new knowledge or by the need for an expert for mapping and sketching a certain domain of knowledge in an ontological structure. In small dimension and complexity domains, these costs do not prevent the manual construction of an ontology. However, in applications for wider domains, the manual preparation of an ontology may be unfeasible, and serious challenges and obstacles may be faced not allowing the extraction of knowledge and its materialization in an ontology [28]. As a response, automatic mechanisms were gradually introduced throughout the different stages of development of the ontology learning process, addressing tasks in which the application of natural language processing, and artificial intelligence programs brought great added value. Gradually a new expertise field emerged. Today, we recognize it as Ontology Learning [6, 7].

Afterwards, all these elements will be used to compose an ontology to house the knowledge we need. However, given the current state of technology in the domain, rarely a process of extracting an ontology can be considered fully automatic, as it often requires the attention of one or more users to validate, evaluate and adjust the parameters of the programs used, according to the results we want to get. In practice, human intervention is desirable for guaranteeing the quality of the ontology, being also dependent on the degree of difficulty of the extraction process. This is as complicated as the nature and complexity of the knowledge domain and consequently dependable of the granularity of the ontological structures required for its representation [8]. In short, supervised ontology extraction processes are usually referred to be semiautomatic processes.

The structure of a semi-automatic process was already defined for a long time. Somewhat inspired by the process of manual ontology construction, Brewster [29] used the image of a "layer cake" for representing the order in which extraction tasks would be carried out, organizing them in an increasing order of execution difficulty – terms >> synonyms >> concepts >> hierarchies >> relationships >> axioms. At the base of the "cake" are the simplest tasks, such as the identification of terms, and at the top the more complicated ones, such as the definition of axioms, representing logical rules for the knowledge domain. Several authors discussed this organization, evaluating its structure and application. Tiwari and Jain [19] simplified the proposal of Brewster [29], considering that some tasks can be performed in the same process step. For example, we can execute the task of identifying terms and synonyms simultaneously, since both tasks are similar in terms of linguistics and extraction methods application. As a result, we have a layer cake with a smaller number of layers – terms and synonyms >> concepts >> relationships >> axioms.

**Fig. 1.** Main tasks of an ontology learning process – adapted from [7].

More recently, Asim et al. [7] adapted the organization of Tiwari and Jain [19], adding two new tasks, namely data pre-processing and evaluation of the ontology extraction process (Fig. 1). In the first task, text pre-processing cleans and prepares text according to the selected extraction algorithm requirements, removing possible cases of ambiguity, or structural or semantic inconsistency that could compromise the final ontology [30]. In the next task, linguistic or statistical mechanisms are applied for extracting terms and concepts to be implemented in the ontology, grouping them into clusters, without any relationship established among them. Subsequently, these elements will be analyzed and combined in order to found possible relationships with each other, based on the dependencies between terms and concepts contained in the text [8]. The task of extracting axioms is the next. This is the most complex and demanding task of the entire process. Usually, it requires very specialized tools, which can use programming mechanisms in inductive logic [31] or Hidden Markov Models [32], among others. Finally, using of data driven or application driven techniques, all the identified ontological elements and their relationships are validated [26]. In short, this analysis and evaluates the adequacy level of the ontology. The approach of Asim et al. [7] served as a guide in the development process we will present and describe in the next section.

## 4   An Ontology for Ancient Remedies

### 4.1   The Application Case

The travels of the Portuguese around the world during the age of discovery allowed them allowed to access to a large variety of knowledge of different peoples and cultures, related to a wide variety of domains, such as medicine, biology, or gastronomy, among others. The knowledge they acquired was recorded in manuscripts and prints that are part of the history of the Portuguese. In many cases, some of these documents remain unknown and without the recognition they deserve within the scope of their domains [14]. One of these manuscripts is the number 142, which is stored in the District Archive of Braga, in Portugal. It is an anonymous manuscript, which includes in one of its parts (notebook II) hundreds of texts, written in classical Portuguese, including receipts of remedies, advice and medicinal secrets, from Portugal, Europe but also from Brazil and Asia, collected during the 16th and 17th centuries. These remedies, prepared in convent apothecaries but also in the kitchens of each family house, still have a lot to offer to today's pharmacological and medicinal fields. They make known to us numerous botanical specimens, with geographically and linguistically varied names, animals and minerals, in addition to the medicinal, daily, agricultural and veterinary practices common in past centuries.

*P**ª** faser Nascer Cabellos.*

*Tome' Ran's, e lagartigxas, ponhanas a torrar no forno dentro de hua panella pisenas como estiuere' be' torradas, e frigiaõ em aseite huas poucas de moscas, e depois ama anasando hua gemma de ouo deitemlhe deste aseite, e poós, e por 3es dias ponhaõ emprasto disto as noites donde quisere' q nasaõ os cabellos.*

**Fig. 2.** A remedy's recipe to grow hair – *"P**ª** faser Nascer Cabellos"*[1]

In Fig. 2, we can see a fragment of the original text of a remedy's recipe, in classical Portuguese (semi diplomatic version). This is just a small example of the ancient medicine texts that we have available for analysis. With a brief analysis of the text it is possible to identify the various ingredients used in the recipe as well as to get to know their preparation and application processes. Obviously, the analysis of a text like this one it is easy to perform, as is the manual extraction process of the knowledge structures presented in the text. According to the content of the text presented in Fig. 1 and abstracting concepts and relationships, we can say that:

(1..1) RECIPE needs > (0..n) INGREDIENT
(1..1) RECIPE involves > (0..n) OPERATION
(1..1) RECIPE uses > (0..n) UTENSIL
(1..1) OPERATION uses > (0..n) INGREDIENT
(1..1) OPERATION requires > (0..n) UTENSIL

In fact, beyond knowing how to read and interpret a text written in classical Portuguese, it is not necessary a great expertize or knowledge to create an ontology for receiving such knowledge. However, when we have to deal with a few hundred texts, the process becomes a little more arduous and complex. In this case, opting for a manual approach for extracting knowledge is not feasible or achievable in useful time. Knowing this, we easily decided to design and develop a system for extracting the knowledge contained in remedies texts, which, in a supervised way, would provide ontology for representing such knowledge correctly and completely. The ontology will allow for a

---

[1] An English translation of the recipe: *"Take frogs and geckos; let roast them in the oven in, a pan; crush them when toasted; fry a few flies in olive oil; after kneading an egg yolk, put the oil and some powders; for 3 days, apply this at night, in the place where you want hair grow."*.

sustained analysis of the different concepts (and their relationships) related to different remedies and, in particular, to their ingredients, and preparation and application processes. Thus, it will be possible to demonstrate, in a simple and visual way, the process of making medicines used at the time, and study the herb, tree or plant, seed, diseases and symptoms, health practices, etc., that were used. For linguistics, the ontology will be a very useful instrument, allowing them to know the writing style followed in each of the recipes, the vocabulary and the way it was used at the time, the structure of the sentences, among many other things, allowing for analyzing and comparing with what is used today.

We define the scope of the ontology using a set of informal competency questions, involving the main aspects of a remedy (recipe, ingredients, utensils, operations, etc.) for validating the knowledge acquired during the ontology extraction process. Questions like "How to prepare the prescription of a remedy?", "How to apply a remedy?", "What ingredients are used in the preparation of a remedy?", or "What operations do you have to perform to prepare a remedy?, were the basis for evaluated the ontology across the several versions of the ontology learning process. In the next section, we will describe this process.

## 4.2  Extracting the Ontology

It is not necessary to make a detailed reading to verify that the texts of remedies mentioned previously contain immense information about the processes of making medicines that took place in the 16th and 17th centuries. From this, we are able to acquire very relevant knowledge about the medicines that were at that time produced, as well as their form of using and application. Providing an ontology with all this knowledge, will be useful for researchers, teachers, students and other users, to know, for example, the different names of an herb, tree or plant, or a seed used in convent apothecaries for treating diseases, or other health practices, from Portugal and Europe, but also from Brazil, and Asia, at that time. After assessing the effort that would be necessary to spend for treating and analyzing manually the referred texts, we found that this work would not be feasible, as it would not produce any results in the short term. Thus, we opted for developing a semi-automatic ontology learning process for extracting knowledge elements for the desired ontology of remedies.

To project and implement the ontology learning process, we adopted the model proposed by Asim et al. [7], as a working base and a general configuration for preparation and extraction tasks. However, given the specific characteristics of our application case, we adjusted or modified some of the tasks for using other text analysis approaches. For example, in the extraction of terms and concepts task we used Hearst patterns [11]) for making the extraction of hyperonym and hyponym relations in texts. Let see, then, how we proceed to get the ontology of old medicines that we will be present later.

### Preprocessing Texts
According to the extraction plan we defined, we began preprocessing the texts containing the various preparation processes of remedies. However, before that we needed to analyze carefully the texts for understanding which models and techniques could be applied without distort the meaning of the text. This is fundamental for ensuring the reliability

of the ontology and guaranteeing that it is as close as possible of the domain's knowledge. Since texts are written in classical Portuguese, we decided to restrict preprocessing tasks as much as possible, in order to maintain intact the meaning of the text in.

Preprocessing began with the elimination of spaces, line changes and special characters presented in the texts, for ensuring that they did not interfere with the next tasks, text tokenization and analysis of part of speech. For accomplishing these two tasks we used spaCy [33], a natural language processing library, based on the performance it has shown in other similar applications, when compared to other similar alternatives, such as NLTK [34]. In addition, spaCy also offers pre trained and variable size pipelines ready to apply to any textual data, including tokenization, part of speech tagging, or named entity recognition (NER) tasks, among others. Additionally, we also removed other characters, such as apostrophes, which are identified by spaCy as individual tokens, as well as other cases, such as the inclusion of specific textual patters, such as the pattern "[3]" that does not add any meaning to the phrase in which it is inserted. We can see a concrete case of remedy recipe ("other"), which was worked according to the process we just explained. The text of the original recipe (in classical Portuguese) is:

> *"Outro.*
> *[10]*
> *Pª resoluer nascidas, farinha de semeas, oleo Rosado, vinho. Outro. Cosimento de barbasco, oleo rosado com hu' pouco de asafraõ, farinha de trigo galego feito huas papas. Outro pera faser arebentar em 24 horas. hua gemma de ouo anasada com asucar mto be' ate q' fique grosa; estendase em hu' paninho, e ponhase, renovandose como estiuer seca, e ella faz buraco, e chama a mala, e continuena depois de aberto, o tempo q'quisere', -pq' atte a rais chupa."*

After applying the prediction models and techniques we selected, the text above was transformed in the following:

> "Outro.P resoluer nascidas, farinha de semeas, oleo Rosado, vinho. Outro. Cosimento de barbasco, oleo rosado com hu pouco de asafraõ, farinha de trigo galego feito huas papas. Outro pera faser arebentar em 24 horas. Hua gemma de ouo anasada com asucar mto be ate q fique grosa; estendase em hu paninho, e ponhase, renovandose como estiuer seca, e ella faz buraco, e chama a mala, e continuena depois de aberto, o tempo q quisere, pq atte a rais chupa."

This new version of the text is easier to interpret and maintains its original meaning. The modifications made did not have a major impact on the meaning of the text, providing a clear text, easier to interpret and process by the tools we chose. After this cleansing step, we fragmented the texts accordingly their sentences. Although spaCy offers components to detect and segment the sentences of a text, the result we got with it was not always correct, revealing some incorrectly segments of sentences. We believe this situation occurred because texts are written in classical Portuguese. Thus, we had to segment sentences using the '.' character as segmentation reference. At the end, each processed text was stored in a document store supported by Mongodb. The use of MongoDB was essentially due to its ability for scaling and rapid processing of queries, in inserting and exploring data operations [35]. Figure 3 shows all the tasks performed during text preprocessing.

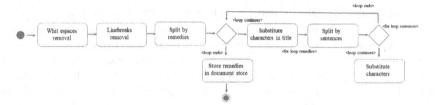

**Fig. 3.** Text preprocessing tasks

## Extracting Concepts and Relationships

After preprocessing texts, we proceeded the extraction of concepts and relationships tasks, createing a specific implementation of a pipeline for NER. We trained the NER model using a data set extracted from remedy texts after being annotatted appropriately. The pipeline was personalized (Fig. 4) and is feed with the sentences of the texts. The pipeline structure closely follows the approach by Honnibal and Montani [33].

**Fig. 4.** Pipeline for concepts and relations extraction [33]

The first component of the model, tok2vec (token-to-vector), is responsible for separating the text into individual tokens. Then, each of the tokens is represented in a vector of a representation space for word embedding. Using a CNN neural network (Convulutional Neural Network) we got the vector representation. The neural network and the embeddings will be shared by the successive components, in order to reduce the size of the models, since the embeddings are only calculated and copied once. Furthermore, this solution allowed reducing the system's processing time. Next, the morphologizer module identifies and classifies the part of speech tags for each token founded. This component uses tok2vec for adding a new layer to the network, containing a softmax activation function to produce part of speech tags predictions. After identifying the tags, the parser component learn dependencies between the different vectors. Once again, we used tok2vec again to create a new model called the transition-based parser. This model can be used either to perform named entity recognition or dependency parsing. Finally, the lemmatization module simplifies the text by reducing words to their basic form. At the end of the process, we got a doc object, containing the sequence of the token objects related to each word. For each token object, it will be possible to consult information regarding the output of each component of the pipeline, being able to access to the part of speech tags or the lemmatized form of the word, among other things.

### Lexical-Syntactic Patterns

For extracting concepts and relationships referred in the texts, we used Hearst patterns [11], which are lexical-syntactic patterns specially oriented to extract hypernym and hyponym relationships from the text. Hearst applied these patterns to encyclopedic and journalistic corpora, obtaining 63% of good quality relationships. The work carried out by Hearst was a pioneer in the use of lexical patterns in the extraction of semantic relationships. There are other relevant works concerning Hearst patterns application to texts written in Portuguese. Authors such as Freitas and Quental [36], Baségio [37], Taba and Medeiros [38] or Machado and Strube de Lima [39], developed very interesting works in this domain, in particular Baségio, which directed its research to the Portuguese language used in Brazil.

The concept (and their relationships) process began with a manual analysis of the texts, for interpreting and identifying possible lexical-syntactic patterns and then extract the hypernym and hyponym pairs. Taking into account the requirements and the goal of the ontology, we applied extraction using a survey of the ingredients that made up a recipe for a remedy, and, later, for identifying ingredients' quantities and recipes' preparation methods, if any. We defined the lexical-syntactic patterns using part of speech tags. The spaCy tool provides a matcher object that can be used to find words in texts that instantiate some of the defined patterns. Then, we used these patterns in conjunction with the matcher object for improving concept and relationship identification. Table 1 shows some of the patterns we used in the ontology learning process.

**Table 1.** Examples of Hearst patterns used in the ontology learning process.

| Nr | Hearst Patterns |
|----|-----------------|
| i | com(erlaðla) (B1,)* (B2(elou))* B3 |
| ii | such NP as {NP,}* {(orland)} {NP} |
| iii | (B1,)* tomado |
| iv | beb(erleralaðlalidalido) (B1,)* (B2(elou))* B3 |
| v | NUM (onsaslonças) de (B1,)* (B2(elou))* B3 |

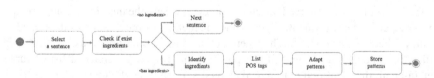

**Fig. 5.** Identification of patterns for ingredients

Additionally, we assumed the existence of a common hypernym, having the value of the ingredient, and then extract the hyponyms related to the existing hypernym from the text being processed. Figure 5 illustrates this process. To demonstrate this process, we will analyze a specific sentence from one of the remedy prescriptions used in the ontology extraction process. The sentence we selected is:

*"**Macela, Coroa de Rei, Maluaisco,** ou **Maluas,** cosido tudo com agoa e metido este cosimento em hua bexiga de boi posta sobre a pontada."*

Thus, after we have selected the phrase, we identify the ingredients making possible to define a lexical-syntactic pattern. In the sentence presented, we identify four distinct ingredients ("Macela", "Coroa de Rei", "Maluaisco" and "Maluas"), which will be integrated later into the composition of the lexical-syntactic pattern. Next, we identify the syntactic elements necessary for defining a pattern that allows us to extract the ingredients identified previously. As we can see, in the selected sentence the ingredients identified were founded before the key words "cosido tudo", which refers a sewn operation. This allows us to verify and generalize, with some certainty, that before these words we can find ingredients. After identifying the pattern, we analyze other recipes to adjust its definition, if occurred some variations caused by the contexts of other recipes. Having the keywords of the pattern, we dispose the doc object information, coming from the spaCy analysis of the sentence used, and we consulted the part of speech tags. In order to generalize the creation of patterns, they were created using a block containing the most common tags for supporting the extraction process. These blocks comprise four tags, related to nouns (NOUN), to proper nouns (PROPN), to adjectives (ADJ) and to verbs (VERB). This format was created based on the patterns presented and described in [39].

**The Ontology**

After finished the definition of lexical-syntactic pattern, we applied them to each of the sentences of the texts used in the extraction process. Whenever we detected an instantiation of a pattern in a sentence, we recorded the occurrence ensuring that we did not keep repeated patterns, whether they were partially or fully instantiated. Then, pattern instantiations were analyzed for extracting the ingredients they referenced. It was necessary to apply some filters for selecting and extracting the ingredients from the texts, in order to get a consistent list, without repetitions. The instantiation of each pattern returned a list of strings, containing the names of the ingredients and other words included in the sentence. According to the position of the ingredients in the string list, we checked for the existence of other specific strings (or just characters) that were not part of the ingredient name. For example, occurrences of commas, or conjunctions such as "and" and "or" were removed. From this process, we got the ingredients of the recipes processed, as well as the quantities used and the method of preparation of the remedies. All these elements are distinct. They were obtained by different patterns, with different unification models. At the end of the process, the system generated a list of tuples containing all the identified ontological elements. Each type of elements has a specific tuple having a particular structure. For example, based on the sentence presented above, we got tuples like:

- ('macela', 'is-a', 'INGREDIENT')
- ('macela', 'has-operation', 'cosido')
- ('coroa de rei', 'is-a'. 'INGREDIENT')
- ('coroa de rei', 'has-operation', 'cosido')

Then, this process was repeated for all the sentences of the texts. At the end, the tuples were prepared and exported to a graph-oriented database created in Neo4J. To visualize the ontology, we chose to use the interrogation and visualization mechanisms Neo4J provides. The native characteristics of this system, similarly to other graph-oriented database management systems, allows for receiving and exploring easily structures like ontologies [40]. In Fig. 6, we show a fragment of the ontology graph that was generated, revealing four remedy nodes and their ingredients.

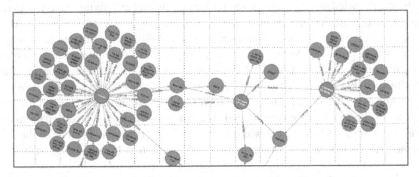

**Fig. 6.** A small view of the ontology create – ingredients segment

## 5  Conclusions and Future Work

The inception and implementation of ontology learning applications are not easy to perform. During the development of an ontology learning process a wide range of challenges raise, often creating barriers in textual data processing and problem solving tasks. However, today we have already available very specialized methods and tools that simplify a lot the process of establishing and characterizing an ontology based on knowledge extracted form texts. During the last few years, the evolution of these techniques and tool was extraordinary. Semiautomatic extraction of ontologies has great advantages when we have to deal with a large number and volume of textual data, whose treatment would not be viable with a manual approach. Automatic approaches allow for reducing the time of knowledge analysis and extraction, contributing to the reduction of the cost of the process of creating an ontology, especially in terms of human resources. However, they are not easy to apply, requiring often the use of very complex tools that require the intervention of experts of natural language processing, text mining and machine learning. Moreover, the nature of the texts, especially the content, text formats, type of writing and vocabulary used, requires a lot of work for configuring, training and tuning, in particular, the algorithms responsible for the extraction of concepts and their relationships, as well as of its subsequent characterization and semantic enrichment.

In fact, in our application case, the main challenge was placed by the nature of the texts, as they were written in classical Portuguese, using a type of writing and vocabulary that we do not use today. This makes the preparation of texts very demanding, both in terms of time, computational resources and expertise in the field of knowledge represented in the texts - XVI-XVII century's remedies recipes, collected by Portuguese during the time of the discoveries. After this phase, the ontology learning process was executed regularly. We adopted a regular work configuration, and iteratively we did all the necessary knowledge extraction tasks (concepts, relationships and axioms). As we going discovered ontological structures, we were also correcting and improving extraction mechanisms, having particular emphasis on lexical-syntactic patterns, refining the process gradually. The current version of ontology, although not complete, reflects adequately the knowledge contained in the recipes of medicines, giving a very concrete image of what remedies contain and represent. Analyzing the texts processed and the results we got, it was possible to demonstrate the reliability and usefulness of the ontology the system provided. Now, we need to incorporate all the remedies texts we had access, extending current ontological elements as well as the representation spectrum of the domain's knowledge. Throughout the various remedies' recipes, we have verified the sporadic existence of new knowledge representation patterns. To treat and incorporate them in the process, we would need to define new lexicon-syntactic patterns for capturing and representing the knowledge gathered using them. This will be studied and implemented in a new version of our ontological system for old remedies recipes.

**Acknowledgements.** This work has been supported by FCT – Fundação para a Ciência e Tecnologia within the R&D Units Project Scope: UIDB/00319/2020.

# References

1. Guarino, N., Oberle, D., Staab, S.: What Is an Ontology? In: Staab, S., Studer, R. (eds.) Handbook on Ontologies. IHIS, pp. 1–17. Springer, Heidelberg (2009). https://doi.org/10. 1007/978-3-540-92673-3_0
2. Keet, M.: An Introduction to Ontology Engineering, University of Cape Town (2018). https:// people.cs.uct.ac.za/~mkeet/OEbook/. Accessed 15 Oct 2022
3. El Kadiri, S., Terkaj, W., Urwin, E.N., Palmer, C., Kiritsis, D., Young, R.: Ontology in engineering applications. In: Cuel, R., Young, R. (eds.) FOMI 2015. LNBIP, vol. 225, pp. 126–137. Springer, Cham (2015). https://doi.org/10.1007/978-3-319-21545-7_11
4. Noy, N., Mcguinness, D.: Ontology Development 101: A Guide to Creating Your First Ontology. Knowl. Syst. Lab. **32** (2001)
5. Drumond, L., Girardi, R.: A survey of ontology learning procedures. In: Proceedings of the 3rd Workshop on Ontologies and their Applications, Salvador, Bahia, Brazil, October 26 2008
6. Cimiano, P., Mädche, A., Staab, S., Völker, J.: Ontology Learning. In: Staab, S., Studer, R. (eds.) Handbook on Ontologies. IHIS, pp. 245–267. Springer, Heidelberg (2009). https://doi. org/10.1007/978-3-540-92673-3_11
7. Asim, M., Wasim, M., Khan, M., Mahmood, W., Abbasi, H.: A survey of ontology learning techniques and applications. Database **2018**, 1758–0463 (2018). https://doi.org/10.1093/dat abase/bay101
8. Wong, W., Liu, W., Bennamoun, M.: Ontology learning from text. ACM Comput. Surv. **44**(4), 1–36 (2012). https://doi.org/10.1145/2333112.2333115
9. Biemann, C.: Ontology learning from text: a survey of methods. LDV Forum **10**, 75–93 (2005)
10. Belhoucine, K.: Mourchid, pp. 113–123. M, A Survey on Methods of Ontology Learning from Text (2020)
11. Hearst, M.: Automatic acquisition of hyponyms from large text corpora. In: Proceedings of the Fourteenth International Conference on Computational Linguistics, Nantes France, July 1992. https://doi.org/10.3115/992133.992154
12. Barros, A.: As receitas de cozinha de um frade português do século XVI, com Prefácio de Raquel Seiça e Colaboração de Joana Veloso e Micaela Aguiar. Coimbra: Imprensa da Universidade de Coimbra, jun 2013

13. Barros, A.: Remédios vários e receitas aprovadas. Segredos vários - Edição semidiplomática e edição interpretativa do Caderno II do manuscrito 142 do Arquivo Distrital de Braga. Imprensa da Universidade de Coimbra / Fundação Calouste Gulbenkian, dec 2016. https://doi.org/10.14195/978-989-26-1282-9

14. Barros, A.: Remédios vários e receitas aprovadas (ms. 142 do Arquivo Distrital de Braga): entre a História da Medicina e a História da Língua, a Ecdótica. In: As Humanidades e as Ciências: Disjunções e Confluências. XV Colóquio de Outono, Publisher: Húmus & Centro de Estudos Humanísticos da Universidade do Minho, Eds Macedo, A., Sousa, C., Moura, V., 2014

15. Chandrasekaran, B., Josephson, J., Benjamins, V.: What are ontologies, and why do we need them? IEEE Intell. Syst. 14(1), 20–26 (1999). https://doi.org/10.1109/5254.747902

16. Uschold, M., Gruninger, M.: Ontologies : Principles , methods and applications Ontologies : Principles, Methods and Applications Mike Uschold Michael Gruninger AIAI-TR-191 February 1996 To appear in Knowledge Engineering Review. vol. 11 no. 2, June 1996 Mike Uschold Tel : Mi. Knowledge Engineering Review (1996)

17. Borst, W.: Construction of engineering ontologies for knowledge sharing and reuse. Twente, sep 1997

18. Gruber, T.R.: Toward principles for the design of ontologies used for knowledge sharing? Int. J. Hum Comput Stud. 43(5–6), 907–928 (1995). https://doi.org/10.1006/ijhc.1995.1081

19. Tiwari, S., Jain, S.: Automatic ontology acquisition and learning. Int. J. Res. Eng. Technol. 03(26), 38–43 (2014). https://doi.org/10.15623/ijret.2014.0326008

20. Sharma, A.: Natural language processing and sentiment analysis. Int. Res. J. Comput. Sci. 8(10), 237 (2021). https://doi.org/10.26562/irjcs.2021.v0810.001

21. Maheswari, M.: Text Mining: survey on techniques and applications. Int. J. Sci. Res. (IJSR) 6(6), 1660–1664 (2017)

22. Zhang, L., Wang, S., Liu, B.: Deep learning for sentiment analysis: a survey. WIREs Data Min. Knowl. Discov. 8(4), e1253 (2018). https://doi.org/10.1002/widm.1253

23. Jones, D., Bench-Capon, T., Visser, P.: Methodologies for Ontology Development (1998)

24. Cristani, M., Cuel, R.: A survey on ontology creation methodologies. Int. J. Semant. Web Inf. Syst. 1(2), 49–69 (2005). https://doi.org/10.4018/jswis.2005040103

25. Uschold, M., Gruninger, M.: Ontologies: principles, methods and applications. Knowl. Eng. Rev. 11(2), 93–136 (1996). https://doi.org/10.1017/S0269888900007797

26. Cecilia Reyes-Peña, C., Tovar-Vidal, M.: Ontology: components and evaluation, a review. Res. Comput. Sci. 148(3), 257–265 (2019). https://doi.org/10.13053/rcs-148-3-21

27. Brank, J., Grobelnik, M., Mladenic, D.: A survey of ontology evaluation techniques. In: Proceedings of the Conference on Data Mining and Data Warehouses (SiKDD 2005), Ljubljana, Jan 2005

28. Maedche, A., Staab, S.: Ontology learning for the semantic web. IEEE Intell. Syst. 16(2), 72–79 (2001). https://doi.org/10.1109/5254.920602

29. Brewster, C.: Ontology Learning from Text: Methods, Evaluation and Applications. Buitelaar, P., Cimiano, P., Magnini, B. (eds.), (DFKI Saarbrücken, University of Karlsruhe, and ITC-irst), Amsterdam: IOS Press (Frontiers in artificial intelligence and appl. Computational Linguistics, 32(4), 569–572 (2006). https://doi.org/10.1162/coli.2006.32.4.569

30. El Ghosh, M., Naja, H., Abdulrab, H., Khalil, M.: Ontology Learning Process as a Bottom-up Strategy for Building Domain-specific Ontology from Legal Texts. In: Proceedings of the 9th International Conference on Agents and Artificial Intelligence, pp. 473–480. SCITEPRESS - Science and Technology Publications, Jan 2017. https://doi.org/10.5220/0006188004730480

31. Hawthorne, J.: Inductive Logic. The Stanford Encyclopedia of Philosophy (Spring Edition), Edward N. Zalta (ed.) (2021)

32. Rabiner, L, Juang, B.: An introduction to hiden markov models. IEEE ASSP Mag. 3(1), 4–16 (1986)

33. Honnibal, M., Montani, I.: spaCy Industrial-strength Natural Language Processing in Python (2017). https://spacy.io/api. Accessed 07 Oct 2022
34. Bird, S.: NLTK: the natural language toolkit. In: Proceedings of ACL 2006, 21st International Conference on Computational Linguistics and 44th Annual Meeting of the Association for Computational Linguistics, Australia, 17–21 July 2006. https://doi.org/10.3115/1225403.122 5421
35. Gyorodi, C., Gyorodi, R., Pecherle, G., Olah, A.: A comparative study: MongoDB vs. MySQL. In: 2015 13th International Conference on Engineering of Modern Electric Systems (EMES), pages 1–6. IEEE, jun 2015. https://doi.org/10.1109/EMES.2015.7158433
36. Freitas, M.: Quental, pp. 1585–1594. V, Subsídios para a Elaboração Automática de Taxonomias (2007)
37. Baségio, T.: Uma Abordagem Semi-automática para Identificação de Estruturas Ontológicas a partir de Textos na Língua Portuguesa do Brasil Uma abordagem Semi-Automática para Identificação de Estruturas Ontológicas a partir de Textos na Língua Portuguesa do Brasil. pages 1–124 (2007)
38. Taba, L.: Medeiros, pp. 2739–2746. C, Automatic semantic relation extraction from Portuguese texts (2014)
39. Machado, P., Strube de Lima, V.: Extração de relações hiponímicas em um corpus de língua portuguesa, Revista de Estudos da Linguagem 23(3):599, December 2015. https://doi.org/10.17851/2237-2083.23.3.599-640
40. López, F., De La Cruz, E.: Literature review about Neo4j graph database as a feasible alternative for replacing RDBMS. Ind. Data 18(2), 135–139 (2015). https://doi.org/10.15381/idata.v18i2.12106

# A Novel Oversampling Technique
# for Imbalanced Credit Scoring Datasets

Sudhansu Ranjan Lenka[1]([✉]), Sukant Kishoro Bisoy[1], Rojalina Priyadarshini[1],
and Jhalak Hota[2]

[1] Computer Science and Engineering, C.V. Raman Global University, Bhubaneswar, India
sudhansulenka2000@gmail.com
[2] KIIT University, Bhubaneswar, India
jhalak.hotafcs@kiit.ac.in

**Abstract.** The imbalanced class distribution of credit-scoring datasets typically makes the learning algorithms ineffective. In this study, NOSTE is proposed, a novel oversampling technique. It first identifies the informative minority instances by eliminating the noisy samples from the minority subset. Then, weight is assigned to the informative minority instances by considering the density and distance factors. Finally, new minority instances are created by determining the average of two different minority instances to make the dataset balanced. In the experimental study, NOSTE performance is validated by conducting an extensive comparison with four popular oversampling methods using three credit-scoring datasets from the UCI repository. The results confirmed that the proposed method brings significant improvement in the classification in terms of F-measure and AUC (Area under the Curve).

**Keywords:** Credit Scoring · Imbalance Class Distribution · Noisy Samples · Oversampling · Classification

## 1 Introduction

In the financial world, credit risk has gained tremendous importance for the growth and sustainability of organizations. The main task of credit risk is to identify the credit defaulters. Through the credit scoring model, banks access the creditworthiness of the applicants before approving their loan applications [1, 2]. Credit scoring is a binary classification problem where the applicants are classified as bad credit or good credit. In financial industries, most of the applicants are good as they repay the loan amount, but very few are bad as they are unable or unwilling to repay the loan amount [3]. Imbalanced data distribution is a condition where the number of positive (or minority) class instances is significantly lowered as compared to that of negative (or majority) class instances. The class distributions in the credit scoring problem are imbalanced, where the number of default applicants is significantly lower than that of non-defaulters [3]. Due to this significant difference in the class distribution, the classifiers are unable to learn

S. Nandan Mohanty et al. (Eds.): ICISML 2022, LNICST 471, pp. 147–157, 2023.
https://doi.org/10.1007/978-3-031-35081-8_12

the minority samples, which makes them more biased towards the majority samples. In such conditions, the overall accuracy of the model is high, but it often misclassifies the minority samples. This misclassification rate significantly increases the economic losses for the banks and financial industries [4].

The resampling technique is one of the common approaches widely used to alter the class distribution of the training set and then the balanced set is used to train the classification models. The resampling method either increases the minority class instances (oversampling) or decreases the majority class instances (under-sampling). Traditional oversampling methods have certain limitations, their approach is synthesized based [5–8]. The most popular oversampling is Synthetic Minority Oversampling Technique (SMOTE) [5]. It generates new samples along the line segment of two randomly selected neighboring minority instances. SMOTE method may pick the noisy samples during new instance generation as a result more noisy samples may get introduced into the dataset. Due to this limitation, different variants of SMOTE have been proposed, such as Borderline-SMOTE (BSMOTE) [7], Adaptive Synthetic Sampling (ADASYN) [6], and Safe-Level-SMOTE (SSMOTE) [9]. Each of these variations uses the k-nearest neighbor (KNN) algorithm to generate new samples by linear interpolation of neighboring samples, but in each method, different approaches are implemented to select the source minority samples. For SMOTE and their variants, we set the number of nearest neighbors, k = 5.

In this study, NOSTE a novel oversampling method has been proposed, whose goal is to make the imbalanced class distribution balanced by generating synthetic minority instances along the line segment of two dissimilar minority instances. The proposed method is very different from the conventional oversampling methods because it generates synthetic instances by computing the average of two dissimilar minority instances. As a result, the newly generated instances are very unique and evenly distributed within the region of minority class samples.

The remaining part of the paper is outlined as follows: Section 2 presents the related work of imbalanced learning approaches. The proposed work method and the algorithm are discussed in Sect. 3. Section 4 presents the experimental setup considering four factors: credit scoring datasets, classifiers, resampling methods, and evaluation metrics. Result analysis has been discussed in Sect. 5 and finally, the conclusion is presented in Sect. 6.

## 2 Literature Review

In many real-world applications, the uneven distribution of instances in each class is a common issue. The most common methods to deal with these imbalanced class distribution issues are the data level, the algorithm level, and the cost-sensitive methods. In this paper, we have applied the data-level method for oversampling. Therefore, we discuss only the data-level methods in this section.

### a. The Data-level Methods

These methods implement different methods in the pre-processing step to make the training set balanced. Resamplings are the most common and effective methods used to handle the imbalanced ratio either by generating synthetic samples (oversampling) [10], or by removing samples (under-sampling) [11] from the dataset. The resampling method balances the dataset, which improves the performance of the traditional classifiers [12]. The undersampling method is useful when the dataset is very large because the loss of information due to the elimination of majority class instances is marginal [13]. In this study, we employed small-sized imbalanced credit-scoring datasets, therefore only oversampling methods are discussed. Oversampling methods balance the class distributions by simply duplicating the existing minority instances, and it may lead to overfitting [14]. SMOTE is a popular oversampling technique, in which for each minority instance, K-nearest neighbors are identified to generate new samples through interpolation [5]. However, SMOTE may suffer from over-generalization. To overcome this over-generalization issue, different variants of SMOTE have been proposed, such as Borderline_SMOTE, Safe-level SMOTE, and ADASYN. Borderline-SMOTE generates new minority samples by interpolating the instances located near the decision boundary. Safe-level SMOTE defines the 'safe level' for each minority instance, and generates new instances closer to this safe level. The safe level of a minority instance is computed by finding the number of other minority instances in its neighborhood. ADASYN method oversamples the instances by assigning more weights to the minority instances that have more number of majority instances in their neighborhood, and thus instances are used in the oversampling. The synthetic instances generated by these methods may overlap with the majority class region, and this may lead to an increase in the misclassification rate of the majority class instances [15]. Another drawback of these methods is that they may generate new instances that are very similar to the existing instances. For example, when $k = 1$, then two very similar instances are used in the sample generation process, which results in the generation of duplicate instances. Additionally, the SMOTE-based methods may not be effective if noisy samples are not properly handled before training.

## 3   Proposed Model

The objective of the proposed oversampling method is to generate new minority instances by averaging two minority instances, not necessarily close to each other. The newly generated sample carries the properties of both instances, rather than simply duplicating the instances that are involved in the oversampling process. The proposed oversampling method, NOSTE involves three basic phases: elimination of noisy minority samples, determination of the weights of each minority instance, and generation of synthetic instances. Algorithm-1 presents the detailed process of NOSTE, in which the first phase is described in step 1, the second phase in steps 2 to 6, and Algorithm-2 describes the final phase. Each phase is discussed in the following sub-sections.

### 3.1   Elimination of Noise Points from Minority Instances

Let $T_{min}$ and $T_{maj}$ represents the minority and majority class subset, respectively. All the minority class instances do not carry equal importance because there may be some noisy points in $T_{min}$. It is, therefore, required to eliminate the noisy samples from $T_{min}$. A minority instance can be treated as a noisy point if it is located in the majority class region, i.e. its nearest neighbor set contains only majority class instances. For each $x_i \in T_{min}$, compute its k1- nearest neighbor $NN(x_i)$ using Euclidean distance, and a point $x_i$ is considered as noisy if $NN(x_i)$ includes only the majority class instances. The informative minority instance set, $T_{imin}$ is defined as:

$$T_{imin} = T_{min} - \{x_i \in T_{min} \text{ and } NN(x_i) \text{ contains only the majority class instances}\} \tag{1}$$

## 3.2 Determine the Weights of the Informative Minority Instances

The instances that are selected in the previous sub-sections may not have equal importance to be used to generate the synthetic instances because some of them may have different discriminative capabilities in the classification process. These differences should be taken into consideration while performing oversampling. In this study, for each $x_i \in T_{imin}$, two factors: density and distance are considered for assigning weights to it. The density factor of $x_i$ is computed by determining the proportion of majority instances present in its k2-nearest neighbors set, i.e.

$$C(x_i) = \frac{|NN_{maj}(x_i)|}{k2} \tag{2}$$

where $|NN_{maj}(x_i)|$ defines the number of majority instances in $NN(x_i)$.

The distance factor of $x_i$ is computed by taking the ratio of the sum of its distances to the majority class instances in its nearest neighbor set to the sum of its distances to all the instances in its nearest neighbor set, i.e.

$$D(x_i) = \frac{\sum_{x_j \in NN_{maj}(x_i)} dist(x_i, x_j)}{\sum_{x_j \in NN(x_i)} dist(x_i, x_j)} \tag{3}$$

where $dist(x_i, x_j)$ defines the Euclidean distance between $x_i$ and $x_j$.

Based on these two factors the weights are assigned to each informative minority instance. For each $x_i \in T_{imin}$ the weight is defined as:

$$W(x_i) = C(x_i) + D(x_i) \tag{4}$$

These weights are used in the next phase to generate the synthetic instances.

## 3.3 The Synthetic Instance Generation Phase

In this phase, the informative minority instances $T_{imin}$ are sequentially arranged based on their weights in decreasing order. Then, the minority instances are partitioned into two halves, such that the first half includes the instances having weights greater than or equal to that of the middle instance, while the second part comprises the remaining instances. The two partitions are defined as:

$$\text{Partition 1} = (x_1, x_2, \cdots, x_{n/2}) \text{ and Partition 2} = (x_{n/2+1}, x_{n/2+2}, \cdots, x_n) \tag{5}$$

where $x_i \in T_{imin}$ and $n = |T_{imin}|$

The instances within the two groups are sequentially labeled, i.e.

$$\text{partition } 1\{label(x_i) = l_i, \text{ for } i = 1, 2, \cdots n/2\} \text{ and}$$
$$partition\, 2\{label(x_i) = l_{i-n/2}, for\ i = n/2 + 1, n/2 + 2, \cdots n\} \tag{6}$$

Two instances $x_a$ and $x_b$ having the same label $l_i$ are picked from partition1 and partition2, respectively. The new instance is generated by computing the mean of $x_a$ and $x_b$, i.e.

$$x_{new} = (x_a + x_b)/2 \tag{7}$$

The same process is repeated for the remaining instances in sequential order and to each new instance, the same label is assigned as that of their parents. The new minority instances are added to the informative minority instance set, which can be further used to generate the new instances. Algorithm 2 presents the descriptions of the synthetic instance generation phase.

Figure 1 shows the detailed procedure of the synthetic instance generation of minority instances. Node $M_1$ and $M_2$ represents the partitions of the borderline minority instances and $C_{li}$ represents the set of synthetic instances generated at each level. In level 0, the synthetic minority instance set $C_{01}$ are generated by sequentially pairing the instances of $M_1$ and $M_2$. In the next level, new instance sets $C_{11}$ and $C_{12}$ are generated by first pairing the instances from the set $M_1$ and $C_{01}$ and later from the set $M_2$ and $C_{01}$, respectively. Consequently, in each level, new instances are generated by pairing the instances of the previous two levels. If each set contains n instances, then in each level $l_i$ it can generate maximum $2^{l_i} \times n$ instances and depending on the imbalances ratio more instances can be generated by pairing the newly generated instances with the previous level instances and the process is repeated until the number of borderline minority instances becomes equal to the number of majority instances. For example in level 2, two sets $C_{22}$ and $C_{23}$ are generated by respectively pairing $(C_{01}, C_{11})$ and $(C_{01}, C_{12})$ sets, and if required more instances can be generated by pairing $(C_{12}, M_1)$ and $(C_{11}, M_2)$ sets.

This method of oversampling ensures that the new instances do not overlap the majority class region. Additionally, the new instances must reside within the boundary of the minority class and also helps to fill the space between the paired instances. The proposed oversampling method generates distinct and unique instances but is related to the paired instances of both partitions, unlike SMOTE algorithm, which oversamples the minority instances by using k-nearest neighbors and the new instances may overlap with majority instances if the neighbors are not closely located. Another advantage of the proposed method over the k-nearest neighbor methods is that the latter method tends to generate synthetic instances in a cluster within the minority class instances and may increase the length of the minority class boundary, thus unable to provide more informative information to the classifier, but the former method generates new instances that are evenly distributed within the convex hull of the minority class instances, thus helps to train the classifier more effectively.

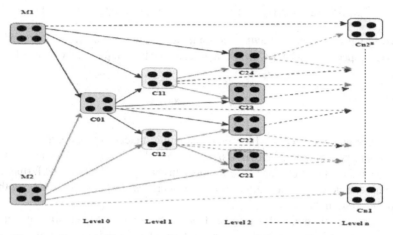

**Fig. 1.** Illustrates the synthetic instance generation process by pairing the previous levels samples

---

**Algorithm 1:** The proposed NOSTE algorithm

**Input:** Imbalanced training set, $T = T_{maj} \cup T_{min}, k1, k2$

**Output:** Balanced training set, $T_{bal}$

**Procedure Begin**

1.  Select the informative minority instances, $T_{imin}$ using Eq.1
2.  for each $x_i \in T_{imin}$ do
3.      Compute the density factor, $C(x_i)$ using Eq.2
4.      Compute the distance factor, $D(x_i)$ using Eq.3
5.      Compute the weights, $W(x_i)$ using Eq.4
6.  end for

7.  Generate synthetic minority instances, $T_{gmin}$ using **Algorithm 2**
8.  $T_{bal} = T_{maj} \cup T_{gmin}$
9.  return $T_{bal}$

**End**

---

**Algorithm 2:** Generation of synthetic minority instances

---

**Input:** $W(\cdot)$ and $T_{imin}$

**Output:** Synthetic minority instances, $T_{gmin}$

**Procedure Begin**

1. Sort the weights of each n informative minority instance in decreasing order.
2. Find the middle instance, $mid = n/2$
3. Divide $T_{imin}$ into partition1 and partition2 using Eq.5
4. To each instance of both the partitions, sequentially unique labels are assigned using Eq. 6.
5. Determine the oversampling size, $T = |T_{maj}| - |T_{imin}|$
6. $C = 0$
7. $T_{new} = \{\}$
8. for $i = 1, \cdots n$ do
9.     Select $x_a$ and $x_b$ from parition1 and partition2, respectively, such that $label(x_a) = label(x_b)$.
10.    Generate new minority instance x using Eq.7
11.    $T_{new} = T_{new} \cup \{x\}$
12.    $C = C + 1$
       end for
13. If $C < T$, pair the instances of the new set $T_{new}$ with the instances of both the partitions and repeat steps 8-12. If still $C < T$, then pair the instances of the current $T_{new}$ with the immediate previous level and later with the predecessor levels and for each subsequent level repeat steps 8- 12.
14. If $C \geq T$, then $T_{gmin} = T_{imin} \cup \{T_{new}\}$
15. return $T_{gmin}$

End

---

## 4   Experimental Study

The main objective of our work is to improve the performance level of the learning algorithms on imbalanced datasets by implementing the proposed oversampling method. To validate the effectiveness of NOSTE, a comparative analysis is performed with different popular resampling methods, such as SMOTE, BSMOTE, ADASYN, Random oversampling (ROS), and no oversampling (NONE).

## 4.1 Datasets

For experimental comparisons, three credit-scoring datasets are used. Table 1 presents brief descriptions of the datasets. The imbalanced credit scoring datasets are collected from two sources. German and Australian credit datasets are sourced from the UCI repository and the Giveme credit dataset is obtained from the Kaggle competition named "Give me some credits".

**Table 1.** Brief descriptions of credit scoring datasets

| Datasets | No. of instances | Imbalanced Ratio |
|----------|------------------|------------------|
| German | 1000 | 2.33 |
| Australian | 690 | 1.25 |
| Giveme | 150000 | 13.9 |

## 4.2 Experimental Design

**Classifier**
In the experiment, four classification algorithms were implemented to show the validity of the results, which are CART Decision Tree (DT), Naïve Bayes (NB), Support Vector Machine (SVM), and Logistic regression (LR). All the algorithms with their default parameters were implemented using the Scikit-learn. The experiments were conducted using 5-fold cross-validation and the process is repeated three times, a total of 15 experiments were conducted and the final result is obtained by averaging each of them.

**Performance Metrics**
In the experiment, F-measure and AUC metrics are used to evaluate the performance of the methods. These two metrics are widely used in the field of binary imbalanced datasets [13]. The performance metrics are defined using four types of classifications, i.e. true positive (TP), true negative (TN), false positive (FP), and false negative (FN). For the definition of these metrics refer to the paper [13].

## 5   Results Analysis

The comparison of NOSTE with other resampling methods is discussed in this section. The average values of F-measure and AUC over all three credit scoring datasets and implementing all four classification algorithms are presented in Table 2 and Table 3. The results and the ranks within the parenthesis of all four resampling methods and without resampling are presented. Additionally, the mean ranks of each method are shown in the last row. The bold fonts indicate the method that performs best for a particular dataset. The results exhibit that NOSTE performs best values in terms of both F-measure and AUC with an average rank of 1.33 and 1.75, respectively.

**Table 2.** Performance of F-measure for different resampling methods

| Dataset | Classification Models | NONE | ROS | SMOTE | ADASYN | BSMOTE | NOSTE |
|---|---|---|---|---|---|---|---|
| German | LR | 58.41(6) | 73.64(2) | 72.84(4) | 72.39(5) | 73.62(3) | **74.54(1)** |
| | SVM | 48.27(6) | 63.57(4) | 65.27(2) | 64.86(3) | 63.49(5) | **66.71(1)** |
| | DT | 51.12(5) | **53.33(1)** | 52.48(3) | 48.61(6) | 52.77(2) | 52.28(4) |
| | NB | 69.38(2) | 67.87(3) | 65.08(5) | 64.12(6) | 65.11(4) | **70.24(1)** |
| Australian | LR | 83.48(3) | 82.76(5) | 83.33(4) | 84.29(2) | 82.70(6) | **85.64(1)** |
| | SVM | 80.89(3) | 79.93(6) | 80.76(4) | 81.32(2) | 80.33(5) | **82.75(1)** |
| | DT | 77.47(5) | 78.84(4) | **83.56(1)** | 78.99(3) | 75.64(6) | 79.84(2) |
| | NB | 74.51(3) | 73.26(6) | 74.88(2) | 73.52(4) | 73.33(5) | **75.89(1)** |
| Giveme | LR | 20.76(6) | 35.82(3) | 35.46(4) | 30.75(5) | 36.51(2) | **37.24(1)** |
| | SVM | 17.12(6) | 33.52(4) | 34.13(3) | 32.72(5) | 35.17(2) | **34.58(1)** |
| | DT | 23.01(6) | 24.89(3) | 24.12(4) | 23.18(5) | 25.91(2) | **32.25(1)** |
| | NB | 34.43(3) | 36.85(2) | 24.72(4) | 19.36(5) | 17.85(6) | **42.25(1)** |
| Mean Ranking | | 4.5 | 3.58 | 3.33 | 4.25 | 4.00 | **1.33** |

**Table 3.** Performance of AUC for different resampling methods

| Dataset | Classification Models | NONE | ROS | SMOTE | ADASYN | BSMOTE | NOSTE |
|---|---|---|---|---|---|---|---|
| German | LR | 70.09(6) | 74.86(4) | 78.59(2) | 78.38(3) | 73.62(5) | **80.12(1)** |
| | SVM | 65.33(6) | 70.52(5) | 72.74(2) | 72.25(3) | 71.52(4) | **73.58(1)** |
| | DT | 62.47(4) | 64.41(2) | 63.14(3) | 48.61(6) | 52.77(5) | **66.24(1)** |
| | NB | 72.22(5) | 70.23(6) | 77.53(2) | 74.24(3) | 73.42(4) | **78.27(1)** |
| Australian | LR | 85.75(3) | 84.64(5) | 85.76(2) | **86.48(1)** | 83.51(6) | 85.47(4) |
| | SVM | 83.41(4) | 82.01(6) | 83.68(2) | 83.51(3) | 82.86(5) | **84.78(1)** |
| | DT | 80.89(5) | 83.29(2) | 82.55(3) | 81.76(4) | 78.79(6) | **85.26(1)** |
| | NB | **79.01(1)** | 78.14(5) | 78.05(6) | 78.34(4) | 78.91(2) | 78.59(3) |
| Giveme | LR | 56.01(6) | 74.19(3) | 74.51(2) | 73.91(4) | 73.84(5) | **75.89(1)** |
| | SVM | 54.75(6) | **74.75(1)** | 74.44(2) | 74.12(4) | 74.39(3) | 73.28(5) |
| | DT | 62.16(5) | 59.94(6) | 63.39(2) | 62.38(3) | 62.23(4) | **64.74(1)** |
| | NB | 69.42(6) | 70.65(3) | 71.26(2) | 69.45(4) | 68.38(5) | **74.56(1)** |
| Mean Ranking | | 4.75 | 4 | 2.5 | 3.5 | 4.5 | **1.75** |

# 6 Conclusion and Future Work

Analyzing the drawbacks of the SMOTE-based oversampling techniques, a novel over-sampling technique NOSTE is proposed to handle the highly-imbalanced credit scoring datasets. The main advantages of the proposed method as compared to the SMOTE-based methods are that: 1) using k-nearest neighbors algorithms the noisy samples are removed from the minority subset, 2) generate diverged and unique minority instances that are evenly distributed within the convex hull of the minority instances, and 3) new minority instances do not overlap the majority class region.

In the experiments, we compare the performance of NOSTE with other popular oversampling techniques. The obtained results show that NOSTE has better ranks than other methods in terms of F_measure and AUC.

In the future study, we intend to apply fuzzy c-means clustering and select the representative minority instances from each sub-cluster to be used in the oversampling process. We are also interested to implement our work in multi-class problems.

# References

1. Luo, C., Wu, D., Wu, D.: A deep learning approach for credit scoring using credit default swaps. Eng. Appl. Artif. Intell. **65**(December), 465–470 (2017). https://doi.org/10.1016/j.eng appai.2016.12.002
2. Sun, J., Lang, J., Fujita, H., Li, H.: Imbalanced enterprise credit evaluation with DTE-SBD: decision tree ensemble based on SMOTE and bagging with differentiated sampling rates. Inf. Sci. (N Y) **425**, 76–91 (2018). https://doi.org/10.1016/j.ins.2017.10.017
3. Brown, I., Mues, C.: An experimental comparison of classification algorithms for imbalanced credit scoring data sets. Expert Syst. Appl. **39**(3), 3446–3453 (2012). https://doi.org/10.1016/j.eswa.2011.09.033
4. Xiao, J., Cao, H., Jiang, X., Gu, X., Xie, L.: GMDH-based semi-supervised feature selection for customer classification. Knowl. Based Syst. **132**, 236–248 (2017). https://doi.org/10.1016/j.knosys.2017.06.018
5. Chawla, N.V., Bowyer, K.W., Hall, L.O., Kegelmeyer, W.P.: SMOTE: synthetic minority over-sampling technique. J. Artif. Intell. Res. **16**, 321–357 (2002). https://doi.org/10.1613/jair.953
6. He, H., Bai, Y., Garcia, E.A., Li, S.: ADASYN: adaptive synthetic sampling approach for imbalanced learning. In: Proceedings of the International Joint Conference on Neural Networks, no. 3, pp. 1322–1328 (2008). https://doi.org/10.1109/IJCNN.2008.4633969
7. Han, H., Wang, W.-Y., Mao, B.-H.: Borderline-SMOTE: a new over-sampling method in imbalanced data sets learning. In: Huang, D.-S., Zhang, X.-P., Huang, G.-B. (eds.) ICIC 2005. LNCS, vol. 3644, pp. 878–887. Springer, Heidelberg (2005). https://doi.org/10.1007/11538059_91
8. Barua, S., Islam, M.M., Yao, X., Murase, K.: MWMOTE - majority weighted minority over-sampling technique for imbalanced data set learning. IEEE Trans. Knowl. Data Eng. **26**(2), 405–425 (2014). https://doi.org/10.1109/TKDE.2012.232
9. Bunkhumpornpat, C., Sinapiromsaran, K., Lursinsap, C.: Safe-Level-SMOTE: safe-level-synthetic minority over-sampling TEchnique for handling the class imbalanced problem. In: Theeramunkong, T., Kijsirikul, B., Cercone, N., Ho, T.-B. (eds.) PAKDD 2009. LNCS (LNAI), vol. 5476, pp. 475–482. Springer, Heidelberg (2009). https://doi.org/10.1007/978-3-642-01307-2_43

10. Douzas, G., Bacao, F.: Self-organizing map oversampling (SOMO) for imbalanced data set learning. Expert Syst. Appl. **82**, 40–52 (2017). https://doi.org/10.1016/j.eswa.2017.03.073
11. Lin, W.C., Tsai, C.F., Hu, Y.H., Jhang, J.S.: Clustering-based undersampling in class-imbalanced data. Inf. Sci. (N Y) **409–410**, 17–26 (2017). https://doi.org/10.1016/j.ins.2017.05.008
12. Krawczyk, B., Galar, M., Jeleń, Ł, Herrera, F.: Evolutionary undersampling boosting for imbalanced classification of breast cancer malignancy. Appl. Soft Comput. J. **38**, 714–726 (2016). https://doi.org/10.1016/j.asoc.2015.08.060
13. He, H., Garcia, E.A.: Learning from imbalanced data. IEEE Trans. Knowl. Data Eng. **21**(9), 1263–1284 (2009). https://doi.org/10.1109/TKDE.2008.239
14. Nekooeimehr, I., Lai-Yuen, S.K.: Adaptive semi-unsupervised weighted oversampling (A-SUWO) for imbalanced datasets. Expert Syst. Appl. **46**, 405–416 (2016). https://doi.org/10.1016/j.eswa.2015.10.031
15. Bennin, K.E., Keung, J., Phannachitta, P., Monden, A., Mensah, S.: MAHAKIL: diversity based oversampling approach to alleviate the class imbalance issue in software defect prediction. IEEE Trans. Software Eng. **44**(6), 534–550 (2018). https://doi.org/10.1109/TSE.2017.2731766

# A Blockchain Enabled Medical Tourism Ecosystem

Nihar Ranjan Pradhan[1]($\boxtimes$), Hitesh Kumar Sharma[2]($\boxtimes$), Tanupriya Choudhury[2]($\boxtimes$), Anurag Mor[2], and Shlok Mohanty[2]

[1] School of Computer Science and Engineering (SCOPE), VIT AP University, Vijayawada 522237, India
nihar.pradhan@vitap.ac.in

[2] School of Computer Science, University of Petroleum and Energy Studies (UPES), Dehradun, Uttarakhand 248007, India
hkshitesh@gmail.com, tanupriya@ddn.upes.ac.in

**Abstract.** Medical tourism is considered as a potential filed for high growth. There are several problems, including the possible ability of patient tourists to monitor critical elements of healthcare quality and professionals. In addition, patient-doctor confidence, process, openness of risks, privacy of the medical record and other threats associated with health in specific treatments come from queries. We study the possible benefits of Blockchain technology in this conceptual paper to answer several outstanding medical tourism concerns. We conclude that technology from Blockchain can serve as the basis for future study. Medical tourism. The four primary objectives that may be reached using Blockchain technology, namely to improve tourism experience, to reward sustainable behavior and to provide benefits for local communities, and to reduce worries about privacy, center on Smart Tourism Destinations. The report also discusses the main hurdles to deploy this new technology successfully. This study seeks to better improve existing understanding regarding blockchain technology's prospective ramifications within the smart tourism field, particular destinations for smart tourism. In this paper, we have provided the strong need of medical tourism and the significance of Blockchain in secured and reliable medical tourism. Medical record sharing on global platform is security concern for doctor and patients. Blockchain Technology can be silver bullet for enhancing medical tourism for Global medical treatment.

**Keywords:** Blockchain Technology · Privacy · Efficiency · Medical Tourism · Healthcare

---

N. R. Pradhan, H. K. Sharma and T. Choudhury—These authors are contributed equally.

# 1 Introduction

The 'sharing economy' also reduces local transit costs internationally, providing alternative, affordable lodging options. In the travel and tourism sectors, emerging technologies provide new consumer focused instruments [2]. The influence of technology is emphasized by tourism research and helps develop continuous initiatives to improve medical satisfaction.

Due to the demand for quick and affordable medical procedures during the past 20 years, medical tourism has gained in importance, appeal, and acceptance. Long public health wait times, high private health insurance premiums, low reimbursement rates, and a lack of local knowledge all contribute to this tendency. Along with life-saving surgeries like organ transplants, medical tourism also offers minor prosthesis and aesthetic procedures. Medical tourism positively affects economic growth in nearby industries including tourism, traffic, pharmaceuticals, and hospitality [1]. This emerging specialist industry aims to exceed passengers' high standards for service. The number of developing countries has increased, and the availability of services at affordable rates is expanding. Additionally, improved income accessibility, technology advancements, and rising competition (Fig. 1).

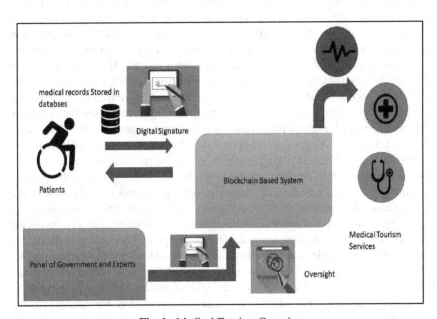

**Fig. 1.** Medical Tourism Overview

The promise of wellness systems, created by this ancient civilization's expertise over many ages, would be completely realised. This is accomplished through portraying India as a hub for spirituality, which has long been a part of Indian culture, as well as for Ayurveda, Yoga, Sidha, Naturopathy, etc. Guidelines for wellness tourism have been created by the ministry of tourism. These standards cover topics including providing high-quality advertising materials, educating and equipping service providers, taking part in national and international wellness-related events, etc. The proliferation of wellness facilities around the nation has increased demand for high-quality care. Medical tourism refers to the rapidly expanding practise of crossing international borders in search of healthcare services. It is also known as medical travel, health tourism, or global healthcare. Elective operations, complicated surgeries, etc. are frequently requested services by tourists. Many hospitals in India have access to cutting-edge medical and diagnostic technology from large international enterprises. The best nurses in the world come from India. Nearly 10,000 nurses are graduated each year from India's nearly 1000 accredited nurse training programmes, the majority of which are affiliated with teaching hospitals.

Blockchain's increased popularity is due to its capacity to build a credible network where the value of Blockchain may be shared. The technique has a broad range of applications across the industry. Academic academics and industrial practitioners that strive to resolve chronic issues in various fields are increasingly paying attention to Blockchain technology. While the influence of Blockchain is an important subject of research that might generate major alterations in the field of tourism, thorough research in its emerging field remains lacking [3]. The quick digitalization of health care is likely to have major consequences for healthcare services for medical tourists with the advent of Blockchain technology. For instance, medical tourism producers are struggling to convince potential clients of the quality and the security of medical centers. Transparency of a Blockchain is due to the fact that each public address is available to observing the holding and transaction.it cannot be amended while the data is kept in the ledger. You don't have the power to change things, no matter who you are. If an error occurs, the error should be reversed by a new transaction. Both transactions are apparent at that moment. In the recorded ledger, the first transaction is seen as a mistake. The confirmed transaction then contributes with additional transactions that create a new data block. If a person wants to give Blockchain information using a specific connection key and a public address, the transaction is signed with a private key. Transparency of a Blockchain is due to the fact that each public address is available to observing the holding and transaction.it cannot be amended while the data is kept in the ledger. You don't have the power to change things, no matter who you are. If an error occurs, the error should be reversed by a new transaction. Both transactions are apparent at that moment. In the recorded ledger, the first transaction is seen as a mistake. The confirmed transaction then contributes with additional transactions that create a new data block. If a person wants to give Blockchain information using a specific connection key and a public address, the transaction is signed with a private key. This type of information is very safe, because it doubles thousands of times and every hacker has to alter over 51% of nodes. Physical movement and transmission of medical information is fundamental requirement for medical tourism. Medical tourism is required for getting treatment from global expertise for the predicted disease.

## 2  Literature Review

Many authors have provided their literature for explaining the significance of Blockchain in medical tourism. In [1] authors have explained the need and availability of various smart healthcare systems in India. They have also explained the requirement of these types of remote medical services in India. In [2] authors have shared their concern about the privacy and security of patients Electronic Health Records (EHR) and the accessibility authentication of the users. They have proposed and implemented Blockchain based technology for securing Telemedicine systems. In [3–5] authors have commonly shared their advance implementation of blockchain based algorithm for user authentication of accessing these remote medical systems. They used the term Threefactor authentication for this security protocols.

Several centuries ago, there was medical tourism, which involved going overseas for medical treatment. Many Europeans visited isolated spas in the 18th and 19th centuries because they were thought to have health-improving qualities [16]. Yoga and Ayurveda are ancient healing practises that have drawn tourists from around the world seeking to enhance their health for more than 5000 years [17]. For more than a millennium, people have travelled to Japan's mineral springs for medicinal treatment [18]. As international travel becomes more and more common, an increasing number of people are doing so in order to get healthcare services.

The researchers conducted study on medical tourism from various angles and in a range of settings. One of the first academic studies in the area [19, 20], suggested that the idea of medical tourism may be exploited as a successful marketing tactic. Studies have made an effort to define the significance of medical travel.

## 3  E-Healthcare or Telemedicine System

Doctors, nurses, pharmacists, and patients can all access a variety of healthcare services through the e-Healthcare system, which is built on information and communication technology [11]. Usually, these services are provided online. Telemedicine, commonly referred to as tele-health or e-medicine, is the delivery of medical services remotely, such as examinations and consultations, using a telecommunications network [22–24]. With the help of telemedicine, medical practitioners can assess, identify, and treat patients without having to visit them in person. Patients can use personal equipment or visit a telehealth kiosk to consult doctors from the comfort of their homes [25, 26]. (Fig. 2).

Three broad categories can be used to categorize telemedicine:

- Dynamic telemedicine/telehealth: enables real-time communication between doctors and patients. These sessions can be held in a designated medical kiosk or at the patient's house. Conversations over the phone or the usage of HIPAA compliant video conferencing software are examples of interactions.
- Through the use of mobile devices that record information on a patient's temperature, blood sugar levels, blood pressure, and other vital indicators, remote patient monitoring, sometimes referred to as telemonitoring, enables patients to be observed in their homes [12, 27].
- One healthcare provider can transmit patient information, such as lab results, with another healthcare provider via store-and-forward, also referred to as asynchronous telemedicine [13].

AI & ML, Cloud Computing, IoT and Blockchain [28–31] these are some advanced technologies support the functionality of Telemedicine systems.

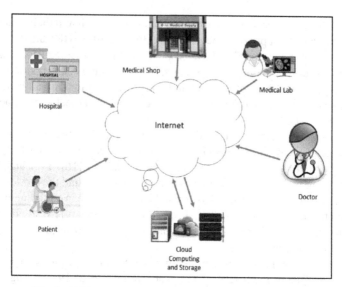

**Fig. 2.** E-Healthcare/Tele-Medicine System (Basic Model)

### 3.1 A. Significance of Cloud Computing in E-Healthcare

A wide range of technology and delivery methods are used in telehealth to provide virtual medical, health, and educational services. 1 Patients with long-term medical issues frequently receive support through telehealth. Both patients and clinicians can benefit from telehealth; it can assist patients in better managing and understanding longterm health conditions, and it can assist clinicians in monitoring their patients' health statuses and intervening as needed when potentially harmful trends or abnormal measurements are noticed (Fig. 2). A cloud computing concept called "cloud storage" places digital data on remote servers that are accessed through the Internet. A hosting provider like AWS (Amazon Web Services), Microsoft, or IBM owns and maintains the physical infrastructure. Along with offering complete data protection and availability, these providers are in charge of maintaining data and applications. Companies can use storage capacity they purchase or lease from suppliers to execute apps and store data.

### 3.2 Significance of Machine Learning in E-Healthcare

Large amounts of data are produced by the growing usage of information technology in healthcare and the digitization of patient data. Numerous systems store data in a variety of formats. The majority of health data about 80% is unstructured. The primary use of the data is the provision of healthcare services, along with planning, management, research, public health, and quality improvement (secondary use). Fast and automated manufacturing of machine-learning algorithms able to evaluate complicated data with precise findings is made possible by the combination of vast volumes of varied data, more computer power, and better approaches. It is necessary to protect the privacy of personal health information. Data must be sufficient, relevant, and limited to what is required to achieve the purposes for which it is processed, according to GDPR. Patients must be fully aware of the purpose behind data processing before they may decide whether or not to consent to the use of their data in an algorithm. The algorithm may make inaccurate predictions. Both overfitting and underfitting are typical causes of this. Because it has discovered random patterns in the training data rather than a larger pattern explaining the fluctuation, the algorithm underperforms on the fresh data when there is overfitting.

## 4 Medical Tourism

Public health care is frequently of fundamental importance in many nations, particularly in industrialized parts of the world, whereas private health insurance is expensive and may penalize those with medical problems that are already in place. With the worldwide technology gap being reduced, the price of medical care has become an important factor for changing medical travelers' patterns and flows. Moreover, numerous medical destinations respond to the "tourist-patients" growing need of inexpensive healthcare and achieve a competitive position and cost advantage in the worldwide market (Fig. 3).

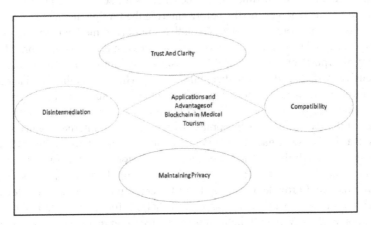

**Fig. 3.** Advantage of Medical Tourism

## 5 Blockchain Technology Potentials in the Field of Medical Tourism

We focus in this essay primarily on the aspects that might affect the field of medical tourism. Increasing demand for medical tourism has allowed medical intermediaries to act as mediators between global patients and suppliers of medical services In the medical tourism business traditional tourist companies retain a strong position, resulting in opportunist behavior. Instead of establishing strong links between medical institutions and patients, the function of the Medical Tourism Intermediaries led to a paternalistic relationship paradigm. These entities' medical tourism packages are typically supplied at high prices, characterized by healthcare providers' actual expenses. In addition, because of their affiliation to specialist medical providers they are sending their patients exclusively, medical middlemen are likely to restrict the available alternatives. Since they specialize in an objective or resource market, they might direct patients using nutrient supplementation and a high referral fee to inappropriate physicians. More problematic are these middlemen in medical tourism who are not actually medical professionals, as they are not legal responsible for any problems. The asymmetric influence of medical tourism intermediaries can be greatly reduced by Blockchain technology. Blockchain technology, for example, allows medical tourists to communicate directly with international healthcare professionals. This allows you to objectively check your credentials, certifications and procedure expenses. Therefore, the technology contains an unrealized potential to reveal new value since it lowers the imbalance between information and medical facility transparency [2, 15, 16]. The use of blockchain technology makes rational and well-informed judgments for potential health tourists. In this planning stage, prospective medical visitors might utilize blockchain-enabled systems, by getting extensive, authentic and verified information on institutions of medical tourism, to improve the search for medical services. This involves validated curriculum vitae of healthcare personnel, accreditation of institutions and certificates for services or procedures. This technique has two advantages: firstly, before entering the foreign medical system, it will improve the confidence of the traveler. Secondly, suppliers of medical tourism may create their brand capital from the outset and keep their consumer's consistent brand image. Blockchain incorporation into the health tourism sector can contribute to trustworthy, comprehensive medical and non-medical information. Throughout their social, cultural, or linguistic history, these systems can support medical tourists in making educated decision-making [2, 15]. The internet is an extension of Internet links to common physical objects. Internet of things Incorporated with electronics, internet connectivity and other physical forms, such gadgets may communicate with, interact with and monitor distant devices through the internet. Because of the rigorous IoT networking requirements, blockchain looks to be. Highly suitable for manipulative network assaults that target saved data and provide a safe platform for communication between devices on each other within the network. This paradigm is helpful for small-scale IoT networks, but it has poor scalability. Additionally, it is expensive to set up extensive IoT networks, maintain centralized clouds, and connect all the equipment. IoT devices must also be resistant to attacks on both the physical and informational levels. Although many of the currently used methods offer security for IoT systems, they are complex and inefficient for low-resource IoT devices. Discover the limitations of existing paradigms and what blockchain pledges leads to the paradigm of IoT-based e-health. Most of the presently used IoT networks depend on the client server architecture, which recognizes, authorizes and links to all devices through cloud server, and has enormous storage and processing capabilities. Moreover, even if the devices are adjacent to one other, all communication between these devices must be over the Internet.

# 6  Digitalization and Interoperability Improvement

As a consequence, online sharing of health information should not ignore interoperability, safety and privacy problems as part of the experience in medical tourism. Blockchain technology can give a full and thorough evaluation of an individual's health by enabling a patient-centric paradigm for information management. This may be done by actively tracking the full history of patients, through sophisticating health records record management and enhanced data access control. An ecosystem built on blockchain technology enables patients outside the world to maintain a higher level of health information control and to actively promote contact between their local and foreign health providers. Blockchain can thereby overcome major interoperability concerns inherited from existing health information technology systems, allowing the unrestricted, fast and safe sharing of health information between medical tourists, international health service providers and other stakeholders. Blockchain can also be considerably improved by the caliber of medical treatments provided to medical tourists. By employing cryptocurrencies, medical tourists can quickly and securely collect payments while lowering the cost of transactions [2, 16]. When medical tourists return home, there may be delays and interruptions since there is no continuity of care for the patients and insufficient interoperability of their external health data. Furthermore, if a patient's complete medical records are not available, there is a higher probability of a diagnosis error. Additionally, the suggested therapy can include drugs that are unavailable in the countries of origin. The persistent issue of medical data fragmentation can be effectively solved by blockchain technology, which can also be used to match prescribed pharmaceuticals.

## 6.1  Electronic Health Records (EHRs)

The EHRs are a computerized collection of medical records for patients. Electronic medical records that will be kept at the hospital or clinical throughout time are saved electronically. All vital clinical data, including MRI, previous medical examination, immunization, laboratory results and all forms of patient's allergy, are contained in these medical records, which is critical for patient care that is kept by a particular care provider [2, 16]. These records are real-time records, patient records that a patient or doctor may easily access.

## 6.2  Methods/Services Offered by Blockchain in Medical Tourism

Blockchain technology is viewed as a fundamental technology since it may be the basis for future social and economic systems. Recent research in the fields of tourism and hospitality has focused heavily on blockchain technology and cryptocurrencies. Only a small number of published studies have examined the effects of blockchain technology on medical tourism, nevertheless, in terms of study on the topic (Fig. 4).

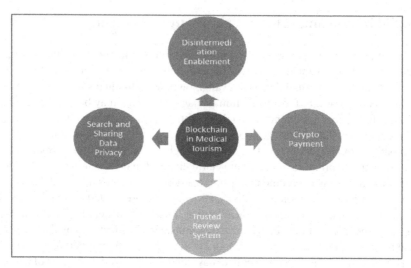

**Fig. 4.** Service offered by Blockchain in Medical Tourism

Regarding patient-doctor trust, procedure and risk openness, and medical record privacy, discuss some unanswered questions in medical tourism. Blockchain and other cutting-edge technology can facilitate the ongoing expansion of medical tourism.

## 7 Challenges

If tele-based administrations begin to confront the genuine situation and answer such frantic issues it should receive a nonexclusive methodology that blends both the world-wide and the neighborhood wellbeing frameworks. This is the solitary way tele-based wellbeing innovation can win hearts and can give a wide scope of clinical medical care administrations through teleconsultations, telediagnosis, teletreatments, by extending more noteworthy information and aptitude in this field through suitable learning and preparing of people associated with medical care. It should be expressed here that it isn't the penultimate answer for the issue, in any case, can help in the improvement of the current circumstance. When telemedical frameworks will be carried out in a complex way, it will assist immature nations with getting to better and sound clinical considera-tion. With this, tele-based medical services ought to have the option to save money on schedule and costs moreover it improves the appropriateness of admission to crises and clinic divisions as needs are. [2, 16].

| Challenge | Meaning |
|---|---|
| Abominable Management | With innovation and clinical practices, there is additionally the need of "being prepared" to acknowledge the resuscitated medical care overseeing frameworks. It is all human brain science, for an invaluable working of tele-based medical care frameworks, there should not be any obstruction, which must be acquired when there is appropriate mindfulness and eagerness inside individuals to acknowledge and receive the adjustment of the human prosperity |
| Inadequacy of Awareness | There is a mistaken understanding of associated medical care innovation (CHT) among individuals. The need of great importance is to grow a more prominent establishment of sufficient information among average folks and experts so fabulous expertise and happy possibilities can be chipped away at |
| Lack of Medic Pupils | To manage the deficiency of clinical crew identified with telehealthcare, more HR can be prepared and used at various levels |

## 8   Conclusion

Medical tourism is one of the social need. As we are well aware that a lot of movement is happening for treatment of disease from one country to another country. The travel made by the humans for their medical treatment come under the medical tourism. As we have defined in this paper that there are many areas where blockchain is used for securing and maintain privacy of the data accessed and stored related to their medical treatment. Each year, millions of Americans seek medical treatment abroad. Medical tourists from the United States frequently travel to Mexico, Canada, as well as countries in Central America, South America, and the Caribbean. The epidemic affected many facets of travel, including medical tourism. In order to address this issue, the study has detailed various prospects for blockchain technology implementation in the current context, such as the decrease of processing times for all government-issued travel-related papers, including visas, and the authenticity guarantee of these documents. The article provides a summary of the various difficulties the pandemic has caused for the medical tourism sector. There are many reasons why a patient might travel for medical treatment, including cost or to have a procedure that would be less expensive abroad.

## References

1. Kustwar, R.K., Ray, S.: eHealth and telemedicine in India: an overview on the health care need of the people. J. Multi. Res. Healthc. 6(2), 25–36 (2020). https://doi.org/10.15415/jmrh. 2020.62004
2. Saha, A., Amin, R., Kunal, S., Vollala, S., Sanjeev, D.: Review on Blockchain technology based medical healthcare system with privacy issues. Secu. Priv. 2, e83 (2019). https://doi. org/10.1002/spy2.83
3. Kamdar, N.M.D., Jalilian, M.P.P., Laleh, M.D.: Telemedicine: a digital interface for perioperative anesthetic care. Anesth. Analg. 130(2), 272–275 (2020). https://doi.org/10.1213/ANE. 0000000000004513

4. Shamshad, S., Mahmood, M.K., Kumari, S., Chen, C.-M.: A secure blockchain-based e-health records storage and sharing scheme. J. Inf. Secu. Appl. **55**, 102590 (2020)
5. Hussien, H.M., Yasin, S.M., Udzir, S.N.I., Zaidan, A.A., Zaidan, B.B.: A systematic review for enabling of develop a blockchain technology in healthcare application: taxonomy, substantially analysis, motivations, challenges, recommendations and future direction. J. Med. Syst. **43**(10), 1–35 (2019). https://doi.org/10.1007/s10916-019-1445-8
6. Shastri, A., Biswas, R.: A framework for automated database tuning using dynamic SGA parameters and basic operating system utilities. Database Syst. J. **3**(4), 25–32 (2012)
7. Shailendra, K.K.: NLP and machine learning techniques for detecting insulting comments on social networking platforms. In: International Conference on Advances in Computing and Communication Engineering (ICACCE) 2018, pp. 265–272. IEEE (2018)
8. Lubkina, V., Marzano, G.: Building social telerehabilitation services. Procedia Comput. Sci. **77**, 80e84 (2015)
9. Sharma, H.K., Khanchi, I., Agarwal, N., Seth, P., Ahlawat, P.: Real time activity logger: a user activity detection system. Int. J. Eng. Adv. Technol. **9**(1), 1991–1994 (2019)
10. Bhushan, A., Rastogi, P., Ahmed, M.E.: I/O and memory management: two keys for tuning RDBMS. In: Proceedings on 2016 2nd International Conference on Next Generation Computing Technologies, NGCT 2016 7877416, pp. 208–214 (2017)
11. Khanchi, I., Ahmed, E.: Automated framework for real-time sentiment analysis. In: International Conference on Next Generation Computing Technologies (NGCT-2019)
12. Singh, T., Kshitiz, K., Singh, H., Kukreja, P.: Detecting hate speech and insults on social commentary using NLP and machine learning. Int. J. Eng. Technol. Sci. Res. **4**(12), 279–285 (2017)
13. Ahlawat, P., Biswas, S.S.: Sensors based smart healthcare framework using Internet of Things (IoT). Int. J. Sci. Technol. Res. **9**(2), 12281234 (2020)
14. Taneja, S., Ahmed, E.: I-Doctor: an IoT based self patient's health monitoring system. In: 2019 International Conference on Innovative Sustainable Computational Technologies, CISCT 2019 (2019)
15. Kamdar, N., Jalilian, L.: Telemedicine. Anesth. Analg. (2020)
16. Rejeb, A., Keogh, J.G., Treiblmaier, H.: Chapter 4 The Impact of Blockchain on Medical Tourism. In: Springer Science and Business Media LLC (2020)
17. Peris-Ortiz, M., Álvarez-García, J. (eds.): Health and Wellness Tourism. Springer, Cham (2015). https://doi.org/10.1007/978-3-319-11490-3
18. Ramos, V., Untong, A.: Spa tourism. In: Jafari, J., Xiao, H. (eds.), Encyclopedia of Tourism. Springer, Cham (2016). https://doi.org/10.1007/978-3-319-01384-8_185
19. Pilkington, M.: The relation between tokens and blockchain networks: the case of medical tourism in the republic of moldova. J. Br. Blockchain Assoc. **4**, 18156 (2021)
20. Goodrich, J.N., Goodrich, G.E.: Health-care tourism—an exploratory study. Tour. Manag. **8**, 217–222 (1987)
21. Singh, A.P., et al.: A novel patient-centric architectural framework for blockchain-enabled healthcare applications. IEEE Trans. Industr. Inf. **17**(8), 5779–5789 (2020)
22. Pradhan, N.R., Singh, A.P., Kumar, N., Hassan, M.M., Roy, D.S.: A flexible permission ascription (FPA)-based blockchain framework for peer-to-peer energy trading with performance evaluation. IEEE Trans. Industr. Inf. **18**(4), 2465–2475 (2021)
23. Pradhan, N.R., Singh, A.P.: Smart contracts for automated control system in Blockchain based smart cities. J. Ambient Intell. Smart Environ. **13**(3), 253–267 (2021)
24. Pradhan, N.R., Singh, A.P., Kumar, V.: Blockchain-enabled traceable, transparent transportation system for blood bank. In: Harvey, D., Kar, H., Verma, S., Bhadauria, V. (eds.) Advances in VLSI, Communication, and Signal Processing: Select Proceedings of VCAS 2019, pp. 313–324. Springer Singapore, Singapore (2021). https://doi.org/10.1007/978-981-15-6840-4_25

25. Pradhan, N.R., Singh, A.P., Verma, S., Wozniak, M., Shafi, J., Ijaz, M.F.: A blockchain based lightweight peer-to-peer energy trading framework for secured high throughput microtransactions. Sci. Rep. **12**(1), 1–5 (2022)
26. Pradhan, N.R., Singh, A.P., Panda, K.P., Roy, D.S.: A novel confidential consortium Blockchain framework for peer to peer energy trading. Int. J. Emerg. Electr. Power Syst. **23**, 673–681 (2021)
27. Pradhan, N.R., Mahule, R., Wamuyu, P.K., Rathore, P.K., Singh, A.P.: A Blockchain and AI based vaccination tracking framework for coronavirus (COVID-19) epidemics. IETE J. Res. **15**, 1–3 (2022)
28. Pradhan, N.R., Kumar, D.A., Singh, A.P.: BlockChain-Based Smart Contract for Transportation of Blood Bank System. The Role of IoT and Blockchain: Techniques and Applications, pp. 253–265, Mar 9 2022
29. Pradhan, N.R., Singh, A.P., Mahule, R.: Blockchain based smart and secure agricultural monitoring system. In: 2021 5th International Conference on Information Systems and Computer Networks (ISCON) 2021 Oct 22, pp. 1–6. IEEE
30. Pradhan, N.R., Rout, S.S., Singh, A.P.: BlockChain based smart healthcare system for chronic–illness patient monitoring. In: 2020 3rd International Conference on Energy, Power and Environment: Towards Clean Energy Technologies 2021 Mar 5, pp. 1–6. IEEE (2021)
31. Pradhan, N.R., et al.: A novel blockchain-based healthcare system design and performance benchmarking on a multi-hosted testbed. Sensors. **22**(9), 3449 (2022)

# Measuring the Impact of Oil Revenues on Government Debt in Selected Countries by Using ARDL Model

Mustafa Kamil Rasheed[1](✉), Ahmed Hadi Salman[1], and Amer Sami Mounir[2]

[1] College of Administration and Economics, Mustansiriyah University, Baghdad, Iraq
{dr_mustafa_kamel,dr.Ahmadhidi}@uomustansiriyah.edu.iq
[2] College of Administration and Economics, Tikrit University, Tikrit, Iraq

**Abstract.** The study examined the relationship between oil revenues and government debt. Most oil-producing countries suffer from a problem in the sustainability of public debt, and the inability of these countries to manage financial resources efficiently, especially oil revenues in order to eliminate the accumulation of government debt.

The study used two indicators: the ratio of oil revenues to GDP, and the ratio of government debt to GDP, and through the use of ARDL model for co-integration, they were applied to five oil countries, and that the study period is (2004–2018). The study concluded that the relationship between oil revenues and government debt was negative, which is identical to the logic of economic theory, but some countries have exceeded the internationally safe ratio of government debt to GDP, which means the inability of the financial policy maker to manage oil revenues well.

The study recommended the importance of the oil resource in order to strengthen the structure of GDP, and encounter the obstacles and problems in the macroeconomic, and that the oil revenues are able to pay off the government debt and improve the national economy.

**Keywords:** Oil Revenues · GDP · Government Debt · ARDLModel · StationaryTest

## 1 Introduction

Oil revenues are an important financial resource in developing economies and should be managed efficiently in order to treat financial problems, the most important of which are the government debt problem, budget deficit and weak financial financing channels. Also, most developing economies suffer from many structural problems in GDP, as the domestic product suffers from weakness in its components, and the lack of total productivity of the elements of production, as well as widespread unemployment and inflation, and the futility of many economic policies, weakness of natural resources and lack of experience of the decision-maker in Managing economic resources, threatening the local economy with many crises.

S. Nandan Mohanty et al. (Eds.): ICISML 2022, LNICST 471, pp. 170–180, 2023.
https://doi.org/10.1007/978-3-031-35081-8_14

The economy's reliance mainly on crude oil harms the composition of the domestic product, which weakens the linkages of economic activities, and thus the tax revenue, which forces the local policymaker to finance government spending through borrowing and then increase government debt under the accumulation of financial surpluses from Oil revenues.

The importance of the study is unbenefited from oil revenues in developing the national economy, strengthening the components of the domestic product and building strong production relationships that stimulate investment and attract local and foreign capital in building the national economy.

The problem statement is that the financial decision-maker ignores the importance of the financial resource for oil revenues, which encourages the spread of administrative and financial corruption, the accumulation of macroeconomic problems, and poor overall productivity. And then the spread of economic crises. And increasing government debt. The study hypothesizes that oil revenues negatively affect government debt. Therefore, it should be used in treating macroeconomic problems. The target of the study is to analyze the index of oil revenues to GDP in the countries of the study sample and to analyze the index of government debt to GDP, and then application econometric study to know the effect of oil revenues in government debt according to ARDL model.

## 1.1  Theoretical Side

The rise in crude oil prices on global markets leads to an increase in oil revenues, which provides an important financial resource for developing countries in general, and oil-producing countries in particular. Because it helps in facing the most important obstacles to sustainable economic development, which is the problem of low domestic saving and thus investment that stimulates national income. Oil revenues can also be directed to support the structure of the industrial sector, without resorting to borrowing, and subsequently causing government debt problems (Dreger et al. 2014, 1). If natural resources are used in a good way, the economy will be developed, economic performance will improve, economic growth rates will rise, and if natural resources are not occupied well, they will negatively affect the overall economy. Therefore, it is sometimes called "the resource curse" (Iimi 2007, p 664–681), just as the negative impact will extend to the stability of the political system, the government's behavior, the decision-maker's ability to make a positive impact. (Benyoub 2018, 4). The dependence of the economy on a single product causes many economic problems. The dependence of oil-producing countries on exporting crude oil leads to a deficit in the current account, a deficit in the general budget, and the creation of government debt that cannot be pay off. The unsustainability of government debt has major implications for the national economy. In addition to the decline in national production, the spread of corruption, the weakness of the economy in encounter fluctuations in global oil prices and external shocks in the economy. (Fatahi et al. 2014; Negahbani 2004; Davoodi 1993). Cordon and Neary (1982) put forth the Dutch disease model, in an attempt to explain the damages suffered by the economy dependent on the natural resource, they asserted that the discovery of the natural resource, and then its price increase, would cause a decline in economic activities and a rise in the exchange rate (Aslam and Shastri 2019, 196).

Government debt is a serious problem in fiscal policy, which affects the behavior of macroeconomic variables, and hence economic growth. In particular, the debate sparked by (Reinhart and Rogoff 2010), regarding the impact of government debt on economic growth. As long as the government debt raises a wide discussion and debate about the ability of the financial decision-maker to avoid problems of the government debt, or reduce its damage to a minimum. And his main question for (Buchanan 1966) is:

"When and who pays for public expenditure financed by debt issue, instead of by taxation or the printing of money?" (Alves 2015, 10).

Many researches indicate that political and economic factors determine the government's credibility in fulfilling its debt-repayment obligations, and among these factors are the budget deficit, economic growth, inflation rates, government debt, rule of law, and the current account deficit (Reed et al. 2019, 21).

## 1.2  Practical Side

2–1- Iraq's ranking was the first for the index (oil revenues: GDP), as Iraq's exports of crude oil increased during the period (2004–2018), The GDP in Iraq is weak in its diversity, and crude oil occupies a large amount of it. The index reached its highest in 2004 (64.1%), and the lowest in 2016 (30.5%), due to the crude oil price crisis in 2014. Saudi Arabia was second in the index, it reached the highest in 2008 (54.3%), and the lowest in 2016 (19.4%). The United Arab Emirates was third, reaching its highest in 2011 (28.8%), and the lowest in 2016 (10.8%). While Russia was fourth, it reached the highest in 2005 (13.1%), and the lowest in 2016 (5.2%). Fifthly, Canada reached the highest in 2008 (2.6%), and the lowest in 2015 (0%). The degree of diversification of GDP is inversely proportional to the degree of dependence on crude oil. The higher the level of the rentier economy, the lower the components of GDP, and vice versa (Figs. 1 and 2).

## 1.3  Econometric Side

### 1.3.1  Specification Stage

According to the logic of the macroeconomic theory, crude oil revenues are one of the components of public revenues, and when oil revenues increase, public revenues increase, and the public budget is in a surplus state, so the government debt decreases, as the government's ability to pay off the public debt increases.

Therefore, oil revenues have an inverse relationship with government debt. The functional relationship is:

$$GVD/GDP = f(OR/GDP, e_t)$$

where:

$GVD/GDP$ = Government Debt : GDP, $OR/GDP$ = Oil Revenue : GDP. $e_t$ = random error.

**Russia** ■ **Canada** ■ **iraq** ■ **Saudi Arabia** ■ **United Arab Emirates**

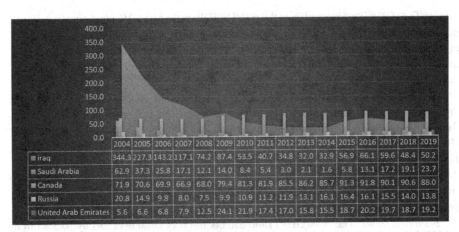

**Fig. 1.** The ratio of oil revenue to GDP in the study sample countries for the period (2004–2018) (%). Source: World Word, Indicators and Statistics, Various years. 2–2-Iraq first in the government debt to GDP index, as it reached the highest in 2004 (344.3%), and the lowest in 2013 (32%). This means that the government debt to- GDP ratio was very high, and more than the global standard ratio (IMF (25%–30%)). Canada second, as it reached the highest in 2016 (91.8%). The lowest in 2007 (66.9%). Saudi Arabia third, as the index ranged between (62.9%–1.6%), and Russia fourth, as the index ranged between (20.85%–7.5%). The United Arab Emirates fifth, as the index ranged between (24.1%–5.6%).

| | 2004 | 2005 | 2006 | 2007 | 2008 | 2009 | 2010 | 2011 | 2012 | 2013 | 2014 | 2015 | 2016 | 2017 | 2018 | 2019 |
|---|---|---|---|---|---|---|---|---|---|---|---|---|---|---|---|---|
| ■ iraq | 344.3 | 227.3 | 143.2 | 117.1 | 74.2 | 87.4 | 53.5 | 40.7 | 34.8 | 32.0 | 32.9 | 56.9 | 66.1 | 59.6 | 48.4 | 50.2 |
| ■ Saudi Arabia | 62.9 | 37.3 | 25.8 | 17.1 | 12.1 | 14.0 | 8.4 | 5.4 | 3.0 | 2.1 | 1.6 | 5.8 | 13.1 | 17.2 | 19.1 | 23.7 |
| ■ Canada | 71.9 | 70.6 | 69.9 | 66.9 | 68.0 | 79.4 | 81.3 | 81.9 | 85.5 | 86.2 | 85.7 | 91.3 | 91.8 | 90.1 | 90.6 | 88.0 |
| ■ Russia | 20.8 | 14.9 | 9.8 | 8.0 | 7.5 | 9.9 | 10.9 | 11.2 | 11.9 | 13.1 | 16.1 | 16.4 | 16.1 | 15.5 | 14.0 | 13.8 |
| ■ United Arab Emirates | 5.6 | 6.6 | 6.8 | 7.9 | 12.5 | 24.1 | 21.9 | 17.4 | 17.0 | 15.8 | 15.5 | 18.7 | 20.2 | 19.7 | 18.7 | 19.2 |

**Fig. 2.** The ratio of government debt to GDP in the study sample countries for the period (2004–2018) (%). Source: World Word, Indicators and Statistics, Various years.

### 1.3.2 Stationary Test

The time series of the variables (YIQ, YSA, YRU, YUAE) were stationary, so we reject the null hypothesis, and we accept the alternative hypothesis, while the time series of the variables (XIQ, XSA, YCA, XCA, XRU, XUAE) were nonstationary, so we accept the null hypothesis, we reject the alternative assumption. These variables have stabilized after making the first difference. All-time series became stationary (Table 1).

**Table 1.** Stationarity results for ADF for model variables

| ADF Test | Level 1(0) Prob. | | | 1 drf. 1(1) Prob. | | |
|---|---|---|---|---|---|---|
| Variables | Int. | Int. + T | Non | Int. | Int. + T | Non |
| YIQ | 0.000 | 0.001 | 0.000 | | | |
| XIQ | 0.3 | 0.3 | 0.2 | 0.055 | 0.12 | 0.004 |
| YSA | 0.6 | 0.01 | 0.5 | | | |
| XSA | 0.6 | 0.2 | 0.3 | 0.03 | 0.2 | 0.001 |
| YCA | 0.8 | 0.4 | 0.9 | 0.053 | 0.003 | 0.008 |
| XCA | 0.2 | 0.2 | 0.4 | 0.1 | 0.03 | 0.000 |
| YRU | 0.1 | 0.01 | 0.1 | | | |
| XRU | 0.4 | 0.1 | 0.4 | 0.07 | 0.3 | 0.003 |
| YUAE | 0.051 | 0.000 | 0.7 | | | |
| XUAE | 0.4 | 0.4 | 0.4 | 0.03 | 0.001 | 0.002 |

Source:Program (EViews 10)

### 1.3.3  Results

1-*Iraq*: The (OR/GDP) ratio affects the (GVD/GDP) ratio by (1.1%) in a negative direction, which means that the increase in oil revenues relative to the GDP leads to a decrease in the ratio of government debt to GDP. Thus, the Iraqi financial administration should make good use of the financial resource that comes from oil revenues, in order to enhance and support the GDP.

The results were statistically significant as a function of the T-Test, F-Test and, Probability Test. The interpretation coefficient ($R^2$) as high as it reached (95%), and the Bond Test was (94.6) is higher than the minimum and the upper limit at a significant level (1%). Second-order tests were good, so there is no Autocorrelation (Breusch-Godfrey Test) The probability of an F-Test reached (0.19), nor Heteroskedasticity (Breusch-Pagan-Godfrey Test) The probability of an F-Test reached (0.49), normal distribution (Jarque-Bera Test), Prob. (0.6), as well as the stability of the model in general (CUSUM Test).

2-*Saudi Arabia*: The (OR/GDP) ratio affects the (GVD/GDP) ratio by (0.3%) in a negative direction, which means that the increase in oil revenues relative to the GDP leads to a decrease in the ratio of government debt to GDP.

The results were statistically significant as a function of the T-Test, F-Test and, Probability Test. The interpretation coefficient ($R^2$) as high as it reached (96%), and the Bond Test was (31.3) is higher than the minimum and the upper limit at a significant level (1%). Second-order tests were good, so there is no Autocorrelation (Breusch-Godfrey Test) The probability of an F-Test reached (0.55), nor Heteroskedasticity (Breusch-Pagan-Godfrey Test) The probability of an F-Test reached (0.4), normal distribution (Jarque-Bera Test), Prob. (0.6), as well as the stability of the model in general (CUSUM Test).

3-*Canada*: The (OR/GDP) ratio affects the (GVD/GDP) ratio by (2.4%) in a negative direction, which means that the increase in oil revenues relative to the GDP leads to a decrease in the ratio of government debt to GDP.

The results were statistically significant as a function of the T-Test, F-Test and, Probability Test. The interpretation coefficient ($R^2$) as high as it reached (97%), and the Bond Test was (8.76) is higher than the minimum and the upper limit at a significant level (1%). Second-order tests were good, so there is no Autocorrelation (Breusch-Godfrey Test) The probability of an F-Test reached (0.11), nor Heteroskedasticity (Breusch-Pagan-Godfrey Test) The probability of an F-Test reached (0.4), normal distribution (Jarque-Bera Test), Prob. (0.87), as well as the stability of the model in general (CUSUM Test).

4-*Russia*: The (OR/GDP) ratio affects the (GVD/GDP) ratio by (0.6%) in a negative direction, which means that the increase in oil revenues relative to the GDP leads to a decrease in the ratio of government debt to GDP.

The results were statistically significant as a function of the T-Test, F-Test and, Probability Test. The interpretation coefficient ($R^2$) as high as it reached (79%), and the Bond Test was (8.9) is higher than the minimum and the upper limit at a significant level (1%). Second-order tests were good, so there is no Autocorrelation (Breusch-Godfrey Test) The probability of an F-Test reached (0.28), nor Heteroskedasticity (Breusch-Pagan-Godfrey Test) The probability of an F-Test reached (0.92), normal distribution (Jarque-Bera Test), Prob. (0.55), as well as the stability of the model in general (CUSUM Test).

4-*United Arab Emirates*: The (OR/GDP) ratio affects the (GVD/GDP) ratio by (0.1%) in a negative direction, which means that the increase in oil revenues relative to the GDP leads to a decrease in the ratio of government debt to GDP.

The results were statistically significant as a function of the T-Test, F-Test and, Probability Test. The interpretation coefficient ($R^2$) as high as it reached (93%), and the Bond Test was (20.9) is higher than the minimum and the upper limit at a significant level (1%). Second-order tests were good, so there is no Autocorrelation (Breusch-Godfrey Test) The probability of an F-Test reached (0.66), nor Heteroskedasticity (Breusch-Pagan-Godfrey Test) The probability of an F-Test reached (0.34), normal distribution (Jarque-Bera Test), Prob. (0.22), as well as the stability of the model in general (CUSUM Test).

## 1.4  Discussion

The amount of the largest effect of oil revenue on the government debt was for Canada, which is reached (2.4%), Iraq, which reached the amount of effect it had (1.1%), and then Russia, which affected it (0.6%), and then Saudi Arabia and the United Arab Emirates.

The Canadian economy is strong, and it has strong links with its economic activities, both inside and outside the economy, and therefore Canada does not face a big problem in settling its debts. As its economy is good and diversified. Hence, its public revenues are also good.

The Iraqi economy is weak, and depends basically on oil, under big decline in overall productivity, and weak linkages of economic activities, and it has a good chance to correct structural imbalances in the macroeconomic, as oil revenues reduce government debt in a better way.

Saudi Arabia's economy is large and diversified, with strong economic links with global markets, and has wide domestic and foreign investments. And have a big control of price in OPEC. Therefore, oil revenue strengthens macroeconomic. And lower government debt, and raise the efficiency of financial management.

The Russian economy is advanced, and it depends on many economic resources based on technology, and the wide diversity in the GDP provides many sources of financing for public revenues, in a way that secures the repayment of government debt, and the econometric study supports the trend of reducing government debt with each increase in oil investment and then oil revenues.

The economy of the United Arab Emirates is strong and diversified and depends on knowledge and quality investment in economic resources. It is also distinguished by the intertwining of the local and foreign sectors, which has strengthened the response to macroeconomic variables in the face of shocks and crises. Therefore, long-term planning in the UAE oil fields strengthened the structure of the GDP. Then the financial administration became able to manage financial surpluses towards strengthening the local economy and supporting its capabilities in global and regional markets, and the econometric study confirmed the ability of oil revenues to extinguish government debt, but the government debt in the UAE was at safe limits during the study period.

## 2  Conclusion

1- Iraq the first in the index of oil revenue/GDP, but it was the first in the government debt/GDP index, which means that the Iraqi economy's dependence on a single productive resource has created a government debt that cannot be repaid, the government debt/GDP index was exceeded safe limits globally. This caused the weakness of the economy, the decline in economic activities, the weakness of public revenues, the continuing deficit of the public budget, and the inability of the Iraqi economy encounter domestic and external shocks and crises.

While the econometric study results confirm that there is a good opportunity for the Iraqi economy to support the national economy, in a condition that there is rational financial management that works to manage the financial resource from oil revenues in strengthening economic activities and improving economic growth rates.

2-Saudi Arabia came second in oil revenue/GDP index, where it is acquiring the largest share of oil production within the OPEC, and its GDP was diversified, so the government debt/GDP index came within the safe limits of the world, except for the period (2004–2005). The econometric study results confirm the ability of Saudi Arabia to benefit from oil revenues in building the capabilities of the Saudi economy and controlling government debt. Therefore, the Saudi economy is one of the strongest economies in the Arab region, and it has diversified investments in many countries of the world.

3-The United Arab Emirates overcome the barrier of dependence on a single resource, its economy planned scientifically and good, in order to become one of the knowledge-based economies, which made it far the danger of government debt. The economy of the United Arab Emirates is diversified and dynamic, has links with global markets, and has depth in the production and distribution activities of various countries of the world. So oil became one of the natural resources invested in the service of the national economy, and this was supported by the econometric study results.

4-The Russian and Canadian economy is an advanced economy, despite that part of its extractive activities depends on the extraction and export of crude oil in international markets. The developed economies general, the Russian and Canadian economies particular, are diverse and dynamic economies that depend entirely on the knowledge and the richness of high-level technology. These economies are scientifically and precisely planned, in order to ensure productive alternatives that support sustainable and environmentally friendly economic development, and the economic decision-maker has the wisdom and ability to put the economy at the forefront.

## 3  Recommendation

1-Undepend on a single resource in the economy, the GDP should be well prepared and diversified, and its production relations strengthened locally and internationally.

2-Strategic planning in building the national economy, based on partnerships between the private and public sectors, supporting the components of output, enhancing local economic activities, and raising the competitiveness of production and exporting goods and services.

3-The government debt does not exceed the GDP outside the safe limits, which puts the economy at economic stability and the ability to pay off the debt.

4-The Iraqi economy needs rational financial management, to save it from its many crises and problems. The GDP is completely distorted, the government is unable to fillet its financial obligations, the government debt is high, there is no sustainability in the government debt, whether domestic or foreign. The persistence of the general budget deficit, the current account deficit, and the high degree of economic exposure, under financial surpluses from oil revenues, which encouraged corruption, damage to property and public institutions, non-rule of the law.

## Appendix (1)

| ARDL Model in Iraq | |
|---|---|
| YIQ $= -1.123211$ XIQ | |
| t-Statistic $(-2.521100)$ Prob. $(0.0284)$ $R^2$: 0.96 $\bar{R}^2$: 0.95 | |
| Bond Test (F-statistic: 94.6) | ECM (CointEq$(-1)$*): $-0.42$ |
| Breusch-Godfrey Serial Correlation LM Test (Prob. F(0.1975) | Heteroskedasticity Test: Breusch-Pagan-Godfrey (Prob. F(0.4983) |

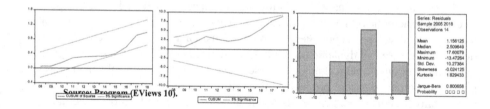

Source: Program (EViews 10).

## Appendix (2)

| ARDL Model in Saudi Arabia | |
| --- | --- |
| YSA = 15.8 − 0.309214 XSA | |
| t-Statistic: (6.9) (−4.5) | |
| Prob.: (0.000) (0.002) | |
| F-Statistic (50.3) $R^2$: 0.96 $\bar{R}^2$: 0.94 | |
| Bond Test (F-statistic: 31.3) | ECM (CointEq(−1)*):−0.24 |
| Breusch-Godfrey Serial Correlation LM Test (Prob. F(0.55) | Heteroskedasticity Test: Breusch-Pagan-Godfrey (Prob. F(0.4) |

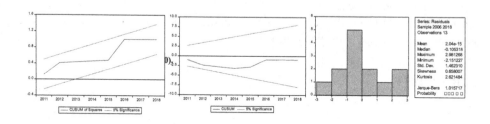

## Appendix (3)

| ARDL Model in Canada |
| --- |
| YCA = 43.1 − 2.466837 XCA + 1.754914 Trend |
| t-Statistic = (2.7) (−2.5) (3.8) |
| Prob. (0.02) (0.04) (0.006) |

(continued)

(*continued*)

| ARDL Model in Canada | |
|---|---|
| F-Statistic (52.1) $R^2$: 0.97 $\overline{R}^2$: 0.95 | |
| Bond Test (F-statistic: 8.76) | ECM (CointEq($-1$)*): $-0.72$ |
| Breusch-Godfrey Serial Correlation LM Test (Prob. F(0.11) | Heteroskedasticity Test: Breusch-Pagan-Godfrey (Prob. F(0.87) |

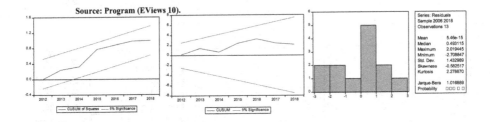

Source: Program (EViews 10).

## Appendix (4)

| ARDL Model in Russia |
|---|
| YRU = 11.24171 − 0.630381 XRU |
| t-Statistic = (4.7) (−3.8) |
| Prob. (0.000) (0.004) |
| F-Statistic (21.8) $R^2$: 0.79 $\overline{R}^2$: 0.76 |

| Bond Test (F-statistic: 8.9) | ECM (CointEq($-1$)*): $-0.43$ |
|---|---|
| Breusch-Godfrey Serial Correlation LM Test (Prob. F(0.28) | Heteroskedasticity Test: Breusch-Pagan-Godfrey (Prob. F(0.92) |

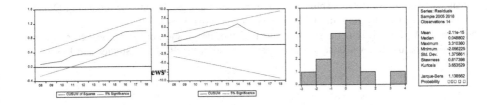

## Appendix (5)

| ARDL Model in United Arab Emirates | |
|---|---|
| YUAE = 8.326582 − 0.182577 XUAE + 10.06831 DO09 | |
| t-Statistic = (3.5) (−2.3) (5.8) | |
| Prob. (0.005) (0.04) (0.000) | |
| F-Statistic (48.8) $R^2$: 0.93 $\bar{R}^2$: 0.91 | |
| Bond Test (F-statistic: 20.9) | ECM (CointEq(−1)*):−0.28 |
| Breusch-Godfrey Serial Correlation LM Test (Prob. F(0.66) | Heteroskedasticity Test: Breusch-Pagan-Godfrey (Prob. F(0.34) |

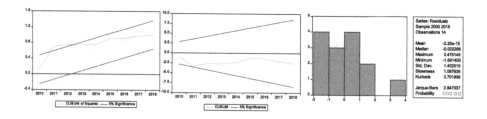

# References

Dreger, C., Rahmani, T.: The impact of oil revenues on the Iranian economy and the gulf states. SSRN Electron. J. (2014)

Davoodi, P.: Trend of the budget deficit in Iran and some important approaches. The research group of the Islamic Consultative Research Center (1993)

Fattahi, S., Ali, H.D., Elnaz, A.: Investigating the sustainability of government debt in Iran's economy. Q. J. Finan. Econ. Policies 2(6), 67–86 (2014)

Alves, J.: The Role of Government Debt in Economic Growth, Hacienda Publica Espanol, Review of Public Economics, Instituto de Estudios Fiscales (2015)

Reed, M., et al.: Analyzing the relationship between budget deficit, current account deficit, and government debt sustainability. J. WEI Bus. Econ. 8, 20–31 (2019)

Benyoub, M.: The Impact of Oil Revenue Investment on Growth, Inflation and Unemployment: The Case of Algeria (2000–2015), MPRA Paper No. 90489, Germany (2018)

Aslam, N., Shastri, S.: Relationship between oil revenues and gross domestic product of Oman: an empirical investigation. Int. J. Econ. Finan. Issues 9(6), 195–201 (2019)

Negahbani, A.: Investigating the effects of the policy of devaluation of the national currency on Iran's trade balance with major trading parties. Institute forBusiness Studies and Research (2004)

# Diagnosis of Plant Diseases by Image Processing Model for Sustainable Solutions

Sasmita Pani[1], Jyotiranjan Rout[1], Zeenat Afroz[1], Madhusmita Dey[1], Mahesh Kumar Sahoo[2], and Amar Kumar Das[3]([✉]) [iD]

[1] Department of Computer Science and Engineering, Balasore College of Engineering and Technology, Balasore, Odisha, India
[2] Department of Computer Science and Engineering, Gandhi Institute for Technology (GIFT) Autonomous, Bhubaneswar, Odisha, India
[3] Department of Mechanical Engineering, Gandhi Institute for Technology (GIFT) Autonomous, Bhubaneswar, Odisha, India
amar.das120@gmail.com

**Abstract.** The first step in preventing losses in agricultural product output and quantity is to identify plant diseases. A significant loss in crop output and market economic value results due to incorrect identification. The farmers used their own eyesight or prior knowledge of plant illnesses to identify plant ailments. When farmers are doing this for a single plant, it is possible, but when it involves many distinct plants, it is much more challenging to detect and takes a lot of effort. Therefore, it is preferable to utilize image processing to detect plants diseases. Image acquisition, picture pre-processing, image segmentation, feature extraction, and classification are all processes in this approach to diagnose the plant disease. In this study, we would like to present the procedures for identifying plant diseases from their leaf photos. We have used VGG 19 model for efficient processing of trained data and test data. This paper aims to support and help the green house farmers in an efficient way.

**Keywords:** diseases · image processing · trained data

## 1 Introduction

India is an agricultural country in which agriculture employs the majority of the population. Agriculture aims to increase productivity and food quality while spending less and profiting more. A complex combination of soil, seed, and agrochemicals results in the agricultural production system. The most significant agricultural products are vegetables and fruits. A quality management control is essentially required in order to obtain more valuable products. Many studies show that plant diseases can reduce the quality of agricultural products. The normal state of the plant is impaired by diseases, which change or stop vital processes like photosynthesis, transpiration, pollination, fertilization, germination, etc. Pathogens, such as fungi, bacteria, and viruses, as well as poor environmental conditions, cause these diseases.

S. Nandan Mohanty et al. (Eds.): ICISML 2022, LNICST 471, pp. 181–192, 2023.
https://doi.org/10.1007/978-3-031-35081-8_15

As a result, diagnosing plant disease at an early stage is critical. This system is based on image processing technology and uses MATLAB as the primary processing tool. In addition, digital image processing, mathematical statistics, plant pathology, and other related fields are taken into account. In image segmentation and system construction, there are numerous innovations when compared to traditional image recognition. Users have a wide range of imaginative interactive options to meet their own needs in order to strengthen the division of the lesion. Meanwhile, linear regression models can be utilized.

Tomato problems are classified into two categories: bacteria or fungi causing 16 diseases and insects causing 5 other types of diseases. Bacterial wilt is caused by the bacteria Ralstonia solanacearum. This bacteria can survive in soil for a very long time and enter roots through wounds created naturally during the emergence of secondary roots, man-made during cultivation or transplanting, or even by insects. Disease development is favored by high humidity and temperature. By rapidly multiplying inside the plant's water conducting tissue, the bacteria fill it with slime. This has an effect on the plant's vascular system, while the leaves may remain green. A cross section of an infected plant stem appears brown with yellowish material coming from it. We have suggested a novel technique in the research study for identifying the disease in tomato crops after examining the leaf image data. The work will solve farmers' problems with plant disease identification without chasing down plant scientists. It will thus assist them in curing the plant's disease in a timely manner, increasing both the quality and quantity of food crops produced and thus contributing to an increase in farmer profit. We obtained the tomato leaves dataset from the village for the experiment. We developed a model to classify the images after downloading the dataset.

The model's performance was evaluated using a variety of parameters, including training accuracy, validation accuracy and loss, loss accuracy, and the number of trainable and number trainable parameters in reference to the pre-trained model.

## 2  Literature Survey

Even though many systems have been developed to date using various machine learning algorithms such as Random Forest, Naive Bayes, and Artificial Neural Network, the accuracy of those models is low, and the work using those classification techniques is done with the mindset of detecting disease for only one species of plant. Farmers continue to use their naked eyes to detect disease, which is a serious problem because the farmer has no idea what type of disease the plant is infected with. Farmers are still dealing with problems, and the methods they use to detect disease are tedious.

Machine learning algorithms are used in a variety of fields, but feature engineering remains the key issue. With the advent of deep neural networks, promising results for plant pathology are now available without the need for laborious feature engineering. Deep neural networks design concerns classification accuracy significantly. This section describes various deep learning techniques used by plant disease researchers. Mohanty et al. [10, 11] used AlexNet [9] to train and classify previously unseen plant diseases. When testing under conditions that were different from those used for training, model accuracy was significantly decreased. Disease can appear on the upper or lower sides of the leaves. Rangarajan et al. [14] trained both AlexNet and VGG19net using the hyper-parameters minimum batch size, weight, and bias learning rate. In the instance of VGG19net, accuracy and minimum batch size are inversely associated. Convolution and pooling layers were combined and deployed as Inception V4 to the GoogleNet architecture for dimension reduction [16]. For fine-tuning, Too et al. added pre-trained weights from ImageNet to this architecture's average pooling layer of 8x8. Furthermore, DenseNets [6], which has 122 layers, is also optimized for the identification of plant diseases. This paper describes a colour image analysis-based method for identifying the visual signs of plant diseases. The RGB image of the sick plant or leaf is first transformed into the H, I3a, and I3b colour transformations as part of the processing procedure.

The I3a and I3b transformations were created as a result of altering the original I1I2I3 colour transformation to satisfy the needs of the plant disease data collection. The segmented image is then determined by looking at the intensity distribution in a histogram. This method is very helpful when the target in the picture data set has a wide range of brightness. The extracted region was post-processed in tests after the image had been segmented to get rid of pixel regions that weren't taken into consideration. In order to capture the disease-related component of the image and extract pertinent disease-related information, image processing techniques are used.

On the other hand, data mining techniques are used to extract pertinent hidden information useful for illness identification based on the derived features [1, 2]. Image processing offers more effective approaches to identify fungus, bacterium, or virus-related plant illnesses. The ability to diagnose diseases through simple eye observations is insufficient. Pesticide overuse, like improper washing, makes people more susceptible to dangerous chronic diseases. The quality of the nutrients that plants receive is also harmed by excessive use. For farmers, it means a significant loss in production. The use of image processing techniques to identify and categorize diseases in agricultural applications is therefore beneficial [3].

Our suggested article comprises a number of implementation phases, including dataset preparation, feature extraction, classifier training, and classification. To distinguish between healthy and unhealthy photos, the produced datasets of diseased and healthy leaves are combined and trained under Random Forest. The Histogram of an Oriented Gradient is used to extract features from an image (HOG). Overall, utilizing machine learning to train the sizable publically accessible data sets gives us a clear technique to detect the disease existing in plants on a massive scale [4]. The goal of this research is to create a computer programme that can mechanically locate and categorize diseases. A stage that involves disease detection is loading a picture and doing pre-processing operations including segmentation, extraction, and classification. For identifying plant diseases, leaf images are used. The majority of tomato plant diseases are discovered in the early stages because they first harm the leaves. Early disease detection on leaves will undoubtedly save impending loss. In this study, the Multi-class SVM algorithm and image segmentation are used to identify four major diseases. Image segmentation is employed to divide up damaged leaf tissue, and the multi-class SVM method is used to accurately classify diseases. Users are advised to seek treatment for disorders that have advanced to their last stages [5, 7]. Plant diseases can be found via image processing. Image acquisition, picture pre-processing, image segmentation, feature extraction, and classification are processes in the disease detection process. The techniques for identifying plant diseases using photographs of their leaves were covered in this essay. This article also included some segmentation and the feature extraction algorithm employed in the identification of plant diseases [8].

# 3   Proposed Model Architecture

## 3.1   System Architecture

Here the disease image is loaded into the model engine. Then the model engine will take all those data according to the disease image our model is used to evaluate the disease name. Some normal images are taken and those images are converted into a colored image using skimage. color so that the disease of that plant can be easily identified. VGG19 is used for creating our model (Fig. 1).

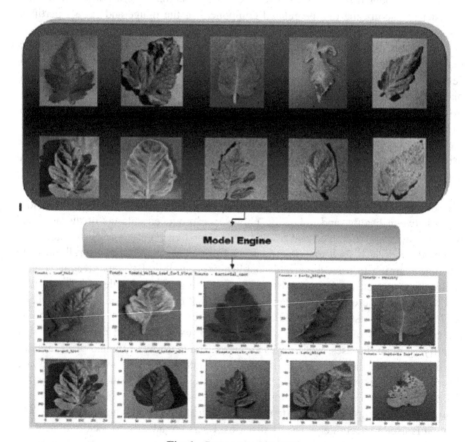

**Fig. 1.** System Architecture

## 3.2  Model Engine Architecture

Here all those disease images are taken and datasets are created. First one is the training data set and the second one is the validating data set. Then training data set as well as the all the dataset is loaded using machine learning and deep learning tools. One model is created that is called Tomato base model.h5. H5 is the extension of this model and tomato base model is the name of our model. Then all our data sets are loaded to train our model for prediction of disease.

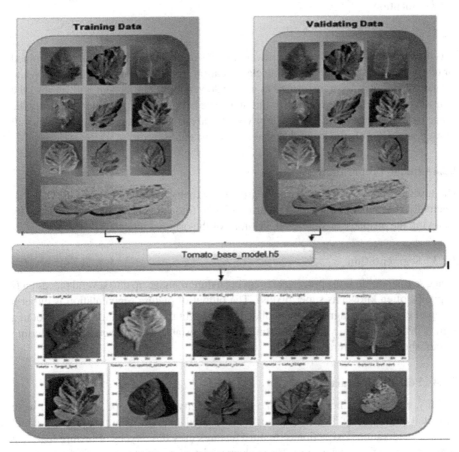

**Fig. 2.** Model-Engine Architecture

Figure 2 first, all diseases photos and data sets have been compiled here. The training data set is the first, and the validation data set is the second. Then, using machine learning, both our training data set and the val data set were loaded. The Tomato base model.h5 model is the only one that has been produced. Our model's extension is H5, and its full name is Tomato base model. Then, in order to train our model for the prediction of plant diseases, we must load all of our data sets.

After our model has been successfully trained, it is tested. Images of diseases are loaded in that test. These photos were captured by our model, and they display the names of the diseases they depict.

The process involves the previous:

1. Acquiring images
2. Image Preparation
3. Segmentation
4. Features extraction
5. Classification

### 3.2.1 Acquiring Images

This process involves feeding our software images of plant leaves that will be examined for disease. As it is simpler to execute classification algorithms on 2-D black-and-white images, the images are transformed to grayscale versions. The system will retrieve the plant snapshot and load the image at this step. The actions that come after acquiring the image include image in JPG format. For visual analysis, higher standard resolutions will be used, and JPEG is the format in which these data are saved.

### 3.2.2 Image Preparation

The unsharp filter is a basic sharpening operator that gets its name from the fact that it actually strengthens edges (and other maximum frequency elements in an image) by removing the unsharp, or smoothed, versions of the original image.

### 3.2.3 Segmentation

Image segmentation is the process of breaking a digital image up into several pieces (sets of pixels, often known as super pixels). The output of picture segmentation is either a group of outlines or fragments that collectively protect the entire image. Each pixel in a zone is in close proximity to a few distinguishing or established characteristics including colour, shape, and texture.

### 3.2.4 Features Extraction

Solidity, extension, minor axis length, and eccentricity are the shape features that were extracted for this study. These characteristics are used to identify the sick area of the leaf under consideration. Extraction of texture features uses three types of texture features: contrast, correlation, and energy. These characteristics are used to identify the sick area of the leaf under consideration. The variation of pixels and their neighboring pixels will then be determined. Feature extraction for colours has a special manner of displaying image representation when it comes to translation, scaling, and rotation. Mean, skewness, and kurtosis are the characteristics utilized for color. Here, RGB is converted to LAB.

### 3.2.5 Classification

Data is divided into three genres: training sets, testing sets, and valuation sets for identi-fication. For each instance or piece of data in the training set, there is one target value and a number of characteristics. We will train our model using training sets and validation sets. To test our model, we use testing sets. Which I have already described in diagrams of system architecture or model architecture.

## 4    Algorithm of the Model

**Ø Step 1:**
Take all the disease images data and process all the disease images data. Create two separate data one is train data another one is val data. Then load all disease images data to the train data and val data using Image Dara Generator.

**Ø Step 2:**
Using matplotlib.pyplot for preprocessing train data. Then try to view some skimage. color images (Fig. 3).

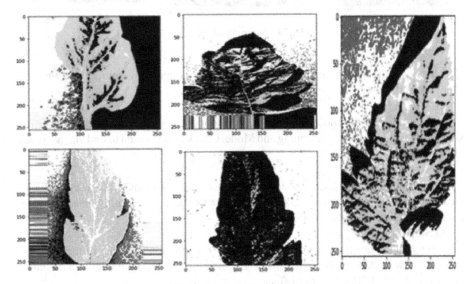

**Fig. 3.** Preprocessed images

**Ø Step 3:**
For printing the normalized data only it is divided by 255. Then try to view some skimage. color images (Fig. 4).

**Ø Step 4:**
Then create one model using keras.applications.vgg19. In Vgg19 pass input shape and include the top. Then print the created model summary.

**Ø Step 5:**
In the model summary add two more layers that are Flatten and Dense. In Dense use "Softmax" activation in the model.

**Ø Step 6:**

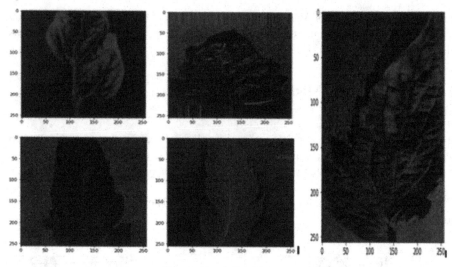

**Fig. 4.** Normalized images

Then compile the model using keras.losses.categorical_crossentropy. In this use adam for optimization and matrices are used for accuracy.

**Ø Step 7:**

Before training the model first do Early Stopping and Model Check Point using keras.callbacks. Here Early Stopping and Model Check Point is used to find val_accuracy of the model.

**Ø Step 8:**

Then train the model using model.fit generator. In this pass our train disease images data set, epochs, steps of epochs, verbose, callbacks and our validating disease images data set, is called validation data.

**Ø Step 9:**

Then find the accuracy of the model as well as validation accuracy of the model in a graphical way. Also evaluate the loss and validation loss of the model in a graphical way using MATPLOTLIB PYPLOT.

**Ø Step 10:**

Then load the model and try to find the final accuracy of our created model. In this scenario final accuracy is evaluated as 96.92307829856873.

**Ø Step 11:**

Now the model is ready to detect the disease of the plant. For testing purpose, load disease plant image then disease name and pictures of the loaded disease plant image is displayed (Table 1).

**Table. 1.** Comparative Study

| Plant Disease Detection using ANN | Plant Disease Detection using CNN | Plant Disease Detection using Image Processing | Plant Disease Detection using Proposed approach |
|---|---|---|---|
| 1. Proposed a "Classification of Pomegranate Diseases Based on Back Propagation Neural Network" which mainly works on the method of Segment the defected area and color and texture are used as the features 2. Here they used neural network classifier for the classification proposed a "Classification of omegranate Diseases Based on Back Propagation Neural Network" which mainly works on the method of Segment the defected area and color and texture are used as the features 3. Using image segmentation, the background is removed from the image. The KNN, ANN, and SVM methods are used to carry out the classification process. Using the closest distance between trained and tested subjects, KNN classifies samples [15, 17].Varun et al. developed models for the extraction noise removal and features extraction. So after that, a multiclass SVM classifier is used. For segmentation, L*A*B* colour spaces are used, which is based on a collection of marks produced by analysing the palette and luminescence components of various sections of the image. The GLCM is applied to extract features. Vijai Singh et al. investigated plant leaf samples taken with a digital camera, including rose/beans (bacterial disorder), lemon (sun burn disorder), banana (early scorch), and beans (fungal).Finally, the genetic algorithm is implemented to obtain the segmentation results. The colour co-occurrence is altered in order to extract useful features from segmented images. The Minimum Distance Criterion is used first for identification, abided by the SVM classifier | 1. The logical next step in automating the identification of plant species, as well as solving many other machine learning challenges, was to eliminate the need for explicit feature selection entirely 2. Deep learning CNNs have recently experienced a significant breakthrough in computer vision because of the accessibility of effective and hugely parallel computing on graphics processing units (GPUs) and the huge amounts of image data required for training deep CNNs with millions of parameters 3. With the exception of prototype and design approaches, CNNs do not require direct and rigorous feature extraction and detection stages. Instead, both are incorporated into an iterative training procedure that incredibly quickly finds an image representation that is statistically appropriate for a given issue 4. Nature is compositional in a similar fashion; small units assemble to create large ones, and each level of clustering increases the structure's diversification. Whether they include or exclude manually created features, such hierarchical representations produce classification results that are largely unattainable using shallow learning techniques | 1. Despite the fact that machine learning methods have many applications, classification algorithm remains the most difficult challenge. Deep neural networks have empowered promising plant pathology solutions to be built without the need for time-consuming feature extraction 2. Deep neural networks significantly improve image classification accuracy. This section describes the various deep learning methods used by scientists to identify plant diseases 3. Mohanty et al. [10, 11] used AlexNet [9] to train and characterise completely undiscovered plant diseases. Prediction accuracy was drastically decreased when testing image conditions varied widely from training image conditions. Disease is rarely visible on the top and bottom sides of the leaves. Rangarajan et al. [14] trained both AlexNet and VGG19net using the hyper-parameters of least sample size, weight, and bias learning rate. Accuracy and minimal level batch size are inversely related in the case of VGG19net For data preprocessing, pooling layers and convolution layer were blended and distributed as Inception V4 to the GoogleNet architecture [16]. Too et al. fine-tuned this architecture's average pooling layer of 8x8 by adding pre-trained weights from Image Net | 1. In this proposed work, image processing is used along with VGG 19 model. Using this model, images can be uploaded and trained very fast and efficiently 2. This model increases image classification process. It will be able to identify diseases that appear in different sections of the leaf 3. Accuracy of the model has been increased |

## 5 Results and Discussion

The accuracy of the model as well as validation accuracy of the model in a graphical way and it is shown in Fig. 5

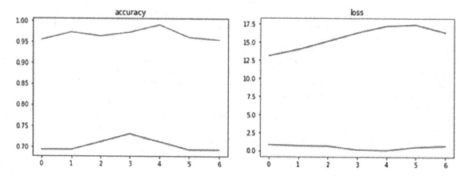

**Fig. 5.** Accuracy and loss of the model

The model loaded and the final accuracy of our created model is obtained. Now the model is ready to detect the disease of the plant. The disease plant image is loaded for testing and then disease name and pictures of the loaded disease plant image is displayed. It is shown in Fig. 6.

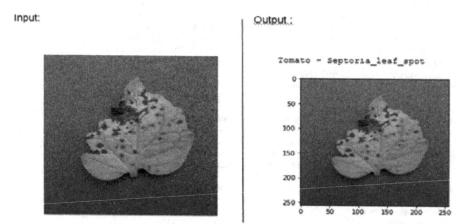

**Fig. 6.** Plant diseased image with disease name

## 6 Conclusion

Through the use of image processing techniques, this work provides effective and precise methods for classifying and detecting plant diseases. The manpower cost and detection time are decreased by this automated method. The farmers can use it to diagnose the illness and take appropriate corrective action. This database will expand in subsequent work to identify more leaf diseases. We have developed a model that is completely original from all others since it makes it simple to examine all varieties of plant diseases. Also system software is developed that allows users to enter an image of their sickness and quickly obtain both the name of the ailment and a cure. So that users' problems can be easily solved and they can produce different good products. Although there are many different versions on the market, this one is superior to all the others. Because numerous other plants, including potato, tomato, banana, and orange ones, have also undergone testing, it gives the disease an image of a disease plant.

# References

1. Mohanty, S.P., Hughes, D.P., Salathé, M.: Using deep learning for image-based plant disease detection. Front. Plant Sci. **7**, 14199 (2016)
2. Rangarajan, A.K., Purushothaman, R., Ramesh, A.: Tomato crop disease classification using pre-trained deep learning algorithm. Procedia Comput. Sci. **133**, 1040–1047 (2018)
3. Too, J., Abdullah, A.R., Mohd Saad, N.: A new co-evolution binary particle swarm optimization with multiple inertia weight strategy for feature selection. Informatics **6**(2), 21. MDPI (2019)
4. Barbedo, J.G.A.: A review on the main challenges in automatic plant disease identification based on visible range images. Biosys. Eng. **144**, 52–60 (2016)
5. Ferentinos, K.P.: Deep learning models for plant disease detection and diagnosis. Comput. Electron. Agric. **145**, 311–318 (2018)
6. Chen, J., Chen, J., Zhang, D., Sun, Y., Nanehkaran, Y.A.: Using deep transfer learning for image-based plant disease identification. Comput. Electron. Agric. **173**, 105393 (2020)
7. Madiwalar, S.C., Wyawahare, M.V.: Plant disease identification: a comparative study. In: 2017 International Conference on Data Management, Analytics and Innovation (ICDMAI), pp. 13–18. IEEE (2017)
8. Martinelli, F., et al.: Advanced methods of plant disease detection. A review. Agron. Sustain. Dev. **35**(1), 1–25 (2015)
9. Wallelign, S., Polceanu, M., Buche, C.: Soybean plant disease identification using convolutional neural network. In: FLAIRS Conference, pp. 146–151 (2018)
10. Shirahatti, J., Patil, R., Akulwar, P.: A survey paper on plant disease identification using machine learning approach. In: International Conference on Communication and Electronics Systems (ICCES), pp. 1171–1174. IEEE (2018)
11. Nagasubramanian, K., Jones, S., Singh, A.K., Sarkar, S., Singh, A., Ganapathysubramanian, B.: Plant disease identification using explainable 3D deep learning on hyperspectral images. Plant Methods **15**(1), 1–10 (2019)
12. UR Rahman, H., et al.: A comparative analysis of machine learning approaches for plant disease identification. Adv. Life Sci. **4**(4), 120–126 (2017)
13. Kothari, J.D.: Plant disease identification using artificial intelligence: machine learning approach. Int. J. Innov. Res. Comput. Commun. Eng. **7**(11), 11082–11085 (2018)
14. Vamsidhar, E., Rani, P.J., Babu, K.R.: Plant disease identification and classification using image processing. Int. J. Eng. Adv. Technol. **8**(3), 442–446 (2019)
15. Pertot, I., Kuflik, T., Gordon, I., Freeman, S., Elad, Y.: Identificator: a web-based tool for visual plant disease identification, a proof of concept with a case study on strawberry. Comput. Electron. Agric. **84**, 144–154 (2012)

# Face Mask Detection: An Application of Artificial Intelligence

Poonam Mittal[1], Ashlesha Gupta[1], Bhawani Sankar Panigrahi[2(✉)], Ruqqaiya Begum[3], and Sanjay Kumar Sen[4]

[1] Department of Computer Engineering, J C Bose University of Science and Technology, YMCA, Faridabad, India
[2] Department of CSE (AI & ML), Vardhaman College of Engineering (Autonomous), Hyderabad, India
bspanigrahi.cse@gmail.com
[3] Department of CSE, Vardhaman College of Engineering (Autonomous), Hyderabad, India
[4] Department of IT, Vardhaman College of Engineering (Autonomous), Hyderabad, India

**Abstract.** COVID-19 has been announced as a new pandemic which has affected almost all the countries of the world. Millions of people have become sick and thousands have died due to the respiratory illness caused by the virus. The virus is known to spread when small droplets from nose or mouth of an infected person gets dissolved in air when he or she coughs or exhales or when a person touches a surface infected with virus. The governments all over the world are working on ways to curb the spread of this virus. Multidisciplinary researchers are working to find the best solutions in their own way. Out of the many solutions wearing surgical facemasks is being one of the best preventive measures to limit the spread of corona virus. These masks support filtration of air and adequate breathability. But the problem is that few people don't use the masks regularly or occasionally due to various reasons like negligence and discomfort etc. This is one of the main causes of high spread of COVID. So, there is a strong need to detect people without mask at public places and to aware them. There are so many initiatives taken by government in this direction, but all have their limitation in one or the other way. So, there is a strong need of a digital solution to ensure that people comply with the government rules of wearing masks in public place sand to recognize unmasked faces on existing monitoring systems to maintain safety and security. Facial recognition systems were being used to identify faces using technology that includes hardware like video cameras. These systems work by combining AI based pattern recognition system along with biometrics to map facial features from an image and compare it with a database of known faces. This research content is also an initiative in this direction to optimize the results.

**Keywords:** COVID-19 · Face Mask · Detection Methods · Deep Learning · Image processing

S. Nandan Mohanty et al. (Eds.): ICISML 2022, LNICST 471, pp. 193–201, 2023.
https://doi.org/10.1007/978-3-031-35081-8_16

# 1  Introduction

Face Mask Detection is a technique which is used to classify that a person is wearing mask or not. Face mask detection can give us insights into the future of the current situation [1–5]. The Face mask detection system [6–8] can be used at Airports, Hospitals, Offices, Workspaces and Public places signal airport authorities to act against the travelers without masks. Face Mask detection techniques mainly follow the following steps:

   i. Detection of people passing through camera.
  ii. Identify mask on the face.
 iii. Providing reliable statistics about whether the person wearing or not wearing the mask.

A variety of face detection systems have been proposed: A real time face mask detection technique was proposed by Harshil Patel which was implemented using Python and OpenCV. The technique executes by applying facial landmark feature to detect face images in the existing video images. Kera [13] and TensorFlow [14] based deep learning techniques are used to categorize the input images into mask or no-mask categories. Since the technique utilizes artificially generated images of the people wearing masks this can't be equivalent to the real images of people wearing masks. So, training model on the Real images can lead to the higher accuracy in detecting the people with the mask and without the mask.

This technique is based on PyTorch and OpenC, used to identify person without mask on image/video-stream. The data is augmented using PyTorch torch vision. The augmented data is then pre-processed using PyTorch transforms. The pre-processed data is then used to train the classifier (MobileNetV2) [7, 12, 13, 15, 18] using PyTorch. The trained classifier is then used to divide video stream images into mask and no-mask categories. The advantage of using PyTorch over TensorFlow is that it provides data parallelism.

Convolution Neural Networks based Image Classification technique has been preferred as it is lightweight and efficient mobile oriented model. The accuracy of the proposed model is 60–70%. It worksin2 phases:

   i. **Object detection**–Neural network SSD issued here for object detection
  ii. **Classification**-MobileNetV2 [12–14] issued here for classification purpose.

This technique also suffers from the limitation like small and blurred image, varying angle of face. To deal the issue of lack of clarity of the images in still frames this method was proposed, where different frames of the video are used for decision making. Additional techniques called as tracking is required to deal the same. All the frames related to a common person are grouped and classifier runs on each frame and then combines the results into a single decision.

In this technique a heuristic approach is used for posing estimation where key-points for many body parts, including the head are extracted. Using head key-point seems more intuitive and simpler. There are some weird glitches pose detections at some frames. These can be filtered out using a threshold for the detection scores. In the cases, where stable detection for all head key-points is not possible, chest key-points seems like the best approach for street cameras in general. Here, pose estimation and extracting heads are used as object detection instead of using an SSD neural network. Now the classification to detect mask/no mask classification is done on the head images. Methods used to classify the images are:

i. **Threshold:** Images are classified on a scale of 100 where classifier outputs with score under20 (*no mask*) or above 80 (*mask*). Others are discarded because the existing solutions ignore the case of misplaced mask.

ii. **Multiple snapshots of video stream:** For each person, count the snapshot which achieves threshold of mask and similarly for non-mask as they walk their path.

Few refinements were also proposed to improve the reliability of the solution. Like margins may be used to refine the image and it darken the outside area. A configurable parameter to classify frontal face may be used to classify only faces so that both eyes can be identified.

## 2  Problem Identification

Need is the key for innovation. Innovation in real world video analytics is at its infant stage. Issues in real world analytics are constantly arising and researchers are trying to get the solution. There is a strong need to find the solutions and to raise the accuracy of existing solutions. Most of the existing solutions work very slow which is a big concern.

i. **Updating the model of pose estimation:** With the advancement of system this is an open area of research which model to use to get better pose estimation.

ii. **Classifier Improvement:** Mask and without mask are successfully implemented but it is very difficult to detect misplaced mask like nose and mouth are visible. Available datasets are ignorant towards this category.

iii. **Person re-identification:** Re-identification techniques are required if the screen freezes. Current video analysts have no solution, but continuous steps are being taken to improve the solution.

## 3  Working of Face Mask Detection

Face mask detection system combines AI techniques with deep learning algorithms along with image processing capabilities. It can be connected to existing surveillance systems to capture face images. The face images are then processed and fed as input to image classifier that uses deep learning models to categorize images into masked and no-mask images. The system can then issue alarm or send warning signals to the officials if someone tries to enter public places without mask.

Convolution Neural Networks are used here to implement Face Mask Detection System as CNN approach models the local understanding of the image properly. Very few parameters are used repeatedly in comparison to a fully connected network. While a fully connected network generates weights from each pixel on the image, a convolution neural network generates just enough weights to scan a small area of the image at any given time. A Convolution neural network (CNN) [8, 14, 15] is mainly used for image processing, classification, segmentation and for other auto correlated data. Each convolution layer contains a series of filters known as convolution kernels. Pixel values are provided as input to the filters where it is a matrix of integers. Each pixel is multiplied by the corresponding value in the kernel, and then the result is summed up for a single value for simplicity representing a grid cell, like a pixel, in the output channel/feature map. To implement the model following steps are followed.

### 3.1 Gathering the Dataset

The first step before beginning implementation of the CNN model using MobileNetV2 is to gather the dataset for the face mask detection. This dataset of about *1,376* images will be used for training the model and also for testing its accuracy. The images with mask are generated artificially by using the facial landmarks.

### 3.2 Processing the Data

As Pandas [15, 18] library has its application for data manipulation and analysis, so here it is used to manipulate the images. Images are stored as large, multi-dimensional arrays (matrices) so here Numpy [17] library is used. These libraries are used for here for data pre-processing as desired for training of CNN model. The steps are as follows:

a. Image path variables extracted from dataset and stored separately in a image path list.
b. Pre-processing and Labelling–Pre-processing steps include resizing to 224 × 224 pixels, conversion to array format, and scaling the pixel intensities in the input image to the range [−1, 1] through pre-process input.
c. Splitting of training data and test data - We have taken the ratio of 80:20 for training and test data respectively. In machine learning, the "Features" are the descriptive attributes which are to be used to predict something and "Label" is the Output we are attempting to predict.
d. Images labelled as the Feature for training the model (X_train) and the class of mask and without mask as the Label (Y_train). Thes arrays X_train and Y_train are converted into Numpy arrays for better processing at later stages.

### 3.3 Classification Using MobileNetV2 Architecture

An improved version of MobileNetV1 is released by Google as MobileNetV2 (a neural network), which is optimized for mobile devices. MobileNetV2 delivers better results while keeping the mathematical overheads as low as possible. Mobile Nets are small, low-latency, low-power models parameterized to meet the resource on strain sofa variety of use cases. Mobile models with a spectrum of different model size can be successfully implemented through MobileNetV2. It is a very effective feature extractor for object detection and segmentation. MobileNetV2 is much faster and more accurate than MobileNetV1.

**Model Architecture-**The basic building block of MobileNetV2 architecture is a bottleneck depth separable convolution with residuals. The architecture of MobileNetV2 in Fig. 1 is comprised of the initial fully convolution layer having 32 filters and having 19 residual bottleneck layers. The architecture of MobileNet is tailored by various researchers as per different performance points. Input image resolution and width multiplier as tunable hyper parameters are tailored to reach the desired precision and performance trade-off. The primary network (width multiplier 1, 224 × 224), has a computation cost of 300 million multiply-adds and uses 3.4 million parameters. The network computational cost ranges from 7 multiply-adds to 585 M MAdds, while the model size varies between 1.7 M and 6.9 M parameters.

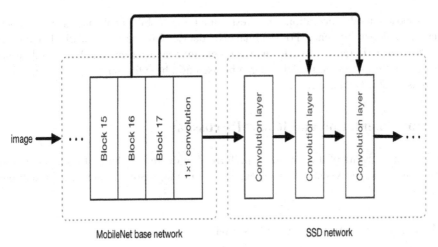

**Fig. 1.** Architecture of MobileNetV2

In comparison to MobileNetV1, MobileNetV2 is more accurate with reduced latency (Fig. 2).

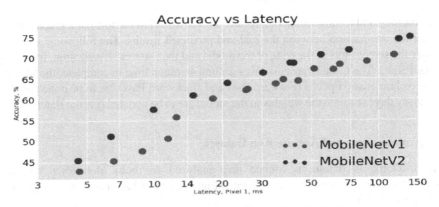

**Fig. 2.** Theoretical comparative view of MobileNetV1 andMobileNetV2 on Accuracy Vs Latency

V2 worked like feature extractor as MobileNetV1 but it requires 5 times fewer parameters and operations in terms of multiply-adds (Fig. 3).

| Model | Params | Multiply-Adds | mIOU |
|---|---|---|---|
| MobileNetV1 + DeepLabV3 | 11.15M | 14.25B | 75.29% |
| MobileNetV2 + DeepLabV3 | 2.11M | 2.75B | 75.32% |

**Fig. 3.** Comparison parameters of MobileNetV1 and MobileNetV2

Proposed model operations are best suited for mobile applications and allows memory-efficient inference. For the ImageNet dataset, MobileNetV2 works like a state of art for a wide range of performance points in ImageNet dataset. It works like an efficient mobile-oriented model that can be used as a base for many visual recognition tasks as in COCO datasets.

## 4   Implementation and Result Discussion

Training and testing of the data set is performed in the initial phase of implementation and then results are visualized and compared with the existing model stop predict the accuracy.

### 4.1   Training and Testing the CNN Model

After the model is implemented, it is trained using the pre-processed trained dataset and generated the predictions for the tested dataset. The CNN model is trained over 20 epochs and batch size of 32 inputs at a time. The Training takes around 40 min.

### 4.2   Making Predictions and Visualizing Results

After training and testing the model, results are visualized in the form of a graph which has set the comparison between the real and predicted results. The following sections include the screenshots of the code of the model and the Dataset visualization, followed by the results. The training process takes around so much time to complete, the time is based on how many Epochs (Forward Pass and Backward Pass) are to be done and for how many days at a time the weights in the model are to be updated (i.e. the Batch Size).

### 4.3   Training Loss and Accuracy on Dataset

Data available in dataset is trained and analyzed for both MobileNet V1 and MobileNetV2 and its comparison is shown in Fig. 4 and model accuracy and comparison is shown in Fig. 5.

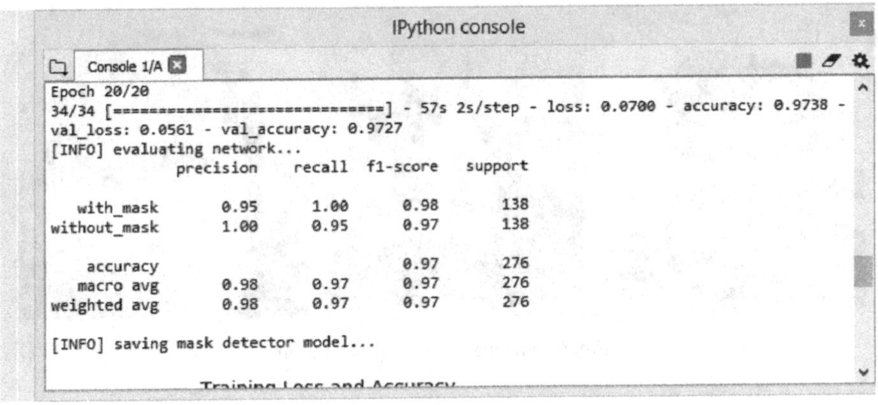

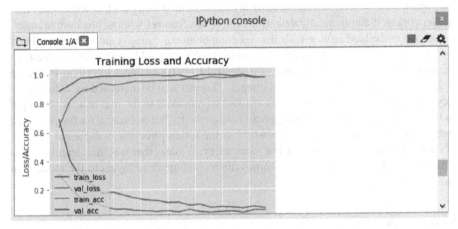

**Fig. 4.** Accuracy comparison of MobileNet V1 and MobileNet V2

**Fig. 5.** Training Loss and accuracy of MobileNetV1 and MobileNet V2

## 4.4 Predictions and Analyzing Accuracy

Once the Model has been trained, we make the predictions by passing the input as frames of the video to the model. The Test Set contains images for classifying the class. The Predictions are made for images. These are then compared with the Actual class (Fig. 6).

**Fig. 6.** Accuracy of mask detection

## 5  Conclusion and Future Enhancements

Face Mask Detection System is successfully implemented using the Convolutional Neural Network as it automatically detects the important features without any human supervision. An embedded device with limited computational capacity finds the best tuned model asMobileNetV2. This technique can also solve the problem of detecting the people without mask in the public places to control COVID 19 spread. System is trained with approximate 1376 AI generated images. This can also be increased for better accuracy. As artificially generated images cannot be equivalent to the real images of people so training model on the real images can lead to the higher accuracy. As the proposed method suffers from few limitations which is the future direction in the same field as: CNN based classifiers are slower but more accurate than other machine learning classifier algorithms. Also, for further improvement, adding more layers to the model can improve accuracy.

## References

1. Mangla, M., Sharma, N.: Fuzzy modelling of clinical and epidemiological factors for COVID-19 (2020)
2. Du, R.-H., et al.: Predictors of mortality for patients with COVID-19 pneumonia caused by SARS-CoV-2: a prospective cohort study. Eur. Respir. J. **55**(5) (2020)
3. Vincent, J.-L., Taccone, F.S.: Understanding pathways to death in patients with COVID-19. Lancet Respir. Med. **8**(5), 430–432 (2020)
4. Ignatius, T.S.Y., et al.: Evidence of airborne transmission of the severe acute respiratory syndrome virus. New England J. Med. **350**(17), 1731–1739 (2004)
5. Tellier, R.: Review of aerosol transmission of influenza a virus. Emerg. Infect. Dis. **12**(11), 1657 (2006)
6. Kazemi, V., Sullivan, J.: One millisecond face alignment with an ensemble of regression trees. IN: Proceedings of the IEEE Conference on Computer Vision and Pattern Recognition (2014)
7. Fernández-Delgado, M., et al.: Do we need hundreds of classifiers to solve real world classification problems? J. Mach. Learn. Res. **15**(1), 3133–3181 (2014)
8. Karpathy, A., et al.: Large-scale video classification with convolutional neural networks. In: Proceedings of the IEEE Conference on Computer Vision and Pattern Recognition (2014)

9.  He, K., et al.: Deep residual learning for image recognition. In: Proceedings of the IEEE Conference on Computer Vision and Pattern Recognition (2016)
10. An Introduction to Convolutional Neural Networks. https://towardsdatascience.com/an-int roduction-to-convolutional-neural-networks-eb0b60b58fd7
11. Simple Introduction to Convolutional Neural Networks. https://towardsdatascience.com/sim ple-introduction-to-convolutional-neural-networks-cdf8d3077bac
12. Dey, S.K., Howlader, A., Deb, C.: MobileNet mask: a multi-phase face mask detection model to prevent person-to-person transmission of SARS-CoV-2. In: Kaiser, M.S., Bandyopadhyay, A., Mahmud, M., Ray, K. (eds.) Proceedings of International Conference on Trends in Computational and Cognitive Engineering. AISC, vol. 1309, pp. 603–613. Springer, Singapore (2021). https://doi.org/10.1007/978-981-33-4673-4_49
13. Venkateswarlu, I.B., Kakarla, J., Prakash, S.: Face mask detection using MobileNet and global pooling block. In: 2020 IEEE 4th Conference on Information & Communication Technology (CICT). IEEE (2020)
14. Vu, H.N., Nguyen, M.H., Pham, C.: Masked face recognition with convolutional neural networks and local binary patterns. Appl. Intell. **52**(5), 5497–5512 (2021). https://doi.org/10. 1007/s10489-021-02728-1
15. Li, C., Cao, J., Zhang, X.: Robust deep learning method to detect face masks. In: Proceedings of the 2nd International Conference on Artificial Intelligence and Advanced Manufacture (2020)
16. Rahman, M.M., et al.: An automated system to limit COVID-19 using facial mask detection in smart city network. In: 2020 IEEE International IOT, Electronics and Mechatronics Conference (IEMTRONICS). IEEE (2020)
17. Kumar, A., Kaur, A., Kumar, M.: Face detection techniques: a review. Artif. Intell. Rev. **52**(2), 927–948 (2018). https://doi.org/10.1007/s10462-018-9650-2
18. Lee, D.-H., Chen, K.-L., Liou, K.-H., Liu, C.-L., Liu, J.-L.: Deep learning and control algorithms of direct perception for autonomous driving. Appl. Intell. **51**(1), 237–247 (2020). https://doi.org/10.1007/s10489-020-01827-9
19. Helaly, R., et al.: Deep convolution neural network implementation for emotion recognition system. In: 2020 20th International Conference on Sciences and Techniques of Automatic Control and Computer Engineering (STA). IEEE (2020)
20. Mangla, M., Sayyad, A., Mohanty, S.N.: An AI and computer vision-based face mask recognition and detection system. In: 2021 Second International Conference on Secure Cyber Computing and Communication (ICSCCC). Organized by NIT Jalandhar, Punjab, India, 21–23 May 2021. https://ieeexplore.ieee.org/document/9478175

# A Critical Review of Faults in Cloud Computing: Types, Detection, and Mitigation Schemes

Ramandeep Kaur$^{(\boxtimes)}$ and V. Revathi

Dayananda Sagar University, Bangalore, India
{ramandeepkaur.res-soe-cse,revathi-cse}@dsu.edu.in

**Abstract.** The continuous rise in for demand services in large-scale distributed systems led to the development of cloud Computing (CC). Because it provides a combination of various software resources, CC is considered dynamically scalable. However, due to the cloud's dynamic environment, a variety of unanticipated problems and faults occur that hinder CC performance. Fault tolerance refers to a platform's capacity to respond smoothly to unanticipated hardware or programming failure. Failure must be analyzed and dealt with efficiently in cloud computing in order to accomplish high accuracy and reliability. Over the years, a significant number of techniques and approaches have been proposed for detecting the faults in CC as well as increasing their tolerance ability. In this review paper, we first provided a brief overview of Cloud computing systems, their architecture, and their working mechanism. Moreover, the services provided by Cloud computing and the issues faced by it are also highlighted in this paper. Also, the taxonomy of various faults that occur in the CC environment along with their mitigation techniques is discussed. Furthermore, it has been analyzed that traditional fault detection methods were not generating effective results which resulted in poor performance in cloud environments. Therefore, an ample number of authors stated to use Machine Learning (ML) based models for fault detection in CC. Nonetheless, ML algorithms were not able to handle a large volume of data therefore the concept of Deep Learning was introduced in fault detection approaches. Moreover, it has been also observed that the performance of DL methods can be enhanced significantly by using optimization algorithms along with them. Some of the recently proposed fault detection and tolerant systems based on ML, DL and optimization have been reviewed in this paper.

**Keywords:** Cloud Computing · Fault detection · Fault mitigation · Machine learning · Fault tolerance

## 1 Introduction

Technology name cloud computing (CC) is a modern technique that refers to browsing, modifying, and configuring software or hardware devices that are installed at far-flung locations. In the year 2009, Buyya and others [1] defined cloud computing as a type of distributed and parallel schema that involves the combination of integrated and virtualized computers that have been dynamically allocated and showcased as one or even more

S. Nandan Mohanty et al. (Eds.): ICISML 2022, LNICST 471, pp. 202–221, 2023.
https://doi.org/10.1007/978-3-031-35081-8_17

centralized computing resources. These systems generally rely on service-level agreements (SLA) that are negotiated between both the end user and the service provider. When considering the definition of Cloud computing given by the National Institute of Standards and Technology (NIST), it is defined as a strategy that enables on-demand network access to programmable computer resources. These resources include PCs, memory, connections, and programs which in return will provide immediately and deliver minimal administrative work as well as network operator involvement [2]. As cloud computing offers high reliability and on-demand services which is universally accepted in today's era. In a typical cloud system, a number of processors, storage and networking devices, and sensors are present which make it capable of processing various requests or applications received from customers. Clients send requests to the cloud system that included requests like storing data or processing apps. Every cloud-based data center is made up of physical machines (PM), including one that hosts a set of virtual machines. Such virtual machines (VMs) process the requests which are made by the client. Due to large data on cloud systems, the servers receive hundreds of requests from consumers each and every second from all over the globe to run millions of applications [3, 4].

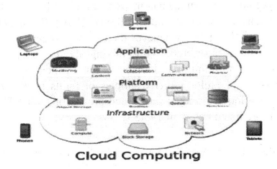

**Fig. 1.** Overview of Cloud computing [5]

The various services as well as an overview of cloud computing are illustrated in Fig. 1. The framework of cloud computing includes the physical layer and abstraction layer. The elements of the physical layer (including, cloud servers, storage, and various other networking components) are required to support the various facilities of the cloud. The software's present in the abstraction layer which is deployed or installed in the physical layer of the system [6] On the basis of services offered by the cloud, it can be categorized into three parts, software a service (SaaS), platform as a service (PaaS), and infrastructure as a service (IaaS). The operating system, networking devices, memory, and processor are some of the resources that the IaaS framework deals with, it also connects the client to the cloud provider. Content delivery networks (CDNs), backup and recovery, computing, and storage are some examples of IaaS. On the other hand, SaaS is an on-demand software application that allows access to different software and applications to clients (like Google docs, Email cloud, billing, customer relationship manager (CRM), financials, and so on). The cloud-like Google app engine has PaaS in it which handles the software applications across the web and permits the customer to generate applications. PaaS allows consumers to handle the complications that are faced during managing and purchasing licenses, network development tools, and many more resources. Some examples of PaaS are business intelligence, database, development and testing, integration, and application development [7–9]. Despite the fact that cloud computing is trending among all industries, some difficulties came into existence that needs to be discussed.

## 1.1 Taxonomy of Faults in CC

With the ever-increasing number of web applications such as Netflix, yelp, and Pinterest installed on public cloud computing stages like Amazon EC2 to allow internet-based services, however, such web applications are prone to errors because of their dynamic, complex, and open nature of cloud systems. This in return affects a large number of customers and also causes financial losses. Among the various concerns that are faced in CC, providing continuous reliability and availability of services in a cloud system is a major challenge. Cloud systems offer services that go far beyond the traditional method which is one of the advantages of the system and these advantages have always been accompanied by some risks and difficulties. For instance, in august 2013 the biggest and most popular organization Amazon.com were unavailable for only about 45 min which results in a financial loss of around 5 million dollars [10]. In a cloud computing system, the breakdown takes place whenever there is a divergence between customer expectations and the services offered. While talking about the types of faults cloud computing is categorized into multiple domains, a few of them is related to network, media, and process-related faults. Other examples of faults in cloud computing are physical faults, service inquiry-related faults, and processor faults. The various faults and their definitions are listed below in Table 1.

**Table 1.** Description of various faults in cloud computing [11]

| Fault types | Description |
|---|---|
| Network type | The faults that arise as a consequence of a network link failure, packet loss or packet corruption, destination failure, and many more types |
| Physical fault | These are the category of faults that are generally found in hardware systems which include faults in memory, faults in the CPU, and many more |
| Media fault | Whenever the media head collapses, these are problems that arise |
| Processor fault | Due to the crashes in the operating system, this type of fault takes place in the processor |
| Process fault | The faults that develop when there are insufficient resources, software problems, and so on |
| Service Expiry Faults | These are errors that happen because of the cloud service expiration for the resource selected when using the application |

Besides this, based on time and resources cloud computing systems face a variety of other faults. Failures such as timing, omission, response, and crash are all forms of failures that happen while computing on operating systems, these failures could be fixed, discontinuous, and temporary (Table 2).

**Table 2.** Lists of faults and their definitions in terms of Computing resources and time [12].

| Fault type | Description |
|---|---|
| Permanent failures | These are the failures that arise because of natural hazards or random shutdown of power due to which several sections of the system might not operate as required |
| Intermittent failures | The error comes out once in a while when the operations are being carried out and it is very hard to recognize the actual harm caused by it |
| Transient failure | The error that appears due to an in-built fault in the system, can be rectified by repealing or rolling back the system to its earlier form. These kinds of defects are commonly detected in the computer system |

Failures cause breaking/shutting down the systems, on the other hand, the distributed and cloud computing systems are distinguished by means of partial faults. The errors that take place in processing or networking elements cause a partial failure which results in the debased performance of the system rather than absolute breakdown. Although this concludes the strong and reliable systems. For a high level of performance in computing systems, the appropriate fault tolerance device is used to control the errors, even though several parts of the system are not running well this fault tolerance allows the system to assist the requirements [13, 14] (Fig. 2).

## 1.2 Fault Tolerance and Mitigation Techniques in CC

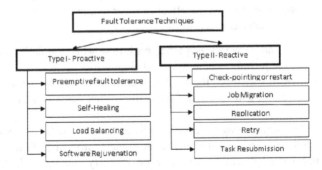

**Fig. 2.** Various kinds of fault tolerance Systems in Cloud Computing

Fault tolerance is a strategy or technology for designing computing systems that function in an effective manner even though some of their components are faulty. While defining a fault-tolerant system, it is stated that the system that is capable to handle a single or even multiple faults related to different sections such as hardware-related faults, design or operation-related errors, etc., is a fault-tolerant system. [15]. The strong likelihood of faults takes place in real-time cloud systems because the processing on computing nodes is usually done distantly. Due to this reason, the requirements of the fault tolerance method are increased to obtain dependability for actual-time computing with a cloud structure. Every fault relies on one another, the connection among these faults, errors, and failures is illustrated in the below figure. The failures are caused by the faults raised in hardware or in software [16]. In a cloud computing system, there are generally 2 types of fault tolerance systems one of them is reactive and the other is termed a proactive type fault tolerance system. These systems make the overall system much stronger and more powerful to tackle faults. Figure 1, demonstrates the different fault tolerance techniques.

**Proactive Fault Tolerance:** The method that determines the doubtful elements and actively takes effective steps such as exchanging the suspicious content before it causes any fault. Further proactive fault tolerance systems are categorized into different types which are discussed below.

1. Preemptive Migration: Under this method, all the systems are constantly estimated and monitored; this project is based on the control loop techniques.
2. Self-Healing: These types of proactive fault tolerance discover and address all the faults that arise while executing the program and fix the failures without any delay. Along with this, a major project is divided into minor sections which operate on a virtual machine as an individual application that deals with the errors expertly.
3. Load Balancing: whenever the definite boundary is exceeded, load balancing procedures are used to equalize the burden of storage and CPU. The processing unit which exceeds its limit is being moved to that processing unit that does not surpass its maximum limit.
4. Software Rejuvenation: The technique which resets the system and makes a new beginning whenever there occurs any error in the system [2, 17].

**Reactive Fault Tolerance:** In this, the effect of error that arises is reduced. There are many types of reactive fault tolerance, such as.

1. Checkpointing/Restart: It works as a label, each time when the fault appears it will reboot its task to the position where it was labeled.
2. Job migration: In this method, the fault is identified for a job operating within a particular device and it will be transferred to some other machine that is suitable for that job.
3. Replication: On various devices, through separate resources, the job is copied in a broad range of times and is executed hence the requests are being fulfilled effectively.
4. Retry: similar virtual machines are required to carry out the task; the work is reduplicated numerous times till the successful outcome.
5. Task Resubmission: for the implementation, the faulted work is once more re-introduced to the same or different device [5, 12].

The Cloud framework needs to be planned in such a way that there must be the least system time off, which in turn ensures the accessibility of services to the cloud users.

To secure access to cloud services, some common policies including a replica of data and checkpointing methods are used. Fault predictions are essential for predictive maintenance because of their capability to stop breakdown events as well as maintain costs [18]. Predictive maintenance, in which the faults are expected and fetching proactive steps [19]. Great possibilities are being formed in machine learning and cloud storage to employ the data from the cloud framework which in turn will guess whenever there are errors in the component. On the basis of tools disorder, physical models, and machine learning methods, mathematical and statistical molding are the famous methods that are used for error predictions. ML-based error detecting and mitigation accesses are examined in the next part of this paper.

# 2  Literature Work

In order to make the CC system more efficient and reliable, it is important to detect the faults and take necessary measures like VM migration and VM load balancing, so that losses can be avoided. Conventional techniques for identifying defects were not reliable or effective due to the complicated and dynamic nature of the CC system. Various researchers have recently applied different ML techniques to forecast failure because such techniques have shown much better and good outcomes than traditional methods. Generally, a classification issue is a prediction problem that states whether there is any fault in the present cloud system or not. Future faults can be anticipated early based on historical failure patterns which in return helps to prevent losses. In this study, numerous machine learning (ML) algorithms that have recently been introduced to forecast faults in a cloud-based context are evaluated.

## 2.1  ML-Based Fault Detection Techniques for Fault Detection

The benefits of cloud systems always had the capability to develop maintenance issues that were increased by a huge number of clients. In current history, many scholars have designed fault tolerance mechanisms to rectify the errors in CC, but the experts were not able to handle all the issues. The authors in [20], proposed a fault detection approach, in which a fuzzy One-class support vector machine and exponentially weighted moving average method were utilized for multi-tiered web applications deployed in CC systems. In order to detect faults in the system, they used the Random Forest technique for selecting features. The suggested scheme was tested and analyzed in the private cloud where a multi-tier application was deployed by using transactional web e-commerce standard and afterward, the faults are injected into it. Experimental findings indicated the efficiency of the proposed fault detection and diagnosis approach. Moreover, the authors in [21], aim at proposing a threshold sensitivity by using support vector machines that creates an effective technique for anticipating failures in the cloud systems, in this new method the faults were avoided for every host based on log files (including CPU utilization, bandwidth, RAM and so on). When the failure threshold levels were 70%, the researchers found that this method was capable to reduce the percentage of migrations to around 76.19%. In [22] the researchers introduced a better and more effective combination based on special SVM. Initially, virtual machines were separated and classified based on their behavioral patterns that use SVM. On the basis of behavioral patterns, by using the gossip protocol and the operation of the case for every group, QoS can be easily anticipated. The outputs of the Cloudsim simulation showed that the proposed strategy enhances processing speed by 0.65 and reduces makespan by 7.22s when compared with similar approaches. The scholars in [23] aim to lower the cost of PMs, to evaluate the resources required the modified best fit describing technique was used. Based on a fitness function, the efficiency of MBFD was optimized by using a genetic algorithm. The Polynomial Support Vector Machine (P-SVM) is used for cross-validation. That has been used for classification purposes, and parameters such as Service Level Agreement and Job Completion Ratio were evaluated. To show the efficiency of the research work a detailed comparison was made in this paper and almost 70% of improvements were noticed. The authors in [24] focused on load balancing among VMs. Certain loads such as network and CPU-based loads, and loads related to memory capacity can be handled effectively using Load balancing approaches. Such algorithm with their features assists cloud computing with multiple features such as handling failovers, improving the scalability of the system, and reducing the overall cost by providing improved resources for the process. In this study, the authors provided details that cover balancing the load using different machine learning approaches such as decision tree, SVM classifier, random forest approach, etc. The results concluded that the SVM was the approach that was handling the processing time in an effective manner by reducing it under the categorization of various user requests. The researchers evaluated and analyzed this technique in a cloud system and observed that it performed better than certain well-known methods and minimized the makespan time. A new framework namely Multi-Class Support Vector Machine was implemented for workflow scheduled in cloud systems by scholars [25] Because the NER problem was extremely hard to solve in cloud architecture. With MC-SVM, the cloud task offered an approach that generates workflow with named entity recognition. Through performing a synchronized and dynamic distribution to cloud resources, the suggested method optimized the allocation of resources mechanism and attempted to fulfill efficacy and cost objectives. The result from testing the provided technique illustrated the system's capacity to effectively manage cloud resources and minimized the makespan and cost. The authors in [26] aim at ML techniques to efficiently utilize hardware resources. Considering the present state of all virtual machines in the computer system, a prediction method named Support Vector Regression (SVR) was utilized to assess whether it is possible to redistribute resources that were planned by the genetic algorithm method. Based on the period in which the fitness function is fulfilled, the experimental results of GA and Particle Swarm were compared to evaluate which technique is better. Moreover, in the cloud architecture, the above-discussed technique provides a required output. To reduce the cloud data center's electricity usage the virtualization approach is an important technology used in CC. In this century the bulk of services was shifted to a cloud system which in turn puts more pressure on data centers, due to which the authors expanded the size of data centers. To tackle this problem, a resource allocation optimization technique was efficient as necessary. In [27] the scholars proposed a method for VM on the basis of a genetic algorithm as well as the random forest, although both the techniques were supervised ML methods. The purpose of this work was to reduce electricity consumption while simultaneously improving load balance among available resources with help of an improved resource utilization approach. A Real-time workload trace was used to design the methodology given by Planet lab. Particularly while compared to other existing methods, the GA-RF approach improves overall energy consumption, execution time, and resource use. In [28], improved cloud reliability and preventive breakdown can be achieved by identifying and anticipating possible issues in the cloud system. Authors have undertaken numerous studies to predict potential loss, and yet no one has combined an automated system that is capable to perform tasks like monitoring, analysis, etc. by itself. Other than this few more considerations can be made such as the measurement of hard drive, and system metrics like patterns of CPU usage. The researchers offered a combined metrics strategy based on AL, as well as four artificial intelligence algorithms to review data from over a hundred cloud systems in order to detect inaccuracy. The result illustrates the benefits of integrating measures, exceeding state-of-the-art. The authors in [29] introduced a fault prediction method whitehat historical data to anticipate the failure-proneness of a component in a cloud system before that occurs. Node breakdown in systems was hard to forecast because that can be caused by a variety of aspects and expressed by a number of spatial and time signals. To resolve these concerns, the researchers proposed MING, a novel technique that integrates, the LSTM model for temporal data, a Random Forest model for spatial analysis, a ranking model that incorporated the alternate results of two modeling techniques as characteristic inputs and is currently ranked the nodes bag by their failure-proneness and a cost-sensitive function that determined the appropriate benchmark for identifying the faulty nodes. Real-world data from a cloud system were used to verify the technique and the outcomes reconfigure the effectiveness of the proposed strategy. The authors effectively implemented the proposed method in real-life situations. In [30] the experts described an unattended error detection strategy based on an ensemble of Bayesian models, which defines the system's typical operational state and recognizes abnormal activities. Once the system administrators have confirmed the irregularities, marked data was available. Afterward, to predict future cloud faults supervised learning with decision tree classifiers was utilized by the authors. According to results obtained in a research center, this method achieved an overall accuracy and even a low false positive rate for preventive fault management. The authors in [31] introduced HORA, a hierarchical online failure prediction technique that integrates component failure forecasters with architectural knowledge. To describe the fault dispersion Bayesian networks were used that included both prediction outcomes and component dependencies obtained from architecture designs. The suggested method was tested by considering 3 different types of faults that were related to memory, overload of systems, and crashing of nodes at an unexpected interval. The whole simulation was carried out by using a Netflix Server-side application that enables distributed RSS reading. By comparing the HORA with the unified method, the researchers found that the area under the ROC curve was improved by almost 9.9%. The authors in [32] investigated how resource consumption metrics from Google cluster traces could be used to detect application faults. To classify the input usage time series into different categories the recurrent neural model was used by the experts, whose results revealed that the model can anticipate batch application faults, which were the most common tasks in the Google network. However, the scholars discovered that the forecast algorithm provides the cloud system sufficient time to take appropriate steps far sooner than the application termination which in turn results in 6–10% of resource efficiency. In [33] the researcher's aim was to identify the fundamental characteristics that were associated with cloud application faults and also provided failure forecasting models that accurately anticipated the conclusion of a task before it finished or failed. To execute this technique the authors analyzed the breakdown characteristics of the Google cluster workload trace. In order to reduce resource waste by improving system workloads that failed or are killed in the cloud system, the fault detection technique was explored more by scholars. In order to recognize application faults in the cloud, the investigators proposed a prediction approach that relies on a specialized class of recurrent neural networks called long- short-term memory. For every operation, it collects resource utilization or data performance with the purpose of forecasting the termination status. In forecasting task failures, the proposed method has an accuracy of 87%, with a true positive rate of 85% and a false positive rate of 11%. On the basis of multi-layer bidirectional long short-term memory whose purpose was to anticipate whether the projects were completed or not, the authors in [3] proposed a fault prediction approach to detect job and task errors. In trace-driven tests, this technique outperforms by 93% accuracy of previous state-of-the-art prediction algorithms an 87% accuracy for task and job failures. The comparison table for the above-mentioned fault detection techniques is given in Table 3.

**Table 3.** Comparison of various SVM-based fault techniques

| References | Techniques Used | Results/Outcomes |
| --- | --- | --- |
| [21] | Threshold sensitive by using a support vector mechanism | When the threshold = 70%, migrations were reduced to 76.19 |
| [22] | A hybrid algorithm based on Gossip architecture by using SVM | Enhanced processing speed by 0.65 and reduces makespan by 7.22s |
| [23] | A genetic algorithm (GA) has been used to optimize the MBFD performance | Efficiency was improved by 70% |
| [24] | SVM with moth flame optimization technique | Minimized the makespan time |
| [25] | Multi-Class Support Vector Machine MC-SVM | Minimized the makespan and cost |
| [26] | Support Vector Regression (SVR), ML technique | Handled huge amounts of data on the cloud |
| [27] | The genetic algorithm as well as the random forest, supervised by ML methods | Reduced power usage and improved load balancing in the cloud |
| [28] | Failure prediction approach based on combined metrics using Artificial intelligence | Enhanced the reliability of Cloud systems |

(*continued*)

**Table 3.** (*continued*)

| References | Techniques Used | Results/Outcomes |
| --- | --- | --- |
| [30] | An ensemble of Bayesian with the unsupervised learning-based fault detection method | Improved accuracy with features of low false rate |
| [31] | HORA, a hierarchical online failure prediction technique | Improved ROC curve by almost 9.9% |
| [32] | Recurrent neural networks | Achieved resource efficiency by 6–10% |
| [33] | LSTM model for fault detection | The overall accuracy of 87%, with a TPR and FPR of 85 and 11%respectively |
| [3] | A method based on multi-layer Bidirectional Long Short-Term Memory | Achieved an accuracy of 97 and 87 for task and job failure prediction |

## 2.2 Some Other Noteworthy Works

Without virtual machines the conclusion of multiple application execution was incorrect, to resolve this issue, the authors in [34] proposed an initial virtual cluster allocation technique on the basis of the properties of VM to minimize the network resource usage as well as the energy utilized by the data center. Afterward, to predict a failed PM the CPU temperature was simulated. The investigators moved the virtual machines from degrading physical machines to a set of ideal PMs. Eventually, the best target PMs were selected as an optimization problem that was solved with an improved particle swarm optimization technique. The result demonstrated the effectiveness and efficiency of this technique. The operating metrics of all tasks executed on virtual machines were observed by authors in [35] by an agent-based monitoring method that has the capacity to fix the issues of degrading the efficiency of VM. Whenever degradation was detected, migration was started which in turn resulted in a high rate of fault tolerance and optimization techniques in terms of complexity and system performance. In [36] the researchers examined the data from the national energy research scientific computing center on the production faults over more than a five-year period. By utilizing the data from the computer failure data repository, the investigators created a successful failure forecasting model that concentrated on the high performance of the cloud system. This technique was capable of predicting future faults in the system by using an Auto-Regressive Moving Average. The result demonstrated that the failure prediction accuracy was 95%, moreover in existing real-time systems; the authors assumed that this technique was feasible and adaptable. The authors in [37] used the Google cluster workload trace to execute (which was already discussed by many other researchers in [33]) how and why problems occurred and forecast future failures. According to the research jobs that failed, consume a disproportionate number of resources, and the long short-term memory network was utilized to anticipate the attributes that determine failure. By using the KNN classification model that was trained on the available data the termination status was forecasted. The scholars in [38] used the Enhanced-Modified Best Fit Decreasing approach to implement a VM method. Cross-validation of assigned virtual machines on real machines using Artificial Neural Networks was the conclusion of the suggested technique. Furthermore, the proposed technique seems to have the merits of recognizing false allocations that arise as a result of wasteful resource consumption and assisting in the reallocation of these VMs. In comparison to the conventional technique, the E-MBFD technique outperforms in terms of decreased power consumption as well as a lower number of service-level agreement violations, according to the experimental evidence. To forecast virtual machine break-down by observing VM deterioration, a Fuzzy min-max Neural Network classification technique was proposed by scholars in [39]. The overloaded hyper box was categorized by using the shortest distance-based KNN classifier. FMNN was enhanced by the pro-posed method which results in reduced computational complexity and a quicker process. The result of framework experimentation demonstrates that VM faults can be detected ahead of time. Following the anticipation of a failure, the choice has been made to move from a problematic node to a reserve node. Thus, at a faster convergence rate, the sug-gested method produces more accurate forecasts. In [40], the faults in data centers and systems must have been identified and forecasted efficiently to activate the mechanism that ensures the errors that occur. When one of the hosted data centers collapses one can anticipate a failure spreading throughout the CC and execute proactive steps to deal with it. Based on information or files one approach for forecasting error was to instruct a machine to anticipate the faults among multiple elements that propagate to other data centers and exacerbate the problem. For each of the systems, parameters (including CPU consumption, RAM usage, and so on) could be maintained, and based on these elements a decision tree was developed that can evaluate whether the elements supplied into the decision tree suggested a failed state or suitable state. The authors introduced a novel methodology for forecasting VM failure based on a time series stochastic model [41]. The detection of virtual machine failure was widely expected due to several proactive fault tolerance mechanisms in cloud systems. But, accurate VM failure prediction is highly difficult and has a significant influence on the proactive fault tolerance system. Thus, a failure prediction mechanism that works on basis of time series by considering the autoregressive integrated moving average was used to predict virtual machine faults. To increase the stability of Virtual machines as well as the overall performance of cloud systems, a fault prediction approach based on AdaBoost-Hidden Markov Model was developed by researchers in [42]. The hidden Markov model was used to investigate the true relationship between the different states of the VMs such as observed and hidden. In addition to this, the impact of the AdaBoost method on the HMM and the effectiveness of forecasting VM failure was also the objective of the study. The suggested method responds to the complex and dynamic cloud system, can reliably predict VM failure state, and enhances the prediction power of VM security status, according to the results.

In [43] the authors used different strategies for anticipating failures so that users can act and repair possible faults before they occur. This technique termed PreFix aimed to detect whether a switch failure occurred in near future during runtime. The predictions were based on current switch system metrics as well as prior switch equipment failure occurrences which are painstakingly labeled by network operators. The major finding was that the error of the same switch model shares certain similar Syslog patterns before they happen which can be extracted using ML approaches to anticipate switch failures. This innovative collection of machine learning features can properly deal with noises, sample imbalance, and computing overhead. Over the course of two years, the authors of this technique evaluated PreFix on a 9397-switch dataset under consideration of 3 different switch models. These models were installed in approximately 20-plus data centers owned by a large worldwide search engine. In PCs and ISP, prefixes outperformed the other failure prediction techniques by an average of 61.81% recall and1.84e-5 false positive ratio. Furthermore, the authors in [44] proposed a new cloud scheduling method with the goal of providing priority scheduling and fault tolerance. This approach has worked for single-server fault tolerance and reallocating problematic server activities to a new server with the least load at the time of the failure. This section also includes different strategies to implement various scheduling methods. Most of the earlier algorithm evaluations were included. In 2008, Mylara Reddy Chinnaiah, N. N. in [45] offered fault-tolerant ways describes the number of communication requests depending on the configuration raised by the various software system. These software-generated configurations were categorized into 2 types one is critical and the other non-critical. Thus, these results in adding 2 factors frequency of configuration interactions and normal interaction frequency. Both factors are helpful in measuring the system's reliability and monitoring the important software function such as financial transactions etc. It is also shown in the study that a huge count of interaction requests and failure of essential requests can cause program failure. In 2018, October-December Jialei Liu [46] introduced a proactive PCFT technique based on particle swarm optimization which was aimed at IaaS cloud architectures based on fat-tree topology. The purpose of this technique was to monitor failed PM and after that, the system looks for an optimum physical machine to migrate the VM from the failing PM. For fault detection, in the physical machine, a CPU temperature model was utilized. Based on Copy on Write- Presave in Cache (CoW-PC) Kalanirnika G R in [47] suggested a VM-Checkpoint technique (a reactive strategy) in which a VM was saved after a failure occurred, and the service was subsequently restored from the last checkpoint indicated in cache memory. To improve the memory checkpointing performance the storage exclusion approach was utilized. In [48] as a proactive fault detection technique, Zeeshan Amin April 2015 utilized the Heartbeat technique combined with an Artificial Neural Network. The technique calculated the time needed for another heartbeat signal to arrive, as well as a safety margin $\alpha$. The formula used in this method is,

$$Th2b = ET + \alpha, \qquad (1)$$

where Th2b is considered to be the calculation of the time interval that occurred between two heartbeat signals. In addition to this ET is termed as an estimated time that will be taken for the arrival of the next heartbeat. In [49] for cloud systems, A. Marahatta 2018 provided a fault-tolerant scheduling approach that was focusing on energy constraints. In order to predict the failure rate, researchers utilized an ML forecasting model to learn and understand the difference between both failure and non-failure-prone jobs. Afterward, the vector reconstruction strategy was employed to rebuild failure-prone activities and projected both rectified failure-prone tasks and non-failure-prone jobs to some of the most suitable hosts. The researchers in [50] suggested an innovative and dynamic fault-tolerant scheduling strategy to help with error-free job scheduling. The provided strategy takes into account the most significant parameters such as the rate of failure and the present workload of the process-able resources for optimal QoS. Recent research showed that the proposed system was more beneficial than the baseline solutions when analyzed in terms of balancing the system load and fault tolerance. Researchers presented a fault tolerance load balancing strategy based on resource load and fault index value in [51]. The given solution was focused on 2 main functionalities the selection of resources in an effective manner and the other on the execution of a task. In the first phase, the best suitable resource was selected for implementation purposes and the resource with the lowest load and less fault occurred is selected in the task execution phase. In order to prove the effectiveness of the proposed scheme, the scheme is compared with existing state of art approaches. The model was simulated in CloudSim and proves its effectiveness in various factors such as response and makespan time, handling overhead, and providing better bandwidth. To avoid the system's real-time failure, the authors in [7] proposed a multi-level fault tolerance scheduling technique. The reliability of VMs was determined during the first step by utilizing non-functional testing and a decision-making algorithm. However, to achieve the reliability requirement, that only considered the most reliable VMs, Reliable Decision K-Nearest Neighbor was used and the scheduling mechanism was utilized to achieve high availability. For this purpose, Teaching-Learning Based Optimization scheduling method was developed, which offered a better-scheduled collection of tasks for the associated customer. The researchers evaluated the suggested method by using the Cloudsim platform. By using a multi-level structure, the result demonstrated that in a cloud context, the system provides good data availability and reliability. The researchers in [52], utilized failure statistics which were published by Backblaze (one of the leading data storage services). Between January 2015 and December 2018, the operational status of heterogeneous servers was collected in this dataset, the data was then screened and highly processed generating 2,878,440 records which include 128,820 faults. The results from the experiment indicated that the ANN model has the best prediction accuracy. In [53] the authors proposed numerous and diversified fault tolerance technique (which enables a process or an element to keep functioning normally even if a failure occur) and monitoring method (that anticipates a defect before it occurs) to increase cloud reliability. Fault tolerance techniques were important for both cloud service providers and clients and this approach contained information on the many approaches and methodologies utilized in FT, as well as a future research direction in cloud Fault tolerance. To improve cloud service reliability, different fault tolerance approaches were proposed in the literature. VM breakdown caused several challenges with cloud service dependability and availability. Moreover, by combining proactive techniques (including VM migration and duplication) and reactive methodologies (like, retry used.) the researchers in [54] contributed a new Threshold-Based Adaptive Fault Tolerance approach to cloud systems. An experimental investigation was carried out by comparing three benchmark fault tolerance methodologies (which include the first fit and least full host selection policies). By using the CloudSim simulator, the proposed approach's study results were seen in terms of several metrics including failure rate, throughput, migration, and execution time. To minimize the user's management complexity, the authors in [55] proposed a fuzzy job distributor for fault detection administration. The suggested technique tries to decrease the probability of system faults by distributing user job requests evenly among available resources, this paper addressed abnormal conditions that could lead to failure in a self-adaptive approach by distributing incoming task requests based on the reliability of processing nodes. When compared to alternative load balancing methods, the experimental outcomes reveal a significant reduction in the occurrence of problems. The researchers in [56] presented an innovative, system-level, modular approach to establishing and maintaining fault tolerance in a Cloud system. A dedicated service layer was utilized to present a comprehensive high-level way to hide the technical details of fault tolerance approaches to application users and developers. This service layer enables the user to declare and determine the necessary level of fault tolerance while obviating a need for awareness of the fault tolerance strategies available in the anticipated Cloud system. The authors in [57], described Cluster-based, fault-tolerant mechanisms to handle the data intensiveness of scientific workflow tasks as well as data-intensive scheduling for research areas in cloud systems. A typical academic workflow was simulated, and the CFD method's outcomes were compared to three well-known heuristic scheduling policies (such as MCT, Max-min, and Min-min). When compared with the previous 3 policies, the CFD technique lowered the make-span by 14.28%, 20.37%, and 11.77%, according to the simulated results, and reduced execution costs by 1.27%, 5.3%, and 2.21%, respectively. In terms of time and cost restrictions, the SLA was not exceeded by the CFD technique, however, that was repeatedly violated by present policies. Table 4 gives a brief comparison of various above-mentioned fault detection and tolerant techniques.

**Table 4.** Comparison of other commonly used fault detection and tolerant techniques

| References | Work done | Technique Used | Results |
|---|---|---|---|
| [34] | Proposed an initial virtual cluster allocation technique, based on VM properties | Improved Particle swarm optimization technique | Minimized the network resource use and the energy consumption by data centers |
| [35] | Proposed an agent-based monitoring system for VMs is developed | VM migration | Resolved the deterioration of VMs |
| [36] | Proposed a failure prediction model for cloud systems dataset collected from NERSC | Autoregressive moving average (ARMA) | Achieved an accuracy of 95% |

(*continued*)

**Table 4.** (*continued*)

| References | Work done | Technique Used | Results |
|---|---|---|---|
| [37] | Effectively studied the causes of failures and techniques to predict those failures by using Google cluster workload trace | LSTM and KNN | Reduced network load |
| [38] | Proposed a method for VM allocation | Enhanced-Modified Best Fit Decreasing (E-MBFD) Algorithm and ANN | Less power usage and SLA violations |
| [39] | Proposed a model for predicting the VM failures | Fuzzy min-max neural network and KNN | Achieved high accuracy with a high convergence rate |
| [40] | Suggested a failure predicting model by understanding the logs passed between clouds | Decision Tree | Predicted the status of the cloud system appropriately |
| [41] | Proposed VM fault detection method via the failure predictor | Time series-based autoregressive integrated moving average | Good failure prediction |
| [42] | Suggested a failure prediction model for CC | AdaBoost-Hidden Markov Model | Effectively predicted failure in virtual machines |
| [44] | Proposed a method for predicting single faults | Scheduling methods | Scheduled priority by using the fault-tolerant property |
| [45] | Suggested a fault-tolerant method that was based on communication requests and configurations | Frequency of configuration interactions (IFrFT), characteristics and frequency of interactions (ChIFrFT) | Observed various reasons for software failure |
| [46] | Suggested a proactive approach that directly interacts with the IaaS cloud structure | PSO and CPU temperature model | Identify and track the faulty PM |
| [47] | Proposed a reactive model for predicting faults in CC | VM-μ Checkpoint mechanism based on CoW-PC (Copy on Write-Presave in Cache) algorithm | Optimized the performance of checkpointing in storage |

(*continued*)

**Table 4.** (*continued*)

| References | Work done | Technique Used | Results |
|---|---|---|---|
| [48] | Proposed a proactive fault tolerance method for cloud systems | Heartbeat strategy with ANN | Predicts the time for the next heartbeat message |
| [49] | Developed an energy-efficient fault tolerance method | ML algorithms and vector reconstruction | The suggested model was able to predict failure effectively |
| [50] | Suggested yet another fault-tolerant method | Cloudsim toolkit | Balances load in CC effectively |
| [51] | A technique for tolerating faults was proposed | Cloudsim toolkit | Enhanced performance in terms of response time, makespan, and throughput |
| [7] | The fault-tolerant method was proposed | Reliable Decision K-Nearest Neighbor (RDK-NN) algorithm teaching-Learning Based Optimization (TLBO) | Tasks are scheduled more effectively |
| [52] | Proposed a fault detection model where they utilized Backblaze data | Self-Monitoring, Analysis, and reporting technology (SMART) along with NB, ANN | ANN is more accurate than NB in predicting faults |
| [54] | New Threshold-Based Adaptive Fault Tolerance (TBAFT) approach | By integrating proactive and reactive fault detection methods in Cloudsim | Reduced failure rate, high throughput |
| [55] | Proposed a fault tolerance technique for dealing with various failures | Fuzzy job distributor or load balancer | Minimized the fault occurrences |
| [57] | Proposed a CFD fault-tolerant method based on clustering | Cluster-based, fault-tolerant, and data-intensive (CFD) scheduling | CFD has less makespan time than MCT, Max-min, and min-min, reducing cost |

## 3   Conclusion

Since the demand for cloud computing services increases day by day, therefore it is crucial to offer uninterrupted services even in presence of faults. The resources in the CC can be scaled dynamically in such a way that cost is reduced and performance is increased. The process of identifying faults and problems in a system is known as fault tolerance. The network should function properly even if a defect, hardware failure, or software failure happens. For dependable cloud computing, failures must be effectively controlled. Additionally, it will provide robustness and dependability. In this context, a number of recently proposed fault detection and tolerance techniques are reviewed in this paper. In addition to this, we have also highlighted the basic concept of CC and various issues related to it. Furthermore, we also analyzed the role of Machine learning and DL and optimization algorithms in detecting the faults in CC and which techniques are mostly employed by researchers in their work. After analyzing the literature, we observed that a conventional number of authors have worked on VM migration, Heartbeat strategy, etc. for detecting and avoiding faults in CC. However, such methods were not able to handle faults effectivity and hence, ML algorithms were used. As there is a number of ML algorithms available, the biggest challenge for researchers was to select the best algorithm. From the literature survey, we concluded that t majority of researchers used SVM in their work for detecting and mitigating the faults in cloud systems. No doubt that ML was showing good results than traditional fault detection systems but it undergoes overfitting issues. Therefore, the authors started to use DL methods for detecting faults in cloud systems. DL-based methods, however, improved the accuracy of fault detection but it also increased latency and reduced battery life. Therefore, some researchers have used optimization-based algorithms in their work for solving multi-objective optimization problems in CC systems. it can be concluded that by integrating optimization algorithms along with effective ML or DL techniques, the accuracy of the fault detection model can be enhanced significantly.

# References

1. Buyya, R., et al.: Cloud computing, and emerging IT platforms: vision, hype, and reality for delivering computing as the 5th utility. Futur. Gener. Comput. Syst. **25**, 17 (2009)
2. Kumari, P., Kaur, P.: A survey of fault tolerance in cloud computing. J. King Saud Univ. Comput. Inf. Sci. **33**(10), 1159–1176 (2021)
3. Gao, J., Wang, H., Shen, H.: Task failure prediction in cloud data centers using deep learning. IEEE Trans. Serv. Comput. (2020)
4. Haresh, M., Kalady, S.: Agent-based dynamic resource allocation on federated clouds. In: Recent Advances in Intelligent Computational Systems (RAICS), pp. 111–114 (2011)
5. Ganesh, A., Sandhya, M., Shankar, S.: A study on fault tolerance methods in cloud computing. In: 2014 IEEE International Advance Computing Conference (IACC). IEEE (2014)
6. Bui, T.-K., Vo, L., Nguyen, C., Pham, T.V., Tran, H.: A fault detection and diagnosis approach for multi-tier application in cloud computing. J. Commun. Networks **22**, 399–414 (2020). https://doi.org/10.1109/JCN.2020.000023
7. Devi, K., Paulraj, D.: Multilevel fault-tolerance aware scheduling technique in cloud environment. J. Internet Technol. **22**(1), 109–119 (2021)
8. Mell, P., Grance, T.: The NIST definition of cloud computing. NIST Special Publication, 800-145 (Draft) (2011). Accessed 11 Oct 2013
9. Cloud Taxonomy. http://cloudtaxonomy.opencrowd.com
10. Wang, T., et al.: Fault detection for cloud computing systems with correlation analysis. In: 2015 IFIP/IEEE International Symposium on Integrated Network Management (IM), pp. 652–658 (2015)
11. Prajapati, V., Thakkar, V.: A survey on failure prediction techniques in cloud computing. No. 4134. EasyChair (2020)
12. Sivagami, V.M., Easwara Kumar, K.S.: Survey on fault tolerance techniques in cloud computing environment. Int. J. Sci. Eng. Appl. Sci. **1**(9), 419–425 (2015)

13. Gokhroo, M.K., Govil, M.C., Pilli, E.S.: Detecting and mitigating faults in cloud computing environment. In: 3rd IEEE International Conference (2017)
14. Charity, T.J.: Resource reliability using fault tolerance in cloud computing, pp. 65–71 (2016)
15. Jhawar, R., Piuri, V., Santambrogio, M.: A comprehensive conceptual system-level approach to fault tolerance in cloud computing. IEEE (2012). https://doi.org/10.1109/SysCon.2012. 6189503
16. Singh, A., Kinger, S.: An efficient fault tolerance mechanism based on moving averages algorithm. IJARCSSE (2013). ISSN: 2277 128X
17. Shah, Y., Thakkar, E., Bhavsar, S.: Fault tolerance in cloud and fog computing—a holistic view. In: Kotecha, K., Piuri, V., Shah, H.N., Patel, R. (eds.) Data Science and Intelligent Applications. LNDECT, vol. 52, pp. 415–422. Springer, Singapore (2021). https://doi.org/10. 1007/978-981-15-4474-3_46
18. Sirbu, A., Babaoglu, O.: Towards data-driven autonomics in data centers. In: Proceedings - 2015 International Conference on Cloud Computing ICCAC 2015, pp. 45–56 (2015)
19. Pop, D.: Machine learning and cloud computing: survey of distributed and SaaS solutions. Inst. e-Austria Timisoara, Tech. Figure 2. Component Failure Analysis Rep 1 (2012)
20. Bui, K.T., et al.: A fault detection and diagnosis approach for multi-tier application in cloud computing. J. Commun. Netw. **22**(5), 399–414 (2020)
21. Fadaei Tehrani, A., Safi-Esfahani, F.: A threshold sensitive failure prediction method using support vector machine. Multiagent Grid Syst. **13**(2), 97–111 (2017)
22. Razzaghzadeh, S., Norouzi Kivi, P., Panahi, B.: A hybrid algorithm based-on Gossip architecture by using SVM for reliability in cloud computing. Soft Comput. J. (2021)
23. Singh, G., Mahajan, M.: VM Allocation in cloud computing using SVM (2019). https://doi. org/10.35940/ijitee.I1123.0789S19
24. Radhika, D., Duraipandian, M.: Load balancing in cloud computing using support vector machine and optimized dynamic task scheduling. In: 2021 9th International Conference on Reliability, Infocom Technologies and Optimization (Trends and Future Directions) (ICRITO), pp. 1–6 (2021). https://doi.org/10.1109/ICRITO51393.2021.9596289
25. Haoxiang, W., Smys, S.: MC-SVM based workflow preparation in cloud with named entity identification. J. Soft Comput. Paradigm (JSCP) **2**(02), 130–139 (2020)
26. Anushuya, G., Gopikaa, K., Gokul Prasath, S., Keerthika, P.: Resource management in cloud computing using SVM with GA and PSO. Int. J. Eng. Res. Technol. (IJERT) ETEDM **6**(04) (2018)
27. Madhusudhan, H.S., Satish Kumar, T., Syed Mustapha, S.M.F.D., Gupta, P., Tripathi, R.P.: Hybrid approach for resource allocation in cloud infrastructure using random forest and genetic algorithm. Sci. Programm. **2021**, 10 (2021). https://doi.org/10.1155/2021/4924708
28. Chhetri, T., Dehury, C.K., Lind, A., Srirama, S.N., Fensel, A.: A combined metrics approach to cloud service reliability using artificial intelligence (2021)
29. Lin, Q., et al.: Predicting node failure in cloud systems. In: ESEC/FSE, Lake Buena Vista, FL, USA. Association for Computing Machinery (ACM) (2018)
30. Guan, Q., Zhang, Z., Fu, S.: Ensemble of bayesian predictors and decision trees for proactive failure management in cloud computing systems. J. Commun. (2012)
31. Pitakrat, T., Okanovic, D., van Hoorn, A., Grunske, L.: Hora: architecture-aware online failure prediction. J. Syst. Softw. (2018)
32. Chen, X., Lu, C., Pattabiraman, K.: Failure prediction of jobs in compute clouds: a google cluster case study. In: 2014 IEEE International Symposium on Software Reliability Engineering Workshops (2014)
33. Islam, T., Manivannan, D.: Predicting application failure in cloud: a machine learning approach. In: 2017 IEEE International Conference on Cognitive Computing (ICCC) (2017)

34. Liu, J., Wang, S., Zhou, A., Kumar, S.A.P., Yang, F., Buyya, R.: Using proactive fault-tolerance approach to enhance cloud service reliability. IEEE Trans. Cloud Comput. **6**(4), 1191–1202 (2018). https://doi.org/10.1109/TCC.2016.2567392

35. Talwar, B., Arora, A., Bharany, S.: An energy efficient agent aware proactive fault tolerance for preventing deterioration of virtual machines within cloud environment. In: 2021 9th International Conference on Reliability, Infocom Technologies and Optimization (Trends and Future Directions) (ICRITO), pp. 1–7 (2021). https://doi.org/10.1109/ICRITO51393.2021.9596453

36. Mohammed, B., et al.: Failure analysis modelling in an infrastructure as a service (Iaas) environment. Electron. Notes Theor. Comput. Sci. **340**, 41–54 (2018)

37. Golani, B., Datta, J., Singh, G.: Prediction of cloud server job failures using machine learning based KNN classification and LSTM modelling methods. Int. J. Eng. Res. Technol. (IJERT) **10**(05) (2021)

38. Shalu, Singh, D.: Artificial neural network-based virtual machine allocation in cloud computing. J. Discrete Math. Sci. Crypt., 1–12 (2021)

39. Qasem, G.M., Madhu, B.K.: Proactive fault tolerance in cloud data centers for performance efficiency. Int. J. Pure Appl. Math. **117**(22), 325–329 (2017)

40. Bambharolia, P., Bhavsar, P., Prasad, V.: Failure prediction and detection in cloud datacenters. Int. J. Sci. Technol. Res. **6** (2017)

41. Rawat, A., Sushil, R., Agarwal, A., Afzal: A new approach for VM failure prediction using stochastic model in cloud. IETE J. Res. (2018)

42. Li, Z., Liu, L., Kong, D.: VM failure prediction method based on AdaBoost-Hidden Markov model. In: IEEE International Conference on Intelligent Transportation, Big Data and Smart City (ICITBS) (2019)

43. Zhang, S.: PreFix: switch failure prediction in datacenter networks. In: Proceedings of the ACM on Measurement and Analysis of Computing Systems (2018)

44. Singla, N., Bawa, S.: Priority scheduling algorithm with fault tolerance in cloud computing. Int. J. **3**(12) (2013)

45. Mylara Reddy Chinnaiah, N.N.: Fault-tolerant software systems using software configurations for cloud computing. J. Cloud Comput. **7** (2018). Article number: 3

46. Liu, J., Wang, S.: Using proactive fault-tolerance approach to enhance cloud service reliability. IEEE Trans. Cloud Comput. **6**(4), 1191–1202 (2018)

47. Kalanirnika, G.R., Sivagami, V.: Fault tolerance in cloud using reactive and proactive. Int. J. Comput. Sci. Eng. Commun., 1159–1164 (2015)

48. Amin, Z., Sethi, N., Singh, H.: Review of fault tolerance techniques in cloud computing. Int. J. Comput. Appl., 11–17 (2015)

49. Marahatta, C.C.: Energy-aware fault-tolerant scheduling scheme based on intelligent prediction model for cloud data center. In: 2018 Ninth International Green and Sustainable Computing Conference (IGSC), Pittsburgh, PA, USA, pp. 1–8 (2018)

50. Sathiyamoorthi, V., et al.: Adaptive fault tolerant resource allocation scheme for cloud computing environments. JOEUC **33**(5), 135–152 (2021). https://doi.org/10.4018/JOEUC.202 10901.oa7

51. Shukla, A., Kumar, S., Singh, H.: Fault tolerance based load balancing approach for web resources in cloud environment. Int. Arab J. Inf. Technol. **17**(2), 225–232 (2020)

52. Ragmani, A., et al.: Adaptive fault-tolerant model for improving cloud computing performance using artificial neural network. Procedia Comput. Sci. **170**, 929–934 (2020)

53. Gupta, A.K., Mamgain, A.: Machine learning based approach for fault tolerance in cloud computing. Int. J. Adv. Res. Ideas Innov. Technol. **4**, 59–62 (2018)

54. Rawat, A., et al.: A new adaptive fault tolerant framework in the cloud. IETE J. Res., 1–13 (2021)

55. Arabnejad, H., Pahl, C., Estrada, G., Samir, A., Fowley, F.: A fuzzy load balancer for adaptive fault tolerance management in cloud platforms. In: De Paoli, F., Schulte, S., Broch Johnsen, E. (eds.) ESOCC 2017. LNCS, vol. 10465, pp. 109–124. Springer, Cham (2017). https://doi.org/10.1007/978-3-319-67262-5_9

56. Jhawar, R., Piuri, V., Santambrogio, M.: Fault tolerance management in cloud computing: a system-level perspective. IEEE Syst. J. 7(2), 288–297 (2012)

57. Ahmad, Z., Jehangiri, A.I., Ala'anzy, M.A., Othman, M., Umar, A.I.: Fault-tolerant and data-intensive resource scheduling and management for scientific applications in cloud computing. Sensors (Basel) 21(21), 7238 (2021). https://doi.org/10.3390/s21217238

# Video Content Analysis Using Deep Learning Methods

Gara Kiran Kumar[1]([✉]) and Athota Kavitha[2]

[1] Department of Computer Science and Engineering, Anurag University, Hyderabad, India
kirankumarcse@anurag.edu.in
[2] Department of Computer Science and Engineering, Jawaharlal Nehru Technological University, Kukatpally, Hyderabad, India

**Abstract.** With the emergence of low-cost video recording devices, the internet is flooded with videos. However, most videos are uncategorized, necessitating video content analysis. This review effort addresses visual big data feature extraction, video segmentation, classification, and abstract video challenges. Exploring compressive sensing, deep learning (DL), and kernel methods for various tasks in video content analysis include video classification, clustering, dimension reduction, event detection, and activity recognition. DL is used to examine video footage recognition and classification. This study examines the algorithms' flaws and benefits when applied to datasets. The classification approaches used Naive Bayes, support vector machine (SVM), and Deep Convolution Neural Network (DCNN) with Deer Hunting Optimization (DHO). Other approaches have higher false discovery and alarm rates than the DCNNDHO algorithm.

**Keywords:** video content segmentation · video content recognition · classification · Deep Convolution Neural Network (DCNN) with Deer Hunting Optimization (DHO)

## 1 Introduction

In multimedia, a combination of videos and images, generation by individuals, the boom is caused by integrated cameras and handheld devices availability with a large storage capacity complemented using the cloud. Through fast broadband connections and high bandwidth, these contents are shared. Social media's reaching power assists this. By 2025, it was estimated that there were approximately 9 trillion images stored on cameras, storage media, and in the cloud around the globe and that 2.4 trillion additional digital pictures will be taken in 2025 alone. In July 2015, it was reported that more than 400 h of Video were posted to YouTube every minute [1], continuing a similar pattern. The growing deployment of Closed Circuit Television (CCTV) cameras, which capture large quantities of media in public and private spaces to improve surveillance and deter crimes, adds to the phenomenon. Because of substantial real-life applications, a significant research area of interest is video content analysis, which is used to perform its functionalities. Video streams are analyzed automatically using Video Content Analysis

S. Nandan Mohanty et al. (Eds.): ICISML 2022, LNICST 471, pp. 222–243, 2023.
https://doi.org/10.1007/978-3-031-35081-8_18

(VCA). Spatial and temporal events are determined and detected using this. About video content, helpful information is provided using this [2]. For analyzing video contents captured using surveillance systems, this is typically inherent. VCA has been used in a broad range of applications such as traffic control, health care, transportation, detecting intruders, and counting the number of people incoming or leaving locations. With VCA, the monitoring system is improved. It can accurately trace all objects' movements, where they came from, where they went, and when. This work is used to reduce the amount of time spent on video search while also improving the accuracy of the results.

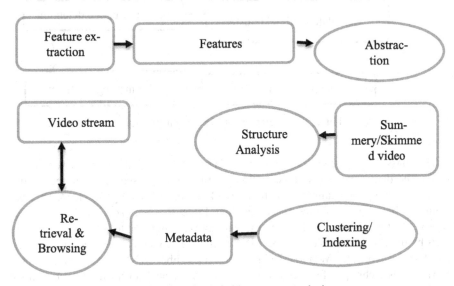

**Fig. 1.** Flowchart of video content analysis.

In a video program, a significant information source is a visual content. In video-content analysis, from multimedia sources, attributes are extracted using an effective strategy [3]. For professional and consumer applications, the video program is characterized by using text, audio, and video components cooperative and combined analysis. Feature extraction is critical in video indexing, as shown in Fig. 1. In content representation, attributes effectiveness is based on indexing schemes' effectiveness. However, mapping extracted features like motion, layout, structure, Shape, Texture, and color into semantics like car-racing, people, and outdoor and indoor scenes is not done quickly. Term video segmentation refers to decaying video data into meaningful elementary parts, which strongly correlates with the real world in video data. The video segmentation result is a segment set that collectively covers the actual entire video data. The significant difference between an image signal and a video signal is that a video signal consists of temporal information, which includes camera motion and introduces the concept of object motion. Therefore Video has temporal nature as well as spatial nature. Segmentation of Video can thus be temporal, spatial, or Spatio-temporal [4]. In the spatial domain, frame segmentation is like a static image. The video frame's sequence segmentation is termed shot detection or temporal segmentation in the temporal domain (Fig. 2).

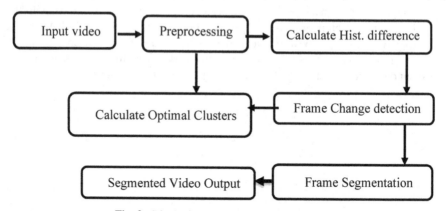

**Fig. 2.** Block diagram of Video Segmentation.

This classification of video segmentation is based on the features available with the input video data. Under this classification, it still has many segmentation techniques based on what type of feature the method is working for segmenting the Video. They are techniques based on semantics, object, content, Edge, Region, pixel, etc. Extraction of low-level features is done at first, and these features are mapped to category or concept labels by training and employing specific classifiers. For video genre identification, the bag-of-visual-words (BoW) model with k-nearest neighbor (KNN) classifiers is adopted in [5]. In this technique, for characterizing video sequence's every frame, a technique based on unsupervised probabilistic latent semantic analysis is used, and it produces a generic framework to analyze sports videos. Frames are classified into any of the following four groups: outer-field, long, mid and close-up view. In mobile video applications, to conform to sports type, four auxiliary datasets are used in the multimodal technique, which includes audio data, spatiotemporal and spatial visual information, and sensor-embedded mobile devices [6]. In infusion models, all possible modality combinations are integrated using auxiliary input data for classifying video types. Numerous research and methodologies are introduced, but the video content classification dataset accuracy is not ensured significantly. Therefore, this survey study suggests feature extraction, video segmentation, and video classification algorithms. So, this comprehensive survey focused on classifying video content dataset performance by using efficient and effective methods. The present study is done in the state of the art of various video content recognition and classification methods.

This study is organized in 4 sections. The literature review is presented in Sect. 2, the experimental results are provided in Sect. 3, and the conclusion of this survey study is given in Sect. 4.

## 2 Related Work

Various authors present different approaches for video classification, video segmentation, and feature extraction. In recent times, current and most often used techniques are discussed in this section.

### 2.1 Review on Feature Extraction Techniques for Video Content Dataset

In content-based visual information retrieval (CBVIR), the typical visual feature extraction applications set is parallelized and optimized by Chen et al. (2007) in [7]. Automatic video management is a mass-market application due to explosive growth in video data. One of the best solutions for this CBVIR. Low-level feature extraction forms the base for this CBVIR system. The MPEG-7 standard is used for feature extraction for high-level semantic concept indexing. A highly computation-intensive task is CBVIR, and in this CBVIR, the highly time-consuming component is the extraction of low-level visual features. In recent data, available multi-core processors' computing power is utilized fully for accelerating CBVIR. This is due to the recent advancements in a multi-core processors. Underlying parallel and optimization methods are examples of video analysis applications, and on multi-core systems, they are used in other applications for enhancing performance. These parallel applications' detailed performance analysis is conducted on a dual-socket, quad-core system. Possible bottleneck causes are identified using this analysis, and for scalability enhancement, this suggests avenues. In realtime performance, applications are made highly powerful in terms of accuracy. In broadcasted sports videos, the Superimposed Caption Box (SCB) interpretation is illustrated by Shih et al. (2008) in [8]. In those videos, the SCB template is not presumably given as s priori. Video content's digested vital information is represented using embedded captions in sports video programs. Known character bitmaps and SCB templates are assumed in most previous studies. This paper's significant contributions include identifying and extracting caption templates, modeling and extracting symbols, and identifying symbols and captions semantic interpretation. SCB contents understanding is done using this algorithm for various commercial sports video programs, as shown in experimental results. To rectify Co-occurrence Histograms of Oriented Gradients (CoHOG) drawbacks, a technique is suggested by Pang et al. (2012) in [9]. With respect to detection accuracy and computation, better results are produced using this technique. Significant contributions of this technique include gradient magnitude information used in addition to orientation information for enhancing detection accuracy significantly. A novel gradient decomposition technique is used, which is regarded as force's decomposition, and a combined approach is used, which is considered force's composite. Deep learning models can automatically learn the optimal features without human interaction. For example, digit identification, image classification, feature learning, visual recognition, musical signal processing, and NLP [10] can benefit from the deep learning framework's robust and accurate feature learning in supervised and unsupervised scenarios. Convolutional neural networks (CNNs) were used to extract visual features for sentiment analysis applications because of their recent success in feature extraction. Using CNN, [11] created a novel visual sentiment prediction system. The method uses transfer learning from a CNN pre-trained on large-scale data for object identification to predict sentiment. The suggested system eliminates the need for domain knowledge for visual sentiment prediction. In 2014, You et al. [12] used 2D-CNN for visual sentiment analysis, fine-tuning deep learning networks to filter out noisy training data. They employed domain transfer learning to boost performance. [13] suggested a deep 3D convolutional network for spatiotemporal feature extraction in 2015. A softmax output layer and eight convolution layers are present in this network. The network has shown excellent spatiotemporal feature extraction. Poria et al. [14] proposed using a convolutional recurrent neural network to extract visual characteristics from multimodal sentiment analysis and emotion identification datasets.

Under the two-stage convolution framework, obtained CoHOG features for suppressing the aliasing effect in a great manner. Usage of integral histogram in two-stage convolution framework enhances feature extraction process speed. A mean spatial filter shows better performance than a linear spatial filter. In the positive class, Incremental Principal Component Analysis (IPCA) (PCA) is employed to minimize CoHOG feature's dimensionality. For key-frame extraction, a framework for modeling semantic contexts is presented by Yong et al. (2013) in [15]. Extracted video frame's semantic context. Monitored its sequential changes and located its significant novelties using a one-class classifier. Working with wildlife video frames, for representing semantic context in scene, image segmentation is done in framework. Then features are extracted, and image blocks are matched. The semantic label's co-occurrence matrix is constructed. Better key-frame extraction is done using high-level semantic modeling, as shown in experimental results compared with low-level features usage. For action recognition, an effective feature extraction technique is developed by Kantorov & Laptev (2014) in [16]. Over-current years, action identification's precision has been enhanced incessantly. Characteristic extraction's low speed and succeeding recognition thwart present techniques from scaling up to a real-size crisis. It concentrates on the initially developed extremely proficient video characteristics through movement information in video compression. Subsequently exploring feature encoding by Fisher vectors and reveal precise action identification with fast linear classifiers. This technique progresses the video feature mining speed, feature encoding speed and action categorization speed by two orders of magnitude with minor reduction in recognition accurateness. Primarily, to evade the long latency owing to frame level calculation, it accepts the ayer parallel restructured box kernel to reinstate iterated Gaussian blur operations. A cascade classifier ensembles bailing-based reliable vehicle classification technique is provided by Zhang et al. (2014) in [17]. For image description, two feature extraction methods are introduced in this designed system. Namely, Pyramid Histogram of Oriented Gradients (PHOG) and Gabor wavelet transform. Image characteristics are hauled out for various vision tasks by implementing Gabor transform. In added discriminating information explanation, PHOG has its advantages. With the refused option, cascade classifier ensembles anticipate an extremely consistent classification technique for holding the state of affairs. If there is sufficient ambiguity, no conclusion is made. The primary ensemble exhibits heterogeneous nature, and it has various classifiers in addition to random forest, Supp, SVMs, Multiple-Layer Perceptrons (MLPs), and CNNs. A second classifier ensemble is used to enhance classification reliability further. This has a base MLPs coordinated using an ensemble Meta-learning method called Rotation Forest (RF). For both ensembles, the rejection option is proficient in concerning consensus degree from bulk voting to confidence measure and nonparticipation for categorizing indefinite samples if consensus degree is inferior to the threshold. For extracting semantic events from sports webcast text, an unsupervised technique is proposed by Chen et al. (2014) in [18]. First, in webcast text descriptions, filtering of unrelated words is done. The significant event classes are formed by clustering these filtered descriptions. At last, for every event class, keywords are extracted. As shown in experimental results, significant event texts are extracted using this technique. Video summarization and indexing are done using these event texts. Further, for text event retrieval, a hierarchical searching technique is given by this. In a large video database, automated video search and video indexing are implemented by Chivadshetti et al. (2015) in [19]. Personalized results are also presented. There are three various phases in this system. Key-frame detection and video segmentation are performed in the first phase to extract meaningful features. Over key-frames, ASR, HOG, and OCR algorithms are applied for extracting textual keywords. Edge, Texture, and color features are extracted in the third phase. All extracted features are stored in the database, and then classification is done concerning query video. At last, on extracted features, performed the search similarity measure. As per the user's interest, personalized re-ranking results with outputs are presented. Between Local Binary Patterns (LBPs) coded frames, based on correlation coefficient quotients, an effective technique is suggested by Zhang et al. (2015) in [20]. This technique has two parts: abnormal point detection and feature extraction. Every video frame is coded using LBP in feature extraction. Then, the correlation coefficient's quotients are computed among sequential LBP-coded frames. Chebyshev inequality is used twice for deleting and inserting localization in abnormal point detection. After this inequality application, decision thresholding is used to detect abnormal points. High detection accuracy with low computational complexity is achieved using this technique, as shown in experimental results. For facial expression analysis, a novel framework is introduced in video sequences by Zhao et al. (2017) in [21], where static and dynamic information is used. For locating facial points, breaking facial regions from the background, and correcting in-plane head rotation, adapted an incremental formulation based on discriminative deformable face alignment. Then, extracted spatial-temporal motion Local Binary Pattern (LBP) feature and for producing descriptors, with Gabor multi orientation fusion histogram, these features are integrated. Facial expressions and dynamic and static texture information are reflected using this. At last, facial expressions are classified by applying a multiclass SVM classifier based on a one-versus-one strategy. Methods using single descriptors are outperformed by this integrated framework, as illustrated in experimentation results. Cohn-Kanade (CK) + facial expression dataset is used in experimentation. On Oulu-CASIA VIS, MMI, and CK + datasets, better performance is shown by this technique when compared with other state-of-the-art techniques. From video frames or images, for computing transform coefficients (features), a novel technique is introduced by Abdulhussain et al. (2019) in [22]. Video frames and the image's local visual contents are represented using these features. Using a standard imaging technique, traditional feature extraction methods are compared. Further, for detecting transitions in Shot Boundary Detection (SBD) applications, video frames employed a fast feature technique. The SBD

## 2.2 Reviews of Video Segmentation Methods

A segmentation technique based on the Genetic Algorithm (GA) is suggested by Kim et al. (2006) in [23]. Moving objects are tracked as well as extracted using this technique automatically. Temporal and spatial segmentation is done mainly in this. Every frame is split as a region with accurate boundaries is formed using spatial segmentation, and every frame is split as a foreground and background area using temporal segmentation. Individuals evolved using Distributed Genetic Algorithms (DGAs) are used for performing spatial segmentation. From the previous frame's segmentation results, initiated the individuals. This is not the case in standard DGAs. Thus mating operator is used for evolving unstable individuals of actual moving objects. According to intensity difference, adaptive thresholding is done between two consecutive frames for temporal segmentation. For object extraction, results of temporal and spatial segmentation are combined. Natural correspondence established using spatial segmentation technique is used for performing the track. A novel technique for segmenting scenes automatically and representing them semantically is introduced by Zhu et al. (2009) in [24]. At first, a rough-to-fine algorithm is used for detecting video shots. Then, within every shot, adaptively selected key-frames with hybrid features and template matching are used to remove redundant key-frames. In the third stage, according to the visual similarity between shot activities and video content's temporal constraint, the same scene is formed by clustering Spatio-temporal coherent shots. At last, scene content is represented semantically on video retrieval under a typical character's full analysis of continuously recorded videos for satisfying human demand. On different TV programs and film genres, performed this algorithm. Interesting video content is retrieved effectively using this method, as shown in experimentation results. Tree-structured graphical models based on occlusion aware semi-supervised video segmentation algorithm are implemented by Budvytis et al. (2011) in [25]. This algorithm is an implementation-friendly one. Pixel labels with their uncertainty estimation are delivered using this algorithm. Supervision is employed for tackling task-specific segmentation problems, where the user predefines the semantic objects. Patch-based undirected mixture model's tree-structured approximation-based video model is used in this problem. A soft label Random Forest classifier and novel time series are included in this feedback. In complex and lengthy road scene sequences, multiclass segmentation problems, and cutting out foreground objects, the model's efficiency is demonstrated using this. There are several applications of this result. For discriminative training models, labeled video data is harvested using these results. For video segmentation, priors are developed using large-scale statistical analysis and articulation/pose/shape learning. A Parametric Graph Partitioning (PGP) based robust as well as effective video segmentation framework is used by Yu et al. (2015) in [26]. Nodes are identified and removed between cluster edges using this fast and parameter-free graph partitioning technique, and it forms a node cluster. Without pre-specified bandwidth parameters and cluster number, Spatio-temporal volume's clustering is performed using PGP other than its computational efficiency. Video segmentation is made highly practical to be used in applications. Sub-volumes are processed using this PGP framework. Performance is enhanced further because of this. In other streaming video segmentation techniques, performance is degraded by sub-volume processing. Chen Xiph.org and SegTrack v2 datasets are used for evaluating this PGP technique. In 3D segmentation running time and metrics, related state-of-the-art algorithms are outperformed. Using deep learning convolutional neural nets, a three-dimensional video segmentation technique is introduced by Piramanayagam et al. (2020) in [27]. For generating initial pixel groups, global boundary maps computed using deep learning techniques are used in addition to the computed local gradient at every pixel location. Traversal to high from low gradient region is done for the same. These initial pixel groups are refined using the local clustering technique. In Video's homogeneous regions, refined sub-volumes are chosen as initial seeds, and according to intensity similarity, they are combined iteratively with adjacent groups. A video's color boundaries terminated volume growth. A multivariate technique is used to merge the over segments obtained in the above steps hierarchically. For every frame, a final segmentation map is produced using this. On a quantitative and qualitative level, concerning computational efficiency and segmentation quality, favorable results are produced using the proposed methodology, as shown in experimental results. A video segmentation benchmark dataset is used in experimentation (Table 2).

**Table 2.** Inferences on existing video segmentation techniques.

| S.No. | Methods | Merits | Demerits |
|---|---|---|---|
| 1 | Distribute Genetic Algorithm (DGA)-based segmentation method [23] | • This algorithm is used to reduce the search time <br> • It reduces the computational cost | • In a few cases, the segmentation accuracy |
| 2 | Video scene segmentation and semantic representation method [24] | • It is used for efficient retrieval of exciting video content <br> • It provides higher segmentation accuracy | • In a few cases, redundant keyframes are an issue |
| 3 | Semi-supervised video segmentation algorithm [25] | • It includes harvesting labeled video data for training discriminative models, shape or pose or articulation learning, and large scale statistical analysis to develop priors for video segmentation | • In a few cases, error rates are a problem |
| 4 | Parametric Graph Partitioning (PGP) [26] | • It increases the video segmentation performance effectively <br> • Running time is fast | • Expensive is an issue |
| 5 | Deep learning convolutional neural nets [27] | • It provides higher quality and computational efficiency | • However, it has a problem with lower resolution |

## 2.3  Reviews of Video Content Classification Algorithms

For online-video sharing Web sites content classification, a text-based framework is suggested by Huang et al. (2010) in [28].Various user-generated data types called comments, descriptions, and titles are used as proxies for online videos. Extracted three text features, namely content-specific, syntactic and lexical features. Three classification methods based on features, namely, Support Vector Machine, Naïve Bayes, and C4.5, are used for video classification. From candidate videos, user-generated data identified by using user-given keywords on YouTube are collected first for evaluating this framework. Then, experiment data is formed by random selection of collected subset data, and they are tagged manually by users. With around 87.2% accuracy rate, based on users' interests, online videos are classified using this technique are shown in experimental results, and videos are discriminated using all three text feature types. In experimentation, Naïve Bayes and C4.5 methods are outperformed by SVM. On video-sharing Websites, accurate video-classification results are beneficial, as demonstrated in results to identify implicit cyber communities. Fan et al. (2016) presented a video-based emotion recognition system in [29] and submitted it to EmotiW 2016 Challenge. In a late-fusion fashion, 3D Convolutional Networks (C3D) and Recurrent Neural networks (RNN) are combined to form a hybrid network, a core module in this system. Variously, motion and appearance information is encoded using C3D and RNN. Specifically, a convolutional neural network (CNN) extracts appearance features over individual video frames and is given to RNN as input, and motion features are encoded later. Video motion and appearance are modeled simultaneously using C3D.In the training set, without using any additional emotion-labeled video clips, around 59.02% accuracy is achieved using this system with the audio module, whereas, EmotiW 2015 winner achieves 53.8% accuracy. As shown in experimentation results, video-based emotion recognition is enhanced significantly by combining C3D and RNN. A novel action recognition technique is presented by Ullah et al. (2017) in [30], where deep bidirectional LSTM (DB-LSTM) and convolutional neural network (CNN) is used for processing video data. From videos, every sixth frame extracts deep features and is used for minimizing complexity and redundancy. Then, the DB-LSTM network is used for learning sequential information available in frame features. For increasing depth, in the backward and forward pass, multiple layers are stacked together in DB-LSTM. Long-term sequences are learned using this technique, and for a certain time interval, features are analyzed for processing lengthy videos. On three benchmark datasets, namely, HMDB51, YouTube 11 Actions, and UCF-10, significant action recognition enhancement is shown using this technique, as illustrated in experimental results compared with other state-of-the-art action recognition techniques. For a crowd, density level classification, violent behavior detection, and simultaneous crowd counting, ResnetCrowd, a deep residual architecture, is presented by Marsden et al. (2017) in [31]. Constructed a new dataset with 100 images, and it is termed as Multi-Task Crowd for evaluating and training multi-objective techniques. For crowd density level classification, violent behavior detection, and simultaneous crowd counting, this new dataset is used as the first computer vision dataset, which is fully annotated. As shown in experimental results, individual task performance is boosted for all tasks using a multi-task approach. In ROC, AUC (Area under the curve), around 90% enhancement is achieved in violent behavior detection. On various other benchmarks, this trained Resnet Crowd model was evaluated, which highlights the crowd analysis model's superior generalization and is trained for multiple objectives. Video content analysis is discussed by Aljarrah et al. (2018) in [32]. This is focused on the rapid increase in real-life applications that use video content analysis to perform its functionalities. It is useful to review the videos recorded using video surveillance systems. An automated content analysis system is used instead of rewinding recorded videos over hours. A searchable text file with video content summarization is produced using this system. Object classification is used in this work for analyzing video surveillance content. A convolutional neural network model is used to detect and classify objects in a video. A text file with detected object classes and appearance time is generated for future usage. Only (I) frames are processed to speed up this heavy computational process. For emotional Big Data, a deep learning-based emotion recognition system is discussed by Hossain et al. (2019) in [33]. There is a video and speech in big data. In this system, for obtaining Mel-spectrogram, the speech signal processing in the frequency domain is done first. This Mel-spectrogram is assumed as an image. Then, a convolutional neural network (CNN) is given with this Mel-spectrogram. From a video segment, extracted some representative frames are fed to CNN in case of video signals. Two consecutive extreme learning machines (ELMs) are used for fusing two CNNs outputs. A support vector machine (SVM) is given for emotion's final classification with this fusion output. Two audio-visual emotional databases are used in this system evaluation. A system with ELMs and CNN's effectiveness is confirmed using experimental results. In videos, crowd event classification is discussed by Shri et al. (2019) in [34]. In computer vision-based systems, it is a highly challenging and important task. Huge video events are recognized using this crowded event classification system. In event classification, a difficult task is the model's decisive. This event classification model shows generalization capability in works with a large video count. In video classification, distinguishable features and powerful portrayals are derived using Deep learning's embodiment. From raw data, the extracted event features using a large number of videos with efficient and effective detection. A power classification model is provided using Convolutional Neural Network (CNN) for event recognition problems. From YouTube, I collected a high-quality 3000 frames for forming a new dataset. This includes four crowd event classes: shopping mall, Jallikattu, cricket, and marriage. Two Deep CNN infrastructures called VGG16 and baseline are used in this system for providing temporal evidence and detecting predefined events. In Video, centrality events are detected, and input video frames are tested automatically using the CNN model. Video event features are extracted using CNN from video input frames, and correct distinguishing of events is done. When compared with other models, around 100% enhanced results are provided using this system. For field sports videos, AlexNet Convolutional Neural Networks (AlexNet CNN) based effective shot classification technique is suggested by Minhas et al. (2019) in [35]. This network has an eight-layer structure, including three fully-connected layers and five convolutional layers, classifying shots as an out-of-field, close-up, medium, and long shots. Over a soccer and cricket video's diverse dataset, evaluated overall validation and training performance. These performances are boosted through feature maps dropout layers and response normalization. Around 94.07% maximum accuracy can be achieved using this model when compared with standard Convolution Neural Network (CNN), K-Nearest Neighbors (KNN), Extreme Learning Machine (ELM), and Support Vector Machine (SVM). To prove this approach's superiority, this method is compared with baseline state-of-the-art shot classification techniques. Khan et al. (2019) developed an affordable in-vehicle snow detection system [36]. In real time, trajectory-level weather information is provided using this system. An SHRP2 Naturalistic Driving Study video data is used in this system, and machine learning approaches are also used. Three classification algorithms, namely random forest (RF), k-nearest neighbor (K-NN), and support vector machine (SVM), two image features based on Texture, namely local binary pattern (LBP), gray level co-occurrence matrix (GLCM), are used for training this snow detection models. An image dataset with three weather conditions, namely heavy snow, light snow, and clear, is used in the analysis. Around 86% of overall prediction accuracy is produced by GLCM features-based models, whereas around 96% of overall prediction accuracy is produced by LBP-based models, which is a greater one. In this study, a cost-effective snow detection system is used, and there is no need to have huge technical support. A single video camera is required for this. In real time, roadway weather conditions are detected with reasonable accuracy using simple mobile apps with a proper data connection. This is due to the advancements made in smartphone cameras. A movie trailer classification based on home action is proposed by Shambharkar et al. (2020) in [37]. This technique uses an optimized deep convolutional neural network in video sequences. At first, images are converted into their grayscale range. Pre-processing is done using adaptive median filtering. From video frames, the background is subtracted using the segmentation technique based on the threshold value, and the foreground portion is extracted. The segmented portion extracts motion features and visual features like Texture and color in the feature extraction stage. At last, for human action classifications, an optimized deep convolutional neural network (DCNN) is used for classifying mined features. DCNN weight values are optimized using introduced deer hunting optimization (DHO). In MATLAB environment, executed the human action classification based on DCNNDHO human action. The experimental results and comparisons are made between them, including the metrics like false discovery rate, F-measure, precision, specificity, sensitivity, false alarm rate, and accuracy. With and without the filtering process also, results are compared (Table 3).

**Table 3.** Inferences on existing video content recognition and classification methods.

| S.No. | Methods | Merits | Demerits |
|---|---|---|---|
| 1 | C4.5, Naïve Bayes, and SVM methods [28] | • This algorithm demonstrated that accurate video-classification results are beneficial for identifying implicit cyber communities on video-sharing Web sites | • In a few cases, it is still too low for such an essential action recognition task |
| 2 | RNN with the C3D method [29] | • It is used to produce higher storage space with better efficiency for larger videos | • This method achieved a lower recognition accuracy |
| 3 | CNN and DB-LSTM method [30] | • This method is capable of learning long term sequences and can process lengthy videos by analyzing features for a certain time interval | • It has a problem with extracting low-level features |
| 4 | ResnetCrowd architecture [31] | • It increases the video classification accuracy | • Expensive is an issue |
| 5 | Convolutional Neural Network (CNN) model [32] | • It is used to speed up this heavy computational process | • However, it has a problem with video classification on a complex background |
| 6 | CNN, ELM, and SVM [33] | • It is used for the better emotion recognition system | • It has an issue with high computational power and a considerable volume of data |
| 7 | Deep learning-based CNN [34] | • It provides higher quality videos for crowd events | • It may suffer from the noisy Variation |
| 8 | SVM, KNN, ELM, and CNN [35] | • This model achieves the maximum accuracy | • Computational complexity is still an issue |
| 9 | GLCM, LBP, RF, SVM and KNN [36] | • It does not require much technical support and only needs a single video camera<br>• It can effectively be used to detect roadway weather conditions in real time with reasonable accuracy | • It is computationally expensive |

(*continued*)

**Table 3.** (*continued*)

| S.No. | Methods | Merits | Demerits |
|-------|---------|--------|----------|
| 10 | DCNNDHO algorithm [37] | • It achieves higher accuracy, precision, and f-measure values | • However, it has an issue with background noise rates |

The deep learning methods will be used for many applications like human action recognition and image retrieval [38–45].

## 3   Experimental Results

In MATLAB 2022a platform, employed an algorithms like CNN, RNN with C3D and DCNNDHO and studied the outcomes. Existing works are used for making comparison. With respect to false discovery rate, F-measure, precision, specificity, sensitivity, false alarm rate and accuracy, performance is evaluated.

**Dataset 1:**
**UCF101** dataset is an extension of UCF50 and consists of 13,320 video clips, which are classified into 101 categories. These 101 categories can be classified into 5 types (Body motion, Human-human interactions, Human-object interactions, Playing musical instruments and Sports). The total length of these video clips is over 27 h. All the videos are collected from YouTube and have a fixed frame rate of 25 FPS with the resolution of 320 × 240.

**Dataset 2:**
The **Kinetics** dataset is a large-scale, high-quality dataset for human action recognition in videos. The dataset consists of around 500,000 video clips covering 600 human action classes with at least 600 video clips for each action class. Each video clip lasts around 10 s and is labeled with a single action class. The videos are collected from YouTube.

### 3.1   Accuracy

Model's overall correctness is determined using accuracy and it is a ratio between total actual classification parameters $(T_p + T_n)$ to sum of all classification parameters $(T_p + T_n + F_p + F_n)$. Accuracy is expressed as,

$$\text{Accuracy} = \frac{T_p + T_n}{(T_p + T_n + F_p + F_n)} \tag{1}$$

Accuracy metric evaluation and its comparison is illustrated in above shown Fig. 3. In that, various techniques are represented in x-axis and accuracy value is expressed in y-axis. Available methods are such as RNN with C3D and CNN algorithms provide lower accuracy whereas DCNNDHO algorithm provides higher accuracy for the UCF and kinetics datasets. Thus the result concludes that the DCNNDHO increases video classification accuracy for both datasets.

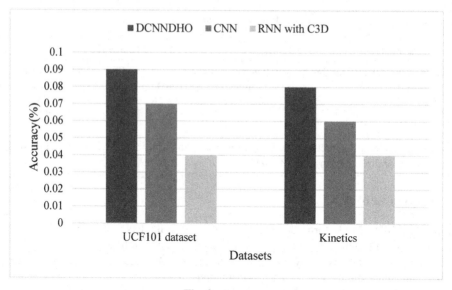

**Fig. 3.** Accuracy.

## 3.2 Precision

Precision value is computed as:

$$\text{Precision} = \frac{\text{True positive}}{\text{True positive} + \text{False positive}} \tag{2}$$

Quality or accuracy is computed using precision value and quantity or completeness is measured using recall value. Computation of highly relevant results than irrelevant results by an algorithm is indicated using high precision value. For a class, ratio between true positives count to total elements which are labelled as positive class's count defines precision value in classification task.

Precision metric evaluation and its comparison is illustrated in above shown Fig. 4. In that, various techniques are represented in x-axis and precision value is expressed in y-axis. DCNNDHO algorithm provides higher precision while other existing RNN with C3D and CNN algorithms provide lower precision values for the given UCF and kinetics datasets. Thus the result concludes that the DCNNDHO algorithm increase the video classification accuracy for the both datasets.

## 3.3 Sensitivity

Actual positive's proportion which are identified correctly defines sensitivity value. This is also termed as recall or true positive rate. In some fields, it is termed as detection probability. It is also stated as a sick people's percentage who are identified correctly as with condition.

$$\text{Sensitivity} = \frac{TP}{TP + FN} \tag{3}$$

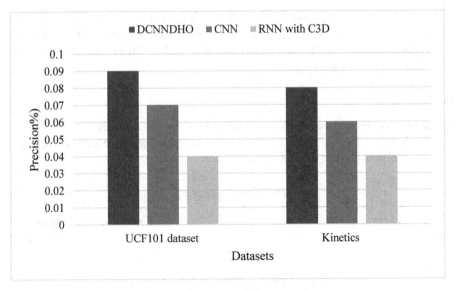

**Fig. 4.** Precision

where, True positive value is represented as TP and False Negative value is represented as FN.

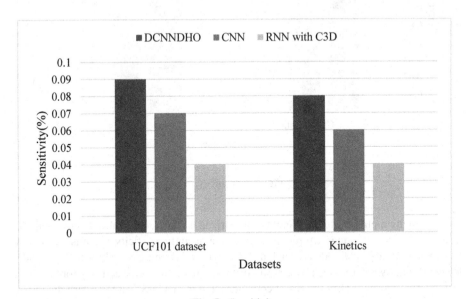

**Fig. 5.** Sensitivity.

Sensitivity metric evaluation and its comparison is illustrated in above shown Fig. 5. In that, various techniques are represented in x-axis and sensitivity value is expressed in y-axis. Available methods are such as RNN with C3D and CNN algorithms provide lower sensitivity whereas DCNNDHO algorithm provides higher sensitivity for the UCF and kinetics datasets. Thus the result concludes that the DCNNDHO increase the video classification accuracy for the both datasets.

## 3.4  Specificity

Actual negatives proportion which are identified correctly as such gives specificity values and it is also termed as true negative rate. It is also stated as, healthy people's percentage who are identified correctly as not with condition.

$$Specificity = \frac{TN}{TN + FP} \tag{4}$$

where, True Negative value is represented as TN and False Positive value is represented as FP.

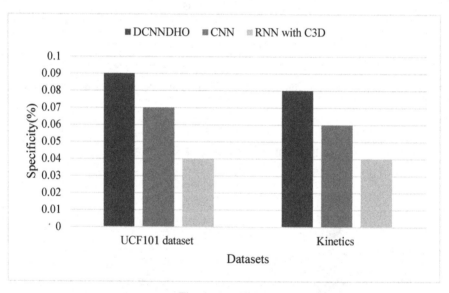

**Fig. 6.**  Specificity.

Specificity metric evaluation and its comparison is illustrated in above shown Fig. 6. In that, various techniques are represented in x-axis and specificity value is expressed in y-axis. Available methods are such as RNN with C3D and CNN algorithms provide lower specificity whereas DCNNDHO algorithm provides higher specificity for the UCF and kinetics datasets. Thus the result concludes that the DCNNDHO increase the video classification accuracy for the both datasets.

Recall and Precision values weighted average defines F1 score. Both false negatives and false positives are considered in this score computation.

$$F\text{-}measure = 2* \frac{(\text{sensitivity} * Precision)}{(\text{sensitivity} + Precision)} \tag{5}$$

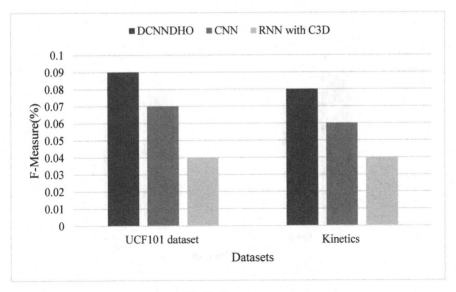

**Fig. 7.** F-measure.

F-measure metric evaluation and its comparison is illustrated in above shown Fig. 7. In that, various techniques are represented in x-axis and F-measure is expressed in y-axis. Available methods are such as RNN with C3D and CNN algorithms provides low F-measure whereas DCNNDHO algorithm provides high F-measure for UCF and kinetics datasets. Thus the result concludes that the DCNNDHO increase the video classification accuracy for the both datasets.

### 3.5 False Discovery Rate

Ratio between false positive results count to total positive test results count defines false discovery rate.

$$\text{False discovery rate} = V/V + S \tag{6}$$

where, false discoveries count is represented as $V$ and true discoveries count is represented as $S$.

False discovery rate metric evaluation and its comparison is illustrated in above shown Fig. 8. In that, various techniques are represented in x-axis and false discovery rate is expressed in y-axis. Available methods are such as RNN with C3D and CNN algorithms provide higher false discovery rate whereas DCNNDHO algorithm provides lower false discovery rate for the UCF and kinetics datasets. Thus the result concludes that the DCNNDHO increase the video classification accuracy for the both datasets.

### 3.6 False Alarm Rate

Ratio between false alarms count to total alarms or warning count defines thus false alarm rate.

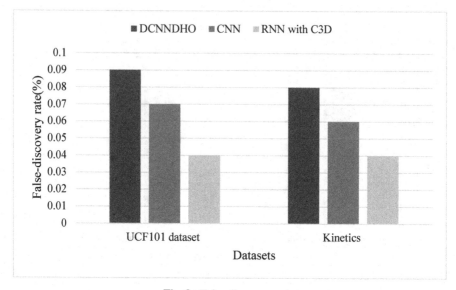

**Fig. 8.** False discovery rate.

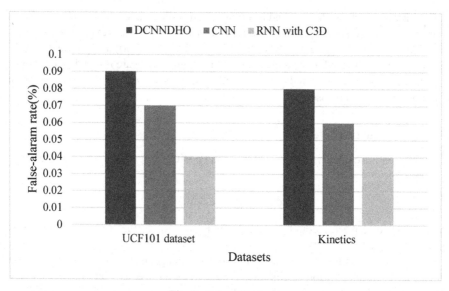

**Fig. 9.** False alarm rate.

False alarm rate metric evaluation and its comparison is illustrated in above shown Fig. 9. In that, various techniques are represented in x-axis and false alarm rate is expressed in y-axis. Available methods are such as RNN with C3D and CNN algorithms provide higher false alarm rate whereas DCNNDHO algorithm provides lower false discovery rate for the UCF101 dataset, and Kinetics dataset. Thus the result concludes that the DCNNDHO increase the video classification accuracy for the both datasets.

# 4 Conclusion

This study examined video content analysis using segmentation, recognition, and classification approaches. Several feature extraction, segmentation, and classification algorithms are analyzed on video content to increase performance. Feature extraction is a crucial stage in extracting essential information from video material. Texture, motion, and color information are extracted for classifier training. Then the video segmentation is optimized using DGA and deep learning methods. Thus, picking characteristics improves classification accuracy. CNN, MLP, SVM, naive Bayes, and KNN are used to classify the dataset. Each algorithm's flaws and benefits are explored. This poll provides a helpful summary of available solutions, with their drawbacks and benefits. However, existing algorithms struggle to identify key aspects and their strengths and limitations in video content classification. The DCNNDHO algorithm is used to increase video classification accuracy. This reduces categorization errors. This improved classifier finds biases and weights between hidden and input neurons. However, deep learning algorithms are not efficient for video content classification in this survey. Hybrid optimization techniques can also be presented to improve video content detection and classification.

# References

1. Gaunt, K.D.: YouTube, twerking & you: context collapse and the handheld co-presence of black girls and Miley Cyrus. J. Popular Music Stud. **27**(3), 244–273 (2015). ISBN 9781315689593
2. Loukas, C.: Video content analysis of surgical procedures. Surg. Endosc. **32**(2), 553–568 (2018). https://doi.org/10.1007/s00464-017-5878-1
3. Bai, L., et al.: Video semantic content analysis based on ontology. In: International Machine Vision and Image Processing Conference (IMVIP 2007). IEEE (2007). https://doi.org/10.1109/IMVIP.2007.13
4. Perazzi, F., et al.: A benchmark dataset and evaluation methodology for video object segmentation. In: Proceedings of the IEEE Conference on Computer Vision and Pattern Recognition (2016). https://doi.org/10.1109/CVPR.2016.85
5. Zhang, N., et al.: A generic approach for systematic analysis of sports videos. ACM Trans. Intell. Syst. Technol. **3**(3) (2012). Article 46
6. Cricri, F., et al.: Sport type classification of mobile videos. IEEE Trans. Multimedia **16**(4), 917–932 (2014)
7. Chen, Y., et al.: Accelerating video feature extractions in CBVIR on multi-core systems. Intel Technol. J. **11**(4) (2007). https://doi.org/10.1535/itj.1104.08. ISSN 1535-864X
8. Shih, H.-C., Huang, C.-L.: Content extraction and interpretation of superimposed captions for broadcasted sports videos. IEEE Trans. Broadcast. **54**(3), 333–346 (2008). https://doi.org/10.1109/TBC.2008.2001143
9. Pang, Y., Yan, H., Yuan, Y., Wang, K.: Robust CoHOG feature extraction in human-centered image/video management system. IEEE Trans. Syst. Man Cybern. Part B (Cybern.) **42**(2), 458-468 (2012)

10. Cambria, E., Poria, S., Bajpai, R., Hussain, A.: A review of affective computing: from unimodal analysis to multimodal fusion. Inf. Fusion **37**, 98–125 (2017)
11. Xu, C., et al.: Visual sentiment prediction with deep convolutional neural networks (2014)
12. You, Q., et al.: Robust image sentiment analysis using progressively trained and domain transferred deep networks. In: Proceedings of the AAAI Conference on Artificial Intelligence, vol. 29 (2015)
13. Tran, D., et al.: Learning spatiotemporal features with 3D convolutional networks. In: 2015 IEEE International Conference on Computer Vision (ICCV) (2015)
14. Poria, S., et al.: Convolutional MKL based multimodal emotion recognition and sentiment analysis. In: 2016 IEEE 16th International Conference on Data Mining (ICDM) (2016)
15. Yong, S.-P., Deng, J.D., Purvis, M.K.: Wildlife video key-frame extraction based on novelty detection in semantic context. Multimedia Tools Appl. **62**(2), 359–376 (2013)
16. Kantor, V., Laptev, I.: Efficient feature extraction, encoding and classification for action recognition. In Proceedings of the IEEE Conference on Computer Vision and Pattern Recognition, pp. 2593- 2600 (2014). https://doi.org/10.1109/CVPR.2014.332
17. Zhang, W., Duan, P., Lu, Q., Liu, X.: A realtime framework for video object detection with storm. In: Ubiquitous Intelligence and Computing, 2014 IEEE 11th International Conference on and Autonomic and Trusted Computing, IEEE 14th International Conference on Scalable Computing and Communications and Its Associated Workshops (UTC-ATC-ScalCom), pp. 732–737 (2014). https://doi.org/10.1109/UIC-ATC-ScalCom.2014.115
18. Chen, C.-M., Chen, L.-H.: A novel approach for semantic event extraction from sports webcast text. Multimedia Tools Appl. **71**(3), 1937–1952 (2012). https://doi.org/10.1007/s11042-012-1323-6
19. Chivadshetti, P., Sadafale, K., Thakare, K.: Content based video retrieval using integrated feature extraction and personalization of results. In: 2015 International Conference on Information Processing (ICIP). IEEE (2015). https://doi.org/10.1109/INFOP.2015.7489372
20. Zhang, Z., et al.: Efficient video frame insertion and deletion detection based on inconsistency of correlations between local binary pattern coded frames. Secur. Commun. Netw. **8**(2), 311–320 (2015). https://doi.org/10.1002/sec.981
21. Zhao, L., Wang, Z., Zhang, G.: Facial expression recognition from video sequences based on spatial-temporal motion local binary pattern and Gabor multiorientation fusion histogram. Math. Probl. Eng. **2017**, 12. Article ID 7206041. https://doi.org/10.1155/2017/7206041
22. Abdulhussain, Sadiq H., et al. "A fast feature extraction algorithm for image and video processing." 2019 international joint conference on neural networks (IJCNN). IEEE, 2019. DOI: https://doi.org/10.1109/IJCNN.2019.8851750
23. Kim, E.Y., Park, S.H.: Automatic video segmentation using genetic algorithms. Recogn. Lett. **27**(11), 1252–1265 (2006). https://doi.org/10.1016/j.patrec.2005.07.023
24. Zhu, S., Liu, Y.: Video scene segmentation and semantic representation using a novel scheme. Multimed. Tools Appl. **42**, 183–205 (2009). https://doi.org/10.1007/s11042-008-0233-0
25. Budvytis, I., Badrinarayanan, V., Cipolla, R.: Semi-supervised video segmentation using tree-structured graphical models. In: CVPR 2011. IEEE (2011). https://doi.org/10.1109/CVPR.2011.5995600
26. Yu, C.-P., et al.: Efficient video segmentation using parametric graph partitioning. In: Proceedings of the IEEE International Conference on Computer Vision (2015). https://doi.org/10.1109/ICCV.2015.361
27. Piramanayagam, S., Saber, E., Cahill, N.D.: Gradient-driven unsupervised video segmentation using deep learning techniques. J. Electron Imaging **29**(1), 013019 (2020). https://doi.org/10.1117/1.JEI.29.1.013019
28. Huang, C., Tianjun, F., Chen, H.: Text-based video content classification for online video-sharing sites. J. Am. Soc. Inform. Sci. Technol. **61**(5), 891–906 (2010)

29. Fan, Y., et al.: Video-based emotion recognition using CNN-RNN and C3D hybrid networks. In: ICMI 2016: Proceedings of the 18th ACM International Conference on Multimodal Interaction, pp. 445–45010 (2016). https://doi.org/10.1145/2993148.2997632

30. Ullah, A., et al.: Action recognition in video sequences using deep bi-directional LSTM with CNN features. IEEE Access **6**, 1155–1166 (2017). https://doi.org/10.1109/ACCESS.2017.2778011

31. Marsden, M., et al.: ResnetCrowd: a residual deep learning architecture for crowd counting, violent behaviour detection and crowd density level classification. In: 2017 14th IEEE International Conference on Advanced Video and Signal Based Surveillance (AVSS). IEEE (2017). https://doi.org/10.48550/arXiv.1705.10698

32. Aljarrah, I., Mohammad, D.: Video content analysis using convolutional neural networks. In: 2018 9th International Conference on Information and Communication Systems (ICICS). IEEE (2018). https://doi.org/10.1109/IACS.2018.8355453

33. Hossain, M.S., Muhammad, G.: Emotion recognition using deep learning approach from audio-visual emotional big data. Inf. Fusion **49**, 69–78 (2019). https://doi.org/10.1016/j.inffus.2018.09.008

34. Shri, S.J., Jothilakshmi, S.J.C.C.: Crowd video event classification using convolutional neural network. Comput. Commun. **147**, 35–39 (2019). https://doi.org/10.1016/j.comcom.2019.07.027

35. Minhas, R.A., et al.: Shot classification of field sports videos using AlexNet convolutional neural network. Appl. Sci. **9**(3), 483 (2019). https://doi.org/10.3390/app9030483

36. Khan, M.N., Ahmed, M.M.: Snow detection using in-vehicle video camera with texture-based image features utilizing K-nearest neighbor, support vector machine, and random forest. Transp. Res. Rec. **2673**(8), 221–232 (2019). https://doi.org/10.1177/0361198119842105

37. Shambharkar, P.G., Doja, M.N.: Movie trailer classification using deer hunting optimization based deep convolutional neural network in video sequences. Multimedia Tools Appl. **79**(29–30), 21197–21222 (2020). https://doi.org/10.1007/s11042-020-08922-6

38. Sreekanth, N., SasiKiran, J., Obulesu, A., Mallikarjuna Reddy, A.: key frame extraction for content based lecture video retrieval and video summarisation framework. European J. Mol. Clin. Med. **7**(11), 496–507 (2020). ISSN 2515-8260

39. Jai Shankar, B., Murugan, K., Obulesu, A., Finney Daniel Shadrach, S., Anitha, R.: MRI image segmentation using bat optimization algorithm with fuzzy C means (BOA-FCM) clustering. J. Med. Imaging Health Inform. **11**(3), 661–666 (2021)

40. Obulesh, A., et al.: Central nervous system tumour classification using residual neural network, Purakala. UGC Care J. **31**(21) (2020). ISSN 0971-2143

41. Obulesh, A., et al.: Traffic-sign classification using machine learning concepts, Tathapi. UGC Care Listed J. **19**(8) (2020). ISSN 2320-0693

42. Thimmaraju, R., Obulesh, A., Reddy, M.S.: Quantum computation and simulation a distinguished demonstration using the BruteForce algorithm. In: 2020 IEEE International Conference for Innovation in Technology (INOCON), pp. 1–6. IEEE (2021). https://doi.org/10.1109/INOCON50539.2020.9298345

43. An, G., Zheng, Z., Wu, D., Zhou, W.: Deep spectral feature pyramid in the frequency domain for long-term action recognition. J. Vis. Commun. Image Represent. **64**, 102650 (2019)

44. Xiao, J., Cui, X., Li, F.: Human action recognition based on convolutional neural network and spatial pyramid representation. J. Vis. Commun. Image Represent. **71**, 102722 (2020)

45. Tiger, M., Heintz, F.: Incremental reasoning in probabilistic signal temporal logic. Int. J. Approximate Reasoning **119**, 325–352 (2020)

# Prediction of Cochlear Disorders Using Face Tilt Estimation and Audiology Data

Sneha Shankar, Sujay Doshi, and G. Suganya$^{(\boxtimes)}$

Vellore Institute of Technology, Chennai, India
{snehashankar.c2020,sujay.doshi2020}@vitstudent.ac.in,
Suganya.g@vit.ac.in

**Abstract.** Cochlear disorder is an audio impairment issue, which causes difficulty in understanding human speech. These disorders can cause difficulty in speech recognition, communication, and language development. Intelligent approaches are proven to be efficient and novel approaches for performing various challenging tasks in the healthcare industry. The primary objective of this study is to use machine learning and computer vision domain, to create a web-based platform enabling early detection of the disorders. Computer vision with a classification model is used for achieving the objective. The model is trained on the static custom audiology dataset formulated from the UCI machine learning repository. Cross-validation over various classification algorithms like Logistic Regression, Decision Tree, Support Vector Classifier, K-Nearest Neighbors, and Multi-Layer Perceptron is performed and is proven that Multi-Layer Perceptron suits the dataset. Application for the purpose is developed using Python flask and is deployed for validation.

**Keywords:** Audio impairment · logistic regression · decision tree · KNN · SVM · multi-layer perceptron · prediction

## 1 Introduction

More than 5% of the total world population, requires hearing loss therapy. According to The World Health Organization, there are approximately 432 million adults and 34 million children who need treatment. It is proposed that by 2050, one out of every 10 people is expected to suffer from various auditory issues such as disabling hearing loss. Diminished sensitivity to sound, such as turning down the level of everything they hear, or reduced clarity, such as garbling everything they hear, are both examples of audio impairments. This is becoming evident due to the continuous usage of earphones during the pandemic and henceforth. The symptoms of cochlear damage often appear before vertigo and are usually overlooked. The goal of this study was to examine the features related to various types of auditory impairments, as well as Meniere's disease, to determine the regularity with which these problems develop. Meniere's disease is an uncommon inner-ear condition that becomes worse over time. The complexity of the

S. Nandan Mohanty et al. (Eds.): ICISML 2022, LNICST 471, pp. 244–251, 2023.
https://doi.org/10.1007/978-3-031-35081-8_19

symptom and its restricted visibility make its diagnosis difficult and it can easily be ignored by the general population. Most people lack access to proper health care or are scared of the exorbitant cost of the consultation to detect any such auditory disorders, while many are just unaware of such a situation persisting in their bodies.

This work aims to develop a product that would attempt to solve the persisting problem of ignorance or unawareness of the auditory disorders (more prominently, cochlear diseases that can be detected with having face tilt as a symptom) present in one's body. Common symptoms such as dizziness, nausea or vomiting, the presence of roaring or ringing sound in the ear, and hereditary disorders related to the ear of the patient are taken as input from the user along with the user's face tilt value, which are the basic requirements for the user's hearing impairment prediction. Early prediction is proposed through the use of a machine learning model trained using a standard dataset. With the rapid advancement of technology and data, the healthcare domain is one of the most crucial study domains in the contemporary era. This paper explains the complete conversion of a dataset from data Pre-processing to Model creation and then to the prediction of output based on user input. Since the dataset was imbalanced oversampling using Random Sampler was implemented. The paper is thus represented as follows. Background and related work is presented in Sect. 2. Section 3 includes the implementation of the project which comprises the objective of the research, proposed work, related algorithms as well as, and research methodology as applied in the study. Section 4 contains results and discussions and the paper is concluded in Sect. 5 with Future works discussed.

## 2  Background Study

Several people around the world are diagnosed with hearing problems and other cochlear diseases. Many of the affected are afraid to even consult a doctor, while others ignore or overlook the symptoms. In a recent study carried out in Delhi, India; it was found that 25.1% of people had an overall prevalence of hearing loss [1]. Also, less than 16% of adults ages 20–69 who need a hearing aid don't use one. That number almost doubles to 30% for adults over the age of 70 who need a hearing aid but don't use it, according to the National Institute on Deafness and Other Communication Disorders [2]. An estimated 38 million Americans have hearing loss [3]. Using Deep Learning (DL) and Machine Learning (ML) techniques, prediction of a very challenging HA type identification for Audiology Patients (AP) is done by researchers [4]. Many efforts and works have been done in Audiological analysis, where the majority of them focus on one or few efficient model(s) for their dataset. Machine Learning Techniques for Differential Diagnosis of Vertigo and Dizziness: A Review [5] analyses the Audiology dataset with SVM, KNN, Decision Trees, Naïve Bayes, and Genetic Algorithm and presented a comprehensive view of all performance. Hearing aid classification based on audiology data [6] presents a comparative study of two machine learning models namely MLP and Bayesian Networks.

Commonly due to changes in the volume of fluid people suffering from any audio impairment tend to develop imbalance leading to the right or left bend. Usually $< 5°$ is considered to be normally caused to due to slight movements and $5° - 20°$ addresses the possibility of audio impairment. The prediction of the auto-Tilt in patients with positional vertigo [7] and Menière's disease [8] by taking inputs i.e. dizziness, nausea, roaring, or ringing or presence of buzzing sound, along with face tilt values from users is discussed in the research works. Computerized dynamic posturography, a method for quantifying balance tests is performed with eyes closed on an unstable surface using a CAPS® system [9]. This indicates the connection between the balance of the body and the audio heard by the person. The authors presented a detailed study about this test and its use in identifying cochlear disease. Detailed research on the importance and need for improvement in technology and research for hearing aid is discussed by researchers [10]. They described the emerging hearing-related artificial intelligence applications and argue for their potential to improve access, precision, and efficiency of hearing healthcare services.

## 3   Proposed Methodology

The objective of the proposed methodology is to present an efficient framework for predicting the type of cochlear disorder at an early stage based on user input and face tilt values. The proposed methodology followed in the research work is depicted in Fig. 1.

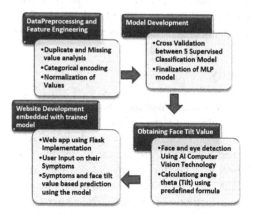

**Fig. 1.** Proposed Methodology

### 3.1   Data Preprocessing and Feature Engineering

In this work, an Audiology Dataset having 70 features representing facial values with an output feature representing the abnormality is used. The dataset is analyzed for missing values and then normalized to ensure proper scaling. Linearity between predictor and response variables is analyzed using scatter plots and correlation analysis. Heatmap is used for visualizing the correlation between features. Figure 2–4 represents some sample analysis done using the dataset. Outlier analysis is done for each feature to understand the existence of abnormal values. Boxplot is used for the analysis and such abnormalities are resolved using minimum and maximum values of corresponding features depending on the extremes the outliers lie in. The frequency of values of each feature is analyzed using a histogram plot. Barcharts are used to understand the number of tuples exist for each output class label.

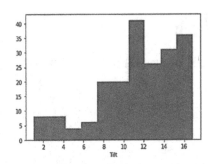

**Fig. 2.** Face Tilt Value Histogram (Univariate Analysis)

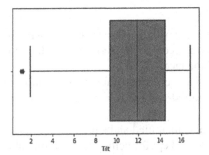

**Fig. 3.** Face Tilt Boxplot (Univariate Analysis)

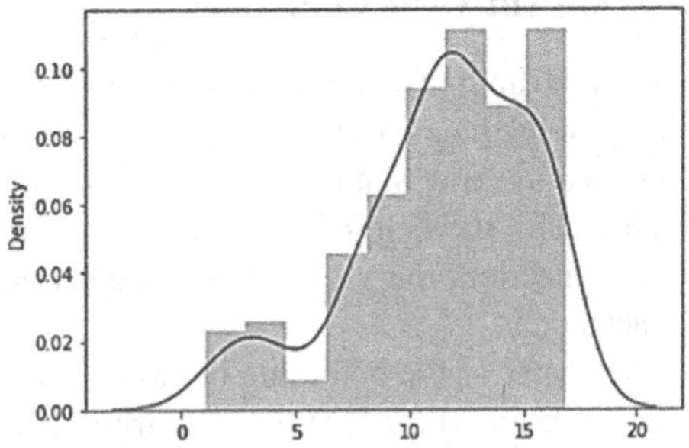

**Fig. 4.** Face Tilt Distplot (Univariate Analysis)

Feature Engineering was then performed to make the dataset suitable for modeling. First, all categorical variables in the predictor category are replaced with numerical values using ordinal encoding. The dataset is identified as imbalanced using Fig. 5. Cochlear_unknown and cochlear_age are identified to be the dominating or majority classes. Hence Oversampling was done using RandomOverSampler to randomly increase the sample numbers of data with the help of the imbalanced-learn package in python. Hence the sample size increased to 1152 data samples with 48 Class labels each.

### 3.2 Model Development

The dataset obtained from phase I is divided into training and testing in 80:20 proportion. Since cross-validation is used for validation, proportion alone is fixed. Various machine learning models including logistic regression, multi-layer perceptron, decision tree, support vector machines, and KNN classifier are used for training the dataset. Every model is trained using 80% of the experience and is tested with 20%. To assure uniformity cross-validation using 5 folds is used.

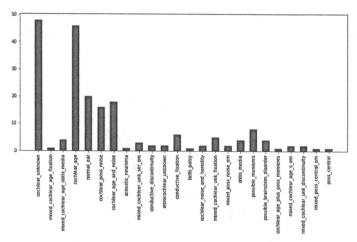

**Fig. 5.** Bar-chart representing the count of output class

### 3.3  Face Tilt Value Collection

- With the help of a webcam from the user's end, the patient's face is detected with the help of the haar cascade classifier dataset, and a green-colored box surrounding it is created to show that the system has detected the face.
- Then with the help of another XML haar cascade classifier trained specifically for eye detection, the user's eyes are detected and red-colored boxes are made around each eye.
- The center of the bounding boxes of eyes is also identified and stored for the calculation required for face tilt. A margin of 5°–20° is kept for getting the face tilt value of the patient.
- To compute tilt, angle an assumption that the face is perpendicular to the joining line of eyes is assumed for further calculations.
- Considering (xi, yi) as the center of eyes, where xi is the horizontal axis and yi is the vertical axis, we can get the angle q, which is the angle from the x-axis, thus the tilt value.

$$q = \tan-1((x2 - x1)/(y2 - y1)) \qquad (1)$$

- In the above-mentioned formula (x1, y1) and (x2, y2) are the centers of eyes calculated and stored previously.
- If the angle is positive then the tilt value is considered to be a right tilt and a negative value indicates a left tilt.

### 3.4  Deployment Procedure

To develop a platform for user Interaction, a python web framework flask was used which helped to create the web application where users can provide their inputs, hence required for detecting the possibility of any audio impairment. HTML and CSS codes were used to create an interactive webpage for users i.e. basically the patients and also the doctors, where doctors from the other end will be responsible to use the model which is better and the one having the highest accuracy. The doctors can analyze our webpage and use the model accordingly which will help in reducing the probability of patients getting misdiagnosed.

Our model was stored in pickle format, a method of serializing objects; machine learning models for saving during run time and loading and deserializing them later for different use. This pickled format of our model was later on passed to the Flask Implementation phase where our web app was developed over this file to give in runtime outputs after giving basic inputs for buzzing, dizziness, etc. Figure 6 represents the method to capture face tilt values. Common symptoms such as dizziness, nausea or vomiting, noise, the presence of roaring or ringing sounds in the ear, and hereditary disorders related to the ear of the patient are taken as input from the user. Along with the above-mentioned inputs we also get the face tilt value which is automatically taken after the user submits the rest of the symptoms from a 10-s live video from their camera. Since the rest of the values required for detection present in our dataset i.e. 59 features cannot be taken from the user as it requires tools and equipment which currently we cannot implement, we take them as random values along with the user input of symptoms and the tilt value. Thus by taking above stated inputs using the created webpage, we predict with the help of the formerly developed model and hence help the patient in detecting their audio impairment.

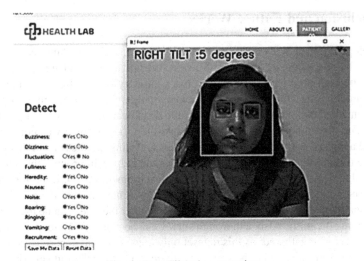

**Fig. 6.** Face Tilt value capturing

## 4 Results and Discussion

The user interactive web application developed was successfully able to predict the cochlear disorder user is suffering from, with the help of all the user input of symptoms and face tilt value. The developed models are validated using test datasets and through cross-validation procedures. Various metrics like Recall, Precision, and F1-score are used for validation. The values of these metrics are calculated using a confusion matrix computed for each model. Table 1 represents the comparison of these metrics for various machine-learning models. Upon analysis, it is found that Multilayer perceptron performs better than other models when tested separately and using 5-fold cross-validation. Thus with the current dataset and model developed we were able to correctly predict the audio impairment issue of the user with the average highest accuracy of 82.5%.

**Table 1.** Comparison of various models.

| Model | precision | recall | f1-score | accuracy |
|---|---|---|---|---|
| SVC | 0.98 | 0.97 | 0.97 | 0.968 |
| MLP | 0.99 | 0.99 | 0.98 | 0.9852 |
| KNN | 0.97 | 0.97 | 0.97 | 0.9661 |
| Logistic Regression | 0.98 | 0.98 | 0.97 | 0.9756 |
| Decision Tree | 0.99 | 0.99 | 0.98 | 0.9852 |

## 5  Conclusion and Future Works

The developed project is a website embedded with A.I. and a machine-learning model developed for the Audiology dataset. This project had a vision of making a product; a website making predictions if a person has audiology defects based on the face tilt value captured using computer vision implementation. Machine learning application was implemented using sci-kit learn library for classification of the data set and model training. The final model chosen was MLP and the model trained was converted to a pickle file and used with Flask to make the website. Using the ideas from this paper on advancing technology added work to the project can help in improving the output with better results. Considering the future, a lot of development can be done for the given project. The "curse of dimensionality" is well-represented in this dataset. Extensive Dimensionality reduction techniques like PCA and other methods can be used to handle the data more efficiently. Also, a thorough survey can be conducted and more prominent data sources can be gathered; as this dataset only contained 200 experiences (rows), so that could be taken care of with the survey. Deep Learning models could also be explored for the given dataset to improve the accuracy and efficiency of the model.

## References

1. Garg, S., Kohli, C., Mangla, V., Chadha, S., Singh, M.M., Dahiya, N.: An epidemiological study on burden of hearing loss and its associated factors in Delhi, India. Ann. Otol. Rhinol. Laryngol. **127**(9), 614–619 (2018). https://doi.org/10.1177/0003489418781968
2. https://www.nidcd.nih.gov/health/statistics/use-hearing-aids-adults-hearing-loss

3. Glassman, J., Jordan, T., Sheu, J.-J., Pakulski, L., Thompson, A.: Health status of adults with hearing loss in the United States. Audiol. Res. **11**(1), 100–111 (2021). https://doi.org/10.3390/audiolres11010011

4. Aljabery, M., Kurnaz, S.: Applying datamining techniques to predict hearing aid type for audiology patients. J. Inf. Sci. Eng. **36**, 205–215 (2020). https://doi.org/10.6688/JISE.202003_36(2).0002

5. Kabade, V., et al.: Machine learning techniques for differential diagnosis of vertigo and dizziness: a review. Sensors **21**(22), 7565 (2021). https://doi.org/10.3390/s21227565

6. Panchev, C., Anwar, M.N., Oakes, M.: Hearing aid classification based on audiology data. In: Mladenov, V., Koprinkova-Hristova, P., Palm, G., Villa, A.E.P., Appollini, B., Kasabov, N. (eds.) ICANN 2013. LNCS, vol. 8131, pp. 375–380. Springer, Heidelberg (2013). https://doi.org/10.1007/978-3-642-40728-4_47

7. https://curve.carleton.ca/873548bb-f077-49d4-a5a6-9a69fddf1284

8. Futaki, T., Ikeda, T.: The auto-tilt test in patients with positional vertigo and Menière's disease. Am J Otol. **10**(4), 289–292 (1989). https://doi.org/10.1097/00129492-198907000-00010. PMID: 2801893

9. Pagnacco, G., Klotzek, A.S., Carrick, F.R., Wright, C.H., Oggero, E.: Effect of tone-based sound stimulation on balance performance of normal subjects: preliminary investigation. Biomed Sci Instrum. **51**, 54–61 (2015). PMID: 25996699

10. Wasmann, J.-W.A., et al.: Computational audiology: new approaches to advance hearing health care in the digital age. Ear Hearing **42**(6), 1499–1507 (2021). https://doi.org/10.1097/AUD.0000000000001041

# Quantum Data Management and Quantum Machine Learning for Data Management: State-of-the-Art and Open Challenges

Sven Groppe[1]([⊠]), Jinghua Groppe[1], Umut Çalıkyılmaz[1], Tobias Winker[1], and Le Gruenwal[2]

[1] Institute of Information Systems (IFIS), University of Lübeck, Lübeck, Germany
{groppe,groppej,calikyilmaz,winker}@ifis.uni-luebeck.de
[2] University of Oklahoma, Norman, USA
ggruenwald@ou.edu

**Abstract.** Quantum computing is an emerging technology and has yet to be exploited by industries to implement practical applications. Research has already laid the foundation for figuring out the benefits of quantum computing for these applications. In this paper, we provide a short overview of the state-of-the-art in data management issues that can be solved by quantum computers and especially by quantum machine learning approaches. Furthermore, we discuss what data management can do to support quantum computing and quantum machine learning.

**Keywords:** Quantum Computing · Data Management · Quantum Machine Learning · Databases

## 1 Introduction

There is a race going on among major quantum computer hardware developers like Google and IBM. This becomes visible when we look at Fig. 1, which shows the timeline of available and future quantum computers dependent on the number of supported qubits. The exponential growth of the number of supported qubits promise quantum applications for end-users by the end of this decade.

The performance of data management tasks is the key for efficient processing of many applications, especially those that are data-driven and large-scale. Nowadays, these applications are essential and ubiquitous, and the amount of data available and their complexity increase drastically. Thus, research to improve data management tasks is vital, even though this area is one of the most well-established ones in computer science. It is obvious that it is important to investigate the possibilities of using quantum computing to solve research and implementation challenges in data management.

S. Nandan Mohanty et al. (Eds.): ICISML 2022, LNICST 471, pp. 252–261, 2023.
https://doi.org/10.1007/978-3-031-35081-8_20

In this paper we discuss the state-of-the-art and open challenges for quantum computing approaches speeding up data management tasks, and data management systems integrating quantum computing approaches. We call the whole area quantum data management. Furthermore, we especially focus on quantum machine learning in our discussion, where machine learning tasks are partly or completely processed on quantum computers.

The remainder of this contribution is organized as follows. Section 2 provides an overview over quantum data management starting with a short discussion about quantum machine learning and its applications in Sect. 2.2. We deal with data management for quantum computing with a special focus on quantum machine learning in Sect. 2.3. Finally, we sum up and conclude in Sect. 3.

## 2  Quantum Data Management

In this section we discuss the state-of-the-art and open challenges of two aspects: 1) quantum computing (including quantum machine learning) for data management tasks, and 2) data management for quantum computing (including quantum machine learning).

### 2.1  Quantum Machine Learning

Extensive surveys [1,15,68] about quantum machine learning show that for nearly every major area of machine learning, a quantum counterpart has been proposed and discussed.

Recent scientific contributions extensively investigate the benefits of applying quantum machine learning over classical machine learning. For example, in comparison to classical support vector machines, an exponential speedup can be achieved by applying quantum support vector machines [51]. Indeed, quantum machine learning methods have the potential to learn on fewer data points than classical methods alone [12]. It is even possible to identify data sets that have a potential quantum advantage in learning tasks by looking at the properties of the data sets [39].

**Applications of Quantum Machine Learning:** The applications of quantum machine learning have a broad spectrum and range from natural science like chemistry and physics [55], to research in software engineering like software supply chain attacks [48], to quantum sciences itself [18] including phase classification, quantum feedback control, representation of many-body quantum states and quantum circuits optimization. In the following sections, we discuss possibilities of using quantum machine learning to support data management tasks.

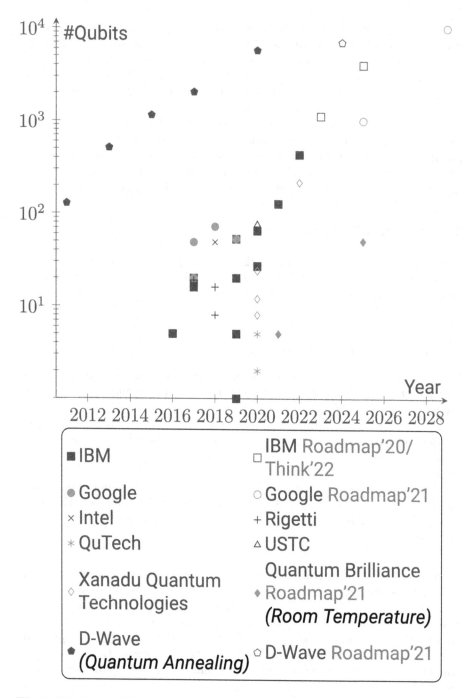

**Fig. 1.** Timeline and Roadmaps of Quantum Computers (Data according to https://en.wikipedia.org/wiki/List_of_quantum_processors. Roadmaps according to https://research.ibm.com/blog/ibm-quantum-roadmap, https://spectrum.ieee.org/ibm-quantum-computer, https://quantumai.google/research, https://www.dwavesys.com/media/xvjpraig/clarity-roadmap_digital_v2.pdf (all visited on 20.6.2022) and [19])

## 2.2   Quantum Computing for Data Management

Whenever a new technology emerges, in order to apply it to an area of one's interest, one would need to analyze the new technology and its benefits. Especially, one would want to identify which tasks in the area of interest would benefit the most from using the new technology. There are quantum counterparts[1] [2,3,5–8,14,20,22,30,34,41,45,52,54,58,62,63] of many classical algorithms for mathematical optimization problems like dynamic programming [23], exhaustive searches [22], simulated annealing, reinforcement learning [9], regression, linear programming [17], random walk [23], genetic algorithm [37], ant colony optimization [16,21] and whale optimization [49]. Some optimization algorithms like QAOA [24] and quantum annealing [42] are developed based on the capabilities and features of quantum computers restricting the input further (here to quadratic binary optimization problems) compared to their more general counterpart in the classical world (here simulated annealing).

Whenever a problem can be reduced to the application of basic mathematical optimization approaches, it can be sped up by quantum computers by replacing classical routines with their quantum computing counterparts promising quadratic speedups in many cases (see e.g. [30,52] up to polylogarithmic factors) or even exponential speedup for some approaches [54].

This straight-forward solution for applying quantum technologies in a domain of interest like data management promises predictable benefits. For example, well-studied subproblems of data management like optimizing queries use many different mathematical optimization approaches as basic routines: Dynamic programming [57], simulated annealing [40], reinforcement learning [33,47,64,66], linear programming [60], random walk [25], genetic algorithm [38] and ant colony optimization [16,21], where this list is not exhaustive. Only few scientific contributions [56,59] deal with applying quantum approaches to query optimization. There are also only few contributions dealing with quantum approaches in other related areas of data management. Another example to the problems in data management is the transaction schedule optimization problem [46]. Although this problem is not as well-studied as query optimization, there are still studies [10,11,29] applying quantum computing approaches for optimizing transaction schedules.

Hybrid multi-model multi-platform (HM3P) databases [27,28] take not only quantum computers, but also other heterogeneous hardware like many-core CPUs, GPUs, FPGAs, Internet-of-Things, and mobile environments into account. Hence, they are a generalization of the idea to integrate quantum computers into database management systems for speeding up the processing of database management tasks.

Besides this straight-forward way to apply quantum technologies in the domain of interest, one might also investigate and research on applying the concepts of a new technology in some new way to the domain of interest. For example, the authors of [53] introduce *quantum databases*, which are deferring

---

[1] We regard here quantum algorithms and quantum-inspired [50] algorithms as quantum counterparts, although quantum-inspired algorithm are designed to run on classical hardware, but are inspired from the quantum computing concept.

the making of choices in transactions until the state of the database must be observed by an application or user.

**Quantum Machine Learning for Data Management:** Investigating some subdomains of data management like query optimization, one may discover the potential use of quantum machine learning in query optimizers. In recent years, there have been many contributions [4,26,32,35,43,65,67] dealing with estimating the runtime of a query or its cardinality, which can be used by a query optimizer to choose the best query execution plan. Other approaches [13,36,47,61,66] propose to directly predict the optimal join order with the benefits of a short runtime of the query optimizer achieving good join orders. Future work includes replacing these classical machine learning approaches with quantum machine learning approaches and investigating the benefits of quantum machine learning in query optimization.

There are many more problems that have been considered to be improved by machine learning approaches [44]. For example, there have been learned tuning methods proposed for improving the tuning performance or resource utilization. For a large number of columns, tables and queries, machine learning approaches provide benefits for the recommendation of creating and maintaining indexes or materialized views in databases. Machine learning methods also predict incoming queries and workload for proactively optimizing the database. Future work might address also these and other topics for evaluating the benefits of quantum machine learning.

## 2.3  Data Management for Quantum Computing

We should look at not only what quantum computing can do to improve data management tasks as discussed in Sect. 2.2, but also what data management systems can provide to support quantum computing applications. We envision a database management system that offers easy access to quantum computing applications by integrating high-level functionalities for quantum computing applications into the data management system. The high-level functionalities include an extension of the language constructs of query languages to call quantum computing subroutines. The data management system should also allow for easy storing and accessing the input and output of quantum computing applications. Furthermore, the data management system should automatically choose the needed and available quantum resources as well as apply hybrid algorithms. These algorithms are tailored in a way that missing resources and support of qubits and circuit depths in quantum computers are overcome by taking over more computations by classical algorithms or simulations of quantum computing on classical hardware.

**Data Management for Quantum Machine Learning:** There is a trend for data management systems to offer machine learning functionalities [31]. While data management systems offer support for traditional requirements like memory management, parallelism and fault tolerance also to machine learning tasks, machine learning tasks pose additional requirements for

- scalable training, where often large-scale data sets are processed in comparison to the (often simple and efficient to perform) application/prediction phase,
- storing models and their parameters after training for their use in the application/prediction phase,
- language constructs for expressing complex machine learning tasks in a simple way while combining these language constructs with query languages, and
- automatic choosing and optimizing models and machine learning tasks.

Open challenges include the integration of quantum machine learning into data management systems and adapting the requirements and solutions to quantum machine learning and available quantum computers with an additional focus on hybrid algorithms. These algorithms combine a quantum algorithm with a classical algorithm to flexibly adapt the available system configuration of classical and quantum hardware.

## 3  Summary and Conclusions

In this paper, we discussed the intersection between quantum computing and data management, and reasoned that the methods developed in each discipline can be used to improve the other. Many studies, some of which we cited in this paper, show that quantum machine learning can dramatically speed up the learning process of some classical machine learning approaches. We also provided a short literature survey on quantum computing approaches to improve the processing times of some data management procedures, namely query optimization and transaction scheduling. We discussed how to embed quantum computing approaches and especially the quantum machine learning functionality into data management systems.

In our future work we aim to implement the quantum counterparts of the well-studied query optimization methods. To achieve this, we plan to analyze the quantum optimization and learning algorithms in depth and develop applicable quantum methods. Also, we aim to broaden the toolbox for transaction schedule optimization both by developing classical algorithms and by further speeding them up via quantum computing.

**Acknowledgments.** This work is funded by the German Federal Ministry of Education and Research within the funding program quantum technologies - from basic research to market - contract number 13N16090.

# References

1. Abohashima, Z., Elhosen, M., Houssein, E.H., Mohamed, W.M.: Classification with quantum machine learning: a survey. arXiv arXiv:2006.12270 (2020). https://doi.org/10.48550/ARXIV.2006.12270
2. Agrawal, R., Kaur, B., Sharma, S.: Quantum based whale optimization algorithm for wrapper feature selection. Appl. Soft Comput. **89**, 106092 (2020). https://doi.org/10.1016/j.asoc.2020.106092
3. Aharonov, Y., Davidovich, L., Zagury, N.: Quantum random walks. Phys. Rev. A **48**(2), 1687–1690 (1993). https://doi.org/10.1103/physreva.48.1687
4. Akdere, M., Çetintemel, U., Riondato, M., Upfal, E., Zdonik, S.B.: Learning-based query performance modeling and prediction. In: 2012 IEEE 28th International Conference on Data Engineering, pp. 390–401. IEEE (2012)
5. Ambainis, A.: Variable time amplitude amplification and quantum algorithms for linear algebra problems (2012). https://doi.org/10.4230/LIPICS.STACS.2012.636
6. Ambainis, A., Bach, E., Nayak, A., Vishwanath, A., Watrous, J.: One-dimensional quantum walks. In: Proceedings of the Thirty-Third Annual ACM Symposium on Theory of Computing - STOC 2001. ACM Press (2001). https://doi.org/10.1145/380752.380757
7. Ambainis, A., Balodis, K., Iraids, J., Kokainis, M., Prūsis, K., Vihrovs, J.: Quantum speedups for exponential-time dynamic programming algorithms. In: Proceedings of the Thirtieth Annual ACM-SIAM Symposium on Discrete Algorithms, pp. 1783–1793. Society for Industrial and Applied Mathematics, January 2019. https://doi.org/10.1137/1.9781611975482.107
8. An, D., Lin, L.: Quantum linear system solver based on time-optimal adiabatic quantum computing and quantum approximate optimization algorithm. ACM Trans. Quantum Comput. **3**(2), 1–28 (2022). https://doi.org/10.1145/3498331
9. Barto, A.G., Sutton, R.S., Brouwer, P.S.: Associative search network: a reinforcement learning associative memory. Biol. Cybern. **40**(3), 201–211 (1981). https://doi.org/10.1007/bf00453370
10. Bittner, T., Groppe, S.: Avoiding blocking by scheduling transactions using quantum annealing. In: Proceedings of the 24th Symposium on International Database Engineering & Applications. ACM, August 2020. https://doi.org/10.1145/3410566.3410593
11. Bittner, T., Groppe, S.: Hardware accelerating the optimization of transaction schedules via quantum annealing by avoiding blocking. Open J. Cloud Comput. (OJCC) **7**(1), 1–21 (2020). http://nbn-resolving.de/urn:nbn:de:101:1-2020112218332015343957
12. Caro, M.C., et al.: Generalization in quantum machine learning from few training data. Nat. Commun. **13**(1) (2022)
13. Chen, J., et al.: Efficient join order selection learning with graph-based representation. In: Proceedings of the 28th ACM SIGKDD Conference on Knowledge Discovery and Data Mining, KDD 2022, pp. 97–107. Association for Computing Machinery, New York (2022). https://doi.org/10.1145/3534678.3539303
14. Childs, A.M., Kothari, R., Somma, R.D.: Quantum algorithm for systems of linear equations with exponentially improved dependence on precision. SIAM J. Comput. **46**(6), 1920–1950 (2017). https://doi.org/10.1137/16m1087072
15. Ciliberto, C., et al.: Quantum machine learning: a classical perspective. Proc. Roy. Soc. A Math. Phys. Eng. Sci. **474**(2209), 20170551 (2018). https://doi.org/10.1098/rspa.2017.0551

16. Colorni, A., Dorigo, M., Maniezzo, V., Varela, F.J., Bourgine, P.E.: Distributed optimization by ant colonies. In: Proceedings of the First European Conference on Artificial Life, pp. 134–142 (1991)
17. Dantzig, G.B.: Linear programming. Oper. Res. **50**(1), 42–47 (2002). https://doi.org/10.1287/opre.50.1.42.17798
18. Dawid, A., et al.: Modern applications of machine learning in quantum sciences. arXiv preprint arXiv:2204.04198 (2022)
19. Doherty, M.: Quantum accelerators: a new trajectory of quantum computers. Digitale Welt **5**(2), 74–79 (2021). https://doi.org/10.1007/s42354-021-0342-8
20. Dong, D., Chen, C., Chen, Z.: Quantum reinforcement learning. In: Wang, L., Chen, K., Ong, Y.S. (eds.) ICNC 2005. LNCS, vol. 3611, pp. 686–689. Springer, Heidelberg (2005). https://doi.org/10.1007/11539117_97
21. Dorigo, M., Birattari, M., Stutzle, T.: Ant colony optimization. IEEE Comput. Intell. Mag. **1**(4), 28–39 (2006)
22. Dürr, C., Høyer, P.: A quantum algorithm for finding the minimum (1996). https://doi.org/10.48550/ARXIV.QUANT-PH/9607014. https://arxiv.org/abs/quant-ph/9607014
23. Eddy, S.R.: What is dynamic programming? Nat. Biotechnol. **22**(7), 909–910 (2004). https://doi.org/10.1038/nbt0704-909
24. Farhi, E., Goldstone, J., Gutmann, S.: A quantum approximate optimization algorithm, November 2014. http://arxiv.org/abs/1411.4028
25. Galindo-Legaria, C.A., Pellenkoft, A., Kersten, M.L.: Fast, randomized join-order selection - why use transformations? In: Proceedings of the 20th International Conference on Very Large Data Bases, VLDB 1994, pp. 85–95. Morgan Kaufmann Publishers Inc., San Francisco (1994)
26. Ganapathi, A., et al.: Predicting multiple metrics for queries: better decisions enabled by machine learning. In: 2009 IEEE 25th International Conference on Data Engineering, pp. 592–603. IEEE (2009)
27. Groppe, S.: Semantic hybrid multi-model multi-platform (SHM3P) databases. In: International Semantic Intelligence Conference (ISIC 2021), New Delhi (hybrid), India, pp. 16–26. CEUR (2021). http://ceur-ws.org/Vol-2786/Paper2.pdf
28. Groppe, S., Groppe, J.: Hybrid multi-model multi-platform (HM3P) databases. In: Proceedings of the 9th International Conference on Data Science, Technology and Applications (DATA) (2020). https://doi.org/10.5220/0009802401770184
29. Groppe, S., Groppe, J.: Optimizing transaction schedules on universal quantum computers via code generation for Grover's search algorithm. In: 25th International Database Engineering & Applications Symposium. ACM, July 2021. https://doi.org/10.1145/3472163.3472164
30. Grover, L.K.: A fast quantum mechanical algorithm for database search. In: Proceedings of the Twenty-Eighth Annual ACM Symposium on Theory of Computing - STOC 1996. ACM Press (1996). https://doi.org/10.1145/237814.237866
31. Günnemann, S.: Machine learning meets databases. Datenbank-Spektrum **17**(1), 77–83 (2017). https://doi.org/10.1007/s13222-017-0247-8
32. Gupta, C., Mehta, A., Dayal, U.: PQR: predicting query execution times for autonomous workload management. In: 2008 International Conference on Autonomic Computing, pp. 13–22. IEEE (2008)
33. Han, Y., et al.: Cardinality estimation in DBMS. Proc. VLDB Endowment **15**(4), 752–765 (2021). https://doi.org/10.14778/3503585.3503586
34. Harrow, A.W., Hassidim, A., Lloyd, S.: Quantum algorithm for linear systems of equations. Phys. Rev. Lett. **103**(15) (2009). https://doi.org/10.1103/physrevlett.103.150502

35. Hasan, R., Gandon, F.: A machine learning approach to SPARQL query performance prediction. In: 2014 IEEE/WIC/ACM International Joint Conferences on Web Intelligence (WI) and Intelligent Agent Technologies (IAT), vol. 1, pp. 266–273. IEEE (2014)

36. Heitz, J., Stockinger, K.: Join query optimization with deep reinforcement learning algorithms. arXiv:1911.11689 (2019)

37. Holland, J.H.: Genetic algorithms. Sci. Am. **267**(1), 66–73 (1992)

38. Horng, J.T., Kao, C.Y., Liu, B.J.: A genetic algorithm for database query optimization. In: Proceedings of the First IEEE Conference on Evolutionary Computation. IEEE World Congress on Computational Intelligence. IEEE (1994). https://doi.org/10.1109/icec.1994.349926

39. Huang, H.Y., et al.: Power of data in quantum machine learning. Nat. Commun. **12**(1) (2021)

40. Ioannidis, Y.E., Wong, E.: Query optimization by simulated annealing. In: Proceedings of the 1987 ACM SIGMOD International Conference on Management of Data - SIGMOD 1987. ACM Press (1987). https://doi.org/10.1145/38713.38722

41. Johnson, M.W., et al.: Quantum annealing with manufactured spins. Nature **473**(7346), 194–198 (11). https://doi.org/10.1038/nature10012

42. Kadowaki, T., Nishimori, H.: Quantum annealing in the transverse Ising model. Phys. Rev. E **58**(5), 5355 (1998)

43. Kim, K., Jung, J., Seo, I., Han, W.S., Choi, K., Chong, J.: Learned cardinality estimation: an in-depth study. In: Proceedings of the 2022 International Conference on Management of Data, pp. 1214–1227 (2022)

44. Li, G., Zhou, X., Cao, L.: Machine learning for databases. In: The First International Conference on AI-ML-Systems. ACM, October 2021. https://doi.org/10.1145/3486001.3486248

45. Liu, M., Zhang, F., Ma, Y., Pota, H.R., Shen, W.: Evacuation path optimization based on quantum ant colony algorithm. Adv. Eng. Inform. **30**(3), 259–267 (2016)

46. Luo, G., Naughton, J.F., Ellmann, C.J., Watzke, M.W.: Transaction reordering. Data Knowl. Eng. **69**(1), 29–49 (2010)

47. Marcus, R., Papaemmanouil, O.: Deep reinforcement learning for join order enumeration. In: Proceedings of the First International Workshop on Exploiting Artificial Intelligence Techniques for Data Management. ACM, June 2018. https://doi.org/10.1145/3211954.3211957

48. Masum, M., et al.: Quantum machine learning for software supply chain attacks: how far can we go? In: 2022 IEEE 46th Annual Computers, Software, and Applications Conference (COMPSAC), pp. 530–538. IEEE Computer Society, Los Alamitos, July 2022. https://doi.org/10.1109/COMPSAC54236.2022.00097

49. Mirjalili, S., Lewis, A.: The whale optimization algorithm. Adv. Eng. Softw. **95**, 51–67 (2016). https://doi.org/10.1016/j.advengsoft.2016.01.008

50. Moore, M., Narayanan, A.: Quantum-inspired computing. Department Computer Science, University Exeter, Exeter, UK (1995)

51. Rebentrost, P., Mohseni, M., Lloyd, S.: Quantum support vector machine for big data classification. Phys. Rev. Lett. **113**, 130503 (2014). https://doi.org/10.1103/PhysRevLett.113.130503

52. Ronagh, P.: The problem of dynamic programming on a quantum computer (2019). https://doi.org/10.48550/ARXIV.1906.02229. https://arxiv.org/abs/1906.02229

53. Roy, S., Kot, L., Koch, C.: Quantum databases. In: Sixth Biennial Conference on Innovative Data Systems Research (CIDR), Asilomar, CA, USA (2013). www.cidrdb.org. http://cidrdb.org/cidr2013/Papers/CIDR13_Paper86.pdf

54. Saggio, V., et al.: Experimental quantum speed-up in reinforcement learning agents. Nature **591**(7849), 229–233 (2021). https://doi.org/10.1038/s41586-021-03242-7

55. Sajjan, M., et al.: Quantum machine learning for chemistry and physics. Chem. Soc. Rev. **51**(15), 6475–6573 (2022). https://doi.org/10.1039/d2cs00203e

56. Schönberger, M., Scherzinger, S., Mauerer, W.: Applicability of quantum computing on database query optimization. In: Frühjahrstreffen Fachgruppe Datenbanken in Potsdam (Poster Presentation), March 2022

57. Selinger, P.G., Astrahan, M.M., Chamberlin, D.D., Lorie, R.A., Price, T.G.: Access path selection in a relational database management system. In: Proceedings of the 1979 ACM SIGMOD International Conference on Management of Data - SIGMOD 1979. ACM Press (1979). https://doi.org/10.1145/582095.582099

58. Subaşı, Y., Somma, R.D., Orsucci, D.: Quantum algorithms for systems of linear equations inspired by adiabatic quantum computing. Phys. Rev. Lett. **122**(6) (2019). https://doi.org/10.1103/physrevlett.122.060504

59. Trummer, I., Koch, C.: Multiple query optimization on the d-wave 2x adiabatic quantum computer. Proc. VLDB Endowment **9**(9), 648–659 (2016). https://doi.org/10.14778/2947618.2947621

60. Trummer, I., Koch, C.: Solving the join ordering problem via mixed integer linear programming. In: Proceedings of the 2017 ACM International Conference on Management of Data. ACM, May 2017. https://doi.org/10.1145/3035918.3064039

61. Wang, H., et al.: April: An automatic graph data management system based on reinforcement learning. In: Proceedings of the 29th ACM International Conference on Information and Knowledge Management, pp. 3465–3468 (2020)

62. Wang, H., Liu, J., Zhi, J., Fu, C.: The improvement of quantum genetic algorithm and its application on function optimization. Math. Problems Eng. **2013**, 1–10 (2013). https://doi.org/10.1155/2013/730749

63. Wang, L., Niu, Q., Fei, M.: A novel quantum ant colony optimization algorithm. In: Li, K., Fei, M., Irwin, G.W., Ma, S. (eds.) LSMS 2007. LNCS, vol. 4688, pp. 277–286. Springer, Heidelberg (2007). https://doi.org/10.1007/978-3-540-74769-7_31

64. Woltmann, L., Hartmann, C., Thiele, M., Habich, D., Lehner, W.: Cardinality estimation with local deep learning models. In: Proceedings of the Second International Workshop on Exploiting Artificial Intelligence Techniques for Data Management - aiDM 2019. ACM Press (2019). https://doi.org/10.1145/3329859.3329875

65. Woltmann, L., Olwig, D., Hartmann, C., Habich, D., Lehner, W.: PostCENN: PostgreSQL with machine learning models for cardinality estimation. Proc. VLDB Endowment **14**(12), 2715–2718 (2021)

66. Yu, X., Li, G., Chai, C., Tang, N.: Reinforcement learning with tree-LSTM for join order selection. In: 2020 IEEE 36th International Conference on Data Engineering (ICDE). IEEE, April 2020. https://doi.org/10.1109/icde48307.2020.00116

67. Zhao, K., Yu, J.X., He, Z., Li, R., Zhang, H.: Lightweight and accurate cardinality estimation by neural network gaussian process. In: Proceedings of the 2022 International Conference on Management of Data, pp. 973–987 (2022)

68. Zhao, R., Wang, S.: A review of quantum neural networks: methods, models, dilemma. arXiv:2109.01840 (2021). https://doi.org/10.48550/ARXIV.2109.01840

# Multivariate Analysis and Comparison of Machine Learning Algorithms: A Case Study of Cereals of America

Rashika Gupta[1]([⊠]), E. Lavanya[1], Nonita Sharma[2], and Monika Mangla[3]

[1] Electronics and Communication Engineering (AI) Department, Indira Gandhi Delhi Technical University for Women, Delhi, India
gupta.rashika@gmail.com
[2] Information Technology Department, Indira Gandhi Delhi Technical University for Women, Delhi, India
nonitasharma@igdtuw.ac.in
[3] Department of Information Technology, Dwarkadas J. Sanghvi College of Engineering, Mumbai, India

**Abstract.** This research work aims to analyze the nutritional value of different cereals available in the market through various machine learning models. This analysis is supplemented with the visualization of data also for enhanced understanding. This understanding enables users to devise market strategies as they are competent to evaluate quality of each product and thus its reception in the market. The works starts with statistical analysis through of the data through various plots which provides insight of the data. Further authors perform a comparative analysis of different cereals based on various parameters. This analysis helps to determine the best cereal according to our requirements. The authors have implemented machine learning models on the data to predict the vitamins of any cereal based on their nutritional value. The implementation of various models viz. Linear regression, decision tree, logistic regression, random forest, and KNN advocates the efficacy of various machine learning models to the given problem.

**Keywords:** Feature selection · linear regression · KNN · random forest · logistic regression · decision tree

## 1 Introduction

All living organisms have been relying on various sources of energy for their life. Among the different sources of energy, whole grain cereals are one of the most sought-after sources of energy and nutrition. These cereals provide various nutrients viz. Protein, vitamins, fiber, and antioxidants. As there are plenty of cereals available, it is important to analyze the nutritional value of each cereal to select the one as per users' requirements. In this paper, authors have attempted to analyze the nutritional value of various cereals through different machine learning models. For the same, authors have considered the

S. Nandan Mohanty et al. (Eds.): ICISML 2022, LNICST 471, pp. 262–271, 2023.
https://doi.org/10.1007/978-3-031-35081-8_21

online available dataset. Ahead of application of machine learning models, authors have performed data preprocessing which extracts the principal features of the considered dataset. The preprocessing involves the detection of null values if any and then dropping those values [1, 21, 23]. This may also include data normalization to bring the entire data in same range so that it becomes meaningful to compare that data. Further, it involves detection of outliers as outliers negatively affect the statistical and mathematical analysis of a machine learning algorithm leading to lower precision and accuracy. Thereafter, various statistical tools and scatter plots may be used to illustrate the data in a graphical manner.

Further, various machine learning models namely linear regression, K-Nearest Neighbors, Random Forest, Decision Trees, and Logistic Regression are implemented [2, 3, 24]. Current work is significant as it analyzes the cereals manufactured by different companies. The obtained information can be used by consumers to make an informed decision about their choice of cereal according to their dietary requirements [4]. It can also be used for strategizing the marketing and researchers' policies of the manufacturers to lead in this competitive scenario [5, 6]. Hence, the implementation of machine learning can also be used in this domain of nutrition and agriculture [7, 22] in addition to several other problems.

Here, the main contribution of the authors is that authors strongly recommend that empirical evaluation and statistical analysis of the data must be performed ahead of application of machine learning models. Employment of rigorous statistical analysis enables to efficiently select the appropriate machine learning model which is cost effective in terms of time and resources.

Current research work is organized in various sections. Section 1 gives a brief introduction to the cereals' nutritional value. The related work by different authors has been presented in Sect. 2. Section 3 is dedicated to the methodology and the results are discussed in Sect. 4. Finally, the conclusion is given in Sect. 5.

## 2   Related Work

Several researchers have attempted to work in this direction to determine the nutritional value of different cereals as there are plenty of cereals available viz. Oats, barley, millet, sorghum, triticale, etc. [8]. All these cereals provide a huge range of vital nutrients namely protein, fiber, minerals, carbohydrates, etc. Among various crops, wheat and rice constitute around 50% of the total production. All cereals consist of an embryo containing the material for production in the new plant. Here, the authors claim that it is very important to store cereals in the required conditions to maintain their nutritional value. Additionally, storage time also impacts the nutritional value i.e. storage for a shorter period leads to less change in nutritional value and vice versa. Further, the nutritional value will be influenced by the milling operation. Here, it depends on the extent to which covering bran and aleurone are taken off. As per the authors in [8], intensive research is required in this field as cereals are the most common source of daily needs. It is also known that regular consumption of cereals may prevent chronic diseases. Although the mechanism that helps to prevent such diseases is not clear.

Further, authors in [9] also believe that cereals have a significant contribution by declaring that although cereals provide a widerange of nutrients, processing may impact their nutritional value. Authors in [9] primarily review the literature that discusses the impact of processing and their mixing with other food items on nutritional value. This study may be helpful to a health professional to give guided advice to their patients. Authors in [10] have presented the significance of barley, known as the fourth floor. Authors claim that barley has high benefits for obesity, diabetes hypertension, etc. owing to its dietary fibers. Additionally, barley is also a good source of starch, minerals, and vitamins and thus can be considered a complete food. Here, the authors present the macro constituents and micro constituents of barley. Its prebiotic effects and nutritional value is also discussed. Further, the authors also discuss required cultivars to preserve their nutritional value.

Authors in [11] perform a comparative analysis of barley with rye, rye wheat, wheat, and oats. For the same, the authors perform a feeding test with mice. Further, a dyebinding (DBC) method is also used to estimate lysine. The focus of the study is to develop high-lysine barleys and high-temperature drying processes for livestock feeds of cereals. DBC method was successful to recover a high-lysine barley line. Further, the authors also discussed the issue of grain deterioration and measures to prevent it. The effect of heat on lysine during various stages namely storage, baking, drying, etc. are also discussed. The study achieves to develop an effective high-temperature drying method that has been adopted in Sweden.

The research is carried forward by authors in [12] by studying the Kodo millet, an ancient grain that grows in arid areas. Kodo millet is very rich in fiber and various minerals. However, processing it may lead to a reduction in nutritional value. In India, several traditional food items are prepared from Kodo millet by blending it with other cereals to enhance its nutritional value.

Additionally, as per the authors in [13], there is a consistent pressure to increase food production in response to population growth. It can be achieved by increasing production capacity or changing consumption habits. For instance, it becomes very difficult to cater to the rising demand for staple cereals like wheat, rice, maize, etc. If the consumption pattern shifts towards cereals like millet and sorghum, it will be highly satisfying as these cereals can be grown in adverse conditions also. Further, these cereals also have a high nutritional value similar to popular staple foods.

Thus, it becomes evident from the research by various researchers that we need to take conscious efforts to cater to the rising demand for cereals without compromising the nutritional demands of the persons.

## 3  Methodology

This section demonstrates the process and various methods used for the analysis of cereals using various machine learning models and data visualization [21]. For implementation, dataset is collected from Kaggle which is compiled by Mr. Chris Craw-ford. The considered dataset has 77 rows and 17 columns. Figure 1 demonstrates the complete methodology followed in the research work. During preprocessing, all null values are handled. The data normalization handles the significant diversity among range of data.

It also handles outliers to remove the noise if any [14]. Further, to find the correlation among various attributes correlation matrix can be obtained that is illustrated in form of heat map. This correlation enables to determine the principal components. Through statistical analysis, authors illustrates the range of data, the maximum, minimum, and average of each attribute, and a comparative analysis of different attributes [15, 23].

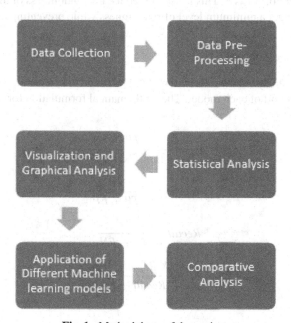

**Fig. 1.** Methodology of the project.

Here, vitamins is the dependent variable. The split of training and testing data is 80:20. Further, 5 machine learning algorithms are applied namely Linear regression [17], Logistic regression, KNN, Decision trees, and Random Forest. In logistic regression, the maximum and maximum iterations are chosen as 12000 [18]. During kNN, the authors have applied the criteria of Minkowski distance of order 2 [19]. Random forest can be considered as a model containing multiple decision trees, which are applied to numerous subsets of the dataset and the average value is taken thereby improving the predictive precision and accuracy of the respective dataset, to produce a more efficient model and analysis [19]. Instead of entire operation being carried by one decision tree, this model uses the prediction from all of the random trees and based on the majority votes of predictions, the final output is predicted. The parameter used in this model is entropy and the number of fragments of decision trees in this model is taken as 20.

Further, decision tree splits the data according to a certain parameter till maximum precision and accuracy are obtained. The tree mainly comprises two constituents, leaves (which are the decision or the outcome) and decision nodes (which are the joints where data is being split), according to the chosen parameter. Two types of criteria can be used-entropy and Gini, and the authors have used the parameter entropy with maximum depth (number of nodes) as 5. This is used to reduce the randomness of the prediction in each step, till we get a minimum level of randomness while preventing overfitting [19].

## 3.1 Comparative Analysis

The authors have analyzed the different models and found the precision, accuracy, recall, F1 score, and support of each model. The mathematical formulation for these metrics is as follows [20]:

$$Accuracy = \frac{TP + TN}{TP + TN + FN + FP} \tag{1}$$

$$Precision = \frac{TP}{TP + FP} \tag{2}$$

$$Recall = \frac{TP}{TP + FN} \tag{3}$$

$$F1\ Score = \frac{2X\ Recall \times Precision}{Recall + Precision} \tag{4}$$

## 4   Results and Discussion

The authors have performed multivariate analysis of cereals using diverse methods of statistical and visualization analysis. It is followed by application of machine learning models, advanced predictive analysis.

### 4.1   Data Analysis and Visualization

Authors have used various tools for data analysis which gives insight about the data. The correlation among various attributes is illustrated in Fig. 2. Correlation is the extent or degree to which any two random variables are linearly related to each other. The correlation coefficient is denoted by r which always lies between -1 to 1 that indicates maximum negative correlation and maximum positive correlation respectively. From Fig. 2, it is evident that Sugar and rating are most negatively correlated while weight and calories are most positively correlated.

Figure 3 depicts a multivariate pair plot. Four different attributes-protein, vitamins, carbohydrates, and fiber have been chosen and plotted against each other, to determine the calories. When an attribute is plotted against itself, we obtain a sinusoidal waveform graph of the normal distribution, while a scatter plot is obtained in all other cases. The variation in the range of the calories has been color-coded, and the scale has been provided. The graph concludes that when carbohydrates are plotted on the dependent axis and the vitamins are plotted on the independent axis, then the calories are minimum when carbohydrates are 10 and vitamins are 0, and the maximum when the carbohydrates are 15 and vitamins are 100. Similarly, in the graph between fiber across the dependent axis, and the protein on the independent axis, the maximum value of calories is obtained when both protein and fiber lie between 2.5 and 5.0, while it obtains its minimum value when protein lies between 2.5 and 5, while fiber is greater than 12.5.

Figure 4 depicts a joint plot of fat and protein with fat on the dependent axis and protein on the independent axis. It is a combination of the scatter plot and bar graphs in the samegraph. The scatter plot is used for finding the extent of correlation and the distribution of the data, while the bar plot gives the variation in the quantity of the attribute. The graph gives the interpretation that protein and fat are positively correlated. Further, Fig. 5 shows a boxplot of the potassium content of the cereals. This is used for detecting outliers, which is a record that lies at an abnormal distance from the remaining data set.

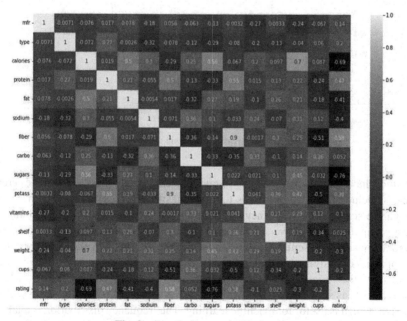

**Fig. 2.** Correlation matrix for the data

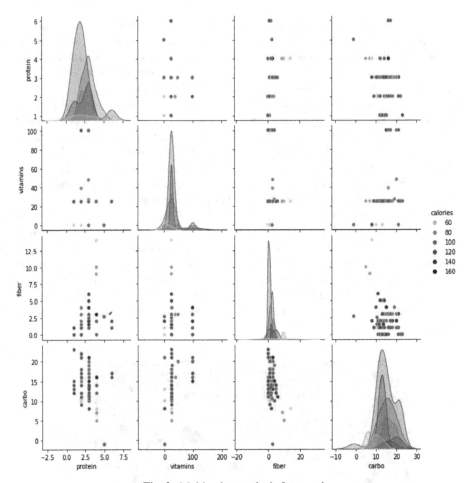

**Fig. 3.** Multivariate analysis for cereals

Authors have found which quantity of fat is present in the highest count of the cereals, and can conclude that 1 mg of fat is the amount of fat present in maximum cereals. Through the scatter plot, frequency distribution and the scattered plot distribution of protein versus fat, and type versus fat can be analyzed. Displayed pair grids and cross grids for the visual representation of the entire dataset. This visualization greatly reduces the complexity of studying and understanding the data. Authors have also made relational plots to show the variation between the manufacturer and fat content in two different types of cereals as shown in Fig. 4. Authors have also made a joint plot along with the regression, which is useful for machine learning. The frequency distribution is analyzed cereals using a histogram Further, outliers can be detected using the boxplot as illustrated in Fig. 5.

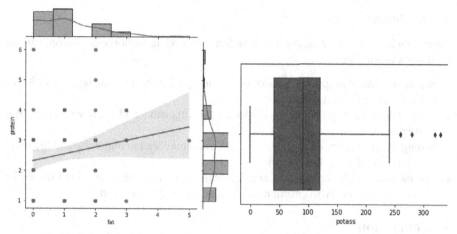

**Fig. 4.** Joint plot of fat vs protein          **Fig. 5.** Boxplot for detecting outliers

## 4.2  Comparative Analysis of Machine Learning Models

The authors have evaluated the effectiveness of all classifiers in terms of precision, accuracy, and F1 score. The Comparative Analysis has been made through the graph of different Machine Learning models used in our project – Linear regression, Logistic regression, K-NN, random forest, and decision trees on different parameters. Each model provides high accuracy of 0.9375 other than the linear regression giving an accuracy of 0.8355865644. The authors have established a comparative analysis of the different models by comparing the value of the training score of each model. The model with the highest train score, Random Forest, is chosen as the best model for the data prediction from the chosen dataset. The details of various metrics obtained are presented in Table 1.

**Table 1.** Comparative Analysis of different models

| Model | Training score |
|---|---|
| Linear Regression | 0.9495 |
| Logistic regression | 0.9672 |
| K-NN | 0.8196 |
| Random forest | 0.9836 |
| Decision trees | 0.9672 |

## 4.3 Challenges

During implementation of various machine learning models, authors experienced various challenges as follows:

- Selection of an appropriate visualization technique for the accurate representation of the data can become a tedious job.
- Data should be appropriately chosen or the precision and accuracy may differ distinctly.
- Wrong data pre-processing and feature selection may lead to imprecise and incorrect predictions in the machine learning models.
- The parameters chosen, and the number of maximum iterations specified should be selected appropriately to ensure maximum accuracy of prediction.

## 5 Conclusion

In this work, the authors have attempted to determine the nutritional value of various bowls of cereal through various methods. The various bowls of cereal like wheat, rice, maize, barley, oats, millets, etc. are discussed. It is clarified from the study by various researchers that although wholesome cereals have high nutritional value; processing may lead to a reduction in the same. Hence conscious efforts must be taken during the processing of the cereals. Also, the need to increase the growth of cereals is briefly discussed given the rising population. For the same, initiatives like the inclusion of non-staple cereals must be taken. The requirement to understand the nutritional value of cereals is important and hence continuous research must prevail in this direction.

## References

1. Sharma, N., Yadav, S., Mangla, M., Mohanty, A., Mohanty, S.N.: Multivariate analysis of COVID-19 on stock, commodity & purchase manager indices: a global perspective (2020)
2. Sharma, N., et al.: Geospatial multivariate analysis of COVID-19: a global perspective. Geo J., 1–15 (2021)
3. Callahan, S.P., Freire, J., Santos, E., Scheidegger, C.E., Silva, C.T., Vo, H.T.: VisTrails: visualization meets data management. In: Proceedings of the 2006 ACM SIGMOD International Conference on Management of Data, pp. 745–747 (2005)
4. Sadiku, M., Share, A.E., Musa, S.M., Akujuobi, C.M., Perry, R.: Data visualization. Int. J. Eng. Res. Adv. Technol. (IJERAT) 2(12), 11–16 (2016)
5. Meyer, R.D., Cook, D.: Visualization of data. Curr. Opin. Biotechnol. 11(1), 89–96 (2000)
6. Mangla, M., Sharma, N., Mehta, V., Mohanty, S.N., Saxena, K.: Statistical analysis for air quality assessment and evaluation: a data mining approach. In: 2021 9th International Conference on Reliability, Infocom Technologies and Optimization (Trends and Future Directions) (ICRITO), pp. 1–5. IEEE (2021)
7. Mangla, M., Shinde, S.K., Mehta, V., Sharma, N., Mohanty, S.N. (eds.) Handbook of Research on Machine Learning: Foundations and Applications. CRC Press (2022)
8. McKevittith, B.: Nutritional aspects of cereals. Nutr. Bull. 29(2), 111–142 (2004)
9. Dewettinck, K., Van Bockstaele, F., Kühne, B., Van de Walle, D., Courtens, T.M., Gellynck, X.: Nutritional value of bread: influence of processing, food interaction and consumer perception. J. Cereal Sci. 48(2), 243–257 (2008)

10. Farag, M.A., Xiao, J., Abdallah, H.M.: Nutritional value of barley cereal and better opportunities for its processing as a value-added food: a comprehensive review. Crit. Rev. Food Sci. Nutr. **62**(4), 1092–1104 (2022)

11. Munck, L.: Improvement of nutritional value in cereals. Hereditas **72**(1), 1–128 (1972)

12. Deshpande, S.S., Mohapatra, D., Tripathi, M.K., Sadvatha, R.H.: Kodo milletnutritional value and utilization in Indian foods. J. Grain Process. Storage **2**(2), 16–23 (2015)

13. Vila-Real, C., Pimenta-Martins, A., Maina, N., Gomes, A., Pinto, E.: Nutritional value of indigenous whole grain cereals millet and sorghum. Nutr. Food Sci. Int. J. **4**(1) (2017)

14. Sharma, N.: XGBoost. The extreme gradient boosting for mining applications. GRINVer-lag (2018)

15. Mitchell, T., Buchanan, B., DeJong, G., Dietterich, T., Rosenbloom, P., Waibel, A.: Machine learning. Ann. Rev. Comput. Sci. **4**(1), 417–433(1990)

16. Jordan, M.I., Mitchell, T.M.: Machine learning: trends, perspectives, and prospects. Science **349**(6245), 255–260 (2015)

17. Sharma, N., Juneja, A.: Combining random forest estimates using LSboost for stock market index prediction. In: 2017 2nd International conference for convergence in Technology (I2CT), pp. 1199–1202. IEEE (2017)

18. Sharma, N., Juneja, A.: Extreme gradient boosting with a squared logistic loss function. In: Tanveer, M., Pachori, R. (eds.) Machine Intelligence and Signal Analysis. pp. 313–322. Springer, Singapore (2019). https://doi.org/10.1007/978-981-13-0923-6_27

19. Oduntan, O.E., Hammed, M.: A predictive model for improving cereals crop productivity using supervised machine learning algorithm, pp. 1–11 (2018)

20. Jensen, S.M., Akhter, M.J., Azim, S., Rasmussen, J.: The predictive power of regression models to determine grass weed infestations in cereals based on drone imagery—statistical and practical aspects. Agronomy **11**(11), 2277 (2021)

21. Arora, A., Gupta, P.K.: Data science and its relation to big data and machine learning. Int. Res. J. Modernization Eng. Technol. Sci. **3**(5), 61–65 (2021)

22. Gupta, P.K., Rishi, R, Biswas, R.: A comparative analysis of temporal data models. Int. J. Adv. Comput. Eng. Network. **1**(8), 34–38 (2013)

23. Gupta, P.K., Singh, J.P., Kaliraman, J.: Master data management emerging issues. Int. J. Eng. Technol. Sci. Res. **4**(6), 268–272 (2017)

24. Gupta, P.K., et al.: Deep learning architecture and algorithms. IN: Proceedings of Techbyte (A National Symposium, held at JIMS, New Delhi, India, pp. 42–47 (2019)

# Competitive Programming Vestige Using Machine Learning

Ajay Dharmarajula[✉], Challa Sahithi, and G. S. Prasada Reddy[ⓘ]

Department of Computer Science and Engineering, Vardhaman College of Engineering,
Hyderabad, Telangana, India
ajaydr16@gmail.com

**Abstract.** Competitive programming improves our problem-solving abil ity. It helps in writing the source code of computer programs that help in solving given problems, and the majority of the problems are mathemat ical or logical in nature. In view of its staggering and different nature, programming requires a particular level of expertise in the examination of estimations, data structures, science, formal reasoning, and related tasks like testing and investigating. In light of the growing regard for expectations for programming, there exist different genuine program ming platforms like HackerRank, CodeChef, CodeForces, Spoj, etc. where students can practice and work on their competitive programming skills. Monitoring the progress on these different platforms becomes hectic as they have to manu ally check each one. Also, there is no tool that helps in predicting their future scores based on their current practice. Another issue is that if the organisations or institutions wanted to monitor their student's progress, it would be tougher as it would have to be done for each student manually. This work will help the stu dents, as well as the organisations or institutions, maintain a proper portal with data to monitor their progress, by which students can improve their competitive programming skills, saving a lot of time compared to the time taken to do this monitoring manually.

**Keywords:** Machine Learning · Web Scraping · Competitive Programming

## 1 Introduction

There is a huge population of youth who are the future of our country but India lacks the skill factor in youth. No doubt everyone is getting educated but they always lack in skills required by industry. In the software industry, the main skill required by each and everyone is Competitive Programming. Organizations/Universities always focus on improvising students' skill sets but in competitive programming, regular observation is required. But this observation when done manually takes a lot of time, and effort and becomes a hectic task.

Foreseeing the scholastic exhibition of students has generally been for quite a while, a sharp area of interest for some specialists. Various investigations have been directed with the goal to measure the connection between the scholastic capability of a student

S. Nandan Mohanty et al. (Eds.): ICISML 2022, LNICST 471, pp. 272–285, 2023.
https://doi.org/10.1007/978-3-031-35081-8_22

and the variables influencing it. Inspecting the components liable for influencing a student's insightful execution wouldn't simply assist us in exploring a better appearance frameworks yet also having the option to help in decreasing the overall drop-out rates among energetic students. Progressions through electronic learning give us overflowing measures of information to see what students realize what elements mean for their scholarly presentation. Online learning archives of the information contains data that could assist us with opening recent fads in educating furthermore, draw bits of knowledge about the current nature of schooling and how could be given a better degree of training than students.

"Competitive Programming Vestige using Machine Learning" is a data analytical paper that uses machine learning methods and will automate these observations and also predicts future results. This paper will scrape the data from every coding platform that a the particular student has registered, store it in the database and then analyse the data as a whole to the student as well as to the organization. This analysis includes future progress, leader board, and many such useful projections for students/organizations to be taken in order to excel. These days, there exists a downpour of web-based programming conditions, for example, programming sites, internet programming instructional exercises and cloud-based Integrated Development Environments (IDEs) giving their clients different apparatuses to sharpen their programming abilities. These programming conditions contain a lot of information about the students' critical thinking history along with data about the nature of programming issues. By examining the previously solved problems of the students, we can endeavour to anticipate the projection of the student. To lead a prescient examination, we gathered information from different competitive programming spaces. Datasets were separated from CodeChef, codeforces, interviewbit, spoj. These are competitive programming sites that give programming difficulties of fluctuating degrees of trouble to its clients and these are additionally involved by many organizations for recruiting possible representatives. These datasets incorporate a similar list of capabilities for assessing student execution. These datasets were independently dissected to derive to foresee the student's progress in individual stages.

## 2 Related Work

There has been a huge load of studies done to predict understudy's academic execution using information mining procedures. The explanation of information mining has turned into a generally famous instrument for surveying a student's execution is on the grounds that, it gives unique instruments to break down the information, and thusly helps us in finding recent fads and connections.

Crafted by R. Kaushal and A. Singh [1], clarifies the significance of programmed appraisal of programming tasks. The creators have fostered a programming entry that means assessing the submitted code naturally and subsequently, grade the understudy in view of their presentation. Their work definitively demonstrates that the execution of such apparatuses in a learning climate, can work on the understudy's execution as far as effectiveness, consistency and precision.

In a comparable work, Medha Sagar, Arushi Gupta and Rishabh Kaushal [2], utilized datasets from HackerEarth and its entryway to examine and survey understudy's execution. The introduced paper draws its motivation from the recently talked about examinations. We have additionally done a relative ex- amination of characterization strategies to choose the most fitting and effective calculation for foreseeing the understudy execution. However, aside from anticipating the presentation, we have fostered an undeniable full-stack application which can be promptly use by students and institutions to get a clearer outcome.

The work of Timmy Devsia, T.P.Vinushree and Hegde Vinayak [3] have accepted the understudy's scholastic history as information and given understudies' impending exhibitions based on semester. Their work definitively proves the accuracy of using the Naive Bayesian algorithm.

In a similar work, M. Sivasakthi [4] worked under data mining which deals with a knowledge flow model for every one of the five classifiers and it grandstands the significance of Prediction and Classification based information mining calculations in the field of programming schooling and furthermore presents a few promising future lines. It could carry advantages and effects on understudies, instructors and scholastic organizations.

## 3  Proposed Approach

### 3.1  Data Set

To lead a prescient examination, we gathered information from different competitive programming spaces. Datasets were separated from CodeChef, codeforces, interviewbit, spoj. These are competitive programming sites that give programming difficulties of fluctuating degrees of trouble for its clients and these are additionally involved by many organizations for recruiting possible representatives. These datasets incorporate a similar list of capabilities for assessing the understudy execution. These datasets were independently dissected to derive to foresee the understudy's progress on individual stages.

### 3.2  Preprocessing

Information Pre-processing incorporates eliminating boisterous information or exceptions. Information is gathered from various coding stages like Codechef, Codeforces and so forth through Web Scraping. One of the means in Data Pre-processing is bringing in libraries. Consequently, for the dataset as web scraping is required, libraries like Beautiful Soup in python helps by supporting Web Scraping. Libraries like NumPy and Pandas are likewise expected for logical computing, manipulation and investigation. For factual modelling(regression) the Scikitlearn library is utilized in Python.

### 3.3  Supervised Learning

Supervised Learning in Machine Learning is a technique through which a machine gains from the it is as of now marked to prepare information which. It is utilized to derive a capacity by learning through the given info information that assists with deciding result for the new inconspicuous information. It assists the prescient models with spreading the word about expectations from the information. Regression and Classification are the two strategies that go under Supervised Learning. Regression method is utilized to anticipate nonstop factors like rating. It is essential to utilize supervised learning since it helps the machine by giving a learning experience that aids in ongoing forecasts. These encounters are likewise useful for the improvement of the presentation. Linear Regression: Linear regression is the most widely recognized calculation that is utilized in Predictive Analysis to foresee consistent factors. Linear Regression is a supervised learning calculation. Displaying the connection between one ward variable and at least one autonomous factors by fitting a linear connection between them is utilized. There are two sorts of linear regression calculations in view of the quantity of free factors utilized. They are Simple linear regression and Multiple linear Regression.

The linear condition would be $Y = a0 + a1 * x$ where y is a dependent (response) variable whose worth is to be anticipated and x is a free factor which is utilized for prediction. Here a0 is the capture and a1 is the incline of the regression line. Here rating is the reliant variable which should be anticipated.

# 4 Proposed Model

## 4.1 Experimental Setup

Web Technologies and Python Frameworks assumes significant part where utilizing of moving tech for our application builds usefulness and productivity. A Full Stack design is utilized to put together everything in a coordinated manner. Using front end as Angular builds Browser streamlining where Angular backings respond, switch Dom where delivering is done at client side, stacking of pages takes less time as it permits parts delivering concurrently. This way part of time will be saved rather than page stacking and page reviving. Backend we involved Flask framework for building an API based cooperation among frontend and backend. Use of flask gives a light weight to the application and APIs can be deployed without any problem. At last, we involved Google's Firestore datafactorr putting away all client subtleties in a key-value style likewise their present scores or evaluations according to their enrolled platforms. This way entire full stack application will be working autonomous to one another and working in a coordinated manner (Fig. 1).

Angular is an improvement stage, based on TypeScript. We construct the total front utilizing Angular where we isolated the application into different parts, designs, pages, factors, modules, and resources. Fostered a login page as the point of arrival once the utilization land on. Users can give his/her credentials to log in to it or probably can tap on register to enrol another user.

When the user sign in the application sidetracks to the user dashboard which we have delivered the page with a huge number. Here every one of the information of different platforms like codechef, codeforces, spoj and a lot more are being pulled from the firestore database however in-fabricated API calls and the response is being delivered into individual parts then, at that point, populated to the dashboard. Same way the predicted graphs additionally being gotten as a response from backend and populated

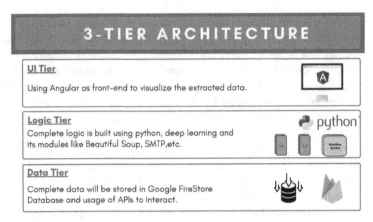

**Fig. 1.** Three Tier Architecture

here on dashboard. Aside from those we have created different extra highlights like top pioneer board information in a type of appropriate organized table.

Same way we have fostered an administrator dashboard where administrator can deal with every one of the students of their organization fetched directly from firestone database at a solitary page and separately can get to any profile. Above all can perform numerous sorts of information scientific operations like greatest, least, looking, arranging, looking through in view of a individual platform, looking through in particular year, picking just a specific year, block unblock a user and parcel of such insightful cycles on a solitary page window (Figs. 2, 3 and 4).

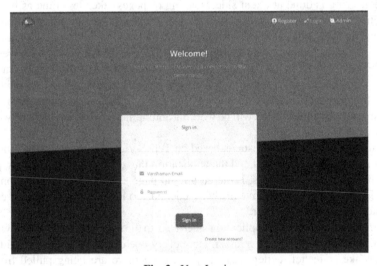

**Fig. 2.** User Login

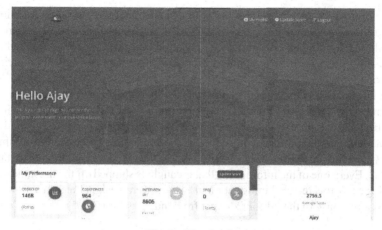

**Fig. 3.** User Login

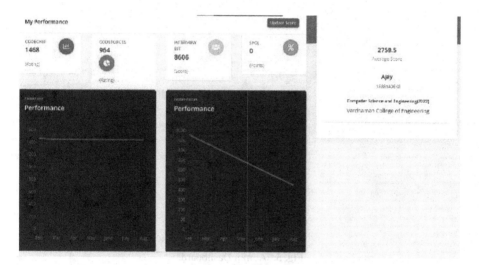

**Fig. 4.** User Dashboard

A web framework is an engineering containing instruments, libraries, and functionalities appropriate to fabricate and keep up with huge web tools utilizing a quick and productive methodology. They are intended to smooth out programs and advance code reuse. To make the server-side of the web application, you want to utilize a server-side language. Python is home to various such structures, renowned among which are Django and Flask. Python Flask Framework is a lightweight miniature structure in view of Werkzeug, Jinja2. It is known as a miniature system since it expects to keep its center usefulness little yet normally extensible to cover a variety of little and enormous applications. Cup Framework relies upon two outer libraries: The Jinja2 format, Werkzeug WSGI tool compartment. Utilizing flask framework, we have fabricated APIs for individual platforms through which utilizing the web scraping idea we are scrapping all the user information or action from the hour of enlistment to work now. Additionally, we ensure that we diminish the quantity of APIs since more the end points are there more will be the traffic and weighty the application becomes. So, we considered just to make just a solitary API for scrapping information and one more API for anticipating the information.

The information being anticipated is finished by considering the dataset as under-studies recently addressed or endeavoured programs and their appraisals. In light of considering and taking that dataset, we have utilized machine learning calculations to anticipate future evaluations or score assuming the understudy or the user go on similarly as now. Given the prediction, user will get to know the amount he/she wants to improve and create. Every one of the information that is caught is shipped off the firestone data set for putting away this rejected information in a key-esteem design. Later this information is sent as a response to the UI for example frontend Angular (Fig. 5).

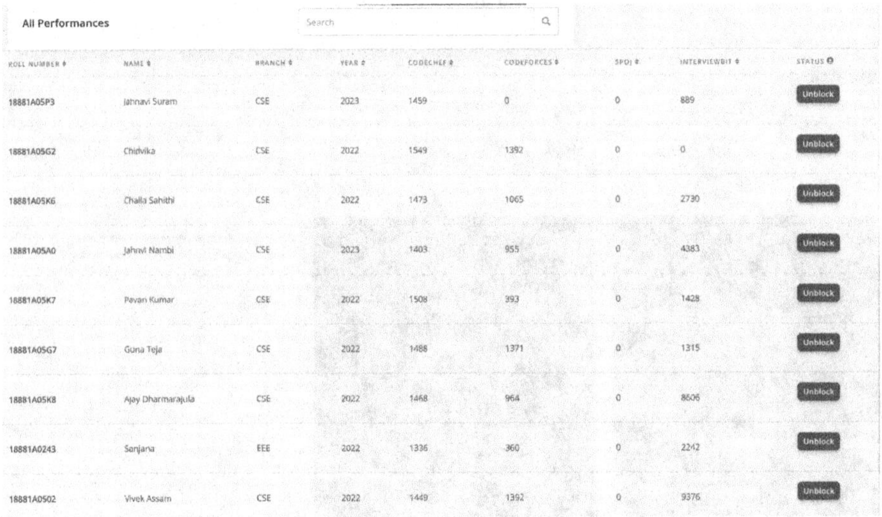

| ROLL NUMBER | NAME | BRANCH | YEAR | CODECHEF | CODEFORCES | SPOJ | INTERVIEWBIT | STATUS |
|---|---|---|---|---|---|---|---|---|
| 18881A05P3 | Jahnavi Suram | CSE | 2023 | 1459 | 0 | 0 | 889 | Unblock |
| 18881A05G2 | Chidvika | CSE | 2022 | 1549 | 1392 | 0 | 0 | Unblock |
| 18881A05K6 | Challa Sahithi | CSE | 2022 | 1473 | 1065 | 0 | 2730 | Unblock |
| 18881A05A0 | Jahnavi Nambi | CSE | 2023 | 1403 | 955 | 0 | 4383 | Unblock |
| 18881A05K7 | Pavan Kumar | CSE | 2022 | 1508 | 393 | 0 | 1428 | Unblock |
| 18881A05G7 | Guna Teja | CSE | 2022 | 1488 | 1371 | 0 | 1315 | Unblock |
| 18881A05K8 | Ajay Dharmarajula | CSE | 2022 | 1468 | 964 | 0 | 8606 | Unblock |
| 18881A0243 | Sanjana | EEE | 2022 | 1336 | 360 | 0 | 2242 | Unblock |
| 18881A05O2 | Vivek Assam | CSE | 2022 | 1449 | 1392 | 0 | 9376 | Unblock |

**Fig. 5.** Admin Dashboard

We have used Heroku for deploying the backend APIs. Utilizing Heroku CLI it turned out to be not difficult to deploy by coordinating GitHub is the repository and every one of the frequent changes is effectively being pushed to the Heroku deployment. With that end, point is made for APIs through which generally GET and POST-based API callings are done without any problem.

We utilized firestore to store every one of the information of the application. It gives many defaults in-constructed APIs through which information can be embedded, erased and fetched. Firestore APIs were utilized to push the user enlistment information and later their platform scores and evaluations including their critical thinking action. We made two documents (for example called tables in SQL) where in one we put away every one of the user's essential subtleties like name, year, institute name, email, password and usernames of the platforms they enlisted in and in another document, we put away every one of the information that is being scrapped from them regarding online judges.

At long last, we deployed and hosted the entire application in firebase utilizing firebase CLI commands. Through this organization any place the institute and regardless of where the student is available all can undoubtedly access with a solitary snap of this facilitated URL and they can further develop their range of abilities by remaining fixed on this particular application.

## 4.2  Proposed Algorithm

The algorithm is a collaboration or set of rules to be gone on in calculations or other decisive reasoning activities, especially by a PC. We have proposed two algorithms for this application one is user algorithm and another one is admin algorithm.

**User Algorithm.** User Algorithm is the algorithm or the set of process that will be performed on the user-side of the application starting from user registration till user logouts. Before going to the user dashboard frontend angular will authenticate whether user is logged in or not, based on that decision it will redirect to user login panel if the user is not logged in. Again, based on users entered credentials it will redirect to dashboard (Fig. 6).

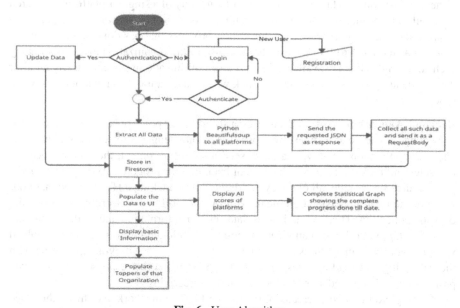

**Fig. 6.**  User Algorithm

In the user dashboard the whatever platform details given while registering the account all those details whether rating or points as per the platform will be populated on to the UI from the firestone database. All the data are completely stored and fetched from

Google's firestone database. Also based the details fetched from the database this application will plot a graph about future six months prediction of that candidate based on his previous attempts on that platform. These complete six months prediction is predicted from the backend that we have developed though flask framework, detail information about the prediction and backend operations will be discussed in backend algorithm below. Apart from prediction application also shows at which rank that student is on as per others students and the complete top leader board of the students of same college. Based on all these projections a user can determine where he/she stands among others and what his/her progress will be in future months if the flow goes like that.

**Admin Algorithm.** Admin Algorithm is the algorithm or the set of the process that will be performed on the admin side of the application starting from admin login till admin logouts. Before going to the admin dashboard frontend angular will authenticate whether the admin is logged in or not same like the above user algorithm, based on that decision it will redirect to the admin login panel if the admin is not logged in. Again, based on the admin's entered credentials it will redirect to the dashboard.

In the admin dashboard whatever data that is been entered by students of that college will be populated from the firestone database through FETCH API. API will send the response as JSON and all the collected data is filtered and populated to the UI. Here all the student's detail along with their platform performances are listed in a tabular form. This tabular form of data is completely filtered as per the admin requirements. Example if the user just wants to know a specific list of data only of a singular platform, or search from only a particular year and many such filters. As an admin, admin can click on or go to any user in their organization to check their progress that has done and predictions. Admin has the right to block a user temporarily in the organization and can do many such admin rights that are available. With such algorithm admin can completely monitor their students' progress by just with a click which saves a lot of manual hours of work time.

**Backend Algorithm.** Not until unnecessarily at some point previously, server- side conveying, or back-end web headway, was the acknowledged strategy for making sites and web applications. You visit a page, send a sales for content, the server processes this sales and makes a response that is sent back to your program. Exactly when a site page renders server-side, all of the cycles drew in with making a HTML page that your web program can understand are dealt with on a far-off server working with the site or web application. This join addresses data sets for information and dealing with any reasoning that your the web application requires. While the faraway server is involved working, your web program is idle, believing that the server will wrap up dealing with the requesting and sending a response. At the point when the response is gotten, web programs translate it and show the output on the screen (Fig. 7).

A complete backend is created utilizing the Flask framework and this is the place where every one of the intelligent activities happen. We fabricated the REST APIs through which front and backend can interface and trade data according to necessity. We have different capacities running at the backend yet significantly we have partitioned the backend into two kinds one is web-scraping and one more is the expectation of gathered data.

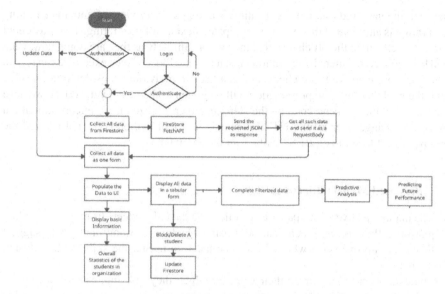

**Fig. 7.** Admin Algorithm

First coming to the web-scraping part we have significantly involved the Beautiful-Soup module of python for accomplishing this. By introducing this module and passing the separate client dashboard URL for individual website we have accumulated the total source code of that page. Later we saw that each field, each worth, or data is available in different classes, div, length, headers so we noted down anything labels that are been implanted to and utilized those label names to get individual data of that comparing esteem. Then, at that point, we have put away every one of the gathered qualities put away and changed over the entire data gathered into a JSON organization and sent back to the frontend and furthermore this gathered data is likewise been pushed to firestore database. As it is an API based cooperation so when the solicitation got from frontend about specific stage and given username. Backend will do the mechanization and sent back the gathered data as a reaction to the frontend.

Presently the subsequent significant part is expectation, precise forecast about rating or score is profoundly unthinkable on the grounds that those last qualities relies upon different elements like what sort of challenge it is, the number of understudies are taking part in it, the number of individuals tackled that issue, the number of settled to some degree, the number of neglected to saw and a great deal of such factors decide the score of any challenge. So, these variables can't be anticipated as it is just can be taken once the challenge is finished. However, we have utilized specific boundaries and attempted to foresee the following a half year expectation of the client. This way client will get to know where he/she is the present moment and will be roused to work more to get a slanted diagram on their advancement. Presently coming to the expectation calculation, we have utilized direct relapse since there is just a single free fand actor through which forecast should be possible. Utilized straight relapse and made a dataset comprising of clients past addressed measurements and past appraisals this way utilizing the connection between the gathered qualities next rating is anticipated, in view of anticipated rating next rating is anticipated this way we anticipated next a half year rating. This way client can comprehend on the off chance that they go on similarly as they are doing now, what will be their advancement by the following a half year. Indeed, even executive can screen and figure out who are those clients and can take an individual consideration for them with the goal that their the presentation will be gotten to the next level. At last, we have facilitated all the backend code on the Heroku server. Utilized the gunicorn module in python to change over all the HTTP demands into real python code and utilized the end-point of it to settle on REST calls from the frontend.

### 4.3 Proposed Model Objectives

- The main objective of our paper is to collect the data of students from various coding platforms they use and then analyse it using Machine learning methods to suggest them the improvements which need to be taken to master the skills without losing interest.
- Students often procrastinate their work by which they lose interest in learning the skills after some time. Hence, they need continuous guidance that is only possible through organization and our paper helps the organization by giving suggestions.
- Our paper predicts the future target of the student based on their daily per- formance which helps the practice to go smoothly.

### 4.4 Proposed Model Outcomes

- Complete Data Analysis of the data scrapped.
- Improved Results in the student's performance.
- Time reduction for organizations' efforts.

## 5   Results and Discussion

Assuming that you're a Computer Science understudy or a coding devotee, odds are more you've heard people examining their Competitive Programming abilities and rankings and accomplishments in different coding difficulties or challenges. Furthermore, really, The competitive Programming ability is one of the couples of abilities that put you aside from the group, and in this manner furnish you with an edge over others during positions or other vocations amazing open doors. Numerous eminent tech monsters including Meta, Google, Amazon, and so forth altogether think about the competitive programming abilities of the competitors and even enlist the up-and-comers through different competitive programming challenges.

Competitive Programming is an activity to step up the Programming and Data Struc- tures and Algorithms abilities through tackling various certifiable programming issues under specific pivotal limitations including time limit, memory requirements, time and space intricacy, and so forth Understudies need to concoct an advanced arrangement inside as far as possible for the given programming issue in your favoured language and the code should finish all the necessary assessment cases. The best part is here you rival different splendid personalities the whole way across the world and improve your programming or DSA abilities as well as different abilities like legitimate and scientific reasoning, critical thinking, using time effectively, breaking an issue into little pieces, and numerous others.

Presently, this is the sort of thing that a significant number of them would've definitely known notwithstanding not being a competitive software engineer - however the issue with most people, particularly undergrads or fledgling developers, is they don't have the foggiest idea about the right and compelling way of beginning with Competitive Programming. Along these lines, with this application school or separate association's organization can without much of a stretch screen the understudies, guide the understudies, actually taking a look at every understudies execution very quickly. Generally assuming this works are done physically like checking and observing every one of the accessible entrances entering the data that would require long periods of long periods of time for every individual cluster then on the off chance that taken of entire school, it would take more time to finish such work. Yet, with utilizing this stage total computerization is accomplished and the work that is taking days to finish is currently will be done in the matter of seconds.

These are a portion of the users on which we have tried the calculation and there isn't a lot of distinction in genuine and anticipated values. This shows the exactness of the application that is sent. Furthermore, as I referenced already in backend algorithm that forecast of these values is profoundly inconceivable as it relies upon different variables that can knows once challenge is finished. In any case, anticipating beforehand is inconceivable yet our calculation will provide users with an assessment of their advancement for the following half year.

| Username | Actual Rating | Predicted Rating |
| --- | --- | --- |
| sahithi 20 | −88 | −101 |
| teja349 | 15 | 1 |
| kp 1104 | 1 | 4 |
| hardik24k9 | −40 | −32 |
| priyanshi garg | 22 | 29 |
| vipresh2000 | −8 | −8 |
| abhimanyu 17 | −75 | −64 |
| taran910 | 19 | 12 |
| yatinagg | 19 | 11 |
| siddhatgarg11 | 21 | 12 |
| vsoni101 | −28 | −19 |
| mscharan14 | −58 | −49 |
| tiwari0000 | −7 | 2 |
| psyche37 | −24 | −31 |
| pramod billa | −60 | −51 |

Above in Fig 3[b] you can notice the forecast of a user and this is how the frontend shows the data graphically. On the off chance that you can notice the client is accomplishing something useful in CodeChef so even following a half year his advancement will tumble down somewhat however not more. Yet, if eyewitness the code forces chart that is populated it shows the user execution will go down quickly in the approaching half year. This shows the user isn't zeroing in on code forces stage more that is the reason he is having low advancement. This perception will be finished by the organization group of his foundation and separate direction will be given to the possibility for his improvement.

## 6   Conclusions

The assumption results will be instrumental in cultivating the programming sharpness of students in a tweaked manner. Observing the factors that could block the progress of students would simplify it to beat the moves that one could look at due to those components. Aside from anticipating the execution of the understudy, we assembled all their diligent effort at only one single application. Aside from foreseeing the outcomes, the introduced work contains itemized investigation to assist instructors with more deeply studying of different elements that influence the exhibition of understudies. From our discoveries, we presume that more modest and more controlled conditions give a superior stage to survey understudy execution. Accordingly, Performance anticipating apparatuses, as portrayed above, can be carried out in a learning climate to assist understudies with performing better in their programming tasks.

As a group of people yet to come residents, to upgrade expertise among youth is the primary saying and with cutting-edge forecasts and authoritative criticisms will help the associations and understudies to improve their programming abilities. India's populace is 1.38 Billion at this point and consistently around 3 Million designer understudies graduates so assuming that we consolidate these for each of the 3 or 4 years of graduate understudies it would be about 1 crore understudies. Indeed, a parcel of understudies need industry necessity abilities and there are different explanations behind it, one of the primary explanations is legitimate checking of understudies that should be possible through this application. Likewise, this application probably won't take care of the total issue yet this would add a stage to their outcome in their excursion. In future, we will chip away at the calculation more to work on the calculation so that a few factors can be anticipated and utilizing that variable exactness can be expanded for those clients whose expectation was not precise

## References

1. Kaushal, R., Singh, A.: Automated evaluation of programming assignments. In: International Conference on Engineering Education: Innovative Practices and Future Trends, AICERA, July 2012. ISBN NO: 978-81-921320-1-3
2. Sagar, M., Kaushal, A.G.R.: Performance prediction and behavioural analysis of student programming ability. In: 2016 International Conference on Advances in Computing, Communications and Informatics (ICACCI). IEEE (2016). ISBN NO: 978-1-5090-2030-0

3. Devasia, T., Vinushree, T.P., Hegde, V.: Prediction of students' performance using Educational Data Mining. In: 2016 International Conference on Data Mining and Advanced Computing (SAPIENCE). IEEE (2016). ISBN No: 978-1-4673-8595-4
4. Sivasakthi, M.: Classification and prediction based data mining algorithms to predict students' introductory programming performance. Published in 2017 International Conference on Inventive Computing and Informatics (ICICI). IEEE (2017). ISBN:978- 1-5386-4032-6,
5. Potluri, S., Mohammad, G.B., Nandan Mohanty, S., Vaishnavi, M., Sahaja, K.: Secure intelligent framework for VANET: cloud based transportation model. Cloud Secur. Tech. Appl., 145–170 (2021). https://doi.org/10.1515/9783110732573-008
6. Gouse Baig Mohammad, S., Kumar, P.R.: Integrated machine learning model for an URL phishing detection. Int. J. Grid Distrib. Comput. **14**(1), 513–529 (2022)

# Machine Learning Techniques for Aspect Analysis of Employee Attrition

Anamika Hooda[1]([⊠]), Purva Garg[1], Nonita Sharma[2], and Monika Mangla[3]

[1] Department of Electronics & Communication Engineering (AI), Indira Gandhi Delhi Technical University for Women, Delhi, India
{anamika107bteceai21,purva117bteceai21}@igdtuw.ac.in
[2] Department of Information Technology, Indira Gandhi Delhi Technical University for Women, Delhi, India
nonitasharma@igdtuw.ac.in
[3] Department of Information Technology, Dwarkadas J. Sanghvi College of Engineering, Mumbai, India

**Abstract.** Employee attrition is the reduction in the employee workforce, which can be defined as the rate of employees leaving the company faster than the rate they are hired. Attrition may be for the whole establishment but sometimes it might be particular for a business field. This happens when there is intervention of technology that contribute in replacing the human workforce. There are several factors contributing to employee attrition, a few being age, number of years in the company, manager, technology change, etc. It is vital to understand the impact of these factors on employee attrition so that necessary action can be taken to avoid this. Thus, Machine learning technique is being used nowadays to inspect and predict the data of several real-life applications. After employing the models, authors performed the analysis on each of them using confusion matrix, F-1 score, recall, precision, etc., and found that the best model is SVM with an accuracy of 85.60%.

**Keywords:** Attrition · Data Analytics · SVM · Logistic Regression · Heatmap · Correlation Matrix

## 1 Introduction

Employees are one of the most significant asset of any organization. The longevity of employees' retention in any organization advocates a healthy work environment. On the contrary, frequent resignations of the employees can be attributed to various reasons. Thus the employees' retention can be directly considered as a measure of satisfaction of employees towards work place. Therefore, it is needed to understand the employees' attrition. Here, employee attrition is the decrease in number of employees [1, 2]. This means that employees leave their organizations before the new staff is hired. Employee attrition can be for the whole company but it can also be particular to a business field. It may be also because the skill sets that are needed change constantly [3].

© ICST Institute for Computer Sciences, Social Informatics and Telecommunications Engineering 2023
Published by Springer Nature Switzerland AG 2023. All Rights Reserved
S. Nandan Mohanty et al. (Eds.): ICISML 2022, LNICST 471, pp. 286–296, 2023.
https://doi.org/10.1007/978-3-031-35081-8_23

More the employee attrition, the more no of workers we need to hire but recruiting employees can be a difficult job. Getting able employees and training them for the job, and after some time they resign is frustrating for the employer. Hence, human resource (HR) managers are there to recognize the factors leading to attrition and take the preventive and corrective measures for reducing attrition. The main focus of this study is to present the aspect analysis of attrition in terms of:

1) Factors leading to employee attrition
2) How it can be decreased
3) Accuracy of four machine learning models used employed in the prediction of attrition.

The models in this project are;

a) Logistic Regression
b) Naïve Bayes
c) SVM Model
d) Random Forest

Logistic Regression is a one of the statistical models often used for classification and predictive analytics. Logistic regression estimates the probability of an event occurring; the next model being the Naïve Bayes algorithm, which is a supervised learning algorithm, based on the Bayes theorem aiming to solve classification problems.

Support vector machines are a set of supervised learning methods used for classification, regression, and outlier detection. Random Forest is a Supervised Machine Learning Algorithm that is used widely in Classification and Regression problems [4, 5].

Authors have employed the dataset of employee attrition from Kaggle [6] to perform various analyses on it. This dataset consists 1470 rows and 35 columns out of which 34 factors are showing their dependency on attrition. Attrition is denoted as Yes/No. There is no null value in our dataset. It has string and integer as data types.

Before employing machine learning models, the research work utilized a heatmap for finding correlations between factors and removing the appropriate ones. After employing the models, the analysis is performed on each of them using confusion matrix, F-1 score, recall, precision, etc. and the results concluded that the best model is SVM with an accuracy of 85.60%.

The current work is organized into various sections. Section 1 introduces the concept of workforce attrition. Similar problems have been undertaken by various researchers. The noticeable research by few researchers has been presented in Sect. 2. The methodology proposed by authors has been elaborated in Sect. 3. Results are discussed in Sect. 4 while the conclusion is presented in Sect. 5.

## 2   Related Work

The significance of employee attrition has been realized since many years and resultantly several authors have tried their hand to understand the association behind. For instance, authors in [7] considered a sample of 297 employees in a private firm. The authors considered various factors such as firm characteristics, location, employee benefits, and work culture etc. Authors performed hierarchical regression analyses and concluded that firms with high benefits and high benefits packages observed slight employee attrition.

The authors in [3] also proposed a model to find association among service and employee attrition. For the same, authors considered data from 64 business units. Authors also determined that a high attrition (specifically for customer-facing employee) will adversely impact the relations with existing customers. This may also impact the revenue generation of the business units. Aligning with this research, authors in [1] also believe that the employees who are leaving from an organization are carrying some tacit knowledge with them which could be advantageous to the competitors. Hence, the organizations must strive to retain the employees and minimize employees' attrition. In order to validate the belief authors considered 309 employees who had left their organization during 1978 to 2006. This dataset was classified into some predefined attrition classes using decision tree models and rule-sets. The classification produced by these 2 classifiers were used for a predictive model so as to predict upcoming employee attrition.

Considering the interest to understand the pattern of employee attrition, machine learning (ML) was also employed for the same considering the demonstrated supremacy of machine learning algorithms. Hence, authors in [2] performed a study to understand employee attrition using ML models. For the same, authors used a synthetic data created by IBM Watson of employees' attrition, an imbalanced dataset. This IBM Watson dataset is processed using support vector machine (SVM), random forest and K-nearest neighbor (KNN). Further, authors also used adaptive synthetic (ADASYN) to address class imbalance. During all experimental setup, the machine learning models demonstrated its efficiency and effectiveness to predict the employee attrition.

Further, authors in [8] also aimed to determine the association between manager's interpersonal skills and employees' attrition. As per the finding by authors in [8], management skills have a strong impact on employee turnover.

Thus it is still to debate that what all factors are there which closely impact the employee attrition and hence needs an extensive research in this domain.

## 3 Methodology

The methodology is depicted in Fig. 1. As evident from Fig. 1, authors have used the IBM Watson dataset of employee attrition from Kaggle [6]. The considered dataset is preprocessing to drop null values and unwanted attributes. Authors converted categorical data with the help of a label encoder [9, 10]. Four models were employed i.e., naïve Bayes, random forest, SVM, and logistic regression, and a heatmap was plotted to determine the correlation between the factors. Analysis of models was done by confusion matrix and then they were evaluated by classification report and accuracy score [11]. Graphs and tables were plotted to get the result and determine the most important attributes for attrition. The following steps are employed in the methodology:

**1. Data Understanding:** The dataset contains the data of 1470 employees. There are 35 attributes present in the database some are – Job level, Percent hiking rate, Years with current manager, Years since promotion etc. There is no null value in our dataset. It has string and integer as data types.

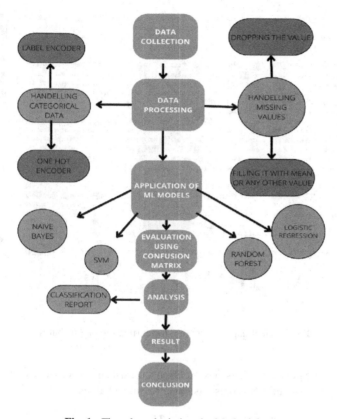

**Fig. 1.** Flowchart depicting the Methodology

**2. Data Pre-processing:** The attributes with string datatype were converted to integer datatype with the help of a label encoder. A heatmap is plotted to check the correlation between attributes and the attributes with higher correlation were removed as shown in Fig. 2. Attributes with no correlation to attrition were also dropped. These attributes were Employee number, employee count, over 18, standard hours, percent salary hike, years in a current role, and total working years. With the help of heatmap, we found the Attributes with no correlation to attrition and the ones which are highly correlated and modified the dataset accordingly.

**3. Modelling:** The Naïve Bayes, Logistic regression, SVM, and Random Forest algorithms are employed.

**4. Analysis:** The confusion matrix is used to check how many times the prediction was these models [12, 13]. We also used a classification report to check the statistical results of the models used. Following metrics were used to make the analysis, Here TP

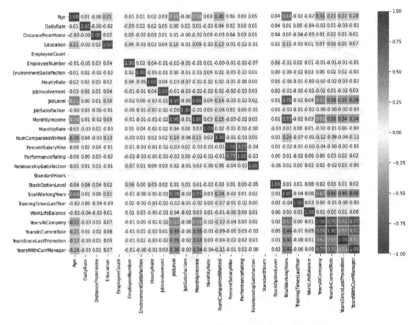

**Fig. 2.** Heatmap representing the correlation of Attributes

represents the true positive values, TN represents the true negative values, FP represents False Positive values and FN represents False Negative values;

$$Accuracy = \frac{TP + TN}{TP + TN + FP + FN} \tag{1}$$

$$Precision = \frac{TP}{TP + FP} \tag{2}$$

$$Recall = \frac{TP}{TP + FN} \tag{3}$$

$$F1Score = \frac{2 * Precision * Recall}{Precision + Recall} \tag{4}$$

**5. Result and conclusion:** After performing the analysis, we get results and conclusions regarding the problem statement.

## 4   Result and Discussion

Ahead of employing the ML models, correlation among various attributes is evaluated. This correlation is illustrated in the heat map shown in Fig. 2. After employing the models, we performed the analysis on each of them using the confusion matrix, F-1 score, recall, precision, etc. The section is divided into two subsections namely Aspect analysis using visualization and Comparative analysis of ML models.

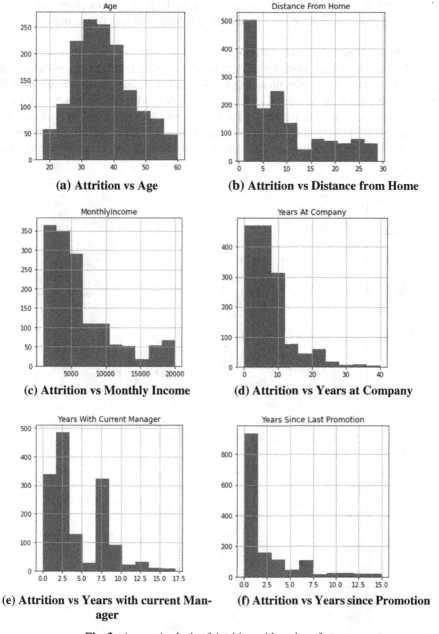

(a) Attrition vs Age

(b) Attrition vs Distance from Home

(c) Attrition vs Monthly Income

(d) Attrition vs Years at Company

(e) Attrition vs Years with current Manager

(f) Attrition vs Years since Promotion

**Fig. 3.** Aspect Analysis of Attrition with various factors

## 4.1 Aspect Analysis Using Visualization

Aspect analysis means analyzing the data with the help of various plots and graphs [14–16]. We plotted various graphs to analyze attributes and understand our data.

**Impact Analysis of Factors on Attrition**
Figure 3 represents the factors affecting Employee Attrition. From the graphs below it is conclude that attrition is maximum among people aged between 30 to 40, living within 10 km, and with a monthly income of less than 6k. People working at the company for less than 12 years, under the same manager for 8 years, and who haven't been promoted for two years are most likely to leave the company. Figure 4 visualizes attrition concerning gender. Here, it can be safely concluded that the attrition among males is 25.6% more

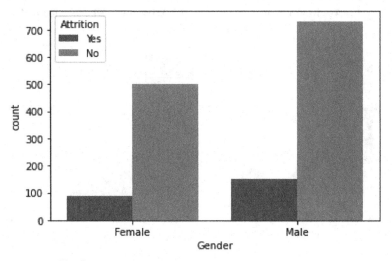

**Fig. 4.** Aspect Analysis of Attrition with respect to Gender

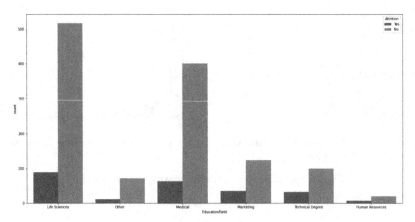

**Fig. 5.** Aspect Analysis of Attrition with respect to Education Field

than among females. Further, Fig. 5 presents the impact of the education field on attrition. Here, we can establish the fact that attrition is most in Lifesciences as compared to other fields and HR has the least attrition. Furthermore, Fig. 6 determines the impact of salary hikes on attrition. Percent salary hike between 11 to 14% leads to more attrition and between 19 to 25%, it's the least.

## 4.2 Comparative Analysis of Various Machine Learning Models

Table 1 displays us the confusion matrix for four models. There are more true positives than false positives and fewer false negatives than false positives [17, 18]. Table 2 displays us the contrast in the classification report of all the models. So, from Table 2 and the bar graph representation in Fig. 7, we can see that with the Logistic Regression method the performance score as the objective variable was 84.98% accuracy, naïve Bayes method the performance score as the objective variable was 82.04% accuracy, SVM method the performance score as the objective variable was with 85.60% accuracy and Random Forest method the performance score as the objective variable was with 85.19%. So, from the above results, we conclude that the best model is SVM with an accuracy of 85.60%.

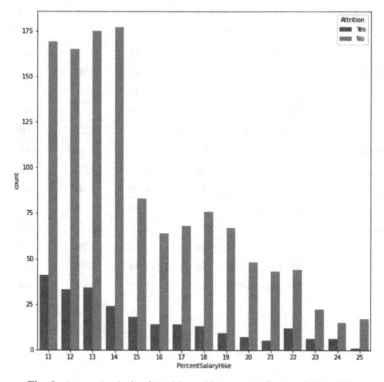

**Fig. 6.** Aspect Analysis of Attrition with respect to Present Salary Hike

**Table 1.** Results in terms of the Confusion Matrix of the models

| Models | | Positive Values | Negative Values |
|---|---|---|---|
| Logistic regression | True | 412 | 4 |
| | False | 69 | 1 |
| Naïve Bayes | True | 370 | 46 |
| | False | 40 | 30 |
| SVM | True | 416 | 0 |
| | False | 70 | 0 |
| Random Forest | True | 407 | 9 |
| | False | 63 | 7 |

**Table 2.** Classification Report of various models

| Models | | Precision | Recall | F1 Score | Support |
|---|---|---|---|---|---|
| Logistic regression | 0 | 0.86 | 0.99 | 0.92 | 416 |
| | 1 | 0.20 | 0.01 | 0.03 | 70 |
| | Macro avg | 0.53 | 0.50 | 0.47 | 486 |
| | Weighted avg | 0.76 | 0.85 | 0.79 | 486 |
| Naïve Bayes | 0 | 0.90 | 0.89 | 0.90 | 416 |
| | 1 | 0.39 | 0.43 | 0.41 | 70 |
| | Macro avg | 0.65 | 0.66 | 0.65 | 486 |
| | Weighted avg | 0.83 | 0.82 | 0.83 | 486 |
| SVM model | 0 | 0.86 | 1.00 | 0.92 | 416 |
| | 1 | 0.00 | 0.00 | 0.00 | 70 |
| | Macro Avg | 0.43 | 0.50 | 0.46 | 486 |
| | Weighted avg | 0.73 | 0.86 | 0.79 | 486 |
| Random Forest | 0 | 0.87 | 0.98 | 0.92 | 416 |
| | 1 | 0.44 | 0.10 | 0.16 | 70 |
| | Macro avg | 0.65 | 0.54 | 0.54 | 486 |
| | Weighted avg | 0.80 | 0.85 | 0.81 | 486 |

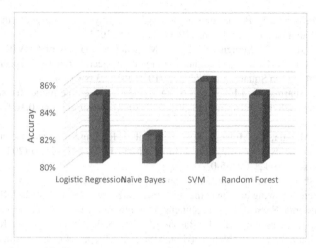

**Fig. 7.** Comparative Analysis of Machine Learning Models concerning Accuracy

## 5 Conclusion

Attrition is unavoidable; its presence is always there. Though, we can find ways to reduce it. Turnover is a costly drain on company resources. Internal attributes are equally responsible, if not more important than external attributes in case of attrition. Constructive leadership can help in the betterment of attrition. From the evaluation, the accuracy of the best-proposed model, SVM is 85.60%. It indicates that the SVM technique is very good at predicting attrition. The SVM model is significant to support the decision-making process and can be efficiently used for improving employee attrition.

## References

1. Alao, D.A., Adeyemo, A.B.: Analyzing employee attrition using decision tree algorithms. Comput. Inf. Syst. Dev. Inform. Allied Res. J. **4**(1) 17–28 (2013)
2. Alduayj, S.S., Rajpoot, K.: Predicting employee attrition using machine learning. In: 2018 International Conference on Innovations in Information Technology (it), pp. 93–98. IEEE (2018)
3. Subramony, M., Holtom, B.C.: The long-term influence of service employee attrition on customer outcomes and profits. J. Serv. Res. **15**(4), 460–473 (2012)
4. Yadav, S., Sharma, N.: homogenous ensemble of time-series models for Indian stock market. In: Mondal, A., Gupta, H., Srivastava, J., Reddy, P.K., Somayajulu, D.V.L.N. (eds.) BDA 2018. LNCS, vol. 11297, pp. 100–114. Springer, Cham (2018). https://doi.org/10.1007/978-3-030-04780-1_7
5. Verma, U., Garg, C., Bhushan, M., Samant, P., Kumar, A., Negi, A.: Prediction of students' academic performance using machine learning techniques. In: 2022 International Mobile and Embedded Technology Conference (MECON), pp. 151–156. IEEE (2022)
6. https://www.kaggle.com/datasets/patelprashant/employee-attrition
7. Bennett, N., Blum, T.C., Long, R.G., Roman, P.M.: A firm-level analysis of employee attrition. Group Org. Manag. **18**(4), 482–499 (1993)

8. Hoffman, M., Tadelis, S.: People management skills, employee attrition, and manager rewards: an empirical analysis. J. Polit. Econ. **129**(1), 243–285 (2021)
9. Sharma, N., Yadav, S., Mangla, M., et al.: Multivariate analysis of COVID-19 on stock, commodity & purchase manager indices: a global perspective (2020). Preprint (Version 1) available at Research Square. https://doi.org/10.21203/rs.3.rs-68388/v1
10. Mangla, M., Sharma, N., Mohanty, S.N.: A sequential ensemble model for software fault prediction. Innov. Syst. Softw. Eng. **18**, 301–308 (2022). https://doi.org/10.1007/s11334-021-00390-x
11. Sharma, N., Mangla, M., Mohanty, S.N., Pattanaik, C.R.: Employing stacked ensemble approach for time series forecasting. Int. J. Inf. Technol. **13**(5), 2075–2080 (2021). https://doi.org/10.1007/s41870-021-00765-0
12. Banik, S., Sharma, N., Mangla, M., Mohanty, S.N., Shitharth, S.: LSTM-based decision support system for swing trading in the stock market. Knowl. Based Syst. **239**, 107994 (2022)
13. Singh, N., Sharma, N., Sharma, A.K., Juneja, A.: Sentiment score analysis and topic modelling for GST implementation in India. In: Bansal, J.C., Das, K.N., Nagar, A., Deep, K., Ojha, A.K. (eds.) Soft Computing for Problem Solving. AISC, vol. 817, pp. 243–254. Springer, Singapore (2019). https://doi.org/10.1007/978-981-13-1595-4_19
14. Sadiku, M., Share, A.E., Musa, S.M., Akujuobi, C.M., Perry, R.: Data visualization. Int. J. Eng. Res. Adv. Technol. (IJERAT) **2**(12), 11–16 (2016)
15. Grinstein, U.M., Wise, A.: Information Visualization in Data Mining and Knowledge Discovery. Morgan Kaufmann, Burlington (2002)
16. Chen, C.H., Härdle, W.K., Unwin, A.: Handbook of Data Visualization. Springer, Heidelberg (2007). https://doi.org/10.1007/978-3-540-33037-0
17. Sharma, N., Juneja, A.: Combining of random forest estimates using LSboost for stock market index prediction. In: 2017 2nd International Conference for Convergence in Technology (I2CT), pp. 1199–1202. IEEE (2017)
18. Mangla, M., Shinde, S.K., Mehta, V., Sharma, N., Mohanty, S.N.: Handbook of Research on Machine Learning: Foundations and Applications. CRC Press, Boca Raton (2022)

# AI-Enabled Automation Solution for Utilization Management in Healthcare Insurance

Gaurav Karki<sup>(✉)</sup> ⓘ, Jay Bharateesh Simha ⓘ, and Rashmi Agarwal ⓘ

REVA Academy for Corporate Excellence (RACE), REVA University, Bengaluru, India
gauravk.ai01@race.reva.edu.in, {jb.simha,
rashmi.agarwal}@reva.edu.in

**Abstract.** As businesses advance toward digitalization by automating an increasing number of procedures, unstructured forms of text in documents present new challenges. Most organizational data is unstructured, and this phenomenon is on the rise. Businesses like healthcare and insurance are embracing business process automation and making considerable progress along the entire value chain. Artificial intelligence (AI) algorithms that help in decision-making, connect information, interpret data, and apply the insights gained to rethink how to make better judgments are necessary for business process automation.

A healthcare procedure called Prior Authorization (PA) could be made better with the help of AI. PA is an essential administrative process that is a component of their utilization management systems, and as a condition of coverage, insurers require providers to obtain preapproval for the provision of a service or prescription. The processing of insurance claim documents can be facilitated using Natural Language Processing (NLP). This paper describes the migration of manual procedures to AI-based solutions in order to accelerate the process. The use of text similarity in systems for information retrieval, question-answering, and other purposes has attracted significant research. This paper suggests using a universal sentence encoder, a more focused strategy, to handle health insurance claims. By extracting text features, including semantic analysis with sentence embedding, the context of the document may be determined. The outcome would have a variety of possible advantages for members, providers, and insurers. AI models for the PA process are seen as promising due to their accuracy and speed of execution.

**Keywords:** Utilization Management · Prior Authorization · Healthcare · Insurance · Claim Processing · Deep Learning · Artificial Intelligence · Automation · Natural language processing

## 1 Introduction

The expenses of the healthcare system have been spiraling out of control for years, and utilization management is a crucial method for insurers and providers to guarantee that adequate care is delivered cost-effectively. Utilization management (UM) is the evaluation of medical care based on evidence-based criteria and health payer requirements. In

S. Nandan Mohanty et al. (Eds.): ICISML 2022, LNICST 471, pp. 297–310, 2023.
https://doi.org/10.1007/978-3-031-35081-8_24

addition to reducing costs, the goal is to give patients the appropriate treatment, from a shorter duration of stay to enhanced release planning. Once insurers have defined their norms and guidelines, the utilization management process centers on controlling prior authorization filings via clinical and peer-to-peer evaluations [1].

The influence of UM processes on payer finances, case management, and health plan member and provider satisfaction is direct. Ineffective utilization control results in annoying care delays and higher operating expenses for health insurance. However, conventional UM systems place member and provider satisfaction and cost control in opposition. More rules or more comprehensive review processes can reduce the high cost of medical care, but at the expense of member and provider satisfaction. Up until now, there has always been a compromise. Now, insurers have the chance to transform their UM processes through the application of automation and AI. By introducing an AI-based solution for utilization management, insurers can simultaneously enhance the member and provider experience while reducing operating expenses and medical costs [2].

PA is a primary process of UM. This is conducted before to at the start of treatment on a particular scenario basis to eliminate needless services. The selected treatment should be considered provisional and subject to modification in the future. PA is an examination of a patient's condition and suggested therapy. Its primary objective is to reduce unnecessary, ineffective, or redundant treatments. PA is utilized for regular and urgent referrals, but not for emergency room admissions. The review might take place either before or after admission, but always before treatment begins. In some situations, a physician's directions may not be followed, which could enrage both the medical staff and the patient.

This paper proposed solution tries to automate the PA procedure. Unlike basic Robotic Process Automation (RPA) systems that just automate individual aspects of the prior authorization process, artificial intelligence may fundamentally alter the way reviewers handle prior authorization requests. If a healthcare provider submits an authorization request, artificial intelligence evaluates this information to the medical necessity criteria to ensure that the patient receives the proper care. If all conditions are satisfied, the request may be automatically authorized, without the requirement for a utilization management reviewer to touch the previous authorization and a clinical evaluation. This can reduce approval times from weeks to hours.

In the field of text similarity, corpus-based techniques have solved the most challenging aspect of natural language processing by achieving human-competitive accuracy. However, later paper has shown that even a little difference in text structure or length can easily mislead the prediction. Term frequency inverse document frequency (TF-IDF) is a common approach presented by some that is believed to compensate for the inaccuracy introduced by the document's format and length, but at the expense of precision. The majority of previous text similarity techniques did not consider the embedding meaning of the words. When working with identical documents other than their wording, the ability of embedding meaning of words becomes useful.

## 2  Literature Review

PA in medical billing aids the healthcare organization in collecting the correct reimbursement for delivered services, hence lowering denials and subsequent follow-up. According to the results of the Prior Authorization Survey conducted by the American Medical Association (AMA) in December 2021 with the participation of 1,000 practicing physicians, the majority of physicians report an increase in the number of PAs necessary for prescription medications and medical services during the preceding years. In both instances as shown in Fig. 1, the proportion of physicians reporting this rise ranged from 84% to 84% [3].

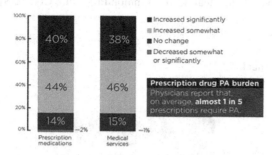

**Fig. 1.** AMA Prior Authorization Physician Survey [3]

Bag-Of-Words (BOW) [4] and Term Frequency-Inverse Document Frequency (TF-IDF) [5] models have been widely used for text encoding by conventional machine learning algorithms in various text analytics domains, such as the legal sector. Kumar et al. observed that the BOW and TF-IDF model yields better results for recognizing the similarity of legal judgments since just the similarity of the legal phrases, as opposed to all the terms in the dataset, are evaluated [6].

Mandal et al. explored multiple advanced vector representation models for legal document sauch as Latent Dirichlet Allocation [7] and word embedding along with the TF-IDF model. Word embedding techniques such as Word2vec [8] and Doc2vec [9], that may better capture the semantics of documents, achieved 69% Pearson correlation coefficients in finding similarities among Indian Supreme Court cases, according to the paper [10].

Word embedding representation has been used in the legal field for a number of years. However, the results reported in the reviewed existing literature [10–12] provide a marginal or non-existent improvement over simple BOW models. This paper investigates the pre-trained, domain-specific deep learning model utilized for text embedding. After exploring for comparable instances, the newly installed embedding yielded superior results.

## 3  Methodology

The method proposes in this work offers an approach for screening PA cases based on local coverage determinations, that are decisions made by a Medicare Administrative Contractor (MAC) whether to approve a case or not. This is an NLP-based model to help insurers by screening the PA cases that give the most similar information and ranking them based on the similarity score in comparison with the Local Coverage Determinations (LCDs) criterions. The Proposed solution consists of the following components as shown in Fig. 2.

1. PA case
2. Requested process id and Healthcare Common Procedure Coding System (HCPCS) code
3. LCDs Criterions
4. Lexicons
5. Text Similarity Check

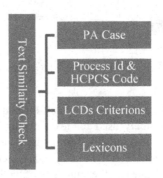

**Fig. 2.** The Proposed Solution's Components

PA cases are collected through any channel between Insurer and provider, including Electronic Medical Record (EMR). Then, getting prepared three JSON files containing all the necessary information to be utilized as input for the text similarity model.

- The first file contains the rules from the LCD criteria used to approve the procedure in relation to the HCPCS code.
- The second file contains the lexicons associated with each rule; these lexicons aid in the identification of required information from PA cases.
- The third file contains both the requested process id and the HCPCS code needed to verify the eligibility of PA case.

The model retrieves text from the lexicon file and PA case and then executes all of the steps outlined in the following Fig. 3.

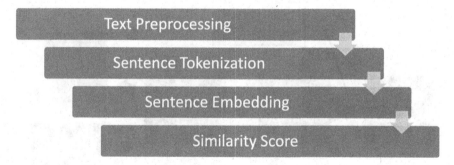

**Fig. 3.** Text Analysis Workflow

## 4 Software Design

As depicted in Fig. 4, the suggested AI-enabled solution consists primarily of three phases. First, the provider submits a PA request, then the PA automation engine examines the case and give the necessary information from the text to assist Registered Nurses (RNs) in making an approval or denial determination. Now examine the automation engine's underlying framework.

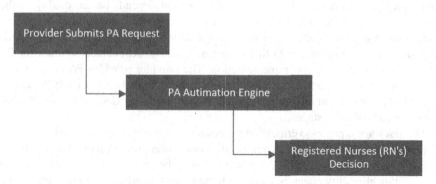

**Fig. 4.** Proposed AI-Enabled PA Process

There are three stages involved in the operation of an automation engine as shown in Fig. 5. The first stage involves process verification; the second stage identifies rules associated with process id and HCPCS code, as a result, finalizes the lexicons for each rule. And the third stage examines textual similarities. If the process verification phase is successful, the subsequent phases are enabled; if it is failed, a case of rejection is possible. Each step is elaborated on and addressed separately.

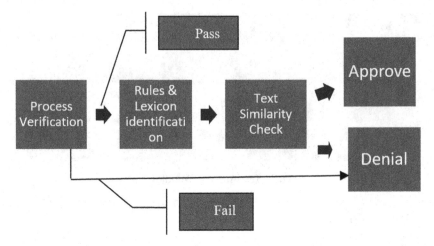

**Fig. 5.** Automation Engine Process

# 5   Implementation

In an effort to create an AI-enabled solution. The first and possibly most crucial phase is data preparation because the quality of the solution depends on the quality of the data used. On the payer side, data is collected in accordance with rules. All essential information is kept in JSON format in a configuration folder containing data collected from insurers in accordance with their requirements. The AI-enabled solution for PA requires two components for implementation. The provider provides PA cases in text format with HCPCS codes. Once a PA case containing the requested HCPCS code is received, the automation engine is engaged. According to the design, the automation engine consists of three stages.

The first stage is process verification as shown in Fig. 6 and this procedure begins with the input of the HCPCS code. Therefore, the automation engine employs a rule-based method to cross-check with JSON files containing the process id and corresponding codes. If this eligibility check is successful, the procedure advances to the subsequent level; otherwise, the case is denied.

The second stage is rules and lexicon identification. HCPCS code facilitates the identification of rules using a rule-based methodology. Consequently, the lexicon is identified relative to each rule using the same method.

The third and last important stage is text similarity. This stage is the central concept of AI utilization in this paper. The text analysis comes into play here.; it aids with text comprehension. Text is provided as input at this stage, after that text preparation occurs. Then, the sentence is tokenized so that the model can convert it into a vector, that is the sentence embedding process. The identical procedure of sentence embedding was used to the lexicon identified in the previous step. Now, after obtaining two sets of vectors, one from lexicons and the other from text, cosine similarity is used to generate similarity metrics. After receiving ranking evidence, RNs can make a decision based on this evidence (Fig. 8).

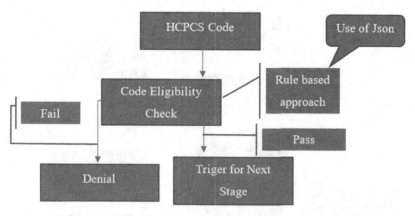

**Fig. 6.** Process Verification Process

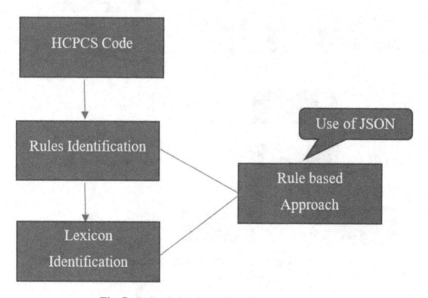

**Fig. 7.** Rules & Lexicons Identifications Process

Sentence embedding is performed to generate a dictionary of pre-processed sentences and their corresponding vectors. Vectors are derived using a model. This model is founded on NLP principles. In this paper, two NLP strategies were utilized to determine the most effective method for achieving our objective.

## 5.1  TF-IDF

In this approach, the frequency of words is rescaled according to their overall frequency in all texts, which penalizes common, ubiquitous words like "the" that appear often throughout all texts. TF-IDF measures how crucial a specific term is to the overall

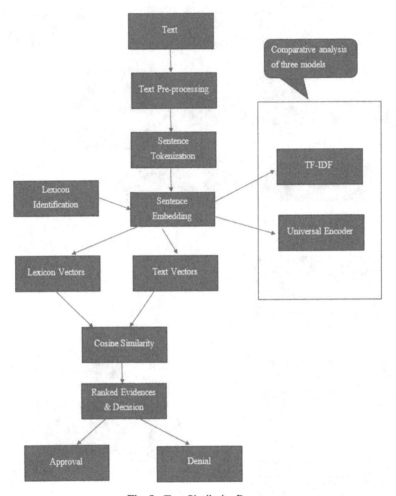

**Fig. 8.** Text Similarity Process

meaning of a text. Multiplying two separate metrics yields a document word's TF-IDF. The Term Frequency (TF) of a document's words. There are numerous methods for calculating this frequency, the simplest of that is a simple count of the occurrences of a word in a document. Then, there are further methods for adjusting the frequency. For instance, as Eq. (1) describes, by dividing the raw count of occurrences of a word by the document's length or by the raw frequency of the document's most frequent word.

$$TF(i,j) = n(i,j) / \sum n(i,j) \tag{1}$$

where,
n(i,j) = number of times nth word occurred in a document

$\Sigma n(i,j)$ = total number of words in a document.

The inverse document frequency (IDF) of a given word across a collection of documents. This reflects the frequency of a word in the entire document set. The closer a term is to 0, the more frequent it is. This metric can be determined by dividing the total number of documents by the number of documents containing a specific word. This metric can then be calculated using the logarithm.

Therefore, this number approaches 0 if the term is prevalent and appears in several documents. Alternatively, it approaches 1 Multiplying these two numbers yields the TF-IDF score of each word in a document. The higher the score, the more pertinent the word is to the document. In mathematical terms, the TF-IDF score is calculated according to Eq. (2).

$$IDF = 1 + \log(N/dN) \tag{2}$$

where,

N = Total number of documents in the dataset.

N = total number of documents in that nth word occur.

## 5.2 Universal Sentence Encoder

A significant amount of work is expended in machine learning research to convert data into vectors. Word2vec and Glove [13] accomplish this by turning a word into a vector. Therefore, the vector corresponding to "cat" will be closer to "dog" than to "eagle." While embedding a sentence with its words, however, the complete sentence's context must be captured in that vector. The "Universal Sentence Encoder" comes into play at this point.

The embedding generated by the Universal Sentence Encoder [14] model especially transfer learning to the NLP tasks. It is trained on a number of data sources in order to acquire skills for a vast array of tasks. The sources include Wiki, web media, online question-and-answer pages, and forums. The input is variable-length English text, while the outcome is a 512-dimensional vector.

Typically, sentence embedding was derived by averaging the embedding of all the words in the phrase; however, this method had limitations and was unsuitable for detecting the true semantic meaning of a sentence. The Universal Sentence Encoder makes sentence-level embedding effortless. It is available in two variants, one trained with the Transformer encoder and the other with the Deep Averaging Network (DAN). In terms of computer resource requirements and accuracy, there is a trade-off between the two. While the one with the Transformer encoder is more precise, it requires more computation. The variant with DAN encoding is computationally less expensive and slightly less precise. This paper utilizes the transformer encoder variant.

## 6 Analysis and Results

A text similarity-based AI solution must be accurate not only in identifying text but also in identifying the meaning of the word in terms of context, as insurance companies deal with complicated documents as a result of sentence formation in the medical history of patients. As shown by Tables 1 and 2, which display the cosine similarity score, a universal sentence encoder thus aids in the capturing of semantic meaning at the sentence level as well as text similarity level. As evident from the validation results, both approaches showed promise in assessing claim approval using text similarity, and reviewers from health insurance companies can approve or decline the claim by confirming that all of the policy's requirements are met in the patient's medical history. This paper shows that, in terms of text similarity, the second approach—using a universal sentence encoder—is more effective than the first—using the TF IDF technique. In this paper, analysis is done by STS Benchmark. This Benchmark offers an empirical assessment of the degree to which similarity ratings obtained by sentence embedding correspond to human judgments. The benchmark necessitates that systems produce similarity scores for an assortment of sentence pairs. The Pearson correlation coefficient is then applied to compare the quality of algorithm similarity scores to human judgments. The statistical method of the Pearson correlation coefficient [15] is commonly used in economics for purposes like trend analysis and classification. Other potential domains of use have been discussed in recent years' literature. Using it, one can determine if strongly two variables are related to one another along a linear axis. And p-value is calculated to check statistically significance. If the correlation coefficient were indeed zero, then the current result would have been seen with a probability equal to the P-value (null hypothesis). A correlation coefficient is considered statistically significant if its associated probability is less than 5%.

## 6.1  TF-IDF

Pearson correlation coefficient = 0.2340
    p-value = 1.015e-19

## 6.2  Universal Sentence Encoder

Pearson correlation coefficient = 0.83
    p-value = 0.0
    And testing and validation purpose only few rules have been considered that are Rule "A", Rule "B" and Rule "C".

- Rule "A" says one or more mobility-related activities of daily living, are severely hindered because of the beneficiary's mobility limitation.
- Rule "B" says a properly adjusted cane or walker would not help the beneficiary with his/her mobility issues to an acceptable degree.
- Rule "C" says there is insufficient upper extremity function for the beneficiary to propel a properly equipped manual wheelchair indoors.

    Results that are from the TF-IDF technique are mentioned in the Table 1.
    Results that are from the Universal Sentence Encoder Technique are mentioned in the Table 2.
    So, the result from the both technique says Universal Sentence Encoder has a high correlation coefficient, p-value, and cosine score compared to TF_IDF.

**Table 1.** Results from the TF-IDF Technique

| Rule Name | Total no. of Matches | Top matching sentence from PA text | Highest Cosine Score |
|---|---|---|---|
| A | 5 | he limited in his ability to partici-pate in all mobility related activities of daily living in the home setting | 0.491431 |
| B | 6 | he la unable to safely or effectively use cane or walker for the distance needed in the home due to fatigue joint pain and numbness | 0.2933 |
| C | 9 | he is unable to self-propel an optimally configures manual wheelchair due to upper extremity weakness and arthritic hand pain | 0.3841 |

**Table 2.** Results from the Universal Sentence Encoder Technique

| Rule Name | Total no. of Matches | Top matching sentence from PA text | Highest Cosine Score |
|---|---|---|---|
| A | 7 | he limited in his ability to partici-pate in all mobility related activities of daily living in the home setting | 0.72 |
| B | 5 | he la unable to safely or effectively use cane or walker for the distance needed in the home due to fatigue joint pain and numbness | 0.70 |
| C | 8 | he is unable to self-propel an optimally configures manual wheelchair due to upper extremity weakness and arthritic hand pain | 0.71 |

The similarity is visualized using a heat map. The graph is a $31 \times 52$ matrix and the color of each element $[i, j]$ is determined by the dot product of the embedding for sentence i and j. The similarity between sentences is displayed via a heat map. This result demonstrates that because the embedding process is carried out at the sentence level, the outcomes from the second approach using the Universal Sentence Encoder have a high color intensity. The two documents being compared are one a medical history and the other a set of policy guidelines. Figure 6 shows the heat map for TF-IDF and Fig. 7 shows the heat map for Universal Sentence Encoder (Figs. 9 and 10).

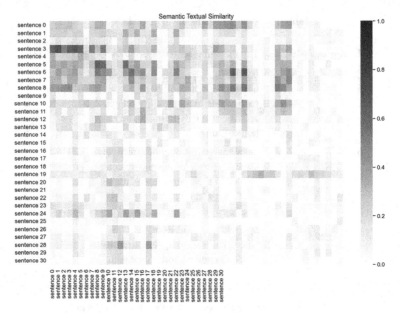

**Fig. 9.** Similarity Visualization for TF-IDF

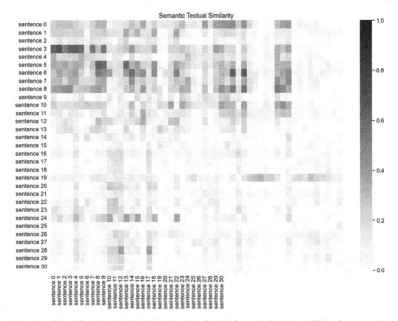

**Fig. 10.** Similarity visualization for Universal Sentence Encoder

# 7 Conclusion

The facts presented in the previous section make it plainly clear that Universal Sentence Encoder's tactics are superior to those of TF IDF. Using the Pearson correlation coefficient, the assessment standard allows for differentiation between the various methodologies. The similarity visualization generates outputs with varying degrees of color intensity that are quite similar. This conclusion is based on the information gathered for the purpose of this paper. On the other hand, the evaluation benchmark makes it obvious that Universal Sentence Encoder approaches can still tackle the challenge even if the difficulty of the text increases. Even though this paper is conducted on PA cases, that are part of the healthcare industry, complexity management is always a concern. This methodology aids in reaching the objectives of the paper. Access to necessary care for patients is frequently delayed as a result of prior authorizations, that may drive patients to abandon their treatment due to the waiting period or other complications related with prior authorization. This work provides a viable method for resolving the issue, as it proposes a method for streamlining AI that minimizes treatment delays and disruptions by reducing the requirement for prior approval. This solution, that is an integral part of the End-to-End Prior Authorization process, eliminates human work that is time-consuming and prone to error. Therefore, the pre authorization team can maximize the health system's capacity to provide faster and better care. Patients, healthcare providers, and insurers, as well as any other parties engaged in the process, can all benefit from an efficient utilization management program. These are the adverbial complements for each:

- Patients gain from decreased treatment costs, more treatment efficacy, and fewer refused claims.
- Fewer denied claims, reduced costs, more effective treatments, improved data, and more efficient resource utilization are all beneficial to the health care industry.

# References

1. Wickizer, T.M., Lessler, D.: Utilization management: Issues, effects, and future prospects. Annu. Rev. Public Health 23, 233–254 (2002). https://doi.org/10.1146/ANNUREV.PUBLHE ALTH.23.100901.140529
2. AI ushers in next-gen prior authorization in healthcare | McKinsey | McKinsey. https://www.mckinsey.com/industries/healthcare-systems-and-services/our-insights/ai-ushers-in-next-gen-prior-authorization-in-healthcare. Accessed 10 Aug 2022
3. American Medical Association. Prior Authorization Physician Survey Update | AMA (2022). https://www.ama-assn.org/system/files/prior. Accessed 10 Aug 2022
4. Ngai, E.W.T., Hu, Y., Wong, Y.H., Chen, Y., Sun, X.: The application of data mining techniques in financial fraud detection: a classification framework and an academic review of literature. Decis. Support Syst. 50(3), 559–569 (2011). https://doi.org/10.1016/J.DSS.2010.08.006
5. Lam, J., Chen, Y., Zulkernine, F., Dahan, S.: Detection of similar legal cases on personal injury. In: IEEE International Conference Data Mining Workshops (ICDMW), pp. 639–646 (2021). https://doi.org/10.1109/ICDMW53433.2021.00084

6.  Kumar, M., Ghani, R., Mei, Z.S.: Data mining to predict and prevent errors in health insurance claims processing. In: Proceedings of the ACM SIGKDD International Conference Knowledge Discovery and Data Mining, pp. 65–73 (2010). https://doi.org/10.1145/1835804.183 5816

7.  Blei, D.M., Ng, A.Y., Jordan, M.I.: Latent dirichlet allocation. J. Mach. Learn. Res. **3**, 993–1022 (2003)

8.  Mikolov, T., Chen, K., Corrado, G., Dean, J.: Efficient estimation of word representations in vector space (2013). arXiv:1301.3781. https://arxiv.org/abs/1301.3781. Accessed 10 Aug 2022.

9.  Le, Q., Mikolov, T.: Distributed representations of sentences and documents. In: International Conference on Machine Learning. http://proceedings.mlr.press/v32/le14.html?ref=https://github.com. Accessed 10 Aug 2022

10. Mandal, A., Chaki, R., Saha, S., Ghosh, K., Pal, A., Ghosh, S.: Measuring similarity among legal court case documents. ACM International Conference Proceeding Series, pp. 1–9, (2017). https://doi.org/10.1145/3140107.3140119

11. Xia, C., He, T., Li, W., Qin, Z., Zou, Z.: Similarity analysis of law documents based on Word2vec. In: Proceedings Companion 19th IEEE International Conference Software Quality Reliability and Security QRS-C 2019, pp. 354–357 (2019). https://doi.org/10.1109/QRS-C.2019.00072

12. Thenmozhi, D., Kannan, K., Aravindan, C.: A text similarity approach for precedence retrieval from legal documents. In: FIRE (Working Notes) (2017). http://ceur-ws.org/Vol-2036/T3-9.pdf. Accessed 10 Aug 2022

13. Pennington, J., Socher, R., Manning, C.D.: GloVe: global vectors for word representation. http://nlp/. Accessed 15 Aug 2022

14. Cer, D., et al.: Universal sentence encoder. In: AAAI, pp. 16026–16028 (2018). https://doi.org/10.48550/arxiv.1803.11175

15. Zhi, X., Yuexin, S., Jin, M., Lujie, Z., Zijian, D.: Research on the Pearson correlation coefficient evaluation method of analog signal in the process of unit peak load regulation

# Real-Time Identification of Medical Equipment Using Deep CNN and Computer Vision

Jaya Rubi[1]([✉]), R. J. Hemalatha[1], and Bethanney Janney[2]

[1] Department of Biomedical Engineering, Vels Institute of Science, Technology and Advanced Studies, Pallavaram, Chennai, India
jayarubiap@gmail.com
[2] Department of Biomedical Engineering, Sathyabama Institute of Science and Technology, Chennai, India

**Abstract.** Sign language is a way of communication in which hand gestures and symbols are used to connect with each other. Communication provides interaction among people to exchange feelings and ideas. Similarly, when it comes to the handling of medical equipment using a robot, sign language should not be a barrier to carrying out such applications. The purpose of this work is to provide a real-time system that can convert Sign Language (ISL) to text format. Most of the work is based on the handcrafted feature. This paper concentrates on introducing a deep learning approach that can classify the signs using the convolutional neural network. First, we make a classifier model using the signs, then using Kera's implementation of convolutional neural network using python we analyze those signs and identify the surgical tools. Then we process another real-time system that uses skin segmentation to find the Region of Interest in the frame. The segmented region is fed to the classifier model to predict the sign. The predicted sign would gradually identify the surgical tool and convert the sign into text.

**Keywords:** Deep CNN · surgical equipment · computer vision · kera's implementation · Gesture recognition · Image processing

## 1 Introduction

Sign language is an important real-time system used amongst several groups of people, especially deaf and dumb people. Sign language or gesture recognition will allow the verbal exchange barrier among exceptional languages like American sign language, Chinese language signal language, Indian signal language, and so forth. The proposed system aims to build a system that can transform these signs with the use of the computer vision technique, further it can be transformed into any language. There are different kinds of studies that focus on building accurate systems and most works are primarily based on pattern recognition. The machines that use simple features and functions aren't always enough in maximum cases and that is the reason this Hybrid approach is delivered to clear up this trouble [8]. However, for a real-time machine, we need quicker strategies

S. Nandan Mohanty et al. (Eds.): ICISML 2022, LNICST 471, pp. 311–319, 2023.
https://doi.org/10.1007/978-3-031-35081-8_25

to solve our problems. Nowadays our computer systems are stepping forward with the speed of processing and the usage of a parallel implementation. Using the Graphics Processing Unit (GPU) system helps solve several issues that may be solved via parallel computing [19, 20]. In the proposed method, we use an area of interest to determine the sign that has been presented in front of the camera, and the analysis and segmentation of this sign are correlated with the medical equipment it is associated with. The proposed proposal has an accuracy of up to 87% and further by increasing the epoch values and training the model the overall output can be improvised and the process of identification can be made much easier.

## 2  Methodology

Sign language is a complicated system with a critical problem known as background noise. Technique to avoid such issues is to run a convolutional neural network at the images. This method is potentially important to increase the efficiency of the classification and apply it to real-world applications [1, 9]. With the proposed methodology the efficiency of the system was increased to 87% (Fig. 1).

**Fig. 1.**  Image analysis

The basic procedure is followed to give the image as input. The camera easily recognizes a handheld object as the initializing process starts. Features were extracted with the specified program designed in python using Kera's implementation [8]. The next process is the classification and prediction of the object or the hand gesture.

Several studies indicated that most object detection problems used image data sets and bounding box maps to train the models. One of the hard troubles in identification and prediction is marking the bounding box map for each image, and this method is pretty high-priced. Moreover, a region-of-interest predictor is proposed using skin segmentation. The Images were cropped from the segmented bounding regions and sent to a classifier for further prediction [10].

The processing of the image is executed in a completely calculative and step-by-step way to acquire clear results. The capturing of the image by the camera is a vital step. It was noted that the lighting conditions and the readability of the camera are major factors that could affect the result. in addition, the complete processing of the picture has been defined in elements to understand the conversions, classifications, and predictions [20] (Fig. 2).

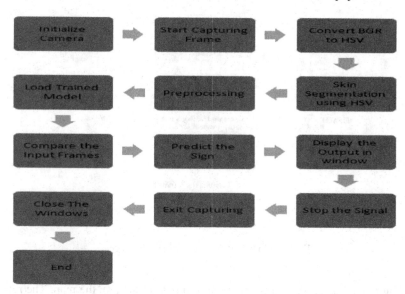

**Fig. 2.** Gesture recognition process using segmentation and boundary detection

The gesture recognition process has three basic steps that could be broadly classified as image capturing, image segmentation and image processing. The initialization happens by starting the camera. As the camera is initiated within a fraction of a second the camera starts to capture the frame. The data collected initialized the camera to capture frames. The images were converted from hue, saturation, and value (HSV) to BGR. This format helps us to display the image in a clear manner [11]. The next process is the skin segmentation process which further helps in the preprocessing stage. The trained model is loaded into the system which helps us to compare the input frames and prediction of the gestures. Once the prediction is complete the signal is stopped and capturing is closed. The below-mentioned Fig. 3 depicts the flow chart for capturing the image and processing it [19].

### 2.1 Data Collection

The first step is data collection. The data collection file must run successfully. As the webcam is initialized a frame would be visible in the upper right corner. The gesture is then made visible in front of the camera. Once the gesture is visible on the screen, it can be captured with the click of the 'c' key to take a picture. Then the data is automatically saved according to the commands used in the program [12].

### 2.2 Training Data

The next important step is to train the data. To avoid overfitting, the model, an epoch of 200 is used. The images should be taken from various angles and positions. This would allow the system to work efficiently. The accuracy of the proposed work is displayed

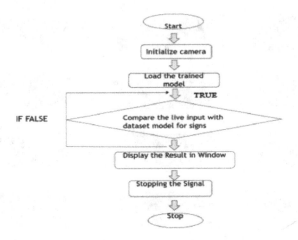

**Fig. 3.** Flowchart for processing the image

according to the comparison of training and test data present on the map. The recommended use is 350 frames per word for the training data and 250 frames per word for the test data folder [17].

It is also important to build a convolutional neural network on Kera's implementation technique. The comparison between deep learning and machine learning is not very widespread. Deep learning has emerged as a totally popular subset of machine learning due to its high performance on unique sorts of facts. One of the potential methods to categorise deep learning is to classify images to construct a convolutional neural network (CNN) [18]. Python's Kera's library makes it very easy to create a convolutional neural network (CNN). The images are fed to the computer systems, and they perceive these images as pixels. Pixels are mostly associated. Certain bunch or groups of pixels may constitute the edge or boundary region. It might also represent certain patterns in an image [13].

The created dataset is handy to be used in Kera's library. This makes it easy for us to load the dataset. The total variety of images in both training and test files furnished within the dataset offers the entire wide variety of images for training and testing respectively [16].

### 2.3 Data Preprocessing

The next process is to transform the given datasets into a particular fomat that would be acceptable to the model during the training process. As the format for the training is achieved the model has to be built for processing. The model type that has been selected to use is Sequential. Sequential models are easy to create in Kera [2]. The model can be built layer by layer which helps in analyzing the system with every step.

Each layer can be added to the model using the add() function. These are convolutional layers that process an input image viewed as a two- dimensional matrix. The number of nodes given is 64 for the initial layer and 32 for the next layer in each layer. This wide variety may be set higher or lower depending on the scale of your data set.

The kernel size is the size of the convolution's filter matrix [3]. The activation function used for the first two layers is ReLU or Rectified Linear Activation. This model will then make its prediction based totally on whichever alternative has the best chance [15] (Figs. 4 and 5).

**Fig. 4.** Training Data Collection gesture 1

**Fig. 5.** Training Data Collection gesture 2

## 2.4  Compiling CNN

The following step is to bring together the complete version by compiling the CNN. Compiling a version requires three parameters: losing, optimizing, and standardizing.

**Fig. 6.** Training Data Collection gesture 3

The usage of an optimizer takes authority over the rate of learning. SGD is often a correct optimizer in most instances. The SGD optimizer adjusts the rate of learning at some point in the training system. To teach the model, use the fit() characteristic on the model with parameters for the training of data (Train X), goal data (Train y), validation statistics, and several epochs [4]. For validation information, we have used the test set provided within the data set. The range of epochs shows how frequently the model iterates over the records. Over epochs, the version improves to a positive factor. After this factor, the model stops improving in the course of each epoch. For this model, we specify the number of epochs to 20.

The complete process of training is done in Kera which is an open-source software library. This library presents a Python interface for artificial neural networks. Kera also serves as a medium for the TensorFlow data library which helps to train any model for the machine learning process. TensorFlow is a free-of-cost, open-source machine learning software library and it potentially helps the machine to understand the gesture [5]. It can be used for a variety of tasks, with a specific focus on deep neural network training and inference [14].

## 3 Results and Discussion

The image data were collected and placed in two different folders. One set of data was placed in the test folder and the other in the training folders. Around 350 images for each gesture were collected in the training folder. Around 250 images were collected per gesture for testing purposes. Each shield has folders for both training and testing modes. These directories are created while the code is running. As far as the program is concerned, the first thing to do is record capture, as shown in Fig. 6.

Here the image is captured and saved in a separate file. As the amount of testing and training data changes, the encoding needs to be changed. This process helps to keep the training model intact (Fig. 9).

Here the image is captured and saved in a separate file. As the amount of testing and training data changes, the encoding needs to be changed. This process helps to keep

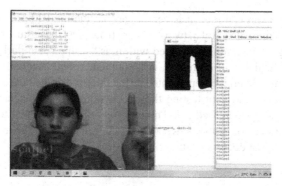

**Fig. 7.** Gesture 1 depicting "SCALPEL"

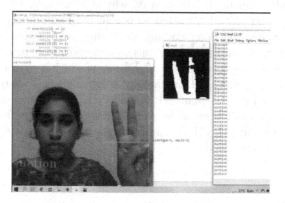

**Fig. 8.** Gesture 2 depicting "SUCTION"

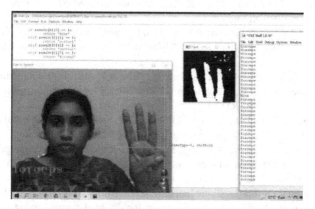

**Fig. 9.** Gesture 3 depicting "FORCEPS"

the training model intact. The loss function used is the categorical cross-entropy for configurations of three or more classes. As the above figures depict the association of each gesture with a surgical tool, it is very clear that the model has been trained well using a deep convolutional neural network. Figure 6. Depicts the gesture 1 and represents the corresponding surgical tool associated with it as "scalpel", similarly Fig. 7 depicts gesture number 2 which will represent an equipment called "suction "device. Lastly Fig. 8 depicts gesture 3 and it is represented as the third tool called the "forceps". Thus, as we train the model and kept testing the epoch values, the efficiency of the model as well as the accuracy increased [6]. The representation of surgical tools along with gestures has numerous applications. Robots can be trained using the model to identify surgical tools and assist doctors in surgeries [7, 8].

## 4  Conclusion

This paper provides valuable information on why sign language interpreting should be included in machine learning models to benefit the future of robotic surgery. A complete model involves collecting, training, and testing data that was used to make final predictions. The most important requirements were convolutional neural networks and TensorFlow. The result is received as a text for the input which is an icon image/gesture. So, in a very straightforward and simple way, a sign language interpreter for three gestures was designed and programmed. Future research areas may involve creating user interfaces with robotic arms using sign language interpreters for manipulation, double-hand gestures, etc. [11, 13]. This model can be used for practicing and mastering robotic arms for robotic manipulation.

## References

1. Zhao, K., Zhang, K., Zhai, Yu., Wang, D., Su, J.: Real-time sign language recognition based on video stream. In: The National Natural Science Foundation (NNSF) of China, 10 September 2020 UTC from IEEE Xplore
2. Panda, A.K., Chakravarty, R., Moulik, S.: Hand gesture recognition using flex sensor and machine learning algorithms. In: 2020 IEEE- EMBS Conference on Biomedical Engineering and Science(2020)
3. Hamza, K.H., Zhang, X., Mu, X., Odekhe, R., Alhassan, A.B.: In: Engineering 2018 IEEE 8th Annual International Conference on CYBER Technology in Automation, Control, and Intelligent Systems (CYBER) (2018)
4. Jin, J., Chung, W.: School of Mechanical Engineering, Korea University, Seoul 02841 Korea. Sensors **19**(2), 289 (2019). https://doi.org/10.3390/s19020289
5. Zhao, D., Yang, J., Koye, M.O., Wang, S.: A novel non-contact abnormal gait recognition approach based on extended set membership filter. IEEE Access **7**, 76471–76753 (2019)
6. Young, K.Y., Cheng, S.L., Ko, C.H., Tsou, H.W.: Development of a comfort-based motion guidance system for a robot walking helper. J. Intell. Robot. Syst. **100**(2), 379–388 (2020)
7. Ahmed, S.F. et al.: Mobility assistance robot for disabled persons using electromyography (EMG) sensor. In: 2018 IEEEInternational Conference on Innovative Research and Development (ICIRD), pp. 1–5 (2018). https://doi.org/10.1109/ICIRD.2018.8376304
8. Roizenblatt, M., Edwards, T.L., Gehlbach, P.L.: Robot-assisted vitreoretinal surgery: current perspectives. Dove Press J. (2018)

9. Meello, R., Jimenez, M., Souza, F., Ribeiro, M.R., Frizero-Neto, A.: Towards a new generation of smart devices for mobility assistance: cloud walker, a cloud-enabled cyber-physical system. In: 7th IEEE International Conference on Biomedical Robotics and Biomechatronics (Biorob) (2018)
10. Miseikis, J., et al.: Lio-a personal robot assistant for human-robot interaction and care application. Published on PMC (2020)
11. Sahoo, A.K., Brahma, B., Pattanaik, A.: Design & development of robotic arm for medical surgery. In: 2nd International Conference on Power and Embedded Drive Control (ICPEDC) (2019)
12. Zhao, X., et al.: A smart robotic walker with intelligent close-proximity interaction capabilities for elderly mobility safety. Front. Neurobot. **14**, 575889 (2020)
13. Ishak, M.K., Kit, N.M.: Design and implementation of robot-assisted surgery based on internet of things (IoT). In: International Conference on Advanced Computing and Applications (ACOMP) (2017)
14. Sagitov, A., Gavrilova, L., Soy, T.T., Li, H.: Design of simple one arm- surgical robot for minimally invasive surgery. In: 12th International Conference on Development in E-System Engineering (DeSE) (2019)
15. Miao, Y., Jiang, Y., Muhammad, G.: Telesurgery robot based on 5G tactile internet. Mob. Netw. Appl. **23**, 1645–1654 (2018)
16. de Smet, M.D., Gerrit, J.L, Faridpooya, K., Mura, M.: Robotic-assisted surgery in ophthalmology. Curr. Opin. Ophthalmol. **29**(3), 248-253 (2018)
17. Jason, D., Wright, M.D.: Robotic-assisted surgery (balancing evidence and implementation). Jama, **318**(16), 1545-1547
18. Jin, J., Chung, W.: Obstacle avoidance of two-wheel differential robots considering the uncertainty of robot motion on the basis of encodes odometry information. Sensors, **19**(2), 289 (2019)
19. Hamza, K.K., Zhang, X., Mu, X., Odekhe, R., Alhassan, A.B.: Modeling and stimulation of transporting elderly posture of multifunctional elderly- assistance and walking-assistant robot. In: 8th International Conference on CYBER Technology in Automation Control and Intelligent Systems (CYBER) (2018)
20. Ahmed, S.F., et al.: Mobility assistance robot for disabled persons using electromyography sensor. In: IEEE International Conference on Innovative Research and Development (ICIRD) (2018)

# Design of a Intelligent Crutch Tool for Elders

A. Josephin Arockia Dhivya$^{(\boxtimes)}$ and R. J. Hemalatha

Department of Biomedical Engineering, Vels Institute of Science,
Technology and Advanced Studies, Chennai, India
{a.dhivya.se,hodbiomedical}@velsuniv.ac.in

**Abstract.** In the last few years physiotherapists has been treating the individuals by taking their decisions quickly which results in complexity, non effective and decrease in recovery rate in rehabilitation. Walking aids play a vital role in helping the patients in certain conditions, they lack balance and leads to complex usage of device. These type of aids helps for individuals suffering from spondylitis, disc bulging and postural In this proposed system we design a solution for patient using walkers, this device helps them to maintain the proper balance. As a proof of concept, we develop a sensors-based solution which can be easily embed where the walker helps to get real time information of the subject and helps in recovery rate. This device will automatically warn the users when they apply more pressure on a sensor using haptic feedback. To design a smart crutch tool for Elders and Accident patients which balances the force applied in terms of stress and strain to warn the patients by means of haptic feedback.

**Keywords:** Posture Correction · Microcontroller · Liquid Crystal Display · Haptic feedback · Force Applied

## 1 Introduction

According to global reports the number of elders are expected to be more than 850 million in 2040. They help to increase the quality of life by improving their gait patterns. It is a portable, low cost device which helps the diseased individuals for their mobility. The device was designed by adding two Flexi-Force sensors to the hand supports of a walker whenever they apply more pressure on a sensor this device will automatically warn the users using haptic feedback.

## 2 Literature Survey

In this paper, a prototype was developed to monitor the axial force and the phase of gait cycle and it also helps to measure the real time parameter of the diseased and its operated in wireless mode.[1].

This paper mainly concentrates on the principle of pendulum for handling the crutch in different angles and motions of different weights [2].

© ICST Institute for Computer Sciences, Social Informatics and Telecommunications Engineering 2023
Published by Springer Nature Switzerland AG 2023. All Rights Reserved
S. Nandan Mohanty et al. (Eds.): ICISML 2022, LNICST 471, pp. 320–324, 2023.
https://doi.org/10.1007/978-3-031-35081-8_26

This paper concentrates on Walking aids play a vital role to maintain mobility and its not recommended for long term use [3].

With the usage of crutches size and shape it is useful for long period usage and it is of more aware and it gives a complete experience [4].

This paper mainly highlights the Gait parameters are used to determine the different levels of gait [5].

## 3  Methodology

We propose a proof-of-concept level sensors-based solution which can be easily embed to the crutch will help to measure the force parameters using flex sensors. They are placed on both the hands and named as F1 and F2.When applying pressure on F1 and F2 there will value variation on LCD.

The drivers (NPN Transistors) is connected with vibration motors which will intimate vibration by using haptic feedback. The output is displayed on LCD Display using power supply. It has analog and digital port. All the digital modules are connected to digital port.

Analog port where varying sensors. LCD display works on 0 and 1 conditions [6]. And it has two operations either it displays the text or it does not display and connected to the digital port of the microcontroller. It is connected to the analog port of the micro-controller. Whenever we press the Flexible force sensor there will an analog value which will vary so we will be setting a threshold value based on the subject. The value will vary only when we connect voltage divider. We are using 10k resistor, Capacitor and voltage regulators are connected to one side and on the other side NPN transistors are connected. It is used to activate or deactivate Haptic feedback motors. Haptic feedback motors. Each motors are connected to each force sensor. Haptic feedback will indicate with vibration when excessive force is applied [7] (Fig. 1).

Analog port is connected to two force sensor which gives the value with variation. Two big flexible force sensor are connected to the analog port of microcontroller. In general purpose board on one side capacitors and voltage regulator is connected and on the other side resistor and NPN transistor are connected.

We need to integrate the power supply and to connect black wire from the power supply board to the battery black terminal and brown wire to the battery red terminal. Once we integrate we will get the power supply, micro controller will turn On and LCD also turn ON. Now LCD display will show the F1 and F2 sensor values. We are using two vibration motors and named as V1 and V2.

We are setting threshold value as greater than 600 Pa. When applying pressure on F1 sensor there will be a analog value variation in LCD display [8]. If the F1 value is <600 Pa the vibration motor will not vibrate, if the F1 value is >600 Pa it will automatically turn ON the vibration motor and give the haptic feedback to alert the user and similarly for F2 force sensor.

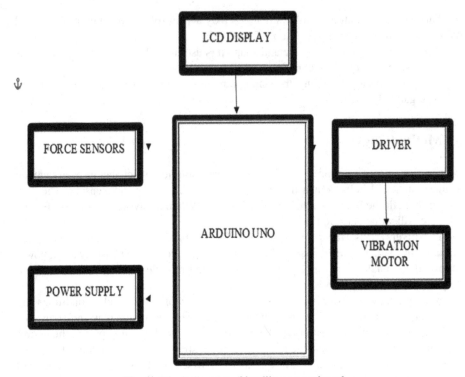

**Fig. 1.** Block diagram of intelligent crutch tool

## 4  Result and Discussion

We have connected both force sensor to the LCD display and we can see that F1 and F2 are at initial state. Now we are applying pressure on F1 sensor and there is an analog value variation in LCD display F1. We are giving threshold value as 600 Pa. If F21 value is <600 Pa vibration motor will not vibrate, if the value is >600 Pa the vibration motor vibrates and alert the user and we are applying pressure on F2 sensor and there is an analog value variation in LCD display F2 [9]. We are giving threshold value as 600 Pa. If F2 value is <600 Pa vibration motor will not vibrate, if the value is >600 Pa the vibration motor vibrates and alert the user [10] (Fig. 2).

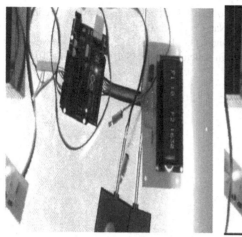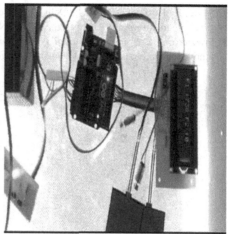

**Fig. 2.** Results obtained when excess force is given in F1 and F2 sensors

## 5  Conclusion

We propose a proof-of-concept level sensors-based solution which can be easily embed to the real walker were used to measure the information like applied pressure on each side using force Sensors. We have designed a crutch tool using haptic feedback which helps to monitor body posture changes and will develop this equipment as a crutch device which helps to monitor body posture changes like gait pattern, sports injury, cerebral palsy etc. to avoid injuries.

## References

1. Perez, C., Fung, J.: An instrumented cane devised for gait rehabilitation and research. J. Phys. Ther. Educ. **25**(11), 36–41 (2011)
2. Khlaikhayai, R., Pavaganun, C., Mangalabrukh, B., Yutapin, P.: An intelligent walking stick for elderly and blind safety protection (2011)
3. Bark, C., Chaccour, K., Darazi, R., El Hassani, A.H., Andres, E.: Design and development of a force-sensing shoe for gait analysis and monitoring (2017)
4. Sengupta, P., Mondal, K., Mahata, H., De, S., Dhara, P.C.: Evaluation of existing walking sticks and recommendations for modified waling stick. Indian J. Phys. Med. Rehab. **30**(3), 70 (2020)
5. Slade, P., Kochenderfer, M.J., Delp, S.L., Collins, S.H.: Sensing leg movement enhances wearable monitoring of energy expenditure. Nat. Commun. **12**(1), 4312 (2021)
6. Jackson, R.W., Dembia, C.L., Delp, S.L., Collins, S.H.: Muscle–tendon mechanics explain unexpected effects of exoskeleton assistance on metabolic rate during walking. J. Exp. Biol. **220**(11), 2082–2095 (2017)
7. Rajagopal, A. et al.: Full-body musculoskeletal model for muscle-driven simulation of human gait. IEEE Trans. Biomed. Eng. **63**(10), 2068–2079 (2016)
8. Hicks, J.L., Uchida, T.K., Seth, A., Rajagopal, A., Delp, S.L.: Is my model good enough? best practices for verification and validation of musculoskeletal models and simulations of movement. J. Biomech. Eng. **137**(2), 020908 (2015)

9.  Slade, P., Kochenderfer, M.J., Delp, S.L., Collins, S.H.: Sensing leg movement enhances wearable monitoring of energy expenditure. Nat. Commun. **12**(1), 4312 (2021)
10. Frizziero, L., Donnici, G., Liverani, A., Alessandri, G., Menozzi, G.C., Varott, E.: Developing innovative crutch using IDeS (industrial design structure). Appl. Sci. **9**(23), 5032 (2019)

# An Approach to New Technical Solutions in Resource Allocation Based on Artificial Intelligence

Tung Nguyen Trong[1(✉)], Nguyen Hai Vinh Cuong[2], Tran-Vu Pham[3],
Nguyen Ha Huy Cuong[4], and Bui Thanh Khiet[2]

[1] Dong A University, 33 Xo Viet Nghe Tinh Street, District Hai Chau, Da Nang City, Vietnam
tungqn@donga.edu.vn
[2] Thu Dau Mot University, Thủ Dầu Một, Binh Duong Province, Vietnam
cuongnhv@tdmu.edu.vn
[3] Faculty of Computer science and Engineering, Ho Chi Minh City University of Technology
(HCMUT), 268 Ly Thuong Kiet Street, District 10, Ho Chi Minh City, Vietnam
ptvu@hcmut.edu.vn
[4] The University of Danang, 41 Le Duan Street, District Hai Chau, Da Nang City, Vietnam
nhhcuong@sdc.udn.vn

**Abstract.** Deadlock is a major problem for systems that allocate resources (AL). There are many solutions to the deadlock problem in distributed systems, the solutions are divided into the following three groups: deadlock-prevention, deadlock-avoidance, and deadlock-detection. AL and related deadlock prevention originate from the design and implementation of operating systems and distributed computing. In this article, we systematize research related to distributed systems, problems of AL, strategies in AL, and solutions to deal with deadlock situations in AL. We present deadlock avoidance algorithms, and deadlock prevention, in addition, we present a deadlock detection algorithm using a two-way search with running time complexity of the horizontal arc $O(m1/2)$ when the edge $(v,w)$ is added to the graph. Compare the two-way search algorithm with the improved algorithm, and finally the experimental results.

**Keywords:** Resource allocation · Heterogeneous · Deadlock detection ·
Deadlock Prevention · Virtual machine

## 1 Introduction

Cloud computing (CC), also known as virtual server computing, is a computing model that uses computer technology and develops based on the Internet. CC provides a high degree of flexibility in deploying, terminating, migrating, and scaling applications and services [1]. Cloud Data Center (CDC) - consists of a series of physical cloud servers connected through high-speed links that provide a variety of cloud computing services such as Software as a Service (SaaS), Platform as a Service (PaaS), and Infrastructure

S. Nandan Mohanty et al. (Eds.): ICISML 2022, LNICST 471, pp. 325–334, 2023.
https://doi.org/10.1007/978-3-031-35081-8_27

as a Service (IaaS) [2, 3]. In addition, CDC provides a variety of customizable settings and additional features to meet the functional and non-functional requirements of end-users. Efficient management and use of cloud resources are of considerable importance to continuously meet application needs while ensuring Quality of Service (QoS) [4].

Ensuring smooth system protection one of the issues that need to be concerned is Deadlock. In a distributed system, when there exists at least one process that requires a resource to be held and is blocked indefinitely by another process, then the system will generate a deadlock. A set of processes that request resources held by other processes are called a deadlock [5]. In distributed systems, dealing with deadlock problems can be divided into three strategies: deadlock-prevention [6, 7], deadlock-avoidance [8–10], and deadlock-detection [11–15]. Deadlock is a major problem for systems that AL in a distributed system. The main problem in deadlock avoidance is checking the safe resource allocation status and checking whether there is a cycle after the allocation. Deadlock prevention is a sequence of actions that ensures the constraints between the processes in the system and the resources imposed on external actors. These constraints monitor to ensure that external actors do not send requests that cause deadlocks [16] (Fig. 1).

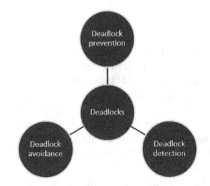

**Fig. 1.** Types of deadlocks in distributed systems

In the past, deadlock avoid has been proposed in [17] using load balancing algorithm to satisfy user requests. A heterogeneous server-based resource allocation algorithm that overcomes deadlock by harvesting available resources from previously provisioned users [18]. The scheduling algorithm AL for services on heterogeneous virtual server platforms, in order to improve the detection algorithm and prevent deadlocks. [19]. Wysk et al. [7] has developed a deadlock detection algorithm by finding optimal time intervals through integer programming. The algorithm uses constraints to ensure agents do not release resources unless specified. Classify the local and global deadlock detection problem in component-based systems as NP-hard [20]. The reinforcement learning method is proposed to find the solution to optimize the schedule in resource allocation, and the processes used in deadlock detection [21].

Difference between cloud computing and grid computing in resource Allocation, batch scheduling problem [22]. Recent studies have mostly focused on application performance and resource variability for infrastructure. In this study, we explore solutions related to the deadlock problem in distributed systems, then propose an improved deadlock detection algorithm using a two-way search algorithm. Comparing the results with the previous algorithm, the evaluation shows that the algorithm has improved performance and efficiency in the system with heterogeneous resources.

The article has the following structure: in Sect. 2, we present related works; in Sect. 3, we present the existing models; in Sect. 4, we present approaches for improving the Two – way algorithm; in Sect. 5, we present our conclusions and suggestions for future work.

## 2 System Model Resource Allocation in Heterogeneous Distributed Platforms

Resource provisioning in cloud computing is divided into two main areas, which are strategy-based and parameter-based. Depending on the characteristics, different purposes to use different strategies Fig. 2.

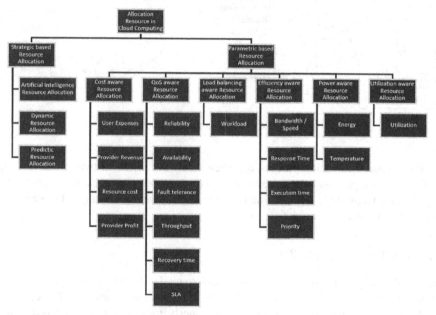

**Fig. 2.** Categorization of resource allocation in cloud computing

The advent of heterogeneous system computing presents many advantages over traditional distributed computing and heterogeneous computing which includes many different types of architectures. Cloud computing has a different resource provisioning model than scheduling, or grid computing [23–26].

## 2.1  The Application

A set of processes p1, p2,…pn transmit messages over the network, each using its processor, different memory, different physical clocks, and different means of communication. Out of order, messages may be duplicated or truncated, processors may fail, or network links may be broken, as defined in a heterogeneous distributed system. A directed graph consists of nodes and edges, in which processes are represented as nodes, the edges of the graph are considered as packets transmitted between nodes, so the distributed system will represent directed graphs.

The background charts for the grid platform. Figure 3 depicts eight processes, each of which is equivalent to an independent processor in memory. The author has modeled the heterogeneous set of resources and linked them as nodes and edges. Example 1 A example simple platform.

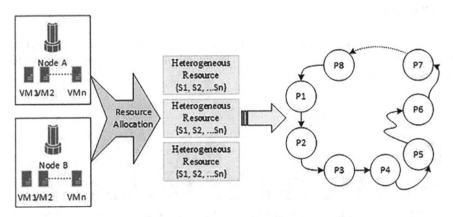

**Fig. 3.**  A example simple platform

The resource allocation process, a process is always in one of two states: running or blocked. The process that is provided with the required resources will execute and stay running. Conversely, a process that requests a resource that is being held by another process will be in a waiting state.

## 2.2  Wait–For–Graph (WFG)

For distributed systems, we use a directed graph to model the state of the system, called a waiting-for-graph (WFG) [24]. In a WFG, Processors are represented as Nodes of the graph, and edges are represented as resource requests, for example, edge E1 is directed to E2, if E1 is waiting for resource E2, waiting for E2 to release the resource. If the directed edges E form a cycle, the processes occupy the resources, there is a cycled WFG graph, and the system will be locked.

## 2.3   The Algorithms Distributed System Resources Detection

**Step 1.** Build an agent whose task is to list the states N1, N2, ....Nm with the property of reachability. In other words, from an agent point A can represent N1, N2, ....Nm, so that all other agents know and can access.

**Step 2.** The Breadth-First-Search (BFS) is created with the nodes below:

{N1}, {N2},...,{Nm}, {N1, N2},..., {Nm − 1, Nm},..., {N2,..., Nm}, {N1, N2,..., Nm}

**Step 3.** Each unique node is checked, based on BFS, and following these steps:

a) All resource-equivalent prerequisites in the node are set to "true".

b) Resource requests in the list of nodes are the cause of the infinite loop, calculate the cost generated and return nodes if there is a path.

Algorithm execution results show occupied resources, these are resources held by other processes. These resources will be the input list to run the deadlock-detection algorithm.

### 1. Mitchell and Merritt's deadlock detection algorithm

Mitchell and Merritt's algorithms belong to the group of edge-chasing algorithms where the probe is sent upwards directly on the edge of the WFG. The algorithm appears in four steps as follows:

- Blocked
- Active
- Transmit
- Detect

The algorithm works by assigning labels to processes, a private label, and a public label. The sequence of the algorithm is as follows: first, a public label is assigned to all processes and initialized to the initial value. Then each process's label is assigned to the corresponding value. When a process P requests a process Q, both processes will be assigned a label greater than that of P and referred to initially. This is the blocking step, at which point P is considered blocked. While process P is blocked, process Q is waiting. Meanwhile, if the above public label on process Q is greater than P, then process P puts the public label on process Q. This is the transition step. In the system, if there is a waiting cycle M, the maximum transition is M - 1 before deadlock is detected.

### 2. Algorithm to Avoid deadlock

To avoid deadlock, we assign a list of groups called "bad groups" to all active agents and name it "To-Avoid-List". In this list, the elements have their sublists. Thus, the list contains the states of the active agents of the deadlock elements detected by the system in the previous steps. In the event of an environmental impact, agents actively check the ToAvoid-List to ensure that the system does not perform a bad transition. When the request process is sent to an active agent, it predicts its next persistent state. The agent's state prediction system actively checks the ToAvoid List, to find if the state is in the sublist. If the alert state is present, a query is sent to the other agents active in the sublist. If the current state of all agents matches the states in the sublist, the end system enters a deadlock state. Therefore, agents actively prevent requests from performing tasks, thereby avoiding deadlocks.

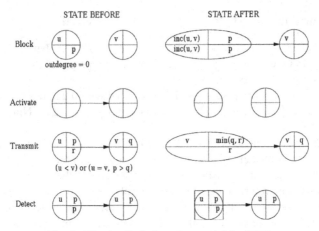

Fig. 4. The deadlock detection model for WFG

## 3. Deadlock detection for resource allocation using Two - way search in heterogeneous distributed platforms

In this study, we propose an algorithm for deadlock detection, saving the properties of a directed graph with n vertices, when a new node is added to the graph by a two-way search algorithm. The minimum time for the algorithm to detect deadlocks takes $O(m1/2)$, the time limit for adding m edges to the directed graph. The results show that when the edge detection algorithm $(v, m)$ always exists a path consisting of edges connecting vertices from $m$ to $v$.

### 2.4  Algorithmic Approach to Deadlock Detection

The two-way purple search algorithm finds the cycles and then rearranges the order of the vertices if there is no cycle in the graph. The efficiency of a two-way search algorithm depends on the number of edges visited during cycle detection in the graph.

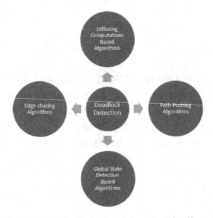

Fig. 5. Deadlock Detection Algorithms In Distributed System

$C_j^{cpu}$, $C_j^{ram}$: Maximum available capacity of CPU, RAM class IaaS provides j

$r_j^{cpu}$, $r_j^{ram}$: The new resource value of IaaS provides j (Fig. 5).

## 3   Our Algorithm to Prevention Deadlock

Consider the process Pi requesting resources, to solve deadlock prevention problems. Where P8 and P2 (Fig. 4) both processes request r1 and r2. Preventing babies from shutting down will help provide the best resources. Efficient resource scheduling prevents deadlocks.

Therefore, the proposed algorithm acts as the engine that provides the necessary content about the process situations whether each is in progress, missing or waiting, and this fact can be expressed by graph through the dependency graph presented in this paper. So, when the process waits - for a broken dependency, the corresponding content will be restored immediately from the system, if not a deadlock will occur.

Set {r1, r2,..., rn} is the set of available resources, processes P access resources R. Each process can access only a subset. Processes are required to follow the rule

- Any session, any process can call *re_resource(rk)* only when it has received all the resources *rj* it needs, that is rj < rk.
- Since process p1 at the moment owns the resource *Ra* and is waiting for the resource *Rb*, it calls *re_resource(Ra)* first and then *re_resource(Rb)*.
- When process *p2* owns resource *Xb* and is waiting for the resource to come out, it first calls *re_resource(Rb)* and then it *re_resource(Rb)*.

In heterogeneous distributed platforms, we propose to prevent deadlock algorithm includes the following steps (Fig. 6):

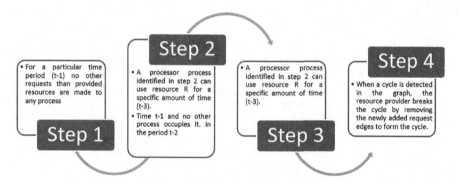

**Fig. 6.** Algorithm to prevention deadlock

## 4   Experiments and Results

In this study, we use a two-way improved cloud computing resource allocation method, experimental results have been verified on CloudSim, the platform is an open-source platform, and the research team has used Java language to implement programming classes implementing algorithms [19]. Experimental results show that the two-way improved algorithm has many advantages Table 1.

**Table 1.** Comparison of the optimal time of our algorithm to Two-way algorithm

| Cloudlet ID | Data center ID | VM ID | TWO-WAY | | | TWO-WAY-IMPROVED | | | Improved |
|---|---|---|---|---|---|---|---|---|---|
| | | | Start | End | Time | Start | End | Time | (%) |
| 0 | 1 | 1 | 0.1 | 100.1 | 100 | 0.1 | 60.1 | 60 | 25% |
| 1 | 2 | 2 | 0.1 | 110.1 | 110 | 0.1 | 70.1 | 70 | 22% |
| 2 | 3 | 3 | 0.1 | 132.1 | 132 | 0.1 | 70.1 | 70 | 31% |
| 3 | 3 | 4 | 0.1 | 145.1 | 145 | 0.1 | 90.1 | 90 | 23% |
| 4 | 1 | 5 | 0.1 | 147.1 | 147 | 0.1 | 100.1 | 100 | 19% |
| 5 | 2 | 6 | 0.1 | 145.1 | 145 | 0.1 | 104.1 | 104 | 16% |
| 6 | 1 | 7 | 0.1 | 152.1 | 152 | 0.1 | 104.1 | 104 | 19% |
| 7 | 2 | 8 | 0.1 | 153.1 | 153 | 0.1 | 110.1 | 110 | 16% |
| 8 | 2 | 9 | 0.1 | 163.1 | 163 | 0.1 | 105.1 | 105 | 22% |
| 9 | 2 | 10 | 0.1 | 168.1 | 168 | 0.1 | 111.1 | 11 | 20% |
| 10 | 3 | 11 | 0.1 | 170.1 | 170 | 0.1 | 110.1 | 110 | 21% |

Comparing the experimental results between the two algorithms, in most cases, the improved algorithm's execution time is better than the lowest 16% and the highest 31% (Fig. 7).

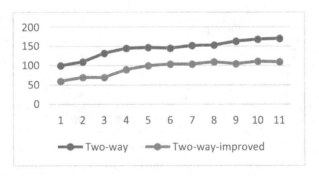

**Fig. 7.** Comparison the optimal time of algorithms

# 5 Conclusion

We learned about deadlock-related issues and introduced deadlock detection, deadlock prevention, and approaches in distributed system resource provisioning.

We proposed a deadlock detection algorithm approach implemented for resource allocation across heterogeneous cloud computing platforms. The experimental results in time complexity $O(min(m1/2))$, which in real cases has improved approximately orders of magnitude. In the study, an improved algorithm for providing resources at the IaaS infrastructure layer on a distributed platform was proposed not homogeneous. Based on an improved two-way search algorithm (Two-Way).

From the experience of this study, we found that the application of appropriate scheduling algorithms will bring optimal performance for cloud computing resources, contributing to the prevention of deadlocks. In the next study, we will study to extend the distributed resource provisioning for virtual server systems. Simultaneously, continue to expand simulation and experimental methods.

**Acknowledgment.** This research is supported and funded by Thu Dau Mot University under Grant Number DT.22.1-010. I am grateful to all of those with whom I have had the pleasure to work during this and other related projects. I would also like to extend our thanks to The University of Da Nang and Dong A university for providing the opportunity to work with experienced professionals in the fields of machine learning and cloud computing.

# References

1. Wu, J., Guo, S., Li, J., Zeng, D.: Big data meet green challenges: greening big data. IEEE Syst. J. **10**(3), 873–887 (2016). https://doi.org/10.1109/JSYST.2016.2550538
2. Banerjee, P., et al.: Everything as a service: powering the new information economy. Computer (Long Beach Calif.) **44**(3), 36–43 (2011). https://doi.org/10.1109/MC.2011.67
3. Rajkumar, M., Mariyadoss, M.K., Kandan, M.: Strategies for Resource Allocation in Cloud Computing: A Review Test Data Compression Methods: A review View project Hadoop Map Reduce View project Strategies for Resource Allocation in Cloud Computing: A Review. https://www.researchgate.net/publication/313160586
4. Kumar, N., Chilamkurti, N., Zeadally, S., Jeong, Y.S.: Achieving quality of service (QoS) using resource allocation and adaptive scheduling in cloud computing with grid support. Comput. J. **57**(2), 281–290 (2014). https://doi.org/10.1093/comjnl/bxt024
5. Khanna, D., Patel, T.P.: Deadlocks avoidance in Cloud computing using enhanced load balancing approach. IJRAR-Int. J. Res. Anal. Rev. (2018). http://ijrar.com/
6. Chao, D.Y., Chen, T.Y., Chen, J.T., Wu, K.C.: A best deadlock control for S3PMR to reach all states. Asian J. Control **14**(1) (2012). https://doi.org/10.1002/asjc.370
7. Leung, Y.T., Sheen, G.-J.: Resolving deadlocks in flexible manufacturing cells (1993)
8. Yu, T.H., Chao, D.Y.: Constructing the closed-form solution of control-related states real-time information for insufficient k-th order systems with one non-sharing resource to realize dynamic modeling large TNCS systems of petri nets. J. Chin. Inst. Eng. Trans. Chin. Inst. Eng. Ser. A **42**(3) (2019). https://doi.org/10.1080/02533839.2018.1562991
9. Roszkowska, E.: Coordination of cyclic motion processes in free-ranging multiple mobile robot systems. In: Bożejko, W., Bocewicz, G. (eds.) Modelling and Performance Analysis of Cyclic Systems. SSDC, vol. 241, pp. 87–104. Springer, Cham (2020). https://doi.org/10.1007/978-3-030-27652-2_5
10. Shanu, S., Sastry, H.G., Marriboyina, V.: Optimal solution approach on large scale data to avoid deadlocks in resource allocations. Mater. Today: Proc. **47**, 7162–7166 (2020). https://doi.org/10.1016/j.matpr.2021.06.357

11. Rout, K.K., Mishra, D.P., Salkuti, S.R.: Deadlock detection in distributed system. Indonesian J. Electr. Eng. Comput. Sci. **24**(3) (2021). https://doi.org/10.11591/ijeecs.v24.i3.pp1596-1603

12. Lu, F., Cui, M., Bao, Y., Zeng, Q., Duan, H.: Deadlock detection method based on Petri net mining of program trajectory. Jisuanji Jicheng Zhizao Xitong/Comput. Integr. Manuf. Syst. CIMS, **27**(9) (2021). https://doi.org/10.13196/j.cims.2021.09.014

13. Knapp, E.: Deadlock detection in distributed databases. ACM Comput. Surv. **19**(4) (1987). https://doi.org/10.1145/45075.46163

14. Lu, F., Tao, R., Du, Y., Zeng, Q., Bao, Y.: Deadlock detection-oriented unfolding of unbounded Petri nets. Inf. Sci. (N Y) **497** (2019). https://doi.org/10.1016/j.ins.2019.05.021

15. Rout, K.K., Mishra, D.P., Salkuti, S.R.: Deadlock detection in distributed system. Indonesian J. Electr. Eng. Comput. Sci. **24**(3), 1596–1603 (2021). https://doi.org/10.11591/ijeecs.v24.i3.pp1596-1603

16. Li, Z., Shpitalni, M.: Smart deadlock prevention policy for flexible manufacturing systems using Petri nets. IET Control Theory Appl. **3**(3) (2009). https://doi.org/10.1049/iet-cta:200 70399

17. Wu, C.W., Lee, K.J., Su, A.P.: A hybrid multicast routing approach with enhanced methods for mesh-based Networks-on-Chip. IEEE Trans. Comput. **67**(9) (2018). https://doi.org/10.1109/TC.2018.2813394

18. Nguyen, H.H.C., Doan, V.T.: Avoid Deadlock Resource Allocation (ADRA) model V VM-out-of-N PM. Int. J. Innov. Technol. Interdisc. Sci. **2**(1), 98–107 (2019). www.IJITIS.org, https://doi.org/10.15157/IJITIS.2019.2.1.98-107

19. Huy, H., Nguyen, C., Le, S., Le, V.S.: Detection and Avoidance Deadlock for Resource Allocation in Heterogeneous Distributed Platforms (2015). www.ijcst.org

20. Minnameier, C.: Local and global deadlock-detection in component-based systems are NP-hard. Inf. Process. Lett. **103**(3), 105–111 (2007). https://doi.org/10.1016/j.ipl.2007.02.016

21. Chen, M., Rabelo, L.: Deadlock-detection via reinforcement learning. Ind. Eng. Manage. **6**(03) (2017). https://doi.org/10.4172/2169-0316.1000215

22. Huy, H., et al.: Technical solutions to resources allocation for distributed virtual machine systems (2015). http://sites.google.com/site/ijcsis/

23. Cưởng, N.H.H., Sơn, L.V.: 'Kỹ Thuật Cung Cấp Tài Nguyên Cho Lớp Hạ Tầng (IAAS) Technical Resources Provision for Infrastructure (2014). http://www.cs.huji.ac.il/

24. Kshemkalyani, A.D., Singhal, M.: Distributed Computing: Principles, Algorithms, and Systems (2008)

25. Kumar, K., Feng, J., Nimmagadda, Y., Lu, Y.H.: Resource allocation for real-time tasks using cloud computing (2011). https://doi.org/10.1109/ICCCN.2011.6006077

26. Professor, D.: A Survey on Resource Allocation Strategies in Cloud Computing (2012). www.ijacsa.thesai.org

# Gesture Controlled Power Window Using Deep Learning

Jatin Rane[✉] and Suhas Mohite

Department of Mechanical Engineering, College of Engineering Pune Technological University, Wellesley Road, Shivajinagar, Pune, Maharashtra 411005, India
{ranejw21.mech,mohitess.mech}@coep.ac.in

**Abstract.** Researchers are working to fill knowledge gaps as new eras are ushering in by the rapid growth of informatics and human-computer interaction. With speech-based communication, touch-free engagement with electronic gadgets is growing in popularity and offers consumers easy-to-use control mechanisms in areas other than the entertainment sector, including the inside of cars, these engagement modes are now being successfully used. In this study, real-time human gesture identification using computer vision is proven, and the possibility of hand gesture interaction in the automobile environment is investigated. With the use of this noncognitive computer user interface, actions can be carried out depending on movements that are detected. By adding Python modules to the system, the design is carried out on a Windows OS. The platforms used for identification are open-cv and keras. The vision-based algorithms recognize the gesture displayed on the screen. A recognition algorithm was trained in keras using the background removal technique and the LeNet architecture. In this paper, four models were created and their accuracy was compared. The convex hull and threshold model outperformed the other models.

**Keywords:** computer vision · open-cv · LeNet · keras · gesture recognition

## 1 Introduction

By evaluating the user's gestures, body postures, or voice and interpreting human intention in to the device control commands, natural user interfaces enable human-machine interaction. The intelligent assistant concept is the result of advances in intelligent systems, artificial intelligence, gesture and voice recognition, dialogue systems, data science, and natural language processing. Such solutions are becoming more common in new cars, and their purpose is to aid drivers in the usage of advanced driver assistance systems (ADAS), such as systems for detecting driver fatigue, blind spot detection, lane detection & departure warning etc.

Natural user interface (NUI) is based on simple and effortless interaction with electronic devices. The interface should be barely noticeable and composed of natural elements. Entire movements cannot be incorporated into the interior of the car, but gestures

S. Nandan Mohanty et al. (Eds.): ICISML 2022, LNICST 471, pp. 335–344, 2023.
https://doi.org/10.1007/978-3-031-35081-8_28

and voice are quite well suited for information exchange with a smart assistant or multimedia system. It should be noted that all these methods of communication may not always be appropriate. When a driver is playing the radio or driving in a noisy conditions, the voice-controlled interface will always fail. In many cases, both hands are used for manoeuvring (steering wheel handling and gear shifting), making additional gestures impossible, thus static gestures with one hand shows their usefulness here.

More than a billion individuals worldwide have some sort of disability, such as hand and speech abnormalities, according to the World Report on Disability from the World Health Organization and the World Bank. Also India has five million people with communication disabilities (Vikas Sheel, Additional Secretary and Mission Director, National Health Mission (NHM)). Most of them struggle significantly on a daily basis. In order to aid the daily activities of individuals with impairments, new types of technologies and equipment are being developed. Thanks to specialized technological solutions like smart systems or driving help gadgets, many of these people can operate automobiles on their own. However, a button console, like that of a power window, multimedia system, is inoperable to a disabled person (due to difficulty to access or due to disability). In this situation, NUI can show its value and usefulness here. In the next section, relevant literature is reviewed in brief.

## 2 Related Works

In an article, Graziano Fronteddu, Simone Porcu, Alessandro Floris, and Luigi Atzori [1] proposed a dataset of 27 dynamic hand gesture types obtained at the full HD resolution from 21 various subjects. The participants were carefully advised prior to actually performing the gestures and watched whereas performing the gesture; if the performed hand gesture seemed to be incorrect, the subjects were required to repeat the movement. Since the proposed dataset contains high-quality recordings of participants correctly performing 27 various hand gestures, it encourages researchers to develop accurate gesture recognition system systems. This proposed dataset is quite useful for training & testing purpose for multi gesture recognition system and have characteristics which are not present in publically available datasets.

Indian sign language (ISL) hand gestures are both static and dynamic in the time domain, claims Dushyant Kumar Singh [2]. Although there is an established standard for Indian sign language, few people actually use it. In this study, the author modelled the most widely used gestures in the Indian society using a convolutional-based convolution neural network. The author trained his model, which was produced by imitating the motions of those gestures, using 20 gestures from the conventional Indian sign language. The trained model is able to produce output in normal language that corresponds to ISL signs. Hence, the challenges associated with conversing with dumb and deaf persons will be lessened by this. These dynamic motions can also be applied in a variety of different disciplines, including the clinical and industrial ones.

In their research, Yassine Rabhi, Makrem Mrabet, and Farhat Fnaiech [3] proposed a human machine interface (HMI) that offers a useful hands-free option. The wheelchair may be controlled by the user by altering its face expressions. Based on the use of machine learning and particular picture preparation techniques, this clever solution. The Viola-Jones combo is first used to identify the face in a video. After that, the expressions seen on the face are categorized using a neural network. The "The Mathematics Behind Emotion" approach can recognize a variety of facial emotions in real - time basis, such as smile and raised eyebrows, and then convert them into inputs for wheelchair operation. Authors also suggested that system can be easily mounted on wheelchair by using microcontrollers like raspberry pi and compatible camera.

To address the issue of a poor rate of gesture image identification, Fei Wang, Ronglin Hu, and Ying Jin [4] suggested a transfer learning-based image recognition system titled Mobilenet-RF. To further enhance the precision of image recognition, they mix Random Forest and the two MobileNet convolutional network models. This process applies the MobileNet model architecture and weight files to gesture photographs first, trains the model, extracts image features, classifies the features obtained by the convolutional network using the Random Forest model, and then yields classification results. When compared to Random Forest, Logistic Regression, K-Nearest Neighbor, and other approaches, the results of the testing are significantly improved.

The project's methodology was determined as a result of this literature review. The methodology for the project is explained in detail in the following section.

## 3 Proposed Method

We demonstrated how to incorporate real-time hand gesture recognition into advanced technology such as Computer Vision in the following technique. This project was created to identify two sets of gestures displayed. The open source computer vision Library, developed by Intel, was used to implement this strategy. For machine learning tasks and ensuring consistency in large matrix processing tasks, Keras and numpy libraries were used. The input is a live webcam to recognize and predict gestures.

The experiment was carried out in specific and flourishing lighting conditions. Before developing datasets from the captured frames, each frame is pre-processed under specific conditions.

The proposed methodology can be divided into several sections: image acquisition, dataset preparation, CNN model development, and arduino interfacing. The following block diagram depicts all of the steps taken in the proposed system. In the next section detailed methodology is explained step by step (see, Fig. 1).

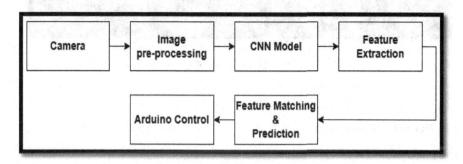

**Fig. 1.** Flow chart of system

# 4  Methodology

## 4.1  Image Acquisition

The first step was to capture the camera frame and identify the region of interest in the image. The challenge is to use an appropriate computer vision method capable of detecting even the smallest difference between similar signals in order to prevent inaccurate translation in real time. In open-cv, there are over 150 color-space conversion methods. However, thresholding and BGR to Gray, are mainly used here. In this paper, we convert the colored RGB format to BGR and then BGR to GRAY because it is more convenient to extract the gesture and easier to process than others.

To capture and store images, a python program was created. The Code was successfully updated for easy data collection, and the in-built python OS module was used to create appropriate folders to store captured images. Images were captured at the rate of 30 fps using laptop in built camera (0.3 megapixel). Following figure shows (see, Fig. 2.) the layout of python program.

```
13        os.makedirs("data/test/increase")
14     ⊖  os.makedirs("data/test/decrease")
15
16     # train or test data
17
18     mode = input("type 'test' for TEST DATA :-\ntype 'train' for TRAIN DATA :- ")
19     directory = 'data/' + mode + '/'
20
21     cap = cv2.VideoCapture(0)
22
23     ⊝while True:
24         _, frame = cap.read()
25         # mirror image
26         frame = cv2.flip(frame, 1)
27
28         # count of existing images
29     ⊖   count = {'increase': len(os.listdir(directory + "/increase")),
30                  'decrease': len(os.listdir(directory + "/decrease"))
31     ⊖        }
32
33         # Printing the count in each set to the screen
34         cv2.putText(frame, "MODE : " + mode, (10, 50), cv2.FONT_HERSHEY_PLAIN, 1, (0, 255, 255), 1)
35         cv2.putText(frame, "IMAGE COUNT", (10, 100), cv2.FONT_HERSHEY_PLAIN, 1, (0, 255, 255), 1)
36         cv2.putText(frame, "increase : " + str(count['increase']), (10, 120), cv2.FONT_HERSHEY_PLAIN, 1, (0, 255, 255), 1)
37         cv2.putText(frame, "decrease : " + str(count['decrease']), (10, 140), cv2.FONT_HERSHEY_PLAIN, 1, (0, 255, 255), 1)
38         cv2.putText(frame, "press 'c' to change mode", (10, 160), cv2.FONT_HERSHEY_PLAIN, 1, (0, 255, 255), 1)
39
40         # Coordinates of the ROI
41         x1 = int(0.5 * frame.shape[1])
42         y1 = 10
```

**Fig. 2.** Python program for data acquisition

## 4.2  Dataset Preparation

The proposed methodology also includes segmentation. In the simplified application, the process displays a binary object that describes the segmentation. Background pixels are black, while foreground pixels are white. In simple implementations, the intensity threshold is the only parameter that determines segmentation.

The main three datasets were created by taking into account conditions such as varying the threshold, using a full-scale colour image, recording various gestures, and employing an image contouring method (convex hull). In addition, an online dataset from kaggle.com was used for training. All four datasets in this project contain 2000 images each for the two gestures increase and decrease. Increase to raise the window and decrease to lower it (Fig. 3).

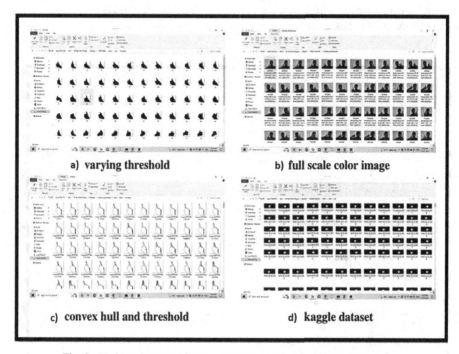

a) varying threshold        b) full scale color image

c) convex hull and threshold        d) kaggle dataset

**Fig. 3.** Various datasets of gestures processed using different techniques

In the next section CNN model development process used in this work is described in brief.

### 4.3 CNN Model Development

CNN was chosen for its weight sharing feature, which reduces the number of trainable network parameters, allowing the network to improve generalization and avoid over fitting. It is also capable of handling spatial data (images) and detecting distinct features from images without any actual human intervention.

A model was developed using jupyter lab. All programming was done using python and various python modules were used such as keras models, keras preprocessing, open-cv, numpy.

The CNN network architecture has layout as enumerated below:

a) First convolutional layer with filter size = 32, kernel (3, 3), and activation function relu is used with maxpool size (2, 2).

b) Second convolutional layer with filter size = 64, kernel (3, 3), and activation function relu is used with maxpool size (2, 2).
c) Third convolutional layer with filter size = 64, kernel (3, 3), and activation function relu is used with maxpool size (2, 2).
d) Then flatten function to 1-D array.
e) Input neuron layer with 128 neurons activation function relu is used.
f) Then dropout layer with 50% dropping rate.
g) Output neuron layer with 1 neurons activation function sigmoid is used.
h) Loss functions is binary crossentropy and adam compiler is used.

```
[5]:  from keras.models import Sequential

[6]:  from keras.layers import Activation, Dropout, Flatten, Conv2D, MaxPooling2D, Dense

[7]:  model = Sequential()

      model.add(Conv2D(filters=32,kernel_size=(3,3),input_shape=input_shape,activation='relu'))
      model.add(MaxPooling2D(pool_size=(2,2)))

      model.add(Conv2D(filters=64,kernel_size=(3,3),input_shape=input_shape,activation='relu'))
      model.add(MaxPooling2D(pool_size=(2,2)))

      model.add(Conv2D(filters=64,kernel_size=(3,3),input_shape=input_shape,activation='relu'))
      model.add(MaxPooling2D(pool_size=(2,2)))

      model.add(Flatten())

      model.add(Dense(128))
      model.add(Activation('relu'))

      model.add(Dropout(0.5))

      model.add(Dense(1))
      model.add(Activation('sigmoid'))

      model.compile(loss='binary_crossentropy',
                    optimizer='adam',
                    metrics=['accuracy'])

[8]:  model.summary()
```

**Fig. 4.** CNN model programming

Every dataset was trained for 100 epochs, and the resulting trained models were saved. Total 4 models were prepared and their performance were compared with each other. The same data collection program was used for prediction purposes, but with modifications based on the respective data collection method used to prepare that dataset. 80% of dataset used for training purpose and 20% is used for testing and respective accuracy of model were evaluated (Fig. 4).

## 4.4 Python Arduino Interfacing

The master-slave concept was used for python-arduino interfacing. After gesture recognition, this command is sent to the computer, where it is processed by the Arduino microcontroller and the appropriate action is taken. To communicate between Python and Arduino, the Pyfirmata library was used.

Power window mechanism and body control module were studied to create a demo of the power window circuit. Then an arduino circuit was created with a 12v DC motor and an L293D motor control module was used to control the motor (Fig. 5).

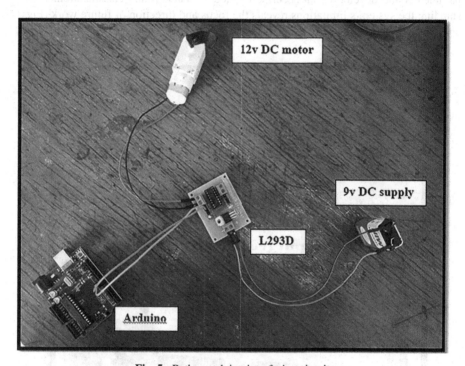

**Fig. 5.** Python arduino interfacing circuit

### 4.5 Testing and Validating

The project setup was tested with various people and in various locations such as the home, classroom, in-cabin, car-cabin, and so on. For the various models that were trained using the various datasets mentioned above.

Convex hull and threshold dataset model works well in all environments, whereas online dataset model performed poorly in all models. All other models performed well at home and in the car, but not well in classrooms due to increased noise in the input image (too many people around). In the next section results obtained by trained models are discussed.

## 5 Result and Discussion

The recognized hand gesture system was tested using hand pictures under various conditions. The methodology describes the overall system's performance using various methods. The limitations of existing systems are overcome by fine-tuning the CNN model parameters and developing an accurate method for background classification. Understanding the system's limitations reveals the focus and direction of future work (Fig. 6 and Table 1).

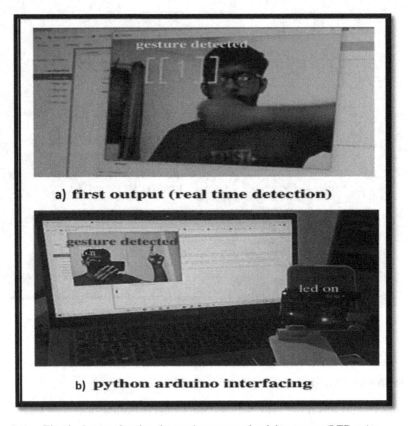

**Fig. 6.** Output showing detected gesture and arduino output (LED on)

The CNN model with convex hull and threshold dataset performs better than other models because it employs better image separation techniques. This model recognize and execute window control in less than second. However, when we start the system, we must wait at least 4–5 s for the model to calibrate the running average.

This lag can be reduced by decreasing the frame average size (currently 30 frames average is used for convex hull & threshold model), but it will have a significant impact on the system's accuracy.

**Table 1.** Results showing models, datasets and their % accuracy

| SR No. | Model (Dataset) | Accuracy (%) |
| --- | --- | --- |
| 1 | Varying threshold | 94 |
| 2 | Full scale colour image | 83 |
| 3 | Convex hull and threshold | 96 |
| 4 | Kaggle.com | 34 |

## 6  Conclusions and Future Scope

On the basis of the project's results, it is feasible to develop a hand gesture recognition system using python and open-cv by putting the concepts of hand segmentation and hand detection method.

In conclusion, this system has accomplished several project goals, including: Using python and open-cv, develop a comprehensive system for sensing, identifying, and evaluating hand gestures; develop a hand gesture sign that is coherent with the project's name; and compare various models to determine the most effective background separation and gesture recognition methods.

Additional gestures will be incorporated to the system's future recommendations so that users with different skin tones and hand sizes can easily complete more tasks also background subtraction, semantic segmentation algorithms can also be used to improve performance.

This system can be put in more sophisticated microcontrollers like the Raspberry Pi and Jetson Nano with the help of Tensorflow Lite to reduce system size and for efficient working.

## References

1. Fronteddu, G., Porcu, S., Floris, A., Atzori, L.: A dynamic hand gesture recognition dataset for human-computer interfaces. a) DIEE, University of Cagliari, 09123 Cagliari, Italy b) CNIT, University of Cagliari, 09123 Cagliari, Italy
2. 3D-CNN based Dynamic Gesture Recognition for Indian Sign Language Modeling Dushyant Kumar Singh CSED, MNNIT Allahabad, Prayagraj-211003
3. Rabhi, Y., Mrabet, M., Fnaiech, F.: A facial expression controlled wheelchair for people with disabilities. University of Tunis, National Higher School of Engineers of Tunis, Laboratory of Signal Image and Energy Mastery (SIME), 5 Avenue Taha Hussein, P.O. Box 56, Tunis 1008, Tunisia
4. Wang, F., Hu, R., Jin, Y.: Research on gesture image recognition method based on transfer learning. Huaiyin Institute of Technology, Huai'an, China
5. Gopal, N., Bhooshan, R.S.: Content based image retrieval using enhanced SURF. In: 2015 5th National Conference on Computer Vision Pattern Recognition, Image Processing and Graphics, NCVPRIPG 2015 (2016)
6. Mathe, E., Mitsou, A., Spyrou, E., Mylonas, P.: Arm gesture recognition using a convolutional neural network. In: 2018 13th International Workshop on Semantic and Social Media Adaptation and Personalization (SMAP) (2018). https://doi.org/10.1109/smap.2018.8501886

7. Shimada, A., Yamashita, T., Taniguchi, R.-I.: Hand gesture based TV control system—towards both user & machine-friendly gesture applications. In: Proceedings of the 19th Korea-Japan Joint Workshop on Frontiers of Computer Vision (FCV 2013), pp. 121–126, February 2013
8. Keskin, C., Kiraç, F., Kara, Y.E., Akarun, L.: Real time hand pose estimation using depth sensors. In: Proceedings of the IEEE International Conference on Computer Vision Workshops (ICCV 2011), pp. 1228–1234, November 2011
9. Zafrulla, Z., Brashear, H., Starner, T., Hamilton, H., Presti, P.: American sign language recognition with the Kinect. In: Proceedings of the 13th ACM International Conference on Multimodal Interfaces (ICMI 2011), pp. 279–286, November 2011

# Novel Deep Learning Techniques to Design the Model and Predict Facial Expression, Gender, and Age Recognition

N. Sujata Gupta[1]([✉]), Saroja Kumar Rout[1], Viyyapu Lokeshwari Vinya[3], Koti Tejasvi[2], and Bhargavi Rani[3]

[1] Department of Information Technology, Vardhaman College of Engineering (Autonomous), Hyderabad, India
gsuji29@gmail.com
[2] Department of Computer Science and Engineering, Vardhaman College of Engineering (Autonomous), Hyderabad, India
[3] Department of Information Technology, Sarvajanik College of Engineering, Surat, Gujarat, India

**Abstract.** For computer and human interaction, human facial recognition is crucial. Our goal is to anticipate the expression of a human face, gender, and age as quickly and accurately as possible in real-time. Understanding human behavior, detecting mental diseases, and creating synthetic human expressions are only a few of the applications of automatic human facial recognition . Salespeople can employ age, gender, and emotional state prediction to help them better understand their consumers. Convolutional Neural Network one of the Deep Learning techniques is utilized to design the model and predict emotion, age, and gender, using the Haar-Cascade frontal face algorithm to detect the face. This model can predict from video in real-time. The goal is to create a web application that uses a camera to capture a live human face and classify it into one of seven expressions, two ages, and eight age groups. The process of detecting face, pre-processing, feature extraction, and the prediction of expression, gender, and age is carried out in steps.

**Keywords:** Convolution Neural Network · Haar-Cascade Classifier · Facial expression · Emotion

## 1 Introduction

Our ambitions have risen since the arrival of modern technology, and they have no limitations. In today's world, there is a wide range of research going on in the field of digital imaging and processing image. The rate of progress has been exponential, and it continues to rise. The facial expression of a person shows the person's mood, state of mind, thinking, and psychopathology, which serves as a communication role in interpersonal connections. The seven major emotions that may be easily classified in human facial expressions are anger, disgust, fear, happiness, neutral, sadness, and surprise [1]. The

S. Nandan Mohanty et al. (Eds.): ICISML 2022, LNICST 471, pp. 345–354, 2023.
https://doi.org/10.1007/978-3-031-35081-8_29

activation of several sets of facial muscles expresses our facial emotions. These seemingly minor, but complex, signals in our expressions often convey a great deal about our mental state. Age and gender classification can be used in many areas in biometrics, security, video surveillance, communication between humans and computers, and in forensic.

The goal of this project is to develop an Automatic Facial Expression, age, and gender Recognition System through a web application that can recognize and categorize human facial photographs with a variety of expressions into seven different expression classes, 2 classes of gender (Male and Female) and 8 classes of ages i.e. (0–2), (4–6), (8–13), (15–20), (25–32), (38–43), (48–53), 60+ [2].

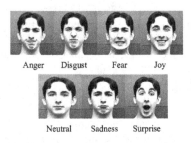

Fig. 1. Seven basic facial expressions.

## 1.1  Problem Definition

Face expressions communicate human emotions and intents, and developing an efficient and effective feature is an important part of the facial expression system. Nonverbal indicators are vital in interpersonal relationships, and facial expressions communicate them. In human and computer interaction, automatic facial expression detection can be a beneficial feature. An autonomous Facial Expression Recognition system must overcome challenges such as face identification and placement in a chaotic scenario, feature extraction from the face, and facial emotion classification.

Convolution neural networks are used in this study to construct a facial expression recognition system. Anger, Disgust, Fear, Happy, Sad, Surprise, and 'Neutral' are the seven facial emotion categories that are used to classify facial photographs. The classifier is trained and tested using the Kaggle data set [1]. The expected gender is either "male" or "female," and the expected age is either (0–2), (4–6), (8–12), (15–20), (25–32), (38–43), (48–53), or (60–100). In the final softmax activation function, there are eight nodes for age and two for gender. When we consider various features like lighting, makeup, and facial expressions, determining the precise age of a person instead of ranging it would be difficult. So, we have used a classification task instead of a regression task.

### 1.1.1  Objective

The project's goal is to create a web application that uses a camera to capture a live human face and classify it into one of seven expressions, two ages, and eight age groups. We used the FER2013 dataset [3] for facial expressions and the Audience benchmark age and gender dataset [4] for age and gender recognition to build CNN for facial expressions, age, and gender classification.

### 1.1.2 Limitations

The facial expression recognition system in this research accurately recognizes all of the expressions except disgust because the data set contains extremely few photos of that label and their training in that label is limited. It's exceedingly difficult to determine a precise age from a single photo due to factors like makeup, lighting, impediments, and facial expressions. According to our observations, the accuracy of detecting age and gender can be improved by increasing the random brightness and fluctuations in RGB. Each photo contains two labels in both training and test data: gender and age. Some of the images of the audience data collection, lack gender or age descriptors.

The rest of the paper is furnished into 3 sections. Section 2 represents the related research and the techniques used by the authors. The methodology of the proposed system is described in Sect. 3. Simulation and results have been depicted in Sect. 4. Section 5 Describes the conclusion and future direction of the research work.

## 2 Literature Review

This research paper proposed an approach to recognizing expressions from faces using binary patterns and cognition. They observed that the eyes and mouth are the main parts to classify an expression. The procedure begins by extracting facial contours using the LBP operator. They used a 3D model to divide the face into six sub-regions. They used the mapped LBP approach to recognize the expression from the sub-parts they divided. They have used a support-vector machine and a softmax activation function for two types of models. Finally, they compared the facial expression dataset Cohn-Kanade (CK +) with the test dataset in which they considered ten members. They observed that their model will remove the image's problematic elements. The expression model outperforms the traditional emotional model by a wide margin [5].

This project is to determine expression by building an artificial neural network based on a different culture. Variations in the appearance of the face, the structure of the face, and facial emotion representation due to cultural differences are the main problems with the facial emotion detection system. Because of these differences, multicultural face expression analysis is required. Several computational strategies are presented in this paper to address these changes and achieve excellent expression recognition accuracy [6].

For intercultural facial expression analysis, they presented an artificial neural network-based ensemble classifier. By merging facial images from the Japanese female facial expression database, the Taiwanese facial expression image database, and the Radboud faces database, a multi-culture facial expression dataset is constructed. Members of the multicultural dataset are Japanese, Taiwanese, Caucasians, and Moroccans, who represent four ethnic groupings. Local binary patterns, uniform local binary patterns, and principal component analysis are utilized to express facial features Figs. 1, 2, 3.

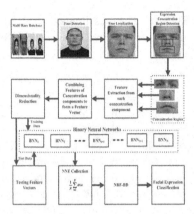

**Fig. 2.** Framework for Multi-Culture Facial Expression Recognition

They have developed a model that recognizes the voice and classifies it into age and gender. Many factors affect the process of automatic speech recognition like the speaker's weight, height, and speech based on a person's mood. There is also a requirement for a very large database that consists of a large number of speakers of different ages and genders. Since there will also be a problem of noise when trying to record the audio of the speaker, high-quality microphones and filters are also required. The result varies when different speakers are used to record the same statement from the same speaker.

Automatic gender and age recognition can be done in a variety of ways. Cepstral characteristics, such as Mel Frequency Cepstral Coefficients, are an example (MFCC). For age recognition. With recorded data, MFCC is known for delivering poor gender and age categorization results. To avoid this issue, the MFCC features are improved by examining the parameters that influence the feature extraction process. MFCC has been employed in a variety of speech applications, including voice recognition and language recognition, and another acoustic characteristic that can be derived is format frequency [7].

This project is to detect the emotions of body movements. They have used these body movement characteristics and developed a two-feature selection framework. They have considered only five basic features namely anger, happiness, sadness, fear, and neutrality. The first layer is the combination of Multivariate Analysis of Variance (MANOVA) and analysis of Variance (ANOVA) to remove unnecessary features for emotion detection. In the second layer, they used a binary chromosome-based genetic algorithm to pick the relevant features that improve in giving the correct label of emotion. Some of the movements they have considered are walking, sitting, and action-independent instances.

Based on experiments of various body movements, this model is outperformed in terms of emotion recognition rate. The accuracy of the action walking is 90%, 96% for sitting, and for other action-independent scenarios, the accuracy is 86.66 [8].

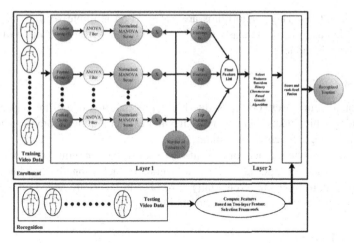

**Fig. 3.** Proposed method for emotion recognition from body movements.

# 3  Methodology

## 3.1  Convolutional Neural Network

A Deep Learning method called Convolutional Neural Network (CNN) takes the image as input. This method allocates the weights to objects of the image, which helps to distinguish one object from the other [9–11]. When compared to other approaches, pre-processing for this approach is less. After the training, the model extracts the features from the images by applying the filters and uses those features for its learning.

Convolution architecture has one input layer, one or more hidden layers, and one output layer. For each layer, there would be CONV, applying activation functions like RELU, and Softmax, applying to pools like max pooling, and mean pooling. There might or might not be parameters for each layer. Each layer takes the input from the previous layer's output. Each layer performs a differential function to give the output to the next layer [12].

## 3.2  Haar Cascade Classifier

Now, Facial recognition is present in every place namely security cameras, and sensors on iPhone X. There are many different human faces and there are many differences between humans to humans and many also similarities. How does facial recognition work to classify all faces?

Haar Cascade classifiers are the classifiers that detect the face of humans in real-time and can differentiate between humans and non-humans. Haar classifier is a machine learning algorithm that accepts input as an image or video and recognizes objects. Haar Cascade's model got trained on many positive images that consist of objects that the classifier wants to identify and also negative images that consist of objects that the classifiers don't want to recognize. Haar features are used to find how a given point is part of an object. To get a strong prediction, a group of weak learners is used with boosting algorithms. These algorithms are executed on multiple sections of an input image or video using cascade classifiers [13, 14]. Open CV can be used to implement the Haar Cascade model [15].

### 3.3 Model

Convolutional Neural Network is used to build a model. It is one of the approaches in Deep learning which takes input as an image and extract features from it. When CNN processes the image, it acts as the human brain.

A convolutional neural network architecture consists of an input layer, one or more hidden layers, and an output layer. All the layers are stacked one by one linearly. The architecture is built by using sequential() in Keras and layers are added one by one by including filters, activation function, and pooling.

### 3.3.1 Input Layer

The images that come to the input layer must be of fixed size. So, pre-processing of images must be done before the images are fed into the input layer. The image's geometry must be fixed to the constant size. A computer vision package OpenCV is used to detect the face from the image. Haar cascade frontal face algorithm already has pre-trained filters of the face and employs AdaBoost to locate and get the face quickly from the image.

### 3.3.2 Convolutional Layers

In each convolution layer, a NumPy array is taken as input which includes parameters like kernel size, and several filters. In total, we have used 4 convolutional layers for expression classification and 3 convolutional layers for forage and gender classification. Convolution produces feature maps that show how pixel values are improved. **Pooling** is one of the convolutional neural network techniques that is used to reduce the dimension. This technique is used so that only the features that mainly affect the label for the classification. Using more and more convolutional layers increases processing time, this layer helps in reducing it. We have used the max-pooling layer of dimension (2,2) and reduced the image size by two.

### 3.3.3 Dense Layers

Dense layers take a huge number of characteristics from input and use them to get the trainable weights and layers. Forward propagation is used to train those weights, and then back-propagation to resolve errors. Parameters like learning rate, batch size, etc. can be used to improve the training pace. Dropout is a way that helps to avoid over-fitting the model that we build. It randomly picks some subset of nodes and assigns weights as zero to them.

### 3.3.4 Output Layer

In the output layer, instead of using the sigmoid activation function which is used for two classes as labels, we have used the softmax activation function which is used when

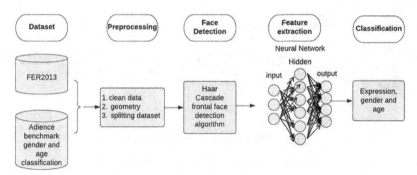

**Fig. 4.** Architecture

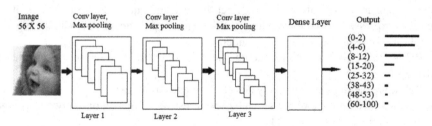

**Fig. 5.** Working model of the expression

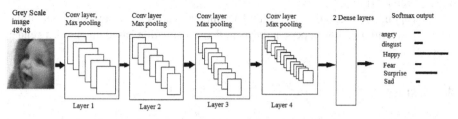

**Fig. 6.** Working model of the age

there are more than two classes as labels. After softmax activation is applied, the model gives the probability for each class Fig. 5. As a result, the model can show the probability of each class is the label for the given input. Finally, the label which gives the highest probability is taken and displayed to the user.

### 3.4 Applications

A web program that detects a person's expression, gender, and age can be utilized on a shopping website to gather product reviews from people of a specific age and gender. So that likely products of a certain age and gender can be separated (Fig. 4).

This software application may be used to store a person's age, gender, and expression in a single database, which can then be utilized for a variety of applications.

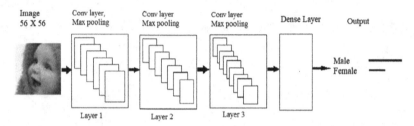

**Fig. 7.** Working model of the gender

Facial expression, gender, and age recognition are also useful in determining which course a person should take depending on his or her mental state, as well as his or her age and gender (Fig. 6).

This application can also be used to determine human behavior in a given situation. It aids in determining how a person reacts to a given situation based on age and gender (Fig. 7).

## 4 Results

Our model downsizes the training and testing images into 48 × 48 for expression and 56 × 56 for age and gender and then processes. The model uses 4 convolutional layers and uses a haar cascade algorithm to detect the face and output the probabilities of all the seven expressions, two for gender and 8 for age and pick up the one with the highest probability for expression, age, and gender.

Below are the given graphs for accuracy and loss of the training dataset and validation dataset.

Below are the steps used to lively detect the image through a web camera and classify the detected face into one of the seven basic expressions [16], one of the two ages, and one of the eight groups of ages [17].

- Download the haar cascade frontal face default.xml and use the location where that is downloaded and store it in a variable (face classifier).
- Use the location where the .h5 file was created after running the model and stored in the variable (classifier).

3.Use the OpenCV method VideoCapture(0) by cv2.VideoCapture, 0 is to capture from the web camera of your currently working PC.
4. Draw a rectangle over the face
5. Get the label based on the emotion which gives the highest probability.
6. Put the text on the rectangle drawn

We have used flask and designed a website whose root page shows the button to capture the face, clicking on it will navigate to another route that on the web camera and lively detects the human face and gives the label for expression, gender, and age Figs. 8 and 9.

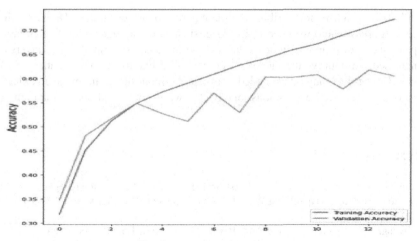

**Fig. 8.** Accuracy of the model

**Fig. 9.** Output of expression, age, and gender

## 5  Conclusion and Futurework

When a model incorrectly predicts an emotion, gender, or age, the right label is often the second closest emotion. The qualities of the human face are related to geometrical structures that are rebuilt as the recognition system's basic matching template, which are significant to varied expressions. In this experiment, we achieved an accuracy of around 70%, which is not terrible when compared to earlier models. However, there are several areas where we need to improve, such as the arrangement of thick layers, the percentage of dropouts in dense layers, and the count of convolutional layers can be increased. To improve the model's accuracy, we'd like to add new databases to the system. This project may be expanded to accept the input file as an image and classify it into one of the seven expressions, one of the two genders, and one of the eight age groups.

# References

1. Jung, H.: January. Development of deep learning-based facial expression recognition system. In: 2015 21st Korea-Japan Joint Workshop on Frontiers of Computer Vision (FCV), pp. 1–4. IEEE (2015)
2. Kwong, J.C.T., Garcia, F.C.C., Abu, P.A.R., Reyes, R.S.: Emotion recognition via facial expression: utilization of numerous feature descriptors in different machine learning algorithms. In: TENCON 2018–2018 IEEE Region 10 Conference, pp. 2045–2049. IEEE (2018)
3. Sambar, M.: FER-2013Dataset. IEEE Access 8 (2020)
4. Kumar, S., Singh, S., Kumar, J., Prasad, K.M.V.V.: Age and gender classification using Seg-Net based architecture and machine learning. Multimed. Tools Appl. **81**, 4228542308 (2022). https://doi.org/10.1007/s11042-021-11499-3
5. Qi, C., et al.: Facial expressions recognition based on cognition and mapped binary patterns. IEEE Access **6**, 18795–18803 (2018)
6. Ali, G., et al.: Artificial neural network based ensemble approach for multicultural facial expressions analysis. IEEE Access **8**, 134950–134963 (2020)
7. Zhao, H., Wang, P.: A short review of age and gender recognition based on speech. In: 2019 IEEE 5th International Conference on Big Data Security on Cloud (BigDataSecurity), IEEE International Conference on High Performance and Smart Computing, (HPSC) and IEEE International Conference on Intelligent Data and Security (IDS), pp. 183–185. IEEE (2019)
8. Ahmed, F., Bari, A.H., Gavrilova, M.L.: Emotion recognition from body movement. IEEE Access **8**, 11761–11781 (2019)
9. Gu, J., et al.: Recent advances in convolutional neural networks. Pattern Recogn. **77**, 354–377 (2018)
10. Albawi, S., Mohammed, T.A., Al-Zawi, S.: Understanding of a convolutional neural network. In: 2017 international conference on engineering and technology (ICET), pp. 1–6. IEEE (2017)
11. Tian, Y.: Artificial intelligence image recognition method based on convolutional neural network algorithm. IEEE Access **8**, 125731–125744 (2020)
12. Howse, J., Joshi, P., Beyeler, M.: OpenCV: Computer Vision Projects with Python. Packt Publishing Ltd. (2016)
13. Shilkrot, R., Escrivá, D.M.: Mastering OpenCV 4: a comprehensive guide to building computer vision and image processing applications with C++. Packt Publishing Ltd. (2018)
14. Hung, J., et al.: Keras R-CNN: library for cell detection in biological images using deep neural networks. BMC Bioinformat. **21**(1), 1–7 (2020)
15. Levi, G., Hassner, T.: Age and gender classification using convolutional neural networks. In: Proceedings of the IEEE Conference on Computer Vision and Pattern Recognition Workshops, pp. 34–42 (2015)

# A Comprehensive Review on Various Data Science Technologies Used for Enhancing the Quality of Education Systems

Olfat M. Mirza[(✉)]

Department of Computer Science, College of Computers and Information Systems,
Umm Al-Qura University, Makkah, Saudi Arabia
ommirza@uqu.edu.sa

**Abstract.** Education is one of the major sources for determining the growth of country with high economic development. But the challenges facing by the education systems are poor decision-making ability, high difficulties in adapting new curriculums, inefficient teaching, and training. These factors could inherently affect the performance of education sectors in terms of increased unemployment, reduced workforce, and dissatisfaction outcomes. In order to solve these problems, this research work aims to deploy the data science technologies for improving the learning strategies in education systems. Here, the data mining techniques are mainly used to extract the relevant or useful information from the data and is widely used for solving the higher education problems. Also, this work investigates some of the challenges associated to the deployment of big data in education systems, which includes consequentialism, scientism, privacy, and security. Moreover, operating characteristics and features of the cyber security model are assessed and validated in Sect. 5. Finally, the overall paper is summarized with its obtainment and future work.

**Keywords:** Data Science Technologies · Education System · Data Mining · Data Warehouse · Big Data · Business Intelligence · Academic Skills

## 1 Introduction

In the present days, education [1] is considered as one of the key element used for improving the progression rate of country with the profitable financial and social incomes. But, the poor decision making [2, 3] could degrade the performance and efficiency of the entire system with reduced accuracy levels. Hence, it is more essential to implement the data science technologies for enhancing the overall growth and efficiency of higher education systems. For this purpose, there are various data science methods have been used in the conventional works, which supports to accomplish an efficient decision making by providing the suitable solutions for the given problems. Moreover, the deployment of data science technologies such as data mining, data warehouse, business intelligence, and big data are extensively used in many application systems [4, 5]. But, the use of

© ICST Institute for Computer Sciences, Social Informatics and Telecommunications Engineering 2023
Published by Springer Nature Switzerland AG 2023. All Rights Reserved
S. Nandan Mohanty et al. (Eds.): ICISML 2022, LNICST 471, pp. 355–366, 2023.
https://doi.org/10.1007/978-3-031-35081-8_30

these techniques in an education system could increase the accuracy of decision making with simple decisions for solving the complex problems. The sample data science technologies [6–8] used for enhancing the higher education sector is illustrated in Fig. 1.

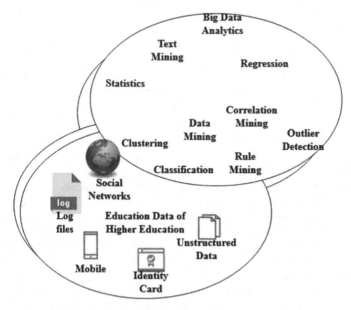

**Fig. 1.** Data science technologies used in higher education system.

The key objectives behind this research work are as follows:

- To investigate the working operations and features of various data science technologies used in an education system.
- To study how the data science methodologies could support improving the learning strategy of education sectors.
- To analyze the efficiency and benefits of using data science methodologies such as data mining, data warehouse, business intelligence, and big data.

The rest of sections structuralized in this paper are as follows: Sect. 2 discusses about the conventional works developed with the data science technologies for education systems. Section 3 presents the clear description of each data science methodology used for improving the learning strategy of higher education institutions. Then, Sect. 4 presents the results and discussion of the existing methodologies used in an education system. Finally, the overall paper is concluded with its obtainment and future scope in Sect. 5.

## 2 Related Works

This section some of the existing works related to the deployment of data science technologies used in an education system. Also, it discusses about the purpose of various methodologies helps to improve the learning and monitoring skills.

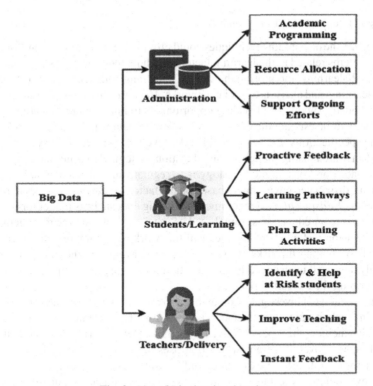

**Fig. 2.** Use of Big data in education.

*Daniel* [9] presented a clear review on big data methodologies used for improving the education system, and this work intends to create the awareness on various problems facing by the educational researchers. Also, the reconceptualization based big data model has been discussed for enhancing both the quality of instructions and research. Moreover, the big data could be more useful for improving the educational system, which is graphically represented in Fig. 2.

Moreover, the different types of issues related to the deployment of big data for education research are as follows: technical, ontology, conception, epistemology, digital divide, methods, data analysis, ethics and privacy. *Chweya, et al.* [10] discussed about the benefits of using big data and IoT in education system for boosting the smart training with quality materials. Typically, the IoT and big data are considered as the developing technologies and plays a vital role in education system. Here, the highlights related to the linking of these two technologies were presented, which helps to improve the training strategies of both learning and teaching. *Aldowah, et al.* [11] conducted a detailed review on Educational Data Mining (EDM) and Learning Analytics (LA) model for improving the quality of higher education system by the following ways:

1. Computer supported behavior analysis
2. Computer supported predictive analysis
3. Computer supported visualization analysis

4. Computer supported learning analysis

Moreover, the data mining techniques could provide the suitable solutions for solving certain problems related to the learning factor, which includes the types of collaborative learning, self-learning, monitoring the student's learning ability, evaluation of materials used for learning, and analysis of social networks. *Moscoso-Zea, et al.* [12] suggested the data warehousing model for providing opportunities to improve the education systems. Also, it aims to investigate the effectiveness of using data warehousing model according to the specifications. *Bhanti, et al.* [13] deployed an e-governance system with the help of data warehousing model for an education system. Here, the main intention of using the data warehousing methodology is to regulate and control the authorities and students in a distributed environment based on the factors of efficiency, accessibility, and transparency. *Tulasi, et al.* [14] recommended the big data analysis model for enhancing the students' higher education system based on the factors of resource management and efficient decision making. The key factor of this work was to improve the success rate of students by finding the risks at the earlier stages. Moreover, the innovative models are mainly deployed in an educational institution for solving the complex issues as well as transforming the education policies.

*Ahmad, et al.* [15] investigated about the performance of various classification based data mining techniques used for accurately predicting the academic performance of students, which includes the types of Naïve Bayes (NB), Decision Tree (DT), and rule based approaches. Moreover, this framework comprises the stages of data gathering, integration, transformation, pattern extraction, and classification. This work mainly concentrates on extracting the most useful patterns by using the education data mining models, where the hidden information is also extracted from the educational dataset. *Sin and Muthu* [16] utilized the concept of learning management system with big data technologies for monitoring the students' online activities. Typically, there are different types of techniques have been used in the present days for improving the educational systems, which includes the regression models, nearest neighbour, clustering, and other learning-based classification techniques. In addition to that, this work objects to perform the skill estimation and behaviour detection processes by using the predictive learning models. *Hasan, et al.* [17] suggested the business intelligence models for education systems, which covers the broad factors of technology, organization, and social. Here, some intelligent solutions have been provided for obtaining growth in educational system.

From the survey, it is identified that the existing works could highly utilized the big data and dimensionality techniques for enhancing the performance of education systems.

## 3   Data Science Methodologies

Gndgb This section investigates some of the recent data science techniques used for improving the efficiency of education system, which includes the technologies of data mining models, big data models, business intelligence and data warehousing techniques. The detailed description of these methodologies is presented in the following subsections:

## 3.1    Data Mining Techniques used in Education System

Data mining is one of the most suitable methodology used for improving academic intervention system. Generally, the data mining techniques are highly depending on the processes of clustering, classification, valuation, and conception. The data mining techniques are mainly used to extract the relevant or useful information from the data and is widely used for solving the higher education problems. *Bhise, et al.* [18] suggested the educational data mining technology for improving the better understanding of students. Here, the main purpose of using this technology is to extract the useful information from the education dataset for analysing the behaviours and trends of students related to education. *Kumar, et al.* [19] intended to predict the performance of students by using an educational data mining techniques. The key factor of this paper is to accurately predict the progress rate of students and to improve their performance in academics with the help of data mining models. Here, the different types of data mining techniques used for predicting the performance of students are listed in below:

1. Decision Tree (DT).
2. Artificial Neural Network (ANN).
3. Random Forest (RF).
4. Support Vector Machine (SVM).
5. Naïve Bayes (NB).
6. Linear regression.
7. K-Nearest Neighbor (KNN).
8. Random tree.

Also, various attributes that affect the performance of prediction accuracy are investigated in this work, which includes internal attributes, external attributes, family income, gender, GPA, SPM grades, academic information, and internal assessment Fig. 3.

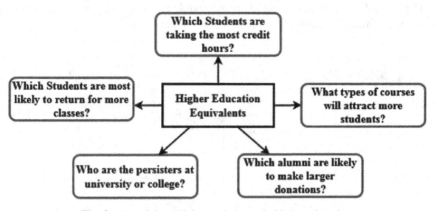

**Fig. 3.**  Use of data mining techniques in higher education.

## 3.2  Big Data Models

Big data is one of the popular data science technology used in different types of applications such as organizational sectors, educational environment, healthcare systems, and transportations for efficiently processing the large number of data. The key dimensionalities of big data are variety, velocity, volume, complexity and veracity. In paper [20], the big data model has been utilized for enhancing the process of education, where the university education environment is taken for analysis. *Manohar, et al.* [21] utilized the big data analytics technique for predicting the performance of students based on the probability measure. Here, the big data methodology is mainly used to assess the success factor of students with respect to the parameters of past performance, subject choice, demographic, and credit scores. Moreover, it helps to provide the solutions for the problems of data fog state, data cleaning, refining, and lack of data governance. *Johnson, et al.* [22] suggested the big data technique for improving the education strategy of higher institutions by enhancing the better understanding of students. Also, it investigates some of the challenges associated to the deployment of big data in education systems, which includes consequentialism, scientism, privacy, and security. *Li, et al.* [23] presented an adaptive big data based learning methodology for supporting students to cultivate their learning abilities. This framework comprises the modules of prediction, display, adaptive, intervention, content delivery, and learning module. Here, it is stated that the big data is a kind of advanced learning paradigm used for improving the standard of education by capturing the learners' activities. The major benefits of using the big data technology in education systems are as follows:

- It helps to acquire an efficient data learning and storage.
- It enables the diversification of test types.
- It increases the visualization of knowledge growth.
- It permits timely supervision and personalization.

The typical flow of using big data methodology in an educational system for improving the learning capabilities of students is illustrated in Fig. 4.

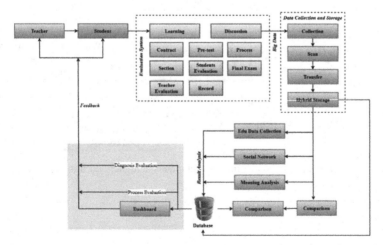

**Fig. 4.**  Flow of analysis using big data technology.

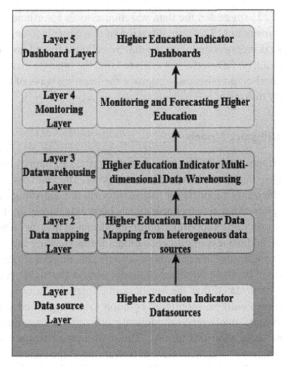

**Fig. 5.** BI model used in higher education system.

## 3.3 Data Warehousing Models

Typically, data warehousing is a kind of information model that is mainly used for making the strategic decisions based on business intelligence. Also, it performs the data operations of extraction, cleaning, transportation, and aligning for providing the complete data support to the end users. *Taylor, et al.* [24] utilized a project based data warehousing model for analysing the criticalities in an education system. The main purpose of this paper is to completely provide the data-driven support for enhancing the decision making process with better understanding [25]. Here, the key benefits of using the data warehousing techniques in an educational system are presented in detail, which includes:

- It enhances the process of critical thinking and deep learning.
- It increases the ability of students to solve real-world problems.
- It supports better understanding and growth of technical skills.
- It establishes teamwork activities among students with intelligent ideas.
- It efficiently increases satisfaction, joyfulness, and motivation.

In paper [26], the big data and data warehousing methodologies have been investigated for enabling an efficient data storage and accessing in an education systems. Also, it discussed about the different processing concepts of big data method for analysing the problematic features, which includes map reduce, no SQL, and new SQL.

*Santoso, et al.* [27] suggested the data warehouse tools for efficiently handling the academic data of universities. The main intention of this paper is to analyse that how the big data framework is incorporated with the data warehouse for enhancing the decision-making process. Based on this study, it is analysed that the big data incorporated with the data warehouse model could efficiently improve the learning ways of education system with better decision making.

### 3.4  Business Intelligence Models

The business intelligence model has been widely applied in many higher educational institutions for improving an academic decision making. The main purpose of using this technology is, it efficiently supports for the monitoring the analysing the recent trends of education indicators. Also, this technology has been extensively applied in the large-scale industries for providing support to intelligent decision making. *Khatibi, et al.* [28] suggested an advanced business intelligence model for monitoring the higher education pointers by incorporating the internal and external data sources. Figure 5 depicts the layered architecture of business intelligence model used in the higher education system. *Guster, et al.* [29] have stated that the business intelligence model is one of the most suitable option for providing an intelligent solution to the higher education system. In paper [30], the business intelligence models are utilized for increasing the technical efficiency of higher education institutions. The main aim of this work is to enhance both the system proficiency and management operations of the education institutions by efficiently trade the funds and resources. Moreover, various key performance indicators are utilized in this analysis for validating the business models used in the education systems, which includes the types of course work, graduation rate, student enrolment, exam assessment, and academic workloads.

## 4  Results and Discussion

This section evaluates the performance rate and efficiency of the data science techniques used in the education systems. Also, it examines the advantages and disadvantages of each technology based on its working operations and key characteristics. Figure 6 compares the performance efficiency of various data science technologies such as Business Intelligence (BI), Big Data, Modern Data Warehouse (DWH), Education Data Mining (EDM), and Data Warehouse (DWH). Based on the analysis, it is observed that the big data technology provides an increased efficiency for improving the learning strategy of higher education systems, which is moderately greater than the other models Table 1.

Table 2 and Fig. 7 shows the accuracy level various data mining techniques such as Decision Tree (DT), Naïve Bayes (NB), Random Forest (RF), K-Nearest Neighbor (KNN), and Neural Network (NN) used in the education systems. From the results, it is identified that the NB and KNN techniques outperform the other techniques with increased accuracy value.

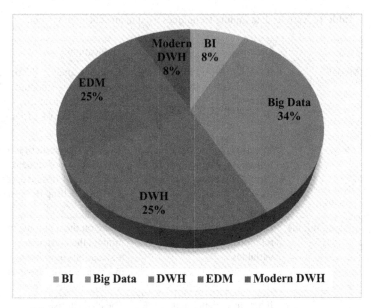

**Fig. 6.** Recent data science technologies support education sector.

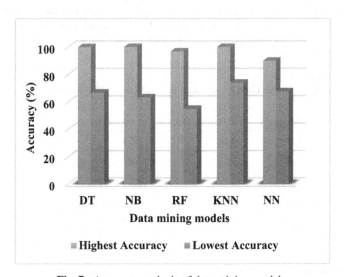

**Fig. 7.** Accuracy analysis of data mining models.

**Table 1.** Various data mining techniques used in an education system.

| Methods | Description | Applications |
| --- | --- | --- |
| Clustering Model | It is mainly used to split the whole data into the group of clusters | It helps to analyse the behaviour of new joining students. Also, it is used to estimate the similarities across various schools |
| Prediction | It is used to predict the value from the combination of data using the predictor variable | By using the prediction model, the behaviour of students can be analysed (For instance, off task activities, betting the system, and skidding) |
| Relationship based mining | It helps to discover the relationship among many variables | Based on the relationship mining, the curricular associations have been discovered with improved learning model |
| Data discovery | It acts as a component used for clustering or classification | The characteristics and behaviour of students have been analysed based on the discovery of data models |
| Data Distillation | The purpose of using data distillation to identify the suitable features of data | It helps to improvise the student learning process |

**Table 2.** Highest and lowest accuracy of various data mining models.

| Methods | Highest Accuracy | Lowest Accuracy |
| --- | --- | --- |
| DT | 99.9 | 66.8 |
| NB | 100 | 63.3 |
| RF | 96.7 | 55 |
| KNN | 100 | 74 |
| NN | 89.8 | 67.6 |

## 5   Conclusion

Due to the increased demand of data science technologies, which have been extensively used in many application systems such as education, transportation, healthcare and other large industries. Normally, there are various techniques have been used for improving the learning strategy of higher education system. Also, it helps to improve the students' learning ability by deploying an advanced model. In which, the data mining techniques are highly depends on the processes of clustering, classification, valuation, and conception. The data mining techniques are mainly used to extract the relevant or useful information from the data, and is widely used for solving the higher education problems. Similar to that, the big data model is also one of the suitable for improving the level of adoption of education system. The main purpose of using this technology is, it efficiently supports for monitoring the analyzing the recent trends of education indicators. Also, this technology has been extensively applied in the large-scale industries for providing support to intelligent decision making. During the performance assessment of these techniques, the efficiency of all data science methodologies is validated and compared. Based on these results, it is evident that the proposed KNN and NB models could offer an increased accuracy, when compared to the other techniques.

# References

1. Alom, B.M., Courtney, M.: Educational data mining: a case study perspectives from primary to university education in australia. Int. J. Inform. Technol. Comput. Sci. **10**(2), 1–9 (2018)
2. Agarwal, R., Dhar, V.: Big data, data science, and analytics: The opportunity and challenge for IS research. 3, INFORMS, 2014, pp. 443–448
3. Pandey, U.K., Bhardwaj, B.K.: Data Mining as a Torch Bearer in Education Sector. arXiv preprint arXiv:1201.5182, 2012
4. Gokalp, M.O., Kayabay, K., Akyol, M.A., Eren, P.E., Koçyiğit, A.: Big data for industry 4.0: A conceptual framework. pp. 431–434
5. Bajpai, N., Biberman, J., Sharma, A.: Information and Communications Technology in the Education Sector in India (2019)
6. Sree, G.S., Rupa, C.: Data mining: performance improvement in education sector using classification and clustering algorithm. Int. J. Innov. Res. Develop. (ISSN 2278–0211), **2**(7), 101–106 (2013)
7. Dwivedi, S., Roshni, V.K.: Recommender system for big data in education, pp. 1–4
8. Drigas, A.S., Leliopoulos, P.: The use of big data in education. Int. J. Comput. Sci. Issues (IJCSI) **11**(5), 58 (2014)
9. Daniel, B.K.: Big Data and data science: a critical review of issues for educational research. Br. J. Edu. Technol. **50**(1), 101–113 (2019)
10. Chweya, R., Ajibade, S.S.M., Buba, A.K. and Samuel, M.: IoT and Big Data Technologies: Opportunities and Challenges for Higher Learning. Int. J. Recent Technol. Eng. (IJRTE) **9**(2), 909 (2020)
11. Aldowah, H., Al-Samarraie, H., Fauzy, W.M.: Educational data mining and learning analytics for 21st century higher education: a review and synthesis. Telematics Inform. **37**, 13–49 (2019)
12. Moscoso-Zea, O., Paredes-Gualtor, J., Luján-Mora, S.: A holistic view of data warehousing in education. IEEE access **6**, 64659–64673 (2018)
13. Bhanti, P., Kaushal, U., Pandey, A.: E-governance in higher education: concept and role of data warehousing techniques. Int. J. Comput. Appl. **18**(1), 875–895 (2011)
14. Tulasi, B.: Significance of big data and analytics in higher education. Int. J. Comput. Appl. **68**(14), 2013
15. Ahmad, F., Ismail, N.H., Aziz, A.A.: The prediction of students' academic performance using classification data mining techniques. Appl. Math. Sci. **9**(129), 6415–6426 (2015)
16. Sin, K., Muthu, L.: Application of big data in education data mining and learning analytics--a literature review. ICTACT J. Soft Comput. **5**(4), (2015)
17. Hasan, N.A., et al.: Business intelligence readiness factors for higher education institution. J. Theor. Appl. Inf. Technol. **89**(1), 174 (2016)

18. Bhise, R.B., Thorat, S.S., Supekar, A.K.: Importance of data mining in higher education system. IOSR J. Human. Social Sci. (IOSR-JHSS), **6**(6) 18–21 (2013)
19. Satapathy, R., Cambria, E., Hussain, A.: Literature Survey. In: Sentiment Analysis in the Bio-Medical Domain. SC, vol. 7, pp. 21–38. Springer, Cham (2017). https://doi.org/10.1007/978-3-319-68468-0_2
20. Michalik, P., Štofa, J., Zolotova, I.: Concept definition for Big Data architecture in the education system, pp. 331–334
21. Manohar, A., Gupta, P., Priyanka, V., Uddin, M.F.: Utilizing big data analytics to improve education.
22. Johnson, J.A.: The ethics of big data in higher education, the international review of information. Ethics **21**, 3–10 (2014)
23. Li, Y., Zhai, X.: Review and prospect of modern education using big data. Procedia Comput. Sci. **129**, 341–347 (2018)
24. Taylor, E., Goede, R.: Using critical social heuristics and project-based learning to enhance data warehousing education. Syst. Pract. Action Res. **29**(2), 97–128 (2016)
25. Sedkaoui, S., Khelfaoui, M.: Understand, develop and enhance the learning process with big data. Inform. Disc. Delivery **47**(1), 2–16 (2018)
26. Ptiček, M., Vrdoljak, B.: Big data and new data warehousing approaches, pp. 6–10
27. Santoso, L.W.: Data warehouse with big data technology for higher education. Proc. Comput. Sci. **124**, 93–99 (2017)
28. Khatibi, V., Keramati, A., Shirazi, F.: Deployment of a business intelligence model to evaluate Iranian national higher education. Social Sci. Human. Open **2**(1), 100056 (2020)
29. Guster, D., Brown, C.G.: The application of business intelligence to higher education: technical and managerial perspectives. J. Inform. Technol. Manage. **23**(2), 42–62 (2012)
30. Alpar, P., Schulz, M.: Self-service business intelligence. Bus. Inf. Syst. Eng. **58**(2), 151–155 (2016)

# AI/ML Based Sensitive Data Discovery and Classification of Unstructured Data Sources

Shravani Ponde$^{(\boxtimes)}$ (iD), Akshay Kulkarni (iD), and Rashmi Agarwal (iD)

RACE, REVA University, Bengaluru 560064, India
{shravanip.ba03,rashmi.agarwal}@reva.edu.in,
akshaykulkarni@race.reva.edu.in

**Abstract.** The amount of data produced every day is enormous. According to Forbes, 2.5 quintillion data is created daily (Marr, 2018). The volume of unstructured data is also multiplying daily, forcing organizations to spend significant time, effort, and money to manage and govern the data assets. This volume of unstructured data also leads to data privacy challenges in handling, auditing, and regulatory encounters thrown by governing bodies like Governments, Auditors, Data Protection/Legislative/Federal laws, regulatory acts like The General Data Protection Regulation (GDPR), The Basel Committee on Banking Supervision (BCBS), Health Insurance Portability and Accountability Act (HIPPA), The California Consumer Privacy Act (CCPA) etc.

Organizations must set up a robust data protection framework and governance to identify, classify, protect and monitor the sensitive data residing in the unstructured data sources. Data discovery and classification of the data assets is scanning the organization's data sources both structured and unstructured, that could potentially contain sensitive or regulated data.

Most organizations are using various data discovery and classification tools in scanning the structured and unstructured sources. The organizations cannot accomplish the overall privacy and protection needs due to the gaps observed in scanning and discovering sensitive data elements from unstructured sources. Hence, they are adapting to manual methodologies to fill these gaps.

The main objective of this study is to build a solution which systematically scans an unstructured data source and detects the sensitive data elements, auto classify as per the data classification categories, and visualizes the results on a dashboard. This solution uses Machine Learning (ML) and Natural Language Processing (NLP) techniques to detect the sensitive data elements contained in the unstructured data sources. It can be used as a first step before performing data encryption, tokenization, anonymization, and masking as part of the overall data protection journey.

**Keywords:** Data Discovery · Data Protection · Sensitive Data Classification · Data Privacy · Unstructured Data Discovery · Classification Model

S. Nandan Mohanty et al. (Eds.): ICISML 2022, LNICST 471, pp. 367–377, 2023.
https://doi.org/10.1007/978-3-031-35081-8_31

# 1   Introduction

The volume of the data owned by organizations is increasing daily, and data management is becoming a considerable challenge. CIO estimates that 80–90% of the data is in unstructured format (David, 2019). According to Forbes, 95% of businesses struggle to manage unstructured data (Kulkarni, 2019).

Meanwhile, data leakages, data breaches, and data security violations are also increasing drastically, which sometimes results in the organizations having to pay heavy penalties from the auditing and regulatory compliance aspects (Hill, 2022), which might also result in reputation loss.

## 1.1   Data Protection Laws and Regulations

Below are three pertinent Data Protection Laws:

### The General Data Protection Regulation (GDPR)

European Union's (EU) GDPR is the law that imposes privacy regulations on any organization that accumulates or processes personal information related to individuals in the EU. Personal information includes but is not limited to names, email, location, ethnicity, gender, biometric data, religious beliefs, etc. All organizations are required to be GDPR compliant as of May 2018. The fines in case of GDPR violations are very high €20miilion or 4% of the global revenue (Wolford, 2020).

### The California Consumer Privacy Act (CCPA)

The CCPA of 2018 gives Californian consumers control over how an organization collects their personal information. The personal information includes but is not limited to name, social security number, products purchased, internet browsing history, geolocation data, etc.

The CCPA provides consumers with three principal "rights." The first right is the "right to know" how the organization collects, uses, or shares personal information. The second right is the "right to opt-out" of selling personal data. The third right is the "right to delete" personal information collected about the consumer (Bonta, 2022).

### The Health Insurance Portability and Accountability Act of 1996 (HIPAA)

HIPAA by the Department of Health and Human Services (HHS) gives consumers rights over their health information. Consumers have the right to get a copy of their health information, check who has it, and learn how it is used and shared. These regulations apply to health care providers, insurance companies, etc., (Office for Civil Rights (OCR), 2022).

Organizations are facing rapid growth of unstructured data, leading to the below challenges:

- Location of the unstructured data
- Classification per organization's policies
- Retention and disposal
- Monitoring of unstructured data

## 1.2  Data Discovery and Classification

Table 1 Gives a high-level overview of Data Discovery and Classification. It is very crucial to identify an organization's data assets scattered across the Enterprise. Organizations need to establish a robust data protection framework by defining security classification policies, Data Discovery methodologies, Data Privacy Standards and a practical Data Governance framework.

**Table 1.** Overview of Data Discovery and Data Classification.

Overview of Data Discovery and Data Classification

| Data Discovery | Data Classification |
|---|---|
| 1. Identifying and Locating sensitive data in structured and unstructured sources via discovery rules<br>2. Identifying the data which is most at risk of exposure, such as PII, PHI | 1. Categorizing the sensitive data - Internal, Public, Confidential, and Restricted<br>2. Classifying the sensitive data enables a faster search of the data assets across the enterprise |

## 1.3  Data Protection Lifecycle

Organizations must identify, classify, protect and monitor sensitive data assets. To achieve this systematically, organizations need Data Protection Lifecycle (DPL) which helps organizations manage sensitive data. By accurately tracking sensitive data, organizations have a foundation to protect sensitive information and face future data privacy and protection challenges.

Figure 1 shows DPL, used to discover, classify, protect and protect sensitive data. By accurately tracking sensitive data, organizations have a foundation to protect sensitive information and face future data privacy and protection challenges.

## 1.4  Types of Sensitive Data

Sensitive data is confidential information that must be protected and inaccessible to outside parties. It can be of different types based on an organization's data classification policies (Steele, 2021):

- Personally Identifiable Information (PII)
- Sensitive Personal Information (SPI)
- Protected Health Information (PHI)
- Non-public Personal Information (NPI)

Table 2 Provides examples of different types of sensitive data.

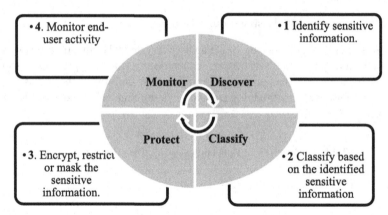

**Fig. 1.** Data Protection Lifecycle

**Table 2.** Types of Sensitive Data.

Types of Sensitive Data

| PII | SPI | PHI | NPI |
|---|---|---|---|
| 1. Name | 1. SSN | 1. Medical Information | 1. Bank Account Number |
| 2. e-mail address | 2. Driver License | 2. Physical Health | 2. Credit Card Number |
| 3. Phone Number | 3. Passport Number | Information | |
| 4. Date of Birth | 4. Religious beliefs | 3. Mental Health | |
| 5. Address | 5. Political Opinion | Information | |
| | 6. Genetic data | | |
| | 7. Biometric data | | |

## 2 Literature Review

Data is considered capital in today's digital economy and holds tremendous value. "Data is regarded as the new oil," said Clive Humby. Organizations are increasingly relying on a robust data management strategy to use data and create value. One of the critical aspects of data management is to manage sensitive data across the enterprise. (Goswami, 2020) states that 69% of consumers are concerned about how personal data is collected in mobile apps. (Gartner Top Strategic Technology Trends for 2022, 2022) lists' Privacy-enhancing computation techniques' as one of the top technology trends for 2022. As per Gartner securing personal data is critical due to evolving privacy and data protection laws and growing consumer concerns. (Yaqoob, Salah, Jayaraman, & Al-Hammadi, 2022) outline data privacy as one of the critical challenges to healthcare data management.

As per Oracle (What Is Data Management?, 2022), today's organizations' data management systems include databases, data lakes, data warehouses, the cloud, etc. Big data management systems have emerged as more and more data is collected every day from sources as disparate as video cameras, social media, audio recordings, and Internet of Things (IoT) devices. Compliance regulations are complex and multijurisdictional, and they change constantly. Organizations need to be able to review their data quickly; in particular, personally identifiable information (PII) must be detected, tracked, and monitored for compliance with increasingly strict global privacy regulations. (Mehmood, Natgunanathan, Xiang, Hua, & Guo, 2016) illustrate the infrastructure of big data and the privacy-preserving mechanisms in each stage of the big data life cycle.

This solution focuses on the capabilities of data governance and data management framework. The framework establishes, enables, and sustains a mature data privacy management solution, which is the core discipline in the data management and governance arena. In (Cha & Yeh, 2018) proposed a data-driven risk assessment approach to personal data protection, which can prevent organizations from overlooking risks to sensitive data. In (Truong, Sun, Lee, & Guo, 2019) design a concept for GDPR compliant Block Chain based personal data management solution. (Xu, Jiang, Wang, Yuan, & Ren, 2014), discusses the approach to privacy protection and proposes a user role-based methodology to privacy issues. (Zhang, et al., 2017) Propose a scalable MRMondrian approach for multidimensional anonymization over big data based on the MapReduce paradigm.

## 3   Problem Statement

Organizations leverage unstructured data across the enterprise, which results in an ever-increasing volume of data that requires protection. A complete data lifecycle is necessary to manage data from its creation to its destruction, ensuring that appropriate protections are applied along the way.

Organizations are scrutinized as to how they manage, control, and monitor stakeholders' data and their preferences. As data breaches increase and sensitive information is compromised, more privacy regulations are developed, from state/ national requirements to potential comprehensive federal privacy laws.

Global privacy legislations require the clients to document and take responsibility for personal data and processing activities. The data discovery and classification program can help them to comply with this requirement.

Below are some of the benefits of sensitive data discovery and classification of unstructured sources:

- Visibility to the sensitive data
- Reduced sensitive data footprint that is not needed
- Enhanced governance and protection of data when stored and transferred internally and externally
- Integrations with data loss preventions, information rights management, defender for end points
- Maintain compliance, apply risk-based protections

Organizations can protect sensitive data if they know where it resides. The data discovery and classification help clients identify where sensitive data is stored and enable the application of risk-based protections.

It is crucial to identify, classify and protect the sensitive data to drive the below initiatives for the organizations as applicable:

- Regulatory Compliance – GDPR, CCPA, etc.

- Auditing purposes
- Data Privacy and protection needs for customers, employees, suppliers, etc.,
- Data governance
- Enterprise metadata management
- Data Remediation
- Data Disposals
- Data Subject Rights

# 4   Proposed Solution

Solve one of the primary data privacy challenges discussed – help organizations manage the sensitive data on unstructured files stored across – Confluence, SharePoint, shared network drives, etc.

a) Detect sensitive elements
b) Document Risk Categorization
c) Document Classification

## 4.1   Detect Sensitive Elements

A sensitive PII data element has three parts – format, pattern, and keywords.
   *Format:* Format of the sensitive data element.
   *Pattern:* The sensitive data elements are pattern-based classifiers that can be identified using regular expressions. A pattern defines what the sensitive data element looks like.
   *Keywords:* Keywords are used to identify the sensitive data element. They represent the occurrences of sensitive data elements in the unstructured data source.

**Social Security Number**
USA Social Security Number (SSN) consists of 9 digits. The first set of three digits is called the Area Number. The second set of two digits is called the Group Number. The final set of four digits is the Serial Number. Table 3 shows the format and sample for identifying an SSN. Table 3 shows the pattern and sample for identifying an SSN.

**Table 3.**   Sensitive Data Element – SSN.

| Sensitive Data Element | | |
|---|---|---|
| SSN | Pattern | Sample |
| | ddd-dd-dddd | 986–43-2453 |
| | ddd dd dddd | 231 24 3168 |

*Format:* Nine digits
   *Pattern:* Search the pattern with formatting that has dashes or spaces (ddd-dd-dddd OR ddd dd dddd)

**Table 4.** Sensitive Data Element – e-mail address.

| Sensitive Data Element | | |
|---|---|---|
| e-mail address | Pattern | Sample |
| | < Letters > @ < letters >. < letters > | Mark.Campbell@gmail.com<br>Lisa.Thomas@hotmail.com |

*Keywords:* ssn, social security number, ssn n, social security #, social security no, Soc sc, s#

**E-mail Address**

*Format:* Search the pattern with letters followed by '@' and '.'

*Keywords:* email, e-mail, email address, e-mail address, email id etc.

The format and pattern for other sensitive elements like Name, Phone number, Date of birth etc., was defined similarly. Regular Expressions (RegEx) are used to identify the sensitive data elements.

## 4.2 Rule Based Document Risk Categorization

The sensitive data elements identified in a document using RegEx (from Sect. 4.1), is used for the document risk categorization. The Table 5 Illustrates the rule-based document categorization approach followed. For example, if a document contains a name along with SSN, PAN, or DOB is categorized as a high-risk document. If a document includes either SSN, Phone number, or e-mail address is categorized as a medium-risk document. If a document contains only a name or DOB is categorized as a low-risk document.

**Table 5.** Rule based Risk Categorization Matrix

| Sensitive Data Element | Document Risk Categorization | | |
|---|---|---|---|
| | High | Medium | Low |
| Name | | | Yes |
| SSN | | Yes | |
| DOB | | | Yes |
| Phone Number | | Yes | |
| email | | Yes | |
| Name + SSN | Yes | | |
| Name + Phone Number | | Yes | |
| Name + email | | Yes | |
| Name + DOB | Yes | | |

### 4.3   Document Classification

Typically, there are four classifications of data. A document can be classified as Public, Internal, Confidential, or Restricted.

**Public**
This type of data is freely accessible to the public.

**Internal**
This type of data is strictly for internal company personnel.

**Confidential**
This type of data is sensitive, and only selective access is granted.

**Restricted**
This type of data has proprietary information and needs the authorization to access it. Inappropriate handling can lead to criminal or civil charges.

Table 6 shows the type of information contained in each document category. For example, an organization's public document can contain financial statements, press releases, etc. In contrast, a restricted document might contain sensitive information like SSN or Bank Account Numbers.

**Table 6.** Document Category.

| Document Category | | | |
| --- | --- | --- | --- |
| Public | Internal | Confidential (Non-Sensitive PII) | Restricted (Sensitive PII) |
| 1. Financial Statements<br>2. Press Release | 1. Training Materials<br>2. Instructions | 1. Name<br>2. Phone Number<br>3. e-mail address | 1. SSN<br>2. Date of Birth<br>3. Bank Account Number |

**Synthetic Data Generation**
Since sensitive information (PII) is unavailable on open sources, synthetic data which mimics PII (Restricted and Confidential) was generated while preserving the format and data type.

**Text Pre Processing**
The unstructured word documents are cleaned and pre-processed to make it ready for modelling. First the text is standardized by converting to lowercase. All the special characters, numbers and stop words are removed. Lemmatization is used to return the base or dictionary form of words (lemma). In this step we transform the words into their normalized form. Figure 2 shows the text cleaning pipeline used for pre-processing the documents.

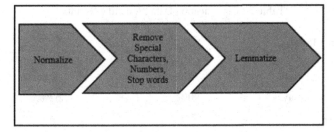

**Fig. 2.** Text pre-processing pipeline

**Feature Engineering**

To analyze a preprocessed data, it needs to be converted into features. Under Feature Engineering, features are created from the cleaned text so that the machine learning model can be trained as shown in Fig. 3.

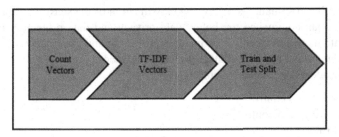

**Fig. 3.** Feature engineering pipeline

## 4.4 Data Modelling Results

Multiclass classification (multinomial classification) refers to supervised machine learning with classification of more than two classes. Since, the documents belong to more than one category, multi-class classification algorithm was used to auto-classify the document.

Table 7 shows the data modelling results for the various classifiers. The best model based on test accuracies is Multinomial Naïve Bayes. After the model training process, the trained model is saved and used to classify the document.

**Table 7.** Classification Data Modelling Results.

| Data Modelling Results | | |
|---|---|---|
| Classifier | Count Vectors Accuracy | TF-IDF Accuracy |
| Multinomial Naïve Bayes | 90% | 62% |
| Random Forest | 80% | 68% |
| K Neighbours | 68% | 50% |
| Decision Tree | 83% | 56% |

## 5  Conclusion and Future Scope

This solution be customized according to privacy and classification needs and deployed on on-premise and cloud infrastructure platforms via APIs.

After the Sensitive data discovery and classification of the sensitive data elements, organizations can commence the below data privacy and data protection needs, and the organizations would establish strong data protection and governance framework to handle regulatory and auditing challenges well in advance.

Enabling access and security controls

- Role based access control
- Password protection control
- API level Encryptions

  Data Protection Capabilities

- Data Masking, Encryption, Tokenization
- Anonymization, Pseudonymization
- Data Loss Prevention (DLP)
- Data Remediation

  Data Subject Rights.

## References

Bonta, R.: California Consumer Privacy Act (CCPA). Retrieved from State of California Department of Justice: https://oag.ca.gov/privacy/ccpa (2022)

Cha, S.-C., Yeh, K.-H.: A Data-Driven Security Risk Assessment Scheme for Personal Data Protection. IEEE, pp. 50510 – 50517 (2018)

David, D.: AI Unleashes the Power of Unstructured Data. Retrieved from CIO (2019, July 9). https://www.cio.com/article/3406806/ai-unleashes-the-power-of-unstructured-data.html

Gartner Top Strategic Technology Trends for 2022. (2022). Retrieved from Gartner: https://www.gartner.com/en/information-technology/insights/top-technology-trends

Goswami, S.: The Rising Concern Around Consumer Data And Privacy. Retrieved from Forbes (2020, December 14). https://www.forbes.com/sites/forbestechcouncil/2020/12/14/the-rising-concern-around-consumer-data-and-privacy/?sh=30741b43487e

Hill, M.: The 12 biggest data breach fines, penalties, and settlements so far. Retrieved from CSO (2022, August 16). https://www.csoonline.com/article/3410278/the-biggest-data-breach-fines-penalties-and-settlements-so-far.html

Kulkarni, R.: Big Data Goes Big. Retrieved from Forbes (2019, 02 07). https://www.forbes.com/sites/rkulkarni/2019/02/07/big-data-goes-big/?sh=278b2aa820d7

Marr, B.: How Much Data Do We Create Every Day? The Mind-Blowing Stats Everyone Should Read. Retrieved from Forbes (2018, May 21). https://www.forbes.com/sites/bernardmarr/2018/05/21/how-much-data-do-we-create-every-day-the-mind-blowing-stats-everyone-should-read/?sh=4e4f805860ba

Mehmood, A., Natgunanathan, I., Xiang, Y., Hua, G., Guo, S.: Protection of Big Data Privacy. IEEE, pp. 1821–1834 (2016)

Office for Civil Rights (OCR). (2022, January 19). Your Rights Under HIPAA. Retrieved from HHS.gov: https://www.hhs.gov/hipaa/for-individuals/guidance-materials-for-consumers/index.html

Steele, K.: A Guide to Types of Sensitive Information. Retrieved from BigID (2021, November 3). https://bigid.com/blog/sensitive-information-guide/

Truong, N.B., Sun, K., Lee, G.M., Guo, Y.: GDPR-Compliant Personal Data Management: A Blockchain-Based Solution. IEEE, pp. 1746–1761 (2019)

What Is Data Management? (2022). Retrieved from OCI: https://www.oracle.com/database/what-is-data-management/

Wolford, B.: What is GDPR, the EU's new data protection law? Retrieved from GDPR.EU (2020) https://gdpr.eu/what-is-gdpr/

Xu, L., Jiang, C., Wang, J., Yuan, J., Ren, Y.: Information Security in Big Data: Privacy and Data Mining. IEEE, pp. 1149–1176 (2014)

Yaqoob, I., Salah, K., Jayaraman, R., & Al-Hammadi, Y.: Blockchain for healthcare data management: opportunities, challenges, and future recommendations. Springer Link, pp. 11475–11490 (2022)

Zhang, X., et al.: MRMondrian: Scalable Multidimensional Anonymisation for Big Data Privacy Preservation. IEEE, pp. 125–139 (2017)

# Bias Analysis in Stable Diffusion and MidJourney Models

Luka Aničin and Miloš Stojmenović[(✉)]

Department of Computer Science and Electrical Engineering, Singidunum University,
Danijelova 32, 11000 Belgrade, Serbia
mstojmenovic@singidunum.ac.rs

**Abstract.** In recent months, all kinds of image-generating models got the spotlight, opening many possibilities for further research direction, and from the commercial side, many teams will be able to start experimenting and building products on top of them. A sub-area of image generation that picked the most interest in the eye of the public is text-to-image models, most notably Stable Diffusion and MidJourney. Open sourcing Stable Diffusion and free tier of MidJourney allowed many product teams to start building on top of them with little to no resources. However, applying any pre-trained model without proper testing and experimentation creates unknown risks for companies and teams using them. In this paper, we are demonstrating what might happen if such models are used without additional filtering and testing through bias detection.

**Keywords:** Artificial Intelligence · AI Generation Models · Bias detection

## 1 Introduction

When Generative Adversarial Networks (GANs) [1] were introduced in 2014, AI-generated art started taking over the world and the headlines by storm. The quality of those images was far from perfect and a long way from reaching the quality of the art that humans could create. However, one research paper at the time, we were getting closer to creating a model that could replace humans in some of the creative works, such as sketching [2], coloring [3], or even restoring old images [4]. In 2020, the companies, for the first time, saw an opportunity on the horizon of replacing some of their human workers with algorithms, and artists started fearing for their jobs and discussing ways how to leverage the new algorithms to enhance their skills and create more sustainable opportunities for their future careers. While this was happening in the artists' world, AI researchers from Open AI introduced a completely new paradigm to the AI-generated models, where one can explain in plain English what they want, and the algorithm would generate an image for them - this marks the release of the first version of the DALL-E model [5]

The release of the DALL-E 2 model at the beginning of 2021 introduces the new research direction, which combines Natural Language Processing and Computer Vision

S. Nandan Mohanty et al. (Eds.): ICISML 2022, LNICST 471, pp. 378–388, 2023.
https://doi.org/10.1007/978-3-031-35081-8_32

techniques to create models that can "understand" English and generate what the end user wants to see from a simple image to fully functioning website pages. While an amazing invention, this model introduces another wave of fear to artists and anger to AI researchers. OpenAI decided to release this model under closed API, without releasing weights and model as an open source. This was an outrageous move from the re- search company back then, especially with a model as useful and big as DALL-E [5]. Fast forward to August 2022; this move was arguably a good decision by OpenAI's team.

In August of 2022, one of the best text-to-image generating models was released by an independent research company, Stability AI [6], under the name of Stable Diffusion [7]. The new model had the capacity to generate images with more details and bigger resolutions compared to the DALL-E. However, these technical differences weren't the only difference between these two projects. The Stable Diffusion model was released under an MIT license, completely open-sourced. Suddenly thousands of researchers had the capacity to generate unlimited images using a standard commercial GPU.

The open-sourced characteristic of the Stable Diffusion model sparked the creation of new hackathons that were formed around this model. New startups were created, and projects were started, as well as existing companies considering utilizing these kinds of AI models in their projects. All these changes are on the right track to creating unprecedented monetary uptake for the economy. However, when blindly applying pre-trained models in a project introduces risks with a bigger downturn than its generated value. The Stable Diffusion model was trained on the LAION-Aesthetics V2 dataset [8], which has pre-conceptualized biases from the real world built inside of its statistics. By using a raw model without inspecting its potential biases, companies expose themselves to potential problems if a user finds generated art to be exclusive or offensive to their gender or race. In this paper, we are testing two of the most popular text-to-image AI models, Stable Diffusion and MidJourney [9], with a goal in mind of increasing the awareness of built-in biases in their predictions and helping their users prevent potential legal actions against them.

Our main contributions are summarized below:

1. We analyzed and demonstrated biases that might introduce inequality and problems to users of two of the most popular AI Generating models - Stable Diffusion and MidJounrey
2. Proposed a simple solution to mitigate potential biases in AI-generating algorithms

## 2  Overview of Bias Detection in Pre-trained Models

Bias takes many shapes and sources [10]. Since the focus of this paper are text-to-image models, we will give most of our attention to biases that can be represented textually as well as visually - gender and racial biases.

Why is the de-biasing of a machine learning model that important, and why now? With the Internet being widely available these days, companies see that as a faster and cheaper growth opportunity. While true, having an AI model as a part of the product, biases that are not present in the company's home country become an inevitable risk for that company.

People from different areas, cultures, and age groups are exposed to the model's predictions and its pre-conceptualized "beliefs", which leads to the assimilation of multiple terms - bias, fairness, and inclusivity. If the model's predictions do not account for different regions where it will be used, that becomes an unhandled risk for the company and its products.

## 2.1 Where Does Bias Come From?

When creating a dataset, researchers have a goal to represent the problem at hand, and all external factors, using only data samples (e.g., images, rows in tables, audio or video recordings), which is an extremely difficult task to do. While researchers achieve very impressive results with this approach, most of the companies and research groups come from western, English-speaking countries, which by default limits the exposure to the eastern cultures for their research.

The model we will focus on in this paper is a great example of this influence. Stable Diffusion, which was trained on the LAION-2B English dataset. This led to having white and western cultures present in most of the predictions of the model, we show this in the results section of this paper. This source of bias was recognized by the creator of the Stable Diffusion as well and marked in the model card in the model's GitHub repository [11].

# 3 Previous Work

At the time of writing this paper, there were no prior works in bias analysis for Stable Diffusion and MidJourney models. However, our research approach and analysis were built on prior work from OpenAI and their DALL-E de-biasing efforts, as well as bias analysis in NLP pre-trained models, such as BERT [12].

## 3.1 Reducing Bias in DALL-E

Every dataset, when created, will be biased to some degree. The amount of bias in a dataset, only depends on how researchers can detect it beforehand and handle it. For this reason alone, bias reduction is a common practice when creating a production-grade machine learning system.

With the introduction of models that combine text and images as a single training sample, the number of blind spots where biases can be present increases exponentially.

One example of this problem is that with the same text description, we could have multiple images that are very similar in nature but can introduce bias to the results. For example, having multiple images with the description "Dog playing a fetch" may bias the dataset if all the examples have the background of woods. If we focus on the description part in this example, it is not very specific; thus, the "dog" part can represent any breed, and if all examples for this description have a golden retriever in them, the model may learn to generate only golden retrieves once a similar prompt is provided.

Having these types of biases may not cause serious damage to the company using that model. However, having a gender or racial bias is a different story. When OpenAI released the DALL-E model, the model had the same amount of gender and racial bias as the models analyzed in this paper. However, the positive side of the DALL-E model was the fact that it was closed-sourced, and OpenAI had full control over the dataset, weights, and its results.

Through several cycles of closed and public testing, the OpenAI team was able to detect common sources of bias and were able to mitigate them as much as possible [13]. Their approach relied on creating a set of filters and human checks before sending predictions to a user. While these checks and filters solved the problem to some degree, it wouldn't be a long-lasting solution and certainly wouldn't be applicable to new versions and models that OpenAI is working on. To tackle this issue in a more lasting way, their researchers created a content policy [14] (Fig. 1).

**Fig. 1.** This image is taken from OpenAI's blog, which explains changes in the DALL-E model and the process they used to remove biases in their predictions. The example shown is when a user prompts the model with a **firefighter.** Six images on the left represent model predictions with bias, whereas six images on the right represent a more robust model with bias mitigated.

### 3.2   Detecting Bias in Pre-trained NLP Models

In 2021, three universities partnered on a research paper to create a system for gender bias detection in pre-trained NLP models [15], while the focus of their research was the BERT model. Researchers created a gender detection system that uses Attention Weights to understand which part of a sentence points to gender-specific words such as - him, her, he, she, etc. Their research proved that a pre-trained NLP model, learned pre-conceptualized biases such as that a specific job corresponds to a specific gender (e.g., nurse strongly correlated with female gender-related words) (Fig. 2).

While only focusing on the text part of the text-to-image problem, this research clearly demonstrated that publicly available datasets and models need additional care before using them in production settings. Building on this research, we demonstrate that similar bias is present in the text-to-image generative models and that most of the bias comes from the context and attention weights influenced by textual prompts.

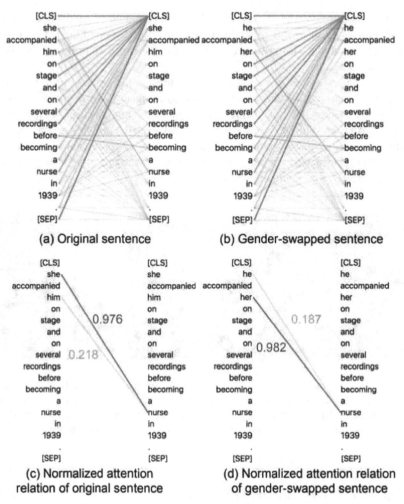

(a) Original sentence

(b) Gender-swapped sentence

(c) Normalized attention
relation of original sentence

(d) Normalized attention relation
of gender-swapped sentence

**Fig. 2.** The figure is taken from the paper *Detecting Gender Bias in Transformer-based Models: A Case Study on BERT*. It shows the attention weights of the BERT model and how those connect feminine words to jobs such as a nurse.

## 4   Results of Bias Analysis in Art Generating Models

There are many sources and reasons why a dataset becomes biased. Human error while creating a dataset is a common source of bias. For example, people get tired and incorrectly label a sample, or if a labeling team has its own biases, those will also end up in the dataset. However, human-generated errors are specific and unique to each team, so we are not focusing on them in this research.

The goal of each dataset is to represent the real world as closely as possible so that we can learn from it. If we have a bias in the real world, that bias will be sown in the dataset as well. One of the common biases we talk about these days is gender inequality in jobs. For example, if one thinks of a nurse, there is a high chance to think of a girl in that role.

In this analysis, we are focusing on two biases, gender, and racial bias, with a goal to showcase the pitfalls and potential risks of using a pre-trained model without proper testing and risk management.

## 4.1 Gender Bias Inequality

To discover gender bias, we started with a hypothesis that models will favor one gender over the other in cases of professions that people generally associate with each gender. For the Stable Diffusion model, to be as objective as possible, we always used a random seed when generating. And shown examples in this paper are hand-picked based on quality only, not content.

**Fig. 3.** These images represent outputs from Stable Diffusion and MidJourney models for the prompt **a professor.** Images on the left are generated by Stable Diffusion, Images on the right represent the output from the MidJourney model.

The first prompt we used to test both models was **"a professor"** without any additional information. Results for this prompt are shown in Fig. 3. We ran inference on this prompt for multiple seeds, and in all cases, we got white males as a result - for both models. To compare our findings for the professor prompt, as a second prompt, we chose **"a teacher"**, results for this prompt are shown in Fig. 4. Stable Diffusion has generated less quality results for this prompt, but for the samples which are generated correctly, teachers were assumed to be a woman, as seen in the top left corner in Fig. 4. As for the MidJourney model, it was able to consistently generate high-quality samples of teachers, either alone or in front of the class, but all of them were women. As for the racial bias, we haven't noticed it as we were in the case of the first prompt.

The same inequality was recognized in other professions as well. We recorded the same results for prompts such as Computer Scientist, Firefighter, CEO, Dancer, and Doctor.

**Fig. 4.** These images represent outputs from Stable Diffusion and MidJourney models for the prompt a teacher. Images on the left are generated by Stable Diffusion, Images on the right represent the output from the MidJourney model.

Besides job-related biases, we tested models with prompts representing nouns people use to describe each gender. That led us to test prompts such as **an intelligent person, a strong person** and, **a beautiful person.** We could capture the same gender bias for job positions, but only in the Stable Diffusion model, where MidJourney generated some random results, which in most cases were not human-like.

As seen in the left part of Fig. 5, the Stable Diffusion model generated only women for the **"a beautiful person"** prompt, whereas for the **"an intelligent person"** generated only male-like figures, as demonstrated on the right-hand side of Fig. 5.

**Fig. 5.** These images represent outputs from Stable Diffusion for words used to describe a specific gender. Images on the left are generated by Stable Diffusion with the prompt a beautiful person. Images on the right represent the output from the Stable Diffusion model with the prompt of an intelligent person.

## 4.2 Racial Inequality

The racial bias was much harder to detect as it was not introduced intentionally nor consciously. Datasets used to train tested models were created in the western countries, predominantly in USA, and do not capture eastern cultures that well.

To test if racial bias was present in these models, it was much more difficult to find a good prompt that demonstrated it. In Fig. 6, on the left-hand side, we can see the results of the Stable Diffusion when prompted with "**a woman**", where we can recognize that all generated portraits are of white female figures. On the right side of the same figure, we can see results of the MidJourney model for the prompt "**a parent with a baby**", where we can see that generated images are of white people and mostly women, which, besides racial, demonstrates the gender inequality as well.

**Fig. 6.** These images represent outputs from Stable Diffusion and MidJourney for prompts that show racial bias towards western cultures. Images on the left are generated by Stable Diffusion with the prompt a woman. Images on the right represent the output from the MIdJourney model with the prompt of a parent with a baby.

Similarly, racial bias can be noticed in almost all results shown in the section dedicated to gender bias. One more example that captures gender and racial bias is the prompt "**firefighter**", shown in Fig. 7.

**Fig. 7.** These images represent outputs from Stable Diffusion and MidJourney models for the prompt a firefighter. Images on the left are generated by Stable Diffusion, Images on the right represent the output from the MidJourney model.

## 5 The Potential Impact of Applying Unfiltered Pre-trained Models

Using pre-trained model ease the development process and shortens the time to production drastically. However, using these models with zero change might be risky for a product and business since the researchers, when training these models, had one goal in mind - to create as accurate a model as possible.

As we demonstrated in this paper, raw, open-sourced image generators are biased on multiple levels, and a team that wants to utilize its capabilities for its public products will need to do extra work to handle edge cases and mitigate potential risks for their companies.

In the past, we saw many AI products that got shut down or even sued over social inequalities in their predictions. If a user finds themselves insulted over gender or racial inequalities, they can sue the product over that issue and win easily. To help potential users of Stable Diffusion or MidJourney not end up with the same destinies, we wrote this paper to demonstrate what can happen if one uses models out of the box.

## 6 Potential Solutions

In this section we will go over a few ideas on how to handle these and other types of biases when using pre-trained models.

### 6.1 Fine-Tuning

When working with pre-trained models, it's always a good idea to fine-tune them with custom data for the problem you are trying to solve. Either this will be unique data for your customers or a specific subset of the problem you try to solve. In the case of bias mitigation, a team can go over the original or custom dataset, hand-pick samples to remove some amount of detected bias, and fine-tune the model using a filtered dataset.

## 6.2  Filtering

If you don't have a custom dataset or resources to filter the raw dataset, fine-tuning is not an option. In this case, you can write a filter based on prompts or images that are triggered once a known, biased prompt is called.

Whenever you start with a pre-trained model, we recommend performing detailed testing of the model and its predictions before going to production with it. An untested pre-trained model is an unmitigated risk for your company.

# 7  Conclusion and Future Work

In this paper, we demonstrated two biases present in two of the most popular text-to-image generating models, Stable Diffusion and MidJourney. Discussed what risks each untested model might bring to a company and proposed two solutions that may help teams use these models for their products.

Even though we are discussing the negative sides of pre-trained models in this paper, we think that open sourcing of projects and pre-trained models is the right direction for the science and AI community. However, using them hastily and untested represents risks for the company and community in general because, if we have many AI products that are not inclusive and biased, belief in AI as an industry will decrease.

In the future, we will continue our work on explainable AI theoretically and practically by creating an open-sourced tool that is able to detect bias in models and datasets automatically.

# References

1.  Goodfellow, I.J., Mirza, M., Xu, B., Ozair, S., Courville, A., Bengio, Y.: Generative adversarial networks (2014). arXiv https://doi.org/10.48550/arXiv.1406.2661
2.  Wang, S., Bau, D., Zhu, J.: Sketch Your Own GAN (2021). arXiv https://doi.org/10.48550/arXiv.2108.02774
3.  Anwar, S., Tahir, M., Li, C., Mian, A., Khan, F.S., Muzaffar, A.W.: Image colorization: a survey and dataset (2020). arXiv https://doi.org/10.48550/arXiv.2008.10774
4.  Wan, Z., et al.: Old Photo Restoration via Deep Latent Space Translation (2020). arXiv https://doi.org/10.48550/arXiv.2009.07047
5.  Ramesh, A., et al.: Zero-Shot Text-to-Image Generation (2021). arXiv https://doi.org/10.48550/arXiv.2102.12092
6.  Stability AI Homepage. https://stability.ai. Accessed 25 Sept 2022
7.  Stable Diffusion GitHub repository. https://github.com/CompVis/stable-diffusion. Accessed 25 Sept 2022
8.  LAION-5B Dataset Homepage. https://laion.ai/blog/laion-5b/. Accessed 25 Sept 2022
9.  MidJourney Homepage. https://www.midjourney.com/home/. Accessed 25 Sept 2022
10.  Mehrabi, N., Morstatter, F., Saxena, N., Lerman, K., Galstyan, A.: A Survey on Bias and Fairness in Machine Learning. arXiv https://doi.org/10.48550/arXiv.1908.09635 (2019)
11.  Stable Diffusion Model Card. https://huggingface.co/CompVis/stable-diffusion. Accessed 25 Sept 2022
12.  Devlin, J., Chang, M., Lee, K., Toutanova, K.: BERT: Pre-training of Deep Bidirectional Transformer for Language Understanding. arXiv https://doi.org/10.48550/arXiv.1810.04805 (2018)

13. OpenAI DALL-E Debias blog. https://openai.com/blog/reducing-bias-and-improving-safety-in-dall-e-2/. Accessed 25 Sept 2022
14. OpenAI content policy. https://labs.openai.com/policies/content-policy. Accessed 25 Sept 2022
15. Li, B., et al.: Detecting Gender Bias in Transformer-based Models: A Case Study on BERT. arXiv https://doi.org/10.48550/arXiv.2110.15733 (2021)

# Machine Learning Based Spectrum Sensing for Secure Data Transmission Using Cuckoo Search Optimization

E. V. Vijay[1]([⊠]) and K. Aparna[2]

[1] SRGEC, Gudlavalleru, Andhra Pradesh 521356, India
evvijay451@gmail.com

[2] JNTUACEK, Kalikiri, Andhra Pradesh 517234, India

**Abstract.** This article is about machine Learning (ML) depending spectrum sensing in using cuckoo search optimization method. In Present days as the number of mobile users is increasing, scarcity of spectrum is arising due to allocation of the available spectrum to growing number of the users in cognitive radio. So there is a need to efficiently utilize the limited spectrum that is available for use. Spectrum sensing is one of the prominent method for effective utilization of the spectrum. Among the existing methods of spectrum sensing using Energy detection, Machine learning based sensing is more prominent. For efficiently optimizing the spectrum sensing cuckoo search based optimization has been used in this paper. For analyzing the channels under noise conditions Gaussian function has been considered. Average information per message based classifier is a good technique of detection for spectrum sensing. Classification has been done with the help of support vector machine and K-Nearest Neighbor algorithms. From the obtained results it has been shown that average information based SVM, KNN techniques outperforms the conventional energy detection based techniques and cuckoo search based optimization has yielded better sensing accuracy with minimum loss.

**Keywords:** Machine Learning (ML) · Cognitive radio · Optimization · Gaussian function · spectrum sensing

## 1 Introduction

The current state of the electromagnetic spectrum demonstrates a significant underutilization. Some parts of the radio spectrum have been found to be highly dense. As 5th Generation networks and the IoT advance, numerous equipment may need to be wirelessly connected. Thus, bandwidth - an expensive and limited resource is in high demand. Therefore, efficient bandwidth utilization lowers costs and enhances the numeral of devices which would send data. Spectrum can be found as both in licensed band as well as in unlicensed bands. Owners or primary users of a licensed spectrum control the spectrum. Smart devices, such as cognitive radios (CR), are able of utilizing licensed spectrum if primary unit is not active in its licensed spectrum. Since a CR uses the spectrum only if the PU is inactive, in that case it can be treated as a secondary user (SU) [1].

S. Nandan Mohanty et al. (Eds.): ICISML 2022, LNICST 471, pp. 389–395, 2023.
https://doi.org/10.1007/978-3-031-35081-8_33

To get connectivity to a channel as a secondary user, primarily spectrum sensing (SS) must be conducted in cognitive radio. The SS role is critical since it assures that such CR somehow doesn't create interference towards the licensed spectrum user. SS has been assumed as a detection task wherein detector chooses between two hypotheses: null hypothesis and alternate hypothesis, where null hypothesis denotes the presence of nothing but noise while alternate hypothesis denotes its presence of both signal and noise. Noise statistics, fading due to multiple paths, shadowing, and other factors can all impede a detector's effectiveness in this scenario [2].

In the literature, various approaches for doing SS indeed been suggested. Energy detector (ED), matching filter detector (MFD), lastly cyclostationary feature detector are three prevalent approaches in conventional SS. To recognize PU behavior in a specific frequency band, the received signal energy is judged against to a threshold in ED. Because the ED is the most common and straightforward detector, it has been frequently used. For the detection of the PU presence, the MFD compares the received data to a predefined transmission message. The PU signal's second order cyclostationary qualities are used by the cyclostationary feature detector to detect PU activity. Nevertheless, those approaches have significant drawbacks, like as ED's poor efficiency at less Signal to Noise Ratio, the cyclostationary detector's complexity, and Matched Filter Detector requirement for set of assumptions on the primary user signal, as well as synchronisation between SU and PU. Such detectors' efficacy has been assessed under existing and projected noise situations. Because of its ease of calculation, Gaussian noise which will be additive in nature (AWGN) is frequently used for explain the noise. Nevertheless, in several circumstances, such as ultra-wide band communication systems, the effect of interference and noise was seen to resemble a Generalized Gaussian distribution (GGD). Furthermore, in a real-world scenario, information about the primary signal, distribution of noise, also fading characteristics of the channel is frequently restricted [3–5].

Similarly Under Advanced Spectrum Sensing Techniques, the Techniques are Wide-band Compressive method, Adaptive Compression method, covariance based methods, and Machine Learning Methods are given in literature [6].

To solve the drawbacks of the aforesaid conventional signal processing procedures, we apply supervised machine learning (ML) techniques to Spectrum Sensing. Machine Learning - based Spectrum Sensing is also now being researched The bulk of the solutions discussed in the literature, however, have two key flaws. To begin, these algorithms use the test energy measuring parameter for obtained readings for training the corresponding procedures, and it has been shown to perform badly in less SNRs as well as GGD noise. In this article, we propose using the Average information per symbol vector for signal received to be the feature vector to train and assess some of the most prominent supervised ML techniques for Spectrum Sensing using empirically collected datasets. By considering hypothesis cases also when compared to ED this method works well in the presence GGD Noise and it is good to a not known [7].

Error Detection and correction coding techniques are coming under channel encoding techniques. Even though the channel encoding is an additional overhead to the overall communication system and complexity gets increased. Optimization is now a days one of the emerging field for finding the best possible solution among the existing methods. With the help of optimization method. To use optimization for spectrum sensing channel power Values under various conditions can be given, and optimization can take these values and suggests the best possible value for utilizing the channel that means, when the SU can utilize the channel. So with the help of optimization a better result can be obtained in spectrum sensing. Cuckoo search algorithm is a meta-Heurisitic algorithm which has been inspired by cuckoo birds lay their eggs in other birds nests, which enhances their existence and productivity. This cuckoo search algorithm is one of the best optimization algorithm in order to find the optimal solution with fast convergence [21, 22].

In the subsequent portion, we discuss the ML algorithms used in this paper.

## 2 Design Methodology

In presence of GGD noise we formulated sample static based on the average information per message. In normal cases the average information per message of primary is known, then it easy to obtain Probability of detection. From simulation results it had been shown that GGD noise has less severity on the performance when compared to ED. In case of measured value in channel Hypothesis will be considered. In this case measurement is given to detection processing and then it makes decisions as $H_0$ or $H_1$ that means false alarm will be considered if signal energy or average information per message is below threshold i.e. $H_0$ and decision is in favor of $H_1$. And missed detection is noticed if energy or average information per message is above threshold but decision is in favor of $H_0$.

In this article a different detection technique used which is relied on average information per message. Average information per message is given by

$$K(l) = -(-1/log2) \int_{-\infty}^{\infty} g_l(l) log(g_l(l)) dl \tag{1}$$

where $g_l(.)$ is the pdf of l.

The average information centered check for finding if an available group of samples are belonging to $g_l$ are indicated by.

$\widehat{K(l)} \underset{<}{\overset{>}{\phantom{|}}} T$, for given $g_l$. Where T is the threshold selected aimed at certain $p_f \in (0, 1)$.

i. Detection in the presence of Generalized Gaussian Noise(GGN): Noise signal is chosen to be GGN with probability density function given as

$$g_N(l) = \frac{1}{2 \pounds \Gamma\left(\frac{1}{\xi}\right)} e^{\left(\frac{-|l|^\xi}{\xi}\right)} \tag{2}$$

where the parameter $\xi$ varies from 0 to 2. Where $\Gamma$ is the Euler's gamma function. The maximum likelihood estimate $H_0$ of Average information per message can be approximated as [4]

$$R(q/H_0) = (1/\xi) - \log(\xi) - \log\left(2\Gamma\left(\frac{1}{\xi}\right)\right)$$
$$+ (1/\xi)\log[\left(\frac{\xi}{L}\right) \sum_{o=1}^{L} |Qi - Q'|^\wedge \xi \tag{3}$$

similarly, Probability of detection moreover false alarm equations can also be applied. With the inclusion of this channel encoding techniques overall secure data transmission can be attained.

## 2.1 Support Vector Machines

Support vector machines (SVM) can be employed to classify data into binary categories. The SVM classifies data from group of points belonging to vector space whose dimension is N in nature and in turn it gives a hyperplane dividing the 2 classes. Each subsequent data point will be classified using hyperplane formula. To increase separability, significantly greater order feature combinations are used. Considering various kernels, the hyperplane expression varies. In this paper modified Support vector machine algorithm has been used. The SVM classifier is often trained using several kernels [8].

## 2.2 K-Nearest Neighbors (KNN)

K-Nearest neighbor algorithm comes under supervised machine learning algorithm that categorizes the incoming information relying over Euclidean distance among data to measured or tested & neighbors which are nearest of the data to be trained. It calculates the distance among supplied data points and the training samples for a given sample of data. The number of points in the training data that are nearest towards testing data is K–that means distance weight – represents set. In this method Classification has been performed in terms of representing label and recurring in fundamental set. Though, afore acquaintance of numeral of classes has needed in KNN for getting a better output [9].

## 2.3 Cuckoo Search Optimization Algorithm (CSO)

In this paper in order to apply CSO the following assumptions were made. The levy flight for cuckoo birds has been calculated using the following formulas [15–20, 23–25].

$$\text{þ} = \frac{\varepsilon(1+\mu)*\sin(pi*\frac{\mu}{2})}{\left(\frac{\varepsilon(1+\mu)}{2}\right)*\mu*2^{(\mu-1)/2}} \tag{4}$$

Using power law index n levy steps can be taken using þ.

A total of 200 search agents haven been considered in this paper with maximum number of 50 iterations, and objective function has been used for finding the optimum sensing value in this cuckoo search algorithm by considering the SNR Values.

# 3  Results and Conclusions

In this portion we demonstrate the comparison of ML-based spectrum sensing Technique results. In the below figure, probability detection values have been taken along vertical axis and SNR values in dB were taken along x-axis. In this figure performance comparison for 4 graphs were shown they are modified KNN using Average information per message, Modified KNN using Energy detection technique, Modified SVM using Average information per message and Modified SVM methods respectively. By observing the figures, modified SVM, KNN using Average information per message Probability detection values are superior when compared to general SVM & KNN methods. Hence better detection is possible using ML – based, KNN Techniques [10–12] (Table 1).

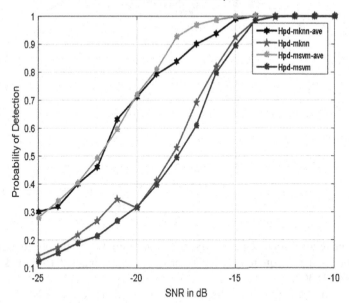

**Fig. 1.** Probability detection using SVM, KNN Techniques

**Table 1.** Comparison table for Spectrum Sensing of SVM & KNN based average information per message [4, 13, 14]

| ML-Method | SNR | | | |
|---|---|---|---|---|
| | −10 dB | −15 dB | −20 dB | −25 dB |
| SVM-AVE | 1 | 0.9898 | 0.7188 | 0.2954 |
| KNN-AVE | 1 | 1 | 0.7049 | 0.3199 |
| SVM-ED | 1 | 0.9159 | 0.3204 | 0.1705 |
| KNN-ED | 1 | 0.9139 | 0.3084 | 0.1236 |

The above table gives the comparison of Modified SVM & KNN methods, and it can be observed that Modified SVM based AVE method gives best results for probability detection for various SNR values.

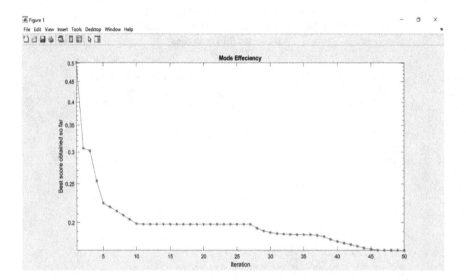

In the above diagram using cuckoo search algorithm, the best scores obtained were shown. In lieu of a given quantity of repetitions, best score obtained using cuckoo search algorithm is 0.18302.

Hence, from the obtained results it can be shown that SVM & KNN Based Spectrum sensing performs better under noise over conventional technique of detection. Performance comparison of graphs as shown in Fig. 1 gives better results for Average information based SS using supervised learning procedures.

## References

1. Saravanan, P., et al.: A supervised learning approach for differential entropy feature-based spectrum sensing. In: 2021 Sixth International Conference on Wireless Communications, Signal Processing and Networking (WiSPNET). IEEE (2021)
2. Yucek, T., Arslan, H.: A survey of spectrum sensing algorithms for cognitive radio applications. IEEE Commun. Surv. Tutorials **11**(1), 116–130 (2009)
3. Gurugopinath, S., Muralishankar, R.: Geometric power detector for spectrum sensing under symmetric alpha stable noise. Electron. Lett. **54**(22), 1284–1286 (2018)
4. Gurugopinath, S., Muralishankar, R., Shankar, H.N.: Differential entropy-driven spectrum sensing under generalized Gaussian noise. IEEE Commun. Lett. **20**(7), 1321–1324 (2016)
5. Qi, H., Zhang, X., Gao, Y.: Channel energy statistics learning in compressive spectrum sensing. IEEE Trans. Wireless Commun. **17**(12), 7910–7921 (2018)
6. Zahabi, S.J., Tadaion, A.A.: Local spectrum sensing in non-Gaussian noise. In: 2010 17th International Conference on Telecommunications. IEEE (2010)
7. Jakkula, V.: Tutorial on support vector machine (SVM). School of EECS, Washington State University 37.2.5, p. 3 (2006)
8. Auria, L., Moro, R.A.: Support vector machines (SVM) as a technique for solvency analysis (2008)
9. Zhang, M.-L., Zhou, Z.-H.: ML-KNN: a lazy learning approach to multi-label learning. Pattern Recogn. **40**(7), 2038–2048 (2007)

10. Guo, G., Wang, H., Bell, D., Bi, Y., Greer, K.: KNN model-based approach in classification. In: Meersman, R., Tari, Z., Schmidt, D.C. (eds.) OTM 2003. LNCS, vol. 2888, pp. 986–996. Springer, Heidelberg (2003). https://doi.org/10.1007/978-3-540-39964-3_62
11. Zhu, X.J.: Semi-supervised learning literature survey (2005)
12. Caruana, R., Niculescu-Mizil, A.: An empirical comparison of supervised learning algorithms. In: Proceedings of the 23rd International Conference on Machine Learning (2006)
13. Machta, J.: Entropy, information, and computation. Am. J. Phys. 67(12), 1074–1077 (1999)
14. Knuth, D.E.: Dynamic Huffman coding. J. Algorithms 6(2), 163–180 (1985)
15. Wang, H., et al.: Spectrum sensing in cognitive radio using goodness of fit testing. IEEE Trans. Wirel. Commun. 8(11), 5427–5430 (2009)
16. Gandomi, A.H., Yang, X.-S., Alavi, A.H.: Cuckoo search algorithm: a metaheuristic approach to solve structural optimization problems. Eng. Comput. 29(1), 17–35 (2013)
17. Joshi, A.S., et al.: Cuckoo search optimization-a review. Mater. Today Proc. 4(8), 7262–7269 (2017)
18. Yang, X.-S., Deb, S.: Cuckoo search: recent advances and applications. Neural Comput. Appl. 24(1), 169–174 (2013). https://doi.org/10.1007/s00521-013-1367-1
19. Yang, X.-S., Deb, S.: Multiobjective cuckoo search for design optimization. Comput. Oper. Res. 40(6), 1616–1624 (2013)
20. Chong, E.K.P., Zak, S.H.: An Introduction to Optimization. Wiley (2004)
21. Gill, P.E., Murray, W., Wright, M.H.: Practical optimization. Soc. Ind. Appl. Math. (2019)
22. Liu, X., Tan, X.: Optimization algorithm of periodical cooperative spectrum sensing in cognitive radio. Int. J. Commun Syst 27(5), 705–720 (2014)
23. Zhang, R., Jiang, X., Li, R.: Improved decomposition-based multi-objective cuckoo search algorithm for spectrum allocation in cognitive vehicular network. Phys. Commun. 34, 301–309 (2019)
24. Yuan, W., et al.: Improved cuckoo search algorithm for spectrum sensing in sparse satellite cognitive systems. In: 2016 IEEE 84th Vehicular Technology Conference (VTC-Fall). IEEE (2016)
25. Xin, Z., Zhang, D., Chen, Z.: Spectrum allocation of cognitive radio network based on improved cuckoo search algorithm. In: Proceedings of the 2nd International Conference on Computer Science and Software Engineering (2019)

# Author Index

© ICST Institute for Computer Sciences, Social Informatics and Telecommunications Engineering 2023
Published by Springer Nature Switzerland AG 2023. All Rights Reserved
S. Nandan Mohanty et al. (Eds.): ICISML 2022, LNICST 471, pp. 397–399, 2023.
https://doi.org/10.1007/978-3-031-35081-8

Printed in the United States
by Baker & Taylor Publisher Services